Legal and Ethical Aspects of
Health Care for the Elderly

Legal and Ethical Aspects
of
Health Care
for the Elderly

Edited by
Marshall B. Kapp, J.D., M.P.H.
Harvey E. Pies, J.D., M.P.H.
A. Edward Doudera, J.D.

Published in cooperation with
the American Society of Law & Medicine

Health Administration Press
Ann Arbor, Michigan
1985

Library of Congress Cataloging-in-Publication Data

Main entry under title:

Legal and ethical aspects of health care for the
    elderly.

    Based on a conference held in June 1983 in Washington,
D.C.; sponsored by the American Society of Law &
Medicine.
        Bibliography: p.
        Includes index.
        1. Aged—Medical care—United States—Congresses.
2. Long-term care of the sick—United States—Congresses.
3. Long-term care facilities—Law and legislation—
United States—Congresses.   4. Aged—Legal status, laws,
etc.—United States—Congresses.   I. Kapp, Marshall B.
II. Pies, Harvey E.   III. Doudera, A. Edward, 1949– .
IV. American Society of Law and Medicine.   [DNLM:
1. Ethics, Medical—congresses.   2. Health Policy—
United States—congresses.   3. Health Services for the
Aged—United States—congresses.   4. Health Services
for the Aged—United States—legislation—congresses.
5. Long Term Care—in old age—congresses.   6. Long
Term Care—in old age—legislation—congresses.
WT 30 L496 1983]
RA564.8.L44   1986   362.1'6'0973   85-17557
ISBN 0-910701-04-0

Health Administration Press
School of Public Health
The University of Michigan
1021 East Huron
Ann Arbor, Michigan 48109
(313) 764-1380

Contents

Contributors

RICHARD W. BESDINE is Director of Geriatric Medical Education at the Hebrew Rehabilitation Center for the Aged in Roslindale, Massachusetts, Assistant Professor of Medicine at Harvard Medical School, and Associate Physician in Medicine at Brigham and Women's Hospital and Beth Israel Hospital. He has acted as a consultant in geriatric program development at several universities including Boston University School of Medicine, George Washington University Medical Center, and Cornell Medical College. He has served on many national and regional committees on health care for the elderly, including the 1981 White House Conference on Aging. Dr. Besdine is also on the editorial boards of the *Annual Review of Gerontology and Geriatrics,* the *Journal of Clinical and Experimental Gerontology,* and the *Journal of Gerontology.* He received his undergraduate degree from Haverford College and his M.D. from the University of Pennsylvania School of Medicine.

ROBERT N. BROWN is an Associate Professor of Law at the University of Detroit School of Law in Michigan. Mr. Brown received both his A.B. and J.D. degrees from the University of Michigan and his LL.M. from George Washington University. Author of *Rights of Older Persons,* Mr. Brown has lectured and written widely on such topics related to health care for the elderly. In 1984–85, he was on a sabbatical at the Urban Institute in Washington, D.C.

CHRISTINE K. CASSEL is an Associate Professor at the University of Chicago School of Medicine. She was formerly Assistant Professor in the Departments of Medicine and Geriatrics and Adult Development at Mount Sinai Medical Center in New York. She received her B.A. from the University of Chicago and her M.D. from the University of Massachusetts Medical School. She has been the recipient of many grants and honors, most recently the Henry J. Kaiser Family Foundation Faculty Scholar Award in General Internal Medicine. Dr. Cassel has served as Chair of the Program Committee of the Society for Health & Human Values and on the Board of Directors of several organizations, including Physicians for Social Responsibility, The Society for the Right to Die, and the Association for the Advancement of Medical Education. She has been a lecturer at many national seminars and is the author of numerous publications.

ELIAS S. COHEN is the Humanist-in-Residence and Social Scientist in Programming at WITF-TV in Harrisburg, Pennsylvania and Director of the Division of Policy and Information Dissemination of Temple University Institute on Aging in Philadelphia, Pennsylvania. He received his B.A. from the University of Wisconsin, his M.P.A. from Syracuse University, and his J.D. from Temple University Law School. Mr. Cohen is former Commissioner of Family Services and Commissioner on Aging for the Commonwealth of Pennsylvania and former Assistant Commissioner of Mental Health for the State of Indiana. He served for six years as Editor-in-Chief of *The Gerontologist,* is a past president of the Gerontological Society of America, and is the author of numerous publications.

CHARLES M. CULVER is Professor of Psychiatry at Dartmouth Medical School, Adjunct Professor of Philosophy at Dartmouth College, and Chairperson of the Ethics Advisory Committee at Mary Hitchcock Memorial Hospital in Hanover, New Hampshire. He received his Ph.D. and M.D. from Duke University. In 1982 he coauthored *Philosophy in Medicine,* published by Oxford University Press. He was a member of the Board of Directors of the American Society of Law & Medicine.

JAMES M. DAVIES is Vice-Chairperson of the Nursing Home Action Group in St. Paul, Minnesota. He is also an advocate of patients' rights.

NANCY NEVELOFF DUBLER is Director of the Division of Legal and Ethical Issues in Health Care, Department of Social Medicine, Montefiore Medical Center in the Bronx, New York. She is also on the faculty of Albert Einstein Medical College. She is Editor of the *Journal of Prison and Jail Health: Medicine, Law, Correction and Ethics* and Associate in the Columbia University Seminar on Social and Preventive Medicine. She received her B.A. from Barnard College and her LL.B. from Harvard Law School. Ms. Dubler has written many articles and spoken at national conferences.

ALAN S. GOLDBERG is an attorney with the firm of Goulston & Storrs in

Boston, Massachusetts, and a member of the Massachusetts and Florida bars. He received his A.B. from Brooklyn College, his J.D. from Boston College Law School, and his LL.M. from Boston University School of Law. Mr. Goldberg is a member of the Board of Directors of the National Health Lawyers Association, and has participated in many of their seminars. He has given presentations at educational programs sponsored by the New England Hospital Assembly, New Jersey Association of Health Care Facilities, Bentley College, New Hampshire Nursing Home Association, Massachusetts Federation of Nursing Homes, American Health Care Association, and the Massachusetts Continuing Legal Education Association–New England Law Institute. He is also a part-time faculty member of Boston College Law School.

JOEL M. HAMME is a partner with the law firm of Pierson, Ball & Dowd in Washington, D.C. He has worked extensively in the health care area and has represented a wide variety of health care providers on reimbursement, licensing, and certification, as well as other statutory and regulatory issues. Mr. Hamme is a frequent lecturer before professional organizations and has written a number of articles in health care publications. He received his B.A. from Dickinson College in Pennsylvania and his J.D. from the University of Pennsylvania Law School.

SUSAN HARRIS is Director of Legal Affairs for the American Health Care Association in Washington, D.C. She received her R.N. from Presbyterian Hospital School of Nursing, her M.P.H. from Johns Hopkins University, and her J.D. from the University of Louisville. Her former positions include Director of Plan Development at Kentucky Health Systems Agency and Senior Planner at Falls Region Health Council. Ms. Harris has spoken at symposia on health policy, long-term care, and patients' rights, and is the author of many publications.

RALPH E. HAZELBAKER is President and Chairman of the Board of Americare Corporation. He has an M.B.A. in corporate finance from Ohio State University. Mr. Hazelbaker is Past President of the Ohio Health Care Association. He has testified on numerous occasions before both the Ohio and West Virginia legislatures in public hearings relating to long-term care regulatory matters and has been a panelist and speaker on numerous radio and television programs dealing with long-term care. In addition, he served as a delegate, by presidential appointment, to the 1981 White House Conference on Aging.

JANE D. HOYT is Chairperson of the Nursing Home Action Group in St. Paul, Minnesota. She is also an advocate of patients' rights.

MARSHALL B. KAPP is Associate Professor of Legal Medicine at Wright State University in Ohio. He is the coauthor of *Geriatrics and the Law: Patient Rights and Professional Responsibilities* (Springer Publishing, 1985) and many articles on law and elderly rights. An active member of professional organizations, Professor Kapp was a participant at the 1981 White House Conference on Aging and was a Visiting Scholar at the Institute of Society, Ethics, and the Life Sciences of The Hastings Center in New York. He currently serves as cochairman of the American Society of Law & Medicine's Committee on the Legal and Ethical Aspects of Health Care of the Elderly. He received his B.A. from Johns Hopkins University, a J.D. from George Washington University, and an M.P.H. from the Harvard University School of Public Health.

PAUL A. KERSCHNER is the former Associate Director, the Division of Legislation, Research and Developmental Services of the American Association of Retired Persons, in Washington, D.C. The holder of a M.P.A. and Ph.D. from the University of Southern California, he is primarily interested in the public policy analysis of aging, health, and long-term care. Dr. Kerschner has spoken extensively around the nation on these subjects as well as participated in numerous research and training endeavors. He has written extensively regarding the aged and served on a variety of related boards and commissions. He is currently a senior consultant to the Villers Foundation of Washington, D.C. and president of the National Foundation for Long Term Care.

CHARLOTTE A. LEAVITT is Director of the Continuing Care Department of Framingham Union Hospital in Framingham, Massachusetts. She received her diploma in nursing from Massachusetts General Hospital School of Nursing and her B.S.N. from Northeastern University. She is the author of an article on the role of continuing care nurses on the Massachusetts State Advisory Committee of the Case Management and Screening Program, published by the American Hospital Association. Mrs. Leavitt has served as President of the Massachusetts Continuing Care Association, Cochairperson of the Boston Regional Continuing Care Nurses Association, and as Region I Director, American Association for Continuity of Care. She is a member of the American Nurses Association, the Massachusetts Nurses Association, and Sigma Theta Tau.

LAWRENCE R. LEONARD is an Associate with the law firm Watson, Ess, Marshall & Enggas in Kansas City, Missouri, where he practices medical malpractice defense law. He received his B.A. from the University of Virginia in 1978 and his J.D. from Boston University School of Law in

1982. He was Student Editor-in-Chief of the *American Journal of Law &*
Medicine, which originally published his chapter.

JOANNE LYNN is Assistant Clinical Professor of Health Care Sciences and
Medicine, the Division of Geriatric Medicine, George Washington University, and Medical Director of the Washington Home Hospice. She was
formerly Assistant Staff Director of the President's Commission for the
Study of Ethical Problems in Medicine and Biomedical and Behavioral
Research and principal author of the report *Deciding to Forego Life-*
Sustaining Treatment. She also made significant contributions to the Commission's reports *Defining Death* and *Making Health Care Decisions.* In addition to authoring numerous publications, she has spoken at national
conferences and appeared on CBS Nightwatch, CBS Morning News, and
Good Night America. Dr. Lynn received her B.S. from Dickinson College
in Pennsylvania, her M.D. from Boston University School of Medicine,
and her M.A. in Philosophy and Social Policy from George Washington
University.

SCOTT A. MASON is President and founder of National Health Advisors,
Ltd., a management consulting firm in McLean, Virginia. He holds a
B.A. from Duke University, a M.P.A. in health planning and administration from Pennsylvania State University, and a doctoral degree in health
services administration from George Washington University. He has
worked as staff specialist for multihospital systems at the American Hospital Association and as Corporate Director with Samaritan Health Service in Arizona. A frequent speaker at professional conferences, he has
also published articles on such topics as multihospital development, strategic planning, and diversification. Dr. Mason is a member of the American Association of Hospital Consultants and of the American College of
Hospital Administrators.

BOBBE SHAPIRO NOLAN is a member of the Medical Advisory Board for
the Ohio Department of Public Welfare and a staff attorney with the
Dayton Legal Aid Society. She received her J.D. degree in May 1985 from
the University of Dayton in Dayton, Ohio. She received her B.S.N. from
Wright State University in Dayton in 1976 and her certificate as a geriatric
nurse practitioner in 1977 from Rush University College of Health Sciences in Chicago, Illinois. Ms. Nolan's chapter was originally published in
the October 1984 issue of *Law, Medicine & Health Care.*

LARRY A. ODAY is an attorney with the firm of Wood, Lucksinger &
Epstein in Washington, D.C. He holds a B.A. from Case Western Reserve
University and a J.D. from Chicago–Kent College of Law. He has served

as Director of the Bureau of Program Policy and Director of the Division of Congressional Affairs, both of the Health Care Financing Administration of the Department of Health and Human Services. Mr. Oday is a member of the American Bar Association and the District of Columbia and Illinois Bar Associations. He received certification from the Michigan House of Representatives for "Outstanding Performance" in Government Relations in 1977.

PHILLIP A. PROGER is a partner with the law firm of Baker & Hostetler in Washington, D.C. and Adjunct Professor of Law at the Georgetown University Law Center. He received his undergraduate degree from the University of Maryland and his J.D. from the University of Maryland School of Law. He is the author of numerous articles on antitrust law and has served as Program Chairman of the National Health Lawyers Association's Annual Seminar on Antitrust in the Health Care Field as well as Vice Chairman of the Section Seven Committee of the Antitrust Section of the American Bar Association.

WINSOR C. SCHMIDT, JR. is Associate Professor of the Department of Public Administration at Florida State University. He received his B.A. from Harvard University, his J.D. from the American University, and his LL.M. from the University of Virginia. He is a member of the District of Columbia Bar and the American Bar Association, among other professional organizations, and is on the Board of Directors of the Florida Chapter of the Mental Health Association. Mr. Schmidt has written many books and articles in journals, speaks frequently at national conferences, and has acted as a consultant on mental health issues.

STANLEY S. WALLACK is Director of the Center for Health Policy Analysis and Research at Brandeis University and Director of the University Health Policy Consortium that comprises Brandeis, Boston University, and Massachusetts Institute of Technology. He received his undergraduate degree from Antioch College and his Ph.D. in economics from Washington University in St. Louis. He has written numerous publications in the fields of economics and health care. Dr. Wallack has served as Commissioner of the National Commission on the Cost of Medical Care of the American Hospital Association.

TERRIE TODD WETLE is Assistant Professor of Medicine at Harvard Medical School, Executive Officer of the Working Group on Health Policy and Aging, and Associate Director of the Harvard Geriatric Education Center. She received her B.S., M.S., and Ph.D. degrees from Portland State University. She was previously Director of the Program in Long-

Term Care and Assistant Professor at Yale University School of Medicine. She is a member of many professional health care organizations and has participated in community service projects, including acting as chairman of the Long-Term Care Task Force of the Gerontological Society of America and as a member of the Massachusetts Department of Elder Affairs Professional Advisory Committee. Dr. Wetle has written many articles on the elderly and long-term care.

DAVID A. WINSTON is Senior Vice-President of Blyth Eastman Paine Webber Health Care Funding, Inc. and Executive Director of the National Committee for Quality Health Care. Prior to joining Blyth, Mr. Winston was the Minority Staff Director for the Senate Committee on Labor and Human Resources. He headed President Reagan's transition team on health care and played an important role as Special Assistant to the Secretary of the Department of Health and Human Services. He received his B.A. from San Francisco State College and his M.A. from the University of California in Santa Barbara.

Preface

Several hundred years ago, the English essayist Jonathan Swift expressed the irony that, while most of us would like to live forever, few of us would choose to grow old. Today, personal and professional feelings toward the aging process and toward the aged remain paradoxical, even as the total population of our nation and our world inexorably grows older, both in percentages and actual numbers. The elderly are the focus of profound hopes and anxieties, our envy and our pity, our respect for pride and our longing to help. The older cohort is at once healthy yet a disproportionate user of health services, independent yet needy for assistance, vigorous yet vulnerable.

These paradoxical characteristics, and the basic social values that they both represent and foster, present many complex and inescapable legal and ethical issues with which we need to grapple. Do older individuals have a right to access to health care? Who is responsible for satisfying that right? How should health care to the elderly be delivered, and by whom, and at what price? Should the elderly be empowered to make personal health care decisions? When should that power be usurped? Who decides for the elderly, and using what criteria? While many of these fundamental questions are generic in nature, in that they are relevant to virtually all health care providers and consumers, these dilemmas take on an added urgency and unique and challenging nuances when applied to elderly persons.

It seems strange that, despite the increasing attention to and complexity of health care of the elderly in this country, precious little work has been done in an organized, analytical fashion in the realm of legal and ethical issues. With only a few exceptions, professionals involved in policymaking for or direct provision of health care to the elderly are without substantial resources to assist in guiding them toward more principled, thoughtful resolutions of the agonizing problems that arise in serving their older clients. It was largely for this reason that, in June 1983 in Washington, D.C., the American Society of Law & Medicine brought together a group of nationally prominent experts from the fields of clinical medicine and nursing, health policy and administration, bio-ethics, and law to explore for three days some of the most fundamental legal and ethical aspects of health care of the elderly. That conference served as the principal genesis for this volume, although the individual chapters found here have all been substantially revised, updated, ex-panded, and referenced for purposes of publication. In addition, several chapters in this text have been reprinted from other publications. We hope that this product makes some headway in helping—and prod-ding—all who are concerned with and about the well-being of the elderly to think more deeply about the social, legal, and ethical ramifications of their endeavors, and to be able to apply some of the insights to troubling situations that arise in the course of their important daily work.

The book begins on a rather global plane by surveying some of the most pressing social, economic, and political considerations impinging on health care of the elderly. Macro questions of access, organization, and responsibility predominate in the remarks of contributors drawn from the ranks of advocacy, health care industry, and public policy. In Section II, we face head-on the primary reality of contemporary American health care: dollars. We look here specifically at the current means of reimburs-ing long-term care and at some potential alternative methods of financing that might enable larger numbers of consumers to gain access to more kinds of noninstitutional services. Legal issues confronting long-term health providers form the core of Section III, as we look at antitrust problems, quality control mechanisms, malpractice possibilities, and other legal concerns particular to the nursing home industry. These legal imperatives interface with some of the economic and ethical considera-tions noted elsewhere in the book, creating difficult challenges for the conscientious provider.

Emphasis then shifts exclusively to the older consumer. Section IV entails an exploration of the legal and ethical rights of the most vulnera-ble segment of the older population, those who reside in nursing homes or who require protective services in the community. Decisions about health care, research participation, daily living, and the residential place-ment itself confront the institutionalized and the impaired elderly, their families, and their care givers. The authors in this section contribute important ideas about appropriate processes for making those hard choices within the unnatural environment of a long-term care facility or an inadequate community setting. The attempt to balance individual rights delicately against unmet needs takes place here, where an exploration of protective services and guardianship presents starkly the tension we feel between autonomy and paternalism in serving the elderly. When does the principle of beneficence justify overriding one's self-determination? What is the extent of the state's *parens patriae* role in forcing protection on a person who cannot or will not engage in self-protection? These are the issues cogently addressed by the contributors here.

In Section V, two physicians, an attorney, and a philosopher delve into the clinical, ethical, and legal complexities of decision making by the elderly in health care, concentrating primarily on the subject of informed consent to, and refusal of, medical treatment. Given that as many as half of the residents of nursing homes suffer some degree of decision-making impairment, assessing the individual's mental competence, and the legal and ethical significance that we attach to such determinations, weigh heavily in these discussions.

The reader will not find in these pages any central "party line" or prevailing philosophical orientation. Rather, we take pride in the rich diversity of ideas and approaches presented. The unifying theme, the common thread tying together the parts of this volume, is simply this: a recognition that health care of the elderly presents many challenging legal and ethical dilemmas that must soon be tackled, and a commitment to identify, analyze, and resolve those issues in a manner that best promotes the integrity and the well-being of the elderly.

Open discussion of these issues is an essential starting point in achieving just and humane ways to reconcile competing values, wants, needs, and limitations. It has been said that history will ultimately judge the quality of a civilization by how it treats those of its citizens who are in the "twilight" of their lives. The ways that we deal with legal and ethical aspects of health care of the elderly will play a significant part in that historical judgment, and we humbly offer this book as an initial contribution toward moving our own civilization closer to passing muster.

MARSHALL B. KAPP, J.D., M.P.H.

Section I

Social, Ethical, and
Political Perspectives

1

Health Care for the Elderly: Meeting the Challenges

Christine K. Cassel, M.D.

The recitation of the "holy" numbers in geriatrics or gerontology has become rote. At some point in the next century, one in every five persons will be over age 65.[1] The number of people in this country over age 65 will increase from 26 million to 50 million in the next century.[2] Persons 85 years old and older are the fastest growing segment of our population.[3] By 1985, nursing home costs will increase from $20 billion to $75 billion.[4] This demographic phenomenon is often viewed as an odd sort of epidemic, but it is simply the growth of a civilized society. It is, in fact, our future.

This chapter examines the problems and possible solutions which must be considered if we are to accommodate successfully this growing number of senior citizens. Although we may be increasingly burdened by these population shifts, the question remains open: will they offer nothing positive? This is not a rhetorical question, but rather one which deserves careful reflection and realistic assessment.

The social, economic, and medical problems associated with the increasing aged population are varied and difficult, but this demographic change also presents unique opportunities. The challenge is to revitalize and redefine a humanistic ethos at the core of an increasingly technological culture. Health care professionals have the capability and the power to handle the problems of the elderly and to revitalize the humanistic ethos of our society.

One major asset, or source of power, that we have in meeting this demographic challenge is our self-interest. We all age. Aging is not a disease; it is an inherent part of human life. Another asset is that we are not avoiding these issues; rather, we are directing much concern, energy, talent, and intelligence toward the resolution of these common problems.

Health care professionals are concerned about the social phenomenon of the graying of America and the more general policy issues in health care and long-term care, or "continuing care" as it is more graciously referred to by Sir Fergusen Anderson, Professor of Geriatrics at the University of Glasgow.[5]

Health professionals have other incentives to be involved in this area. Geriatrics and gerontology provide great opportunities; work in these fields is at the "cutting edge." This is an area full of excitement, imperatives, and opportunities for creative work. While medicine is beginning to study the major causes of suffering, disability, and premature death in elderly people, many questions remain unanswered. Osteoarthritis, osteoporosis, Parkinson's disease, systolic hypertension, strokes, urological disorders, sexual dysfunction, depression, and senile dementia of the Alzheimer's type (SDAT) are sources of major disability among large numbers of people; these diseases are costing millions of dollars to treat. The cost of the subsequent dependency due to these disabilities is also high. These diseases were formerly considered uninteresting mostly because they were so common, and because their etiologies and pathogeneses (causes and mechanisms) were often not well understood. Today, however, these areas are especially interesting and ripe for creative research. We have overcome our professional aversion to these diseases, and to the aged. In addition, while there were no effective treatments for these common disorders in the past, there certainly are effective ways today to make people feel better and function more fully.

Of course, we should not turn our attention to the issues of aging simply because they embody opportunities for career advancement. This area provides the opportunity for meaningful work, which can be rare in modern technically oriented societies. There is real satisfaction in working on the problems associated with aging, and from this satisfaction we derive a source of power.

THE PRIMARY ISSUES

The medical, ethical, and legal issues in health care of the elderly center on three related themes: paternalism, costs, and death.

Although paternalism has lately acquired a bad connotation, it is nevertheless an important factor when working with severely impaired people of all ages. For example, cognitive impairment, in particular SDAT (which Lewis Thomas has called one of the most important epidemics of our time[6]), requires the paternalistic function. A truly respectful paternalism is founded on an essential humanism—a Samaritan urge to help those in need. It reflects the values of our institutions and our relationships. Paternalism is problematic because it can decrease one's recognition of individuality; we must administer needed care without compromising individual rights. Despite our efforts to do what is best for someone else, we may either miss the target or act at too great a cost to the individual's self-respect.

The figures describing the demographic revolution of this century are rarely discussed without some mention of the increased costs caused by our aging population. But in our concern over cost, we must determine society's proper role in supporting elderly people who may no longer be economically productive. While medical care is expensive, our rhetoric proclaims that every patient is inherently worthy of that care, a notion that supports a humanistic health care system. Policies and legislation, however, are not always based on concepts of equity and do not support adequate health care for all individuals. Every practitioner has had the experience of "bending" a regulation in order to give the patient what he or she needs; this is our definition of "good medical care."

Another important aspect of aging is that the elderly are closer to death than most people, and thus difficult issues arise concerning dying and the elderly. Death used to be a private family matter, which occurred primarily at home.[7] Today, decisions about the management of death are the subject of diverse and intense debates in the courts and are a cause of great contention among health professionals. These decisions have become the subject of federal policy (e.g., Medicare hospice reimbursement regulations[8] or the original Baby Doe regulations[9]). These debates have arisen because of our imperfect technologies which, while postponing death, do so at great expense, and because of conflicting values—for individuals and for society—surrounding dilemmas such as the right to refuse treatment.

The first "death with dignity" law was passed in California in 1976.[10] Kübler-Ross began her pioneering work nearly ten years before that,[11] and theologians and philosophers had been debating questions concerning euthanasia and termination of life support systems considerably before that time. Also in 1976, the case of Karen Ann Quinlan brought the issue of the role of medical technology and the right to die before the eyes of the lay public.[12] Since then it has become clear that the courts cannot settle such issues in a simple and final way, for several cases in different states have been resolved with quite conflicting conclusions.[13] This lack of uniformity is, perhaps, due to the law's inability to come to grips adequately with the specific issues and their significance. An attorney testifying before the President's Commission for the Study of Ethical Problems in Medicine and Biomedical and Behavioral Research gave this warning on the role of the law in these decisions:

> It is the doctor's job to take decisions which may affect the span of human life. Therefore, it is especially important that law be neither too strict nor

too lenient. If it is too strict, it will begin to make doctors criminally responsible for man's mortality; if it is too lenient it will give doctors a "license to
kill." But whether the law does steer a middle course between these two
extremes, or indeed, is capable of doing so . . . is a different matter.[14]

The situation of deciding when to discontinue a respirator for a
person who is irreversibly comatose and in a persistent vegetative state, as
occurred in the *Quinlan* case, is rightfully much discussed. However, this
situation is not as common as the one faced by physicians and nurses in
hospitals and nursing homes every day. These professionals may have to
determine what constitutes the best course when treatment is possible
but when meaningful life is no longer possible, and the patient wants to
die. For example, the prognosis for recovery of a stroke victim is im-
precise. He or she may continue in a vegetative state, or recover to full
participation in life, or function at one of the intervening levels of existence. When capacity for interpersonal communication, mobility, and
control over bodily functions no longer exists, how are we to interpret
persistent gestures forcing away the spoon of the nurse's aide who would
try to feed this person day after day?

Much needs to be discussed by professionals and the general public.
Norman Brown and colleagues in Seattle, Washington, reported in the
New England Journal of Medicine the high incidence of unevaluated and
untreated fevers in nursing home patients.[15] More recently, the same
journal printed a personal account from a physician who agonized about
how to respond to a call from a nursing home about a fever in a very old,
extremely impaired woman.[16] We need to ask whether there should be a
general policy and whether such decisions should be tied to reimbursement policies.

These issues are all related to increasing disability and illness among
the elderly. Both the health professions and society are confused about
the appropriate focus and extent of medical care and protective services
for the most dependent.

THE PREVENTIVE APPROACH TO HEALTH CARE
FOR THE ELDERLY: A CRITIQUE

One of the more optimistic approaches to providing good medical care
for the elderly is the preventive approach. This is intended not to prevent
aging, but to prevent chronic disease and disability, those occurrences
that become more problematic with age. Although based on significant
population data, the preventive approach is limited and, in many ways,
superficial. The prime spokesperson for the preventive theory is James
Fries of Stanford Medical School, who assembled longevity and survival

data from the past century to develop his theory of the compression of morbidity.[17] Largely because of recent successes in sanitation, nutrition, and public health, people live longer today. Nonetheless, those who manage to live to old age, today as in the past, usually die between age 85 to 100. In light of laboratory research suggesting that human cells are programmed genetically to multiply only a certain fixed number of times,[18] it seems logical to conclude that approximately 90 years is the natural limit to the life span of humans who do not get sick beforehand.

The compression of morbidity assumes that if people exercised more, and led more healthy lives in general, they would not "rust out" from disease and abuse. Fries is particularly impressed with the fact that world marathon record holders decline approximately only 30 percent between the ages of 30 and 70.[19] Indeed, healthy living may promote longevity in many cases and certainly can improve the quality of life, but it is no solution to the "problem" of the demographic revolution, for several reasons.

Although there are many fit and splendid old people, they probably do not deserve all of the credit for their longevity. There is ample evidence supporting a significant genetic role in life span. More important, the compression of morbidity theory does not account for the influence of environmental and occupational factors in aging. For example, various kinds of malignancies, pulmonary diseases, and immune disorders may have environmental components.

While it is true that many chronic disorders which plague modern industrial societies are associated with behaviors that are mutable, people do not always act in the best interests of their health. Society itself does not encourage those desired changes in lifestyle. Furthermore, the emphasis on exercise may be misleading and damaging to the human body. While it is recognized that a moderate amount of aerobic exercise enhances the cardiovascular system, this type of exercise is hard on the musculoskeletal system. The accumulated microtrauma incurred over many years of running may result in severe osteoarthritis in old age.

Finally, a focus on personal responsibility carries a concomitant risk that the system will devolve into one that blames the victim. For example, as far as medical research can tell us, a healthy life style and vigorous exercise do not prevent Alzheimer's disease.[20] If this disease continues to affect 5 percent of the population over age 65, it will affect four million by the end of the century.

The preventive approach also attempts to bypass some of the most important ethical issues in long-term care. In its scenario, since we fall to pieces all at once, chronic diseases disappear. One is either vigorous or dead. According to Fries, "High-level medical technology applied at the end of a natural life span epitomizes the absurd. . . . Human interaction, rather than respirators and dialysis and other mechanical support for failing organs, is indicated at the time of the 'terminal drop'."[21] This statement about the "terminal drop" suggests a level of certainty which is unfamiliar to most clinicians, and is not clearly delineated by law. In any case, human interaction, if done well, could cost more than technological intervention. Questions will still arise concerning which medical technologies are extraordinary. It may not be difficult to decide to forego mechanical ventilation or an artificial heart in a 90-year-old with multisystem failure. It will be extremely difficult, however, to decide to forego such measures as a feeding tube or antibiotics which can prolong life considerably in a severely limited and impaired person. Even if correct, the "compression of morbidity" theory does not eliminate ethical problems about life support.

In sum, the preventive approach will not solve our ethical dilemmas in treatment nor make nursing homes obsolete by the end of the century. This theory cannot help us by preventing such diseases as SDAT or by lowering the costs of treatment. Finally, this approach ignores the fact that, despite advances in prevention and treatment, the absolute numbers of those afflicted still will be enormous.

THE SEARCH FOR VIABLE SOLUTIONS

We need creative solutions to deal with the problems of our aging population. We need vision to see the solutions and the ways to effect them. Acknowledgement of the reality of aging is an important first step. We must recognize that, of our 25 million citizens over age 65, up to 90 or 95 percent are healthy enough to live independent lives, to make major contributions to the quality of our social fabric, and to assist in the resolution of the difficult issues presented here. A great source of power lies in this group's perspective, dynamism, and size. Because of its numbers, the group has been increasingly recognized as an important political force. What it lacks, however, is the necessary connection to the rest of society. Health care professionals have the power to create this connection through a subtle but profoundly meaningful shift in their attitudes, which will then be reflected in social structures. One such step is to avoid the locution which refers to the aged as "they" and to acknowledge that they are we.

The values represented and articulated by a truly intergenerational community could be a source of power enabling us to handle the challenges that face our civilization—hunger, overpopulation, illiteracy, economic instability, and the threat of global thermonuclear war. In dealing with the problems of today's world, the perspective of old age can provide patience, a sense of history, and a sense of human continuity. The urge toward immortality does not have to be expressed only in familial structures; it can generate a strong and vigorous orientation to the future.

Moreover, advances in science may diminish the problems that we face. Although science and technology do not hold the answer to all of the problems of chronically disabled or impaired people, modern medicine has made some advances in the care of the aging. Our research and educational institutions are just beginning to examine seriously the problems of chronic disease and disability. Breakthroughs can be expected.

Even if we cannot eradicate all of the chronic diseases and disabilities that plague our elderly, the important work of humanizing health services and society must continue. Paul Starr points out that ever since the birth of the hospital system in the 19th century, the emphasis in medicine has been on acute care problems.[22] The less prestigious, but highly dedicated, profession of public health dealt with socioeconomically related disease and disability. Public health medicine pioneered in humanizing health care by recognizing that humane and compassionate care of underserved populations should incorporate both scientific medicine and social policies. Before the growth of the hospital-dominated system, health care literature was oriented toward getting people back to work. Hospitals then were few in number and housed only the poor or the outcasts who did not "contribute." As physician-dominated hospitals grew, the ethic imperceptibly changed. Hospitals became places for treatment of sickness and disease, which happened to coincide frequently with old age. A health care system dominated by the values of industrial productivity grew in technical capability and institutional orientation to become one in which the treatment of disease and relief of suffering became the overriding, but never explicit, value. Even today, the cost effectiveness studies based on workplace productivity often do not include the social values of relief of suffering and improved quality of life.[23] Now more than ever, these factors will have to underlie any meaningful progress in long-term care.

The relatively recent development of a scientific health care system has spawned some innovative ways to approach the needs of long-term care. As Starr points out, our health care system is the result of a hodgepodge of market forces, professional dominance, and (more recently) intermittent and often arbitrary regulation.[24]

Research capability can be another source of power in dealing with our demographic revolution. Good research asks important questions about the quality of care and the functional abilities of the recipients of that care (rather than merely inquiring about simplistic diagnosis related categories). This kind of research can bring some positive changes for today and support the gerontologists' hope for the future.

Clinical epidemiology can help us find solutions because it provides tools to determine the most efficient and effective ways to set up and to operate health care institutions, ranging from nursing homes to intensive care units. As a newly developing science which incorporates methodologies of statistics and of the social sciences, health services research has not been immediately welcomed by the world of medicine. Surgeons do not want to be told they are performing too many operations, doctors do not want to hear that they can be replaced (and often with improved patient satisfaction) by nurse practitioners, and hospitals do not want to know that their most lucrative procedures make no detectable therapeutic impact on the outcomes of patient care. However, insurance companies and public agencies which fund the greatest share of medical practice do want to know these things, for obvious fiscal reasons. Their interest will encourage the growth of this field.

Few lay individuals in our society are aware that persons in nursing home beds in this country outnumber those in hospital beds, and that one of every four people over age 65 will spend some time in a nursing home.[25] The shortcomings and advantages of home health care and long-term care demand our attention. While geriatric medicine and research are advancing toward the minimization of disabilities (especially incontinence, disruptive confused states, and profound immobility) which make home care impossible, there will always be a substantial number for whom these disorders cannot be reversed by medical intervention. They can, however, be managed by good nursing care. In addition, those individuals who have no care giver at home are at a higher risk of institutionalization, often at a more restrictive level of care than is necessary—because the services that they require are either not available or not reimbursed by Medicare and Medicaid.

A REEVALUATION OF SOCIAL VALUES

When we attempt to find answers merely by examining studies of health care systems, we encounter a major obstacle: our efforts may prove analogous to rearranging the deck chairs on the *Titanic*. That is, we fail to address the serious underlying problems. Social systems of any kind either directly express or imply the values of that society. Regardless, our health care system will exhibit our values, and will not change significantly in response to rhetoric. We have entered what Butler has called the century of old age, wherein "contemporary older people are a kind of pioneer group that is demonstrating adaptation and synthesis to new social and work roles."[26] He sees them not as a burden, but as pioneers, and—of course—if we come to the awareness that we are they, then we also are pioneers.

One of the major frontiers consists of the evolution, clarification, and realization of a coherent social ethic. The shifting demographic pattern is often portrayed in the popular press as a constantly increasing number of dependent elderly needing to be supported by a fixed or less rapidly growing "productive" segment. There are two reasons to question this perception. First, we need a broader definition of productivity and increased options for the voluntary employment of the elderly. Second, the demographic profile is more complex than these reports acknowledge. Consider the following account from Robert M. Ball on the demographic reality and the social choices it implies:

> During the next 25 years or so, the growth in the under-20 group is expected to come to an end. Thus, looking at the total dependency ratio—those under 20 plus those over 65—it is not true that each worker in the future will be supporting a larger and larger number of dependents. If one takes into account not only (those) 65 and over but also those under 20, the total dependency ratio drops between now and 2010, and then returns in 2020 to about where we are today. Even at the expected high point in the size of the aged population, 2035, the estimated total dependency ratio is only 84 per 100. This is lower than the ratios experienced in the 1960s and early 1970s. There is a shift in who the dependents are, but as compared with the recent past, no absolute increase in the ratio of dependents to those aged 20–64.
>
> The issue in the long-range future could well be whether people will be willing to spend more to bring about the kind of world they want for themselves and others when they grow old because they will need to spend less on bringing up children.[27]

Could it be this simple choice of where the money goes, and of whose money is spent? Social choices like these are expressed through state and federal social policies; the choices are part of responsible citizenship.

No calculation can resolve the conflict between liberty and justice inherent in our credo "liberty and justice for all." Philosophers have attempted such a resolution for centuries, even millenia; in many respects, liberty and justice seem reciprocal, not additive, attributes. In order to ensure some justice, a portion of each person's liberty is relinquished. In fact, maintaining this balance is one of the most important functions of law in our society. For example, increasing taxation of the very wealthy could contribute significant resources to providing home care services that would increase the freedom (i.e., the liberty) of the impaired but marginally independent elderly. Is such a distribution of liberty consistent with the goal of justice as we define it? Or does justice mean that each individual is entitled only to the material gains of his or her investments?

The concept of liberty infuses our economic policies, but I believe that health care ought to be allocated according to criteria other than to the highest bidder. The present state of policies for the elderly in this country makes it clear that policy makers are not allocating services consistently or coherently. Our legal tradition supports the rights of individuals and the protections guaranteed by the Constitution. But what does this mean to us and to our aging? Government policies, along with the medical and legal traditions, are still unclear about many of the value conflicts raised by the need for health care and the demographic imperative.

CONCLUSION

No single policy will solve these problems, nor will scientific advances totally eliminate them. The demographic revolution is a time of great change in our world. We cannot begin to predict its significance or its consequences, except to note that social change on such a large scale always produces stress or, more positively, "creative tension." The challenge of the future is not just that of frail, dependent elderly persons but also that of vigorous elderly individuals who will need meaningful roles, respect, and avenues that allow them to contribute their experience and wisdom. Human continuity means that the demographic revolution encompasses "us" as well as "them;" to achieve this continuity, we must seek progress in ethics comparable to this century's progress in technology.

We must also learn to take seriously the discipline of qualitative study. Philosophy as a rigorous part of medicine, law, and health care studies is necessary to maintain civilization rather than simple narcissistic survival. For the law to uphold social values in the face of the complexities of health care for the elderly, policy makers must understand these values and take them into account. For the health care professional, the ability to deal competently with ethics will become a critical part of his or her requisite skills, as will the sensitivity to seek an expert consultant in ethics or in law when needed.

Such are my hopes for the effect of the demographic revolution on the profession of medicine. As an educator, I see that the humanistic ethos is the major source of power for medical students who daily confront the frustrating limits of technology in the care of the aged patient. This ethos is the source of power which will similarly undergird any reasonable approach to the ethical and legal issues in long-term care.

Working on the problems of aging provides an appreciation for the value of human beings and the meaning of life in the community. The field of aging involves one in the work of humanizing our society; it is a job that is not only uplifting but also one that is essential if we are to survive as a nation.

NOTES

1. NATIONAL INSTITUTE ON AGING, SPECIAL REPORT ON AGING (U.S. Gov't Printing Office, Washington, D.C.) (1979) at 12.
2. Leaf, A., *Getting Old*, SCIENTIFIC AMERICAN 22:45–52 (1973).
3. Watts, D., McCally, M., *Demography*, in GERIATRIC MEDICINE (C.K. Cassel and J.R. Walsh, eds.) (Springer-Verlag, New York) (1984), Vol. II, at 3–15.
4. Butler, R.N., *The Triumph of Age: Science, Gerontology and Ageism*, BULLETIN OF THE NEW YORK ACADEMY OF MEDICINE 58(4):347, 349 (May 1982).
5. W.F. ANDERSON, PRACTICAL MANAGEMENT OF THE ELDERLY (Lippincott, Philadelphia) (3d ed. 1976).
6. Thomas, L., *The Problem of Dementia*, in LATE NIGHT THOUGHTS ON LISTENING TO MAHLER'S NINTH SYMPHONY (Viking Press, New York) (1983) at 120–26.
7. R.M. VEATCH, DEATH, DYING, AND THE BIOLOGICAL REVOLUTION (Yale University Press, New Haven) (1976) at 2–4.
8. *See* Smith, D.J., Granbois, J.A., *The American Way of Hospice*, HASTINGS CENTER REPORT 12(2):8–10 (April 1982).
9. Holden, C., *Government Intercedes in "Baby Jane Doe,"* SCIENCE (November 25, 1983) at 908.
10. CAL. HEALTH & SAFETY CODE § 7185 (West 1982). *See* D.W. MEYERS, MEDICO-LEGAL IMPLICATIONS OF DEATH AND DYING (Bancroft-Whitman Co., San Francisco) (1981) at 492 (California Natural Death Act).
11. E. KUBLER-ROSS, ON DEATH AND DYING (Macmillan Co., New York) (1969).
12. *In re* Quinlan, 355 A.2d 647 (N.J. 1976).
13. Lee, M., Cassel, C.K., *Orders Not to Resuscitate: The Ethical and Legal Framework for Decision Making*, WESTERN JOURNAL OF MEDICINE 140(1):117–22 (January 1984).
14. PRESIDENT'S COMMISSION FOR THE STUDY OF ETHICAL PROBLEMS IN MEDICINE AND BIOMEDICAL AND BEHAVIORAL RESEARCH, DECIDING TO FOREGO LIFE-SUSTAINING TREATMENT (U.S. Gov't Printing Office, Washington, D.C.) (1983) at 72, quoting Beynon, H., *Doctors as Murderers*, Vol. 1982, CRIMINAL LAW REVIEW 17–18 (January 1982).
15. Brown, N.K., Thompson, D.J., *Nontreatment of Fever in Extended Care Facilities*, NEW ENGLAND JOURNAL OF MEDICINE 300(22):1246–48 (May 31, 1979).
16. Hilfiker, D., *Allowing the Debilitated to Die: Facing our Ethical Choices*, NEW ENGLAND JOURNAL OF MEDICINE 308(12):716 (March 24, 1983).
17. *See* J.F. FRIES, L.M. CRAPO, VITALITY AND AGING: IMPLICATIONS OF THE RECTANGULAR CURVE (W.H. Freeman & Co., San Francisco) (1981).
18. Meier, P., *The Cell Biology of Aging*, in GERIATRIC MEDICINE (C.K. Cassel and J.R. Walsh, eds.) (Springer-Verlag, New York) (1984), Vol. I, at 3–12.
19. FRIES & CRAPO, *supra* note 17, at 115.
20. Gruenberg, E.M., *Epidemiology of Senile Dementia*, in NIH SECOND CONFERENCE ON THE EPIDEMIOLOGY OF AGING (Publication Number HHS 80–969) (U.S. Gov't Printing Office, Washington, D.C.) (1980) at 91–104.
21. Fries, J.F., *Aging, Natural Death and the Compression of Morbidity*, NEW ENGLAND JOURNAL OF MEDICINE 303(3):130, 135 (JULY 17, 1980).

22. P. STARR, THE SOCIAL TRANSFORMATION OF AMERICAN MEDICINE (Basic Books, New York) (1983).
23. Avorn, J., *Benefit and Cost in Geriatric Care*, NEW ENGLAND JOURNAL OF MEDICINE 310(20):1294–1301 (May 17, 1984).
24. STARR, *supra* note 22, at 379–419.
25. Somers, A., *Long Term Care for the Elderly and Disabled: A New Health Priority*, NEW ENGLAND JOURNAL OF MEDICINE 307(4):221–26 (July 22, 1982).
26. Butler, *supra* note 4, at 355.
27. Ball, R.M., *Rethinking National Policy on Health Care for the Elderly*, in THE GERIATRIC IMPERATIVE (S.R. Somers and D.R. Fabian, eds.) (Appleton Century Crofts, New York) (1981) at 34–35.

2

Ethical Issues: Equitable Distribution and Decision Making

Joanne Lynn, M.D.

At this time in this country, two areas pose major ethical dilemmas for those who provide health care to the elderly: equity in the distribution of health care and decision making. The issue concerning access, briefly, is this: Given that society has limited resources and multiple goals, what kind of life are we willing to provide for the elderly when meeting their needs requires community funds? Decision making raises this issue: How can we be sure that the wishes of the competent elderly are respected, the interests of the incompetent are protected, and determinations of competence are made responsibly?

Before addressing these areas of concern, one should consider ethical dilemmas generally. Many people feel that ethics has to do only with making decisions about values and that anyone's opinion is as good as anyone else's. This first perception is largely true, but the second is clearly wrong. Some reasons and choices are without merit or, at least, are worse than others. An alternate conception holds that ethics is a way to resolve disputes by reason, rather than by power or force. The tools of ethics are clear definition, sharp analysis, and persuasion with logic and argument.[1]

Generally, ethics does not provide a prescription for policy or behavior, and policy makers and implementers must consider current power systems and personal abilities which modify ethical imperatives. Ethics thus defined commonly can lead to understanding, but it does not necessarily lead to easy resolutions of dilemmas. Even a clear view of the ethical principles can be complicated by the realities of frequently anguishing and difficult situations.

Ethics is also a body of literature that provides critiques of reasoning.[2] Geriatric practitioners, for example, could benefit greatly by being pushed to use conceptually clear definitions and to give complete argu-

ments. Overzealous advocates for the elderly, as well as therapeutic ni-
hilists, often employ sloppy reasoning and rhetorical arguments rather
than careful analysis. Yet, little interest in and support for the endeavors
of serious philosophers is evident in geriatrics. Multidisciplinary approaches need to go beyond multidisciplinary health care teams, including also sociologists, philosophers, political scientists, lawyers, and others
who are willing to exert themselves to analyze cases and arguments
critically.

   For example, the language that is used to frame discussions has a
bearing on how we conceptualize those discussions. Consider the difference between the language of obligations and that of rights. Lawyers
often speak in terms of "rights," thinking of the interests they would
argue for on behalf of their clients. As a linguist, a sociologist, or a
philosopher might point out, when we talk of "rights" we talk of adversar-
ies. A right is held against someone else. On the other hand, "obligations"
are "to" someone, and the word implies a collaborative or community-
building relation. There well may be times when it is appropriate to use
either language, but the terms are not equivalent. If ethical discussion
regarding health care of the elderly is phrased in terms of rights, the
image created is adversarial. If talk is put in terms of obligations, the
image is of community. Choosing a term for the persons receiving health
care services also creates an image. Are they to be called clients, patients,
or residents? Again, these are not equivalent terms. "Client" suggests a
business model. "Patient" fits a paternalist model. "Resident" implies a
relatively independent person.

A HISTORICAL PERSPECTIVE

Growth in the number of elderly persons has strained traditional understandings of obligations among people. An ordinary extended family at
the turn of the century was likely to have at most one great-grandmother,
who would live with the family and be supported by them. Now an
extended family might have between five and six great-grandparents living; but largely due to social changes, many of these elderly now live
apart from the younger family.[3] Families are sometimes mutually supportive, providing for the growth and development of children and the support of the elderly. They may also be unacceptable modes of living, in
which people are abusive to one another, in which they limit one another's potential, or in which they fail to provide adequately for one
another. This society allows people the choice of not living in a family by
making it economically viable for people to be divorced, for children to
live separately from parents, and for parents to live independently of
their children. Our society may have gone too far, because it is now often

disadvantageous to live in families in many circumstances. Most Americans live in atomistic settings, often of the minimum size necessary to raise children. Clearly, these changes in lifestyle limit the options for care of the elderly.

Ethical dilemmas are also presented by the increasing complexity of the health care system. A person who was getting old and dying in 1900 was probably helped by family, clergy, and a few neighbors. The people touched directly by the decisions could be involved in making and experiencing them. Now, most such patients would go to a hospital, be attended by many people, and be involved in two or three community care systems. Health care has changed from being based at home or in the doctor's office to a complex and unwieldy system in which an elderly person who has even a few needs may become involved with an astonishing number of helping professionals. All who are affected by decisions cannot possibly have a hand in making them, especially if payment is from public funds gathered from taxpayers. These background considerations shape the context for exploring the key issues posed earlier— equity and decision making.

EQUITY IN THE DISTRIBUTION OF HEALTH CARE

Securing access to good health care for the population necessarily compromises other goals. Consider the conflict between saving costs and securing quality health care. If society were to concentrate on saving money, diseases or care patterns that kill people cheaply would actually be advantageous. The late André Hellegers, M.D., former head of the Kennedy Institute of Ethics, used to stun audiences by saying that smoking should be encouraged as a cost control measure because it tended to kill people just past the prime of life and to do so in a manner that did not consume substantial medical resources. As long as victims avoided the relatively infrequent plagues of severe emphysema, they usually avoided the high costs of long-term dependency. While Helleger's statement may no longer be true,[4] some diseases, for example, arrhythmogenic heart attacks, are cheap, quick killers and frequently affect those who are "just past the prime of life." While we would abhor the society that affirmatively encouraged such diseases, cost-saving enterprises might stimulate a shift of resources to more "productive" areas.

This society would like to have it all: individual health, community health, individual self-determination, and equity in distribution of health services. However, without unlimited resources, pursuit of these objectives is doomed to create conflict. The meaning and priority of each goal will lead to the delineation of changes needed in the health care system.

Access to health care for elderly persons depends largely upon the extent of the community's willingness to provide payment. A preliminary problem is defining "health care." For example, "health care" may well not include most of "long-term care." Long-term care includes providing housing, shelter, nutrition, and general supervision, which many hold to be separate from health care.[5] If health care were to include these services, then housing and nutrition subsidies would occasion the same societal responses as payment for health care. The World Health Organization has actually included these services in its expansive definition of health care.[6] Allocation of health care under such a definition becomes the allocation of all good things. On the other hand, a very restrictive definition, considering only physician-provided drugs or procedures, would eliminate from the scope of concerns many services that have substantial impact on health.

Once the definition of health care is settled, one must decide whether all or part of health care is ethically different from other things, and particularly whether there are reasons for allocating health care (or some kinds of health care) on a special basis. The President's Commission's answer was that health care is especially important to people in that it relieves suffering, provides opportunity to live, provides information concerning the ways that people can live and plan their lives, and gives evidence of mutual empathy and compassion.[7] Of course, some of these attributes are true of adequate clothing and food as well, but health care needs are also more difficult for individuals to handle alone. Ill health generally strikes unpredictably and people are not usually accountable for their ill health. Holding the victim of ill health blameworthy for his or her health status is generally a difficult proposition to justify with empirical evidence. Thus, even for smokers where the data are increasingly definitive, we continue to permit and even support smoking.

Once defined and assessed regarding any special claims, how should health care be distributed? What distributions of health care would be fair? Fairness does not demand equal access to all health care, because each of us does not need the same type and amount of health care. A few lucky people avoid doctors for nine decades or more; others were stricken with polio at the age of six. A strict equality of access is unsupportable. Neither can allocation be made fairly on the basis of needs, because some people are so needy that enormous amounts of resources could be spent for their care and yet be insufficient, while the ordinary sorts of care that most people want and need on a relatively routine basis would not be provided.

The President's Commission decided that an ethically defensible and practical standard would be that all persons should have equal access to an adequate level of health care.[8] Defining the "adequate level" involves consideration of society's resources and other legitimate societal priorities. At present, the Commission held, there would be broad consensus on certain glaring examples of inequities. For example, more than 40 million Americans (mostly the poor and the unemployed) are not insured against devastating medical expenses.[9] Prenatal care is often effectively unavailable.[10] In other areas without broad consensus, society can and should debate the precise definition of "adequate." The availability of health care to all must mean that each potential patient has physical access to care of adequate quality without undue burden. Each of those elements entails, of course, further definition.[11]

In order to limit health care made available to some people so as to ensure equity, one must account for the worth of the health care not given to the potential recipient who was denied. The Commission's report, *Deciding to Forego Life-Sustaining Treatment,* notes that while priorities of the elderly for health care are not clear, it is clear that the elderly are not being asked.[12] At the present time, any patient, no matter how demented, no matter how close to death, can be admitted to an intensive care unit or a dialysis unit and have most of the health care costs reimbursed under Medicare. Yet, other services such as the "Meals on Wheels" program, which can make a difference in someone's life, are often difficult to obtain. It may be that this priority should not be reversed, but the elderly as a group should be given a voice in establishing the priorities. Our service delivery system reflects a medical model patterned upon the needs, wants, and fears of 40- and 50-year-olds; it is not based on the needs, wants, and fears of 70- and 80-year-olds.

In our quest for an effective and efficient health care system, the effects of federal and state health care policies on equity must be assessed. This exercise is complex, and not commonly done. For example, the recent federal hospice care legislation provides a substantial entitlement that may largely go to middle-class cancer patients at the expense of other Medicare recipients.[13] Even though hospice otherwise seems to be a good idea, society should be concerned if a benefit is granted to people with adequate care at the expense of those lacking adequate health care.

Ensuring access may well impinge upon traditional commitments to individual liberties and individual well-being, requiring a rebalancing of values. Thus far, our society has dealt with health care equity as a policy problem and individual decision making as a doctor-patient problem, and has acted as though the two shall never meet. That distinction cannot continue. No logical and ethically defensible system can hold those concerns separate. At some point, a doctor will have to limit health care because of its cost. At present, even if a doctor feels he or she should limit care because of its cost, that motivation is not now a defense to a charge of malpractice.[14]

Finally, efforts to enhance equity will be constrained by Americans who historically have both valued individual free choice highly and designed a system that makes it virtually impossible to deny health care to current patients because of cost. The resulting "system" has excluded some potential patients from receiving care. This was evidenced by the recent maneuver to change Medicaid eligibility requirements for health care reimbursement.[15] These changes make it likely that some people will never become part of the health care system; however, since they will essentially be invisible to health care providers, they will not be "denied" care by the system.

DECISION MAKING

Decision making is a major problem area for ethical dilemmas in caring for the elderly and is the subject of many of the following chapters. Here, the focus will be upon how to effect good practices in health care decision making, concentrating on the three groups of patients highlighted by the following questions: For competent patients, how does one ensure that they have the opportunity to decide about their care? For patients with fluctuating, diminished, or uncertain competence, what procedures best balance maximum self-determination with appropriate protection from the serious harm resulting from an irrational decision? For clearly incompetent patients, what procedures ensure that the decision serves the patient's best interests, ideally on the patient's own terms?

The difference between competence and incompetence is crucial.[16] If the patient is competent, he or she has the right to choose among available options for health care. Only when the patient chooses a course that the physician is unwilling to provide does anyone else have a role in decision making. Moreover, that role ideally extends only to reviewing whether the patient is competent, has received the appropriate information, and has chosen voluntarily.[17] This is a very limited review. On the other hand, when a person is incompetent, other persons must have authority—both in law and in practice—to make the necessary decisions. Generally, individual cases involving incompetent patients do not receive public judicial review unless a surrogate and doctor disagree on a decision or course of treatment. This review for an incompetent patient is not only for the determination of incompetence and the assessment of voluntariness and appropriate information disclosure, but also may extend to a consideration of the actual health care decision being made and whether it is in the patient's best interests. That is a much more problematic review and authority.[18] Thus, the actual competence of each patient is important in determining the patient's involvement in his or her own health care decisions and, complementarily, the authority of others to intervene.

For those who are competent, the first obligation is to facilitate their involvement in decision making. Failures in our usual decision making procedures must be reduced; these include inadequate information, inattention to the enhancement and determination of competence, and undue reliance upon the judiciary. Many improvements can be accomplished if health care providers take decision making seriously.

Second, advance directives, such as living wills or durable powers of attorney, should be encouraged. Using a durable power of attorney, for example, a person who is presently competent can indicate who should make decisions concerning medical care if incompetence subsequently occurs; the document can also indicate what sorts of decisions should be made. The courts and health care providers should give deference to advance directives. An increasing number of states are recognizing by statute the validity and usefulness of these devices.[19] Even in states without a specific law, the patient may well assert the authority to designate a proxy and to specify preferences regarding at least some forms of health care. Many health care providers and lawyers do not yet realize the potential value of such documents.

Finally, decision making can be improved by establishing and using "intermediary institutions," a sociological term referring to institutions that lie between the person and the government, and that often have no clear authority in law but are granted informal deference by the surrounding community. Professional societies could take the initiative and work with hospitals and nursing homes to establish internal, multidisciplinary committees charged with ensuring fundamental fairness and holding practitioners and families to appropriate standards in decision making.[20]

Such efforts would tend to limit the involvement of the legal system to those relatively few cases where there are real conflicts or where there is a substantial chance that a patient's interests are not being served. Not every patient of dubious competence needs to be taken to court for guardianship or for decision making about a treatment. Internal institutional committees could provide a forum in which policies concerning competence determination and surrogate designation can be discussed and applied to specific cases. Institutions should establish procedures that use the legal system only when needed, but that still adequately protect the interests of incompetent patients.

CONCLUSION

Two very different sorts of ethical issues face those who are concerned with health care for the elderly. Regarding the making of choices among health care options, the standards have become fairly clear. The task now before care givers is to effectuate good quality decision making: to ascertain and enhance competence, to improve information transfer, to ensure adequate voluntariness, to protect the interests of incompetent patients, and to maintain privacy and efficiency while doing so.

Regarding the concern to allocate limited health care equitably, society is not yet clear as to the standards by which to judge whether the endeavor is doing well. Much work needs to be done to define the terms, play out their implications, and especially set the priorities for this pursuit of justice with legitimate societal goals.

NOTES

1. *See, e.g.,* T.L. BEAUCHAMP, PHILOSOPHICAL ETHICS: AN INTRODUCTION TO MORAL PHILOSOPHY (McGraw-Hill, New York) (1982).
2. *See, e.g.,* S.J. REISER, A.J. DYCK, W.J. CURRAN, ETHICS IN MEDICINE: HISTORICAL PERSPECTIVES AND CONTEMPORARY CONCERNS (MIT Press, Cambridge, Mass.) (1977) [hereinafter cited as ETHICS IN MEDICINE].
3. *See, e.g.,* Butler, R., *The Teaching Nursing Home,* JOURNAL OF THE AMERICAN MEDICAL ASSOCIATION 246(13):1435 (September 25, 1981).
4. In the decade since his statement, much progress has been made in treating cancer of the lung and coronary artery disease, thus reducing their lethality and increasing the costs of associated care.
5. PRESIDENT'S COMMISSION FOR THE STUDY OF ETHICAL PROBLEMS IN MEDICINE AND BIOMEDICAL AND BEHAVIORAL RESEARCH, SECURING ACCESS TO HEALTH CARE: THE ETHICAL IMPLICATIONS OF DIFFERENCES IN THE AVAILABILITY OF HEALTH SERVICES (U.S. Gov't Printing Office, Washington, D.C.) (1983) at 151 [hereinafter cited as SECURING ACCESS].
6. WORLD HEALTH ORGANIZATION, PREAMBLE TO THE CONSTITUTION, W.A.U. BASIC DOCUMENTS (World Health Organization, Geneva, Switzerland) (26th ed. 1976) at 1, as reprinted in ETHICS IN MEDICINE, *supra* note 2, at 552.
7. ETHICS IN MEDICINE, *supra* note 2, at 16–17.
8. SECURING ACCESS, *supra* note 5, at 4–5.
9. SECURING ACCESS, *supra* note 5, at 109.
10. SECURING ACCESS, *supra* note 5, at 111.
11. *See* SECURING ACCESS, *supra* note 5, at 65–113.
12. PRESIDENT'S COMMISSION FOR THE STUDY OF ETHICAL PROBLEMS IN MEDICINE AND BIOMEDICAL AND BEHAVIORAL RESEARCH, DECIDING TO FOREGO LIFE-SUSTAINING TREATMENT (U.S. Gov't Printing Office, Washington, D.C.) (1983) at 110 [hereinafter cited as FOREGOING TREATMENT].
13. Tax Equity and Fiscal Responsibility Act of 1982, Section 122 P. L. 97–248,42 U.S.C.A. §§ 1395c–1395f (West 1982); Medicare Program: Hospice Care, 48 Fed. Reg. 56008–36 (December 16, 1983); Brody, H., Lynn, J., *The Physician's Responsibility Under the New Medicare Reimbursement for Hospice Care,* NEW ENGLAND JOURNAL OF MEDICINE 310(14):920–22 (April 5, 1984); Churchill,

L., *The Ethics of Hospice Care*, in HOSPICE DEVELOPMENT AND ADMINISTRA-
TION (Glen Davidson, ed.) (Hemisphere Publishing Co., New York) (1984).

14. Malpractice cases turn on whether the physician's behavior was or was not
below the standard of practice of similarly situated practitioners. PROSSER
AND KEETON ON THE LAW OF TORTS (W.P. Keeton, ed.) (West Publishing Co.,
St. Paul, Minn.) (1984) at 185–93. Those standards have been established
without particular regard to costs. The practitioner who chooses to be a
"responsible steward" of community resources and to compromise pursuit of
the patient's interest to do so will have no defense. Indeed, it will seem that
the physician made a particular patient disadvantaged in an idiosyncratic
manner. *But see* Kapp, M., *Legal and Ethical Implications of Health Care Reimbursement by Diagnosis Related Groups*, LAW MEDICINE & HEALTH CARE
12(6):245–53 (December 1984).

15. 42 C.F.R. §§435.400–930 (1983).

16. "Competence" and "incompetence" here are used to mean actual capacity to
make valid choices, not to reflect a court's affirmation of that status. *See* chs.
17, 24 of this text.

17. *See generally* SECURING ACCESS, *supra* note 5, at 190–93.

18. *See, e.g.,* FOREGOING TREATMENT, *supra* note 12, at 130–32, 153–60.

19. In March 1983, 42 states had explicit durable powers of attorney (none of
which are clearly inapplicable to health care), and 13 states and the District of
Columbia had Living Will statutes. *Id.* at app. D., app. E. *See also* Steinbrook, R.,
Lo, B., *Decision Making for Incompetent Patients by Designated Proxy: California's
New Law*, NEW ENGLAND JOURNAL OF MEDICINE 310(24):1598–601 (June 14,
1984).

20. FOREGOING TREATMENT, *supra* note 12, at 160–70; INSTITUTIONAL ETHICS
COMMITTEES AND HEALTH CARE DECISION MAKING (R.E. Cranford, A.E.
Doudera, eds.) (Health Administration Press, Ann Arbor, Mich.) (1984).

3

Assuring Access
to Long-Term Care:
Legal, Ethical, and Other Barriers

Paul A. Kerschner, Ph.D.

In 1975 the U.S. Senate Special Committee on Aging called long-term care for the elderly "the most troubled and troublesome" area of human service delivery.[1] This description is still accurate. Due to a confluence of demographic, political, and social forces, we are witnessing an increasing demand for a system of long-term health care services for the elderly. It has become obvious that our present health care system, including service delivery, methods of funding, and limited scope of planning and programming, can no longer adequately serve present and future aging populations.

Before revising our present system, we first must determine what we mean by long-term care and what our long-term care policy ought to be. The U.S. Department of Health and Human Services (DHHS) defines long-term care as "services required by people who have functional limitations as a result of or in conjunction with chronic illness or conditions."[2] Although our current long-term care policy suggests an institutional orientation, it should include the whole continuum of care. What we mean by "continuum of care" is a system that would incorporate a whole range of support services, both medical and social, and would allow home-based and/or community care, as well as institutional care for those elderly persons who need it. Persons needing long-term care may live in nursing homes, domiciliary care homes, halfway houses, their own homes, or their children's.

Having briefly defined the concept of long-term care, we must consider the issue of access to long-term care, particularly the definition of access and the ethics of access.

THE ETHICS OF ACCESS

In a recent publication entitled *Securing Access to Health Care*,[3] the President's Commission for the Study of Ethical Problems in Medicine and Biomedical and Behavioral Research concluded that access to health care could be expressed in terms of "ethical obligations." The Commission concluded that:

1. [Society] has an ethical obligation to ensure equitable access to health care for all.
2. The societal obligation is balanced by individual obligations.
3. Equitable access to health care requires that all citizens be able to secure an adequate level of care without incurring excessive burdens.
4. When equity occurs through the operation of private forces, there is no need for government involvement, but the ultimate responsibility for ensuring that society's obligation is met . . . rests with the Federal government.
5. The cost of achieving equitable access to health care ought to be shared fairly.
6. Efforts to contain rising health care costs are important but should not focus on limiting the attainment of equitable access for the least well-served portion of the public.[4]

Although this is a somewhat cautious set of conclusions, the Commission did seek to define access in terms of ensuring an adequate level of care without excessive burdens to the individual. The Commission acknowledged that there are many ambiguities regarding the nature of society's obligation to provide health care. For instance, the Commission did not determine what share of health costs individuals should be expected to bear directly, nor did it suggest the extent of our responsibility to use health resources prudently. In addition, the Commission did not determine if it is society's responsibility to ensure that every person receives an equal amount of care services. Must society ensure that everyone has the same opportunity to receive all available care? If not, what level of care is sufficient? And, does society's obligation include a responsibility to ensure both that care is available and that the cost of care will not unduly burden the patient?

In my opinion, the Commission erred in failing to elaborate on what distinguishes long-term care from health care. Thus, when discussing the minimum level of long-term care in a nursing home accredited under Medicare, it stated: "The question of the nature of the social obligation to pay for this type of care, some of which is 'custodial' rather than 'health' care, raises different issues, however, from those presented by the obligation to ensure access to an adequate level of health care."[5] In another chapter of this book, Joanne Lynn states that the Commission did not focus on long-term care issues because they are at the boundary of health care—health care is but one of the services included when we talk about long-term care.[6]

In this regard the Commission was correct; long-term health care involves more than a quantitatively adequate level of health care. Long-term care must not only be adequate in amount, but must also be accessible in appropriate levels and mixes of care. Regarding this attempt, we must remember that human and financial resources are scarce. At one time, the problem of resource allocation for the aged seemed deceptively simple. Since a large segment of our population needed help, the first order of business was to marshal money and services as quickly as possible. In an era when national resources seemed virtually inexhaustible and economic growth appeared eternal, it seemed that moral pressure alone would open the tap to an equitable sharing of health care resources with those who had passed the years of economic productivity.

Today we recognize that health care resources are limited, and we are faced with the task of weighing the distribution of these resources to the elderly against society's other priorities. Helping the elderly is still a positive value, but new questions are being asked regarding limits: how much care, what kind of care, at whose expense, and who decides how it should be allocated?

With these pressing economic realities, the old question of whether there is a right to access to any health care at all has presented itself once again. The President's Commission preferred not to couch access in terms of a right, but rather to express it as an ethical obligation.[7] But clearly, Congress and the state legislatures have conferred benefits and entitlements upon the elderly, and especially those who are poor, disabled, unemployed, or mentally ill. The problem, as Elias Cohen has discussed,[8] is that these benefits and entitlements are not self-executing. This is a problem for elderly persons, particularly those in need of long-term care. Almost by definition, the need for long-term care implies frailty, economic, physical and/or psychological dependence, low physical and psychological energy reserves, impaired mobility, and similar characteristics. Under such conditions, the presumption of vigorous claim assertion or protest when rights are invaded, denied, or withheld is unrealistic. It can only result in societal failure to protect the rights of older adults who do not or cannot protect themselves. Those who are ignorant of their entitlements, those who cannot comprehend the unbelievably complex world of public benefits, those who are reticent, those who perceive public benefit schemes to be charity which renders them the object of pity, and those who do not have economic, transportational, or intellectual means by which to lay claim to the benefits due them become victims of discrimination.

Let us now examine the assertion that there is an ethical obligation to provide an appropriate level of long-term care to the elderly. Before discussing this ethical obligation, one must determine what is an appropriate level of long-term care, and what are the existing barriers to such a level of care.

It is widely held that, in the area of long-term care, an appropriate level of care must combine health care with social care. Although the elderly represent the vast majority of the nursing home population, many elderly neither need nor prefer nursing home care. Many elderly people are inappropriately placed in nursing homes because federal and state reimbursement is available for such care and not for other types of services. Therefore, the development of long-term care has followed funding patterns rather than the needs of the individual. At present, the federal government sponsors more than 100 programs that support or provide long-term care services to the elderly. These programs include public housing, food stamps, unemployment compensation, employment services through the CETA legislation, and a number of other social services provided by the Administration on Aging under the Older Americans Act of 1966.[9] Although these programs were aimed at the poor or unemployed and do not contain age-related eligibility conditions, the elderly receive a large share of benefits because of their low-income status. Yet often access is impeded, the services are fragmented, and eligibility requirements are tied to costly and unwieldy reimbursement formulas. Current health and social care programs are mainly task oriented, level-of-care oriented, or finance oriented, and are designed around a single service. This piecemeal approach to long-term care and support has generated dissatisfaction and underscored the need for a coordinated long-term care system that includes institutional and noninstitutional components. The system must have a broad array of possibilities. Institutionalization remains the appropriate method of care when a certain level of disability has been reached. Home services are not a panacea.

In addition to linking health care and social care services, the concept of appropriate levels of care is intertwined with considerations of choice and the doctrine of the least restrictive alternative.[10] Currently, many older people have very little choice regarding health care services. Their choices are restricted by their physicians' orders and the financial structure of programs presently available. We need to consider what kinds of limitations on choice are most consistent with fulfilling society's moral obligation to provide equitable access to appropriate levels of care. We must decide whether a new financial structure would expand the element of choice and self-determination for older people.

As Elias Cohen has argued, the application of the doctrine of the least restrictive alternative requires that the elderly be made aware of choices of services available to them and that they be allowed to choose in a noncoercive environment.[11] Cohen believes that too often a patient is influenced into a choice by his physicians, nurses, or social workers without being aware of the alternatives. Identification of the most appropriate solution in accordance with the principles of the least restrictive alternative doctrine requires assessing the individual's functioning and then delineating the precise problems, if any, which the impairment presents. Finally, the least restrictive alternative principle suggests a delivery system able to provide the appropriate service, case management, and other necessary supports needed by each individual resident.

Put another way, the least restrictive alternative doctrine incorporates the older individual's right to the choice of treatment when that treatment is needed. It means neither over-providing (e.g., 24-hour skilled nursing home care for one who needs only assistance with dressing and personal hygiene in the morning and at night) nor under-providing (e.g., skilled nursing care for a patient recovering from peripheral nerve damage secondary to diabetes, where intensive rehabilitation therapy and programs are required).

BARRIERS TO ACCESS TO APPROPRIATE LEVELS OF LONG-TERM CARE

Now that we have a framework to ensure access to appropriate levels of long-term care, we must examine some of the barriers within our current system that make attaining that goal very difficult.

THE MEDICAL MODEL

Approaches to long-term care have been fragmented and narrow in scope because they are based on a medical model of health care. Medicare and Medicaid were established to pay for health care services; they rely on the medical model of care. Thus, the focus of the medical model is on services that physicians and nurses provide, even though many chronically disabled persons do not need that kind of skilled care. The medical model has proven to be inappropriate for long-term care because of its emphasis on costly acute care rather than chronic care, on diagnostic and treatment services rather than psychosocial and rehabilitative services, on disease rather than health promotion, and on medical professionals rather than paraprofessionals and social service professionals. Many older people need long-term care that is not medically intensive. But many basic supportive services, such as meal preparation, laundry, and housekeeping, are only reimbursed if they are provided in a nursing home or hospital setting, not in the patient's own home. To the extent that states have had the option under Medicaid to finance less medically oriented services (e.g., personal care), relatively few have done so.

Policy makers have been reluctant to abandon the medical model because of its usefulness as a budgetary control mechanism. Since the potential unmet need for long-term care is so large, many fear that total expenditures would increase dramatically if Medicaid or Medicare paid for supportive nonmedical services. The result is that, in the area of home health care, there are restrictions, such as the "homebound" and "skilled care" requirement, that limit the full use of home health care services. Regulations and definitions associated with these home health care requirements are complex, making them subject to a variety of interpretations.[12]

FRAGMENTATION

Although the public financing of nursing homes is dominated by Medicaid, noninstitutional long-term care services are funded by a multitude of programs and agencies at the federal, state, and local levels, with no single agency having overall responsibility for coordinating long-term care. Several programs finance alternatives to nursing home care for the elderly.[13] There is some overlap of these services, and each program has its own legislatively mandated eligibility requirements, benefit package, provider participation restrictions, administrative structures, and service delivery mechanism. Each program tends to operate independently of the others. Furthermore, no single agency or organization is assigned responsibility for coordinating the care of the individual recipient. As a result, the disabled elderly face a complicated and confusing service system in which it is difficult to coordinate a comprehensive package of noninstitutional services. Moreover, the availability of long-term care services varies greatly, both among and within states. This raises questions of equity, since it appears that most variations in resources do not appear related to variations in need.

MEDICAID ELIGIBILITY CRITERIA

From the perspective of humane public policy, unnecessary institutionalization is unacceptable because, commonly, it subjects individuals to forced regimentation, increased medication, loss of privacy, and a lack of contact with the outside world.

Medicaid eligibility criteria are a primary cause of inappropriate institutionalization. This is because it is easier for an individual to obtain Medicaid benefits in a nursing home than at home, for two reasons. First, in something fewer than a third of the states, the elderly and disabled living in the community cannot become eligible for Medicaid no matter how great their medical or long-term care needs, unless their incomes are so low as to make them eligible for public assistance.[14] However, in some 14 states, the Medicaid eligibility standards are more restrictive than the "welfare" program (Social Security Insurance), and in some 20 states the Medically Needy Program does not exist.

In the other two-thirds of the states, persons not receiving public assistance can receive Medicaid, but only if their medical expenses are large enough to reduce their remaining incomes below the Medicaid eligibility standard.[15] Usually these standards are numerically quite low. Therefore, while persons needing long-term care can become eligible for home health care under Medicaid, they may not have enough income left to meet routine nonmedical needs.

MEDICAID RELATIVE RESPONSIBILITY LAWS

In a controversial 1983 policy, the Department of Health and Human Services (DHHS) announced that adult relatives can be made legally responsible for some of the Medicaid costs involved in providing care to indigent relatives in hospitals and nursing homes in states which have enacted a statute to that effect.[16] The new DHHS policy grants the states discretion to determine which relatives will be asked to share in the costs of these Medicaid services, and to what extent. The DHHS ruling declares that "states may require adult children or other relatives of Medicaid recipients to provide financial support to adult relatives under statutes of general applicability."[17]

In its announcement, DHHS pointed out that the policy would not affect the criteria used in determining a person's eligibility for Medicaid. However, there will be difficulties for the beneficiary related to the administration of the policy and its enforcement. Also, the new policy raises certain ethical questions. For example, should an adult child be forced to pay a portion of the cost of nursing home care provided to a parent even if that child had been abandoned by the parent in childhood? Also, should an adult be forced to pay if he or she personally is elderly and in retirement? These are just a few of the questions that must be answered before the relative responsibility laws can effectively and ethically be enforced.

INSTITUTIONALIZED ELDERLY

Access to appropriate care while in an institution raises both ethical and legal questions. As the President's Commission for the Study of Ethical Problems in Medicine and Biomedical and Behavioral Research has pointed out, some long-term care institutions do not appear to make aggressive life-prolonging care available to some patients.[18] Generally, long-term care facilities share hospitals' commitment to prolonging life, but that emphasis is less strong and less uniform. A study examining the nontreatment of fever in long-term care facilities showed that nearly half of the patients with a fever were not treated (with antibiotics or otherwise) and that the mortality in this group, as expected, was high (59 percent).[19] The study indicated that untreated patients were more likely to have malignancies, to be bedridden and in pain, and to reside in smaller facilities. Nontreatment in such settings seemed to be accepted; the decision making leading to nontreatment was rarely the object of scrutiny. The choice of treatment or nontreatment in these institutions seemed largely to depend on the predilections of its administrators, trustees, and employees.

Further, and again according to the President's Commission, the financial incentives established by various reimbursement systems are another, often unexamined, influence on the decisions made regarding patients in long-term care facilities.[20] These institutions find it much more profitable, for example, to provide rehabilitation services and skilled care of wounds than psychiatric services and recreation. Due in part to these incentives, Medicare spends about 6.6 times as much on each enrollee who dies in a calendar year than on one who lives through the year.[21]

Although it is not clear that the services provided are those that patients would choose, it is clear that patients have little opportunity to alter the mix of services that they receive. Thus, the responsibility of providing the most useful mix of services and informing patients and their surrogates of the opportunities that are available must rest with two groups: those who establish the incentives (that is, the legislators and administrators of Medicaid programs) and those who respond to them (predominantly nursing home administrators and trustees, although the patients' physicians and nurses may have a substantial vote).

HOSPICES

Hospices were created as an alternative to traditional long-term care institutions. They were developed solely for the purpose of assisting dying patients (typically cancer patients who have exhausted all reasonable forms of curative treatment) to live their remaining weeks or months as free of symptoms and as much in control of their lives as possible. Hospice care is premised on dignity for the patient. It holds that home is almost always the best place to die and that traditional medical care facilities, particularly acute care hospitals, do not appropriately address the needs of the dying.[22]

Despite these advantages, the concept of hospice care raises many ethical questions. Like all other institutions, hospices have their particular principles and operate under constraints that necessarily affect both the range of health care options available to patients and the ease of obtaining these options. Most hospices discuss their philosophy and approach with potential patients and their families in order to enhance patient self-determination; many have rather explicit formal consent procedures. Nonetheless, some patients do not realize that hospice admission amounts to a decision to forego many kinds of life-sustaining treatment (such as resuscitation, continuous cardiovascular monitoring, and chemotherapy).

Other difficulties include the institutional separateness of hospices, which can interfere with a patient's return to the traditional care setting should such a step become necessary or desirable. Also, although hospices pride themselves on providing an alternative to the norms of acute care hospitals, their own philosophy of care may make it emotionally (even if not practically) difficult to offer their patients additional alternatives. The enthusiasm and personal involvement of hospice care givers can make patients feel guilty if they reject recommendations, resist plans of care, fail to respond to treatment (that is, fail to report symptom relief), or fail to conform to the institution's norms (a general acceptance of death). In contrast with hospitals, which sometimes pressure patients to continue aggressive therapy after it is no longer warranted, hospices risk pressuring patients to accept death too readily and to forego potentially life-sustaining therapies too soon.

Recent federal legislation authorizing reimbursement for hospice services under Medicare may promote further inequities in access to hospice care.[23] For example, the severe limits on reimbursement for inpatient care favor patients who will not need such care because they have substantial and supportive families and homes. Yet, there are certainly other patients with comparable medical burdens or with no families who, on grounds of equity, have a stronger claim to public support. Also, the fact that a physician's opinion must indicate that a patient has less than 180 days to live acts as a severe constraint on the types of patients who now qualify for hospice care.

UNMET NEEDS AND THE ROLE
OF THE FAMILY

Under current programs, many people who require some form of long-term care, particularly noninstitutional care, do not receive these services. Our ability to quantify this population is hampered by the availability and willingness of family and friends to provide informal care. The vast bulk of noninstitutional long-term care is provided by family and friends. Clinical records show that dependent elderly persons are usually placed in institutions only after their families have suffered considerable stress over a long period of time while providing care for them. With an increasing number of potential care givers in the work force, the stress of caring for elderly family members and its associated guilt are becoming even more apparent. If the availability of family members or their willingness to provide care declines in the future, the need for formal long-term care services will escalate.

The dilemma seems to be that, while most families feel morally obligated to care for their dependent elderly, sometimes our society can discourage the family's assumption of that role. Moreover, while we give lip service to the familial obligation, we fail to provide adequate incentives or rewards to encourage families to persist with their "responsibility." In fact, the willingness of many observers to point an accusing finger at the family for the deteriorating situation of the elderly may symbolize evasion of the problems that need to be faced.

"INSURING" ACCESS TO LONG-TERM CARE

Much of the recent attention to long-term care is due to the rising cost of that care. While the number of elderly and disabled people requiring long-term care continuously rises, so does the cost of providing this care. Although government funds pay for slightly more than half of all nursing home costs nationally, most of it through Medicaid, many people still pay for part or all of their nursing home care with their own money. In 1981, private individuals paid for 43 percent of the nation's nursing home costs.[24] Direct out-of-pocket expenditures accounted for virtually all private payments; private insurance payments and other private sources accounted for only about 1 percent of all expenditures.[25] The greatest cost for long-term care is said to be borne by families who take care of their elderly at home, a cost impossible to pinpoint accurately.

While the expenditure increases in recent years have been great, future demand for long-term care is expected to be even greater. If present utilization rates continue, the total nursing home population will rise 54 percent by the turn of the century.[26] This forecast does not include the possible impact of other trends, which may reduce the availability of informal care and thus increase the need for formal services. Furthermore, due to the overall aging of the population, the need for long-term care services may grow much faster than government tax revenues, making it even more difficult for the government to maintain services.

Although private insurance is available in most areas of health care, it has not been generally available to help meet the costs of long-term care. There has been some talk of a new Medicare benefit: Medicare Part C. Such a policy benefit would probably supplement most benefits of Medicare Parts A and B, and would replace the home health benefits of those parts, along with providing other long-term care services. However, with the contemplated cutbacks in Medicare benefits, it is difficult to imagine the program being augmented by a third part any time in the near future.

The other alternative for "insuring" access is the development of private insurance. This has not been a terribly popular alternative to date, due to fears of open-ended benefits and open-ended liabilities. There is also the concern that home health care may not necessarily be treated as an alternative to institutionalization. That is, once the opportunities for home health care are expanded, many persons who have not used such services in the past will use them now, causing a great expansion in services. Consequently, underwriting for such services has not been available because of the risk-avoiding nature of insurers.

Despite their resistance to insuring for long-term care, private insurance companies do realize that there is a growing need for long-term health care insurance in the marketplace. There are signs that some insurance companies may be giving thought to long-term care and how they can effectively meet a portion of the costs involved.

CONCLUSION

Older Americans now face many barriers to long-term health care. There has, however, been some progress toward eliminating these barriers. Despite the Medicare/Medicaid bias toward institution-based services, some modest progress has been made in reorienting the emphasis of these programs. States opting to "waive" the federal approach and develop their own approaches have been able to provide a wider range of community and home-based services in lieu of nursing home care, including such services as case management, personal care services, adult day care, and respite care. This may be an opportunity to redirect the focus of the long-term care components of their Medicaid programs.

The need for long-term care services does not seem likely to diminish. As the costs of health and social services continue to rise, and as gaps in access persist and possibly widen, the pressures on the system will intensify and will require even more difficult financial, social, ethical, and legal choices.

NOTES

1. Nursing Home Care in the United States: Failure in Public Policy: Hearings Before the Subcommittee on Long-Term Care of the Senate Special Committee on Aging, 94th Cong., 1st Sess. 3 (Fed. 1975) (Supporting Paper No.3).
2. UNDERSECRETARY'S TASK FORCE ON LONGTERM CARE, WORKING PAPERS ON LONGTERM CARE (U.S. Gov't Printing Office, Washington, D.C.) (1981).
3. PRESIDENT'S COMMISSION FOR THE STUDY OF ETHICAL PROBLEMS IN MEDICINE AND BIOMEDICAL AND BEHAVIORAL RESEARCH, SECURING ACCESS TO HEALTH CARE: THE ETHICAL IMPLICATIONS OF DIFFERENCES IN THE AVAILABILITY OF HEALTH SERVICES (U.S. Gov't Printing Office, Washington, D.C.) (1983) [hereinafter cited as SECURING ACCESS].
4. *Id.* at 4–5.
5. *Id.* at 151.
6. *See* Lynn, J., ch. 2 of this text.
7. SECURING ACCESS, *supra* note 3, at 4.
8. *See* Cohen, E., ch. 16 of this text.
9. 42 U.S.C. §3001 (1976); Califano, J., *The Aging of America: Questions for the Four Generation Society,* ANNALS OF THE AMERICAN ACADEMY OF POLITICAL AND SOCIAL SCIENCE (July 1978) at 98.
10. *See generally* Shelton v. Tucker, 364 U.S. 479 (1960); "In a series of decisions this court has held that, even though the governmental purpose be legitimate and substantial, that purpose cannot be pursued by means that broadly stifle fundamental personal liberties when the end can be more narrowly achieved." *Id.* at 488.
11. Cohen, *supra* note 8.
12. 42 C.F.R. §§409.40–409.45.
13. For example, New York State has two programs: Nursing Homes without Walls, (OBRA) (1981), and 82176 Home and Community Based Waivers.
14. *See* SHORT TERM EVALUATION OF MEDICAID: SELECTED ISSUES (Urban Systems Research & Engineering, Inc., Cambridge, Mass.) (1984) (report to U.S. Department of Health and Human Services) at 61–121.
15. *Id.*
16. HEALTH CARE FINANCING ADMINISTRATION, STATE MEDICAID MANUAL, PART 3—ELIGIBILITY §3812—TREATMENT OF CONTRIBUTIONS FROM RELATIVES TO MEDICAID APPLICANTS OF RECIPIENTS (U.S. Gov't Printing Office, Washington, D.C.) (1983).
17. *Id.*
18. PRESIDENT'S COMMISSION FOR THE STUDY OF ETHICAL PROBLEMS IN MEDICINE AND BIOMEDICAL AND BEHAVIORAL RESEARCH, DECIDING TO FOREGO LIFE-SUSTAINING TREATMENT: MEDICAL, ETHICAL, AND LEGAL IMPLICATIONS (U.S. Gov't Printing Office, Washington, D.C.) (1983) at 109–10 [hereinafter cited as FOREGOING TREATMENT].
19. Brown, N., Donovan, T., *Non-Treatment of Fever in Extended-Care Facilities,* NEW ENGLAND JOURNAL OF MEDICINE 300(22):1246 (May 31, 1979).
20. FOREGOING TREATMENT, *supra* note 18, at 110.

21. J. LUBITZ, *et al.*, USE AND COSTS OF MEDICARE SERVICES IN THE LAST YEAR OF LIFE (U.S. Gov't Printing Office, Washington, D.C.) (1981).
22. *See generally* Smith, D.H., Granbois, J.A., *The American Way of Hospice*, HASTINGS CENTER REPORT 12(2):8–10 (April 1982).
23. 42 C.F.R. § 418.
24. Jennings, M.C., Krentz, S.E., *Private Payment for Long-Term Care: The Untapped Mechanism*, TOPICS IN HEALTH CARE FINANCING 10(3):1, 4–5 (Spring 1984), *citing* Gibson, R.M., Waldo, D.R., *National Health Expenditures: 1981*, HEALTH CARE FINANCING REVIEW 4(1):1–35 (1982).
25. *Id.*
26. Jennings, Krentz, *supra* note 26, at 3, *citing* Willging, P.R., Neuschler, E., *Long-Term Care: Debate Continues on Future of Federal Financing of Long-Term Care*, HOSPITALS 56(13):62 (1982).

4

The Hospital–Nursing Home Interface: Coordinating Continuity of Care

Charlotte A. Leavitt, B.S.N.

"Continuity of care" and "discharge planning" are terms that 10 to 15 years ago were unknown in the health care field. If their function was served under another rubric, there was clearly no need to have a special hospital department to manage them. Today, federal and state regulations[1] and JCAH requirements[2] mandate that hospitals practice discharge planning. A new national association has been created to represent and educate the growing number of health care personnel working on coordinating continuity of care.[3] Private insurance companies have become involved and, in this era of cost containment in health care, state Medicaid programs have also developed systems to assure that monies are being used most appropriately. For example, the Massachusetts Case Management Screening Program, a program established in 1978 by the Medicaid Division of the Department of Public Welfare, seeks to ensure that Medicaid clients are placed in long-term care *institutional* settings only when there is no appropriate *community* care, and that the institutional setting is the appropriate level of care.

Our health care institutions are part of a complex system that changes frequently and that requires constant attention to be used most effectively. Within this system, physicians are fully occupied with the business of diagnosing and treating. Therapists are using their expertise to rehabilitate, nurses are providing continuous care, and social workers are helping patients and families with the crises brought on by illness. All of these caretakers influence the patient's continuity of care, but none assumes that role as his or her major responsibility. Therefore, patient and family need help in getting care and finding their way through the system. This is the role that this new and expanding group of health professionals—continuity of care coordinators—fill.

THE NEED FOR COORDINATION

What does "coordinating continuity of care" mean? What is its purpose? By examining the definitions of coordinating and continuity we get a clue to the process. To coordinate is "to arrange in proper order or relation, to act together harmoniously;" while continuity means "a continuous or connected whole, uninterrupted succession, unbroken series." To act together harmoniously with the patient and the family toward a connected whole or unbroken succession of care is certainly the objective of continuing care. The succession of care settings includes all parts of the acute and long-term care system: acute hospitals, rehabilitation and chronic hospitals, day care, skilled nursing facilities, intermediate care facilities, rest homes, home health care, foster care, respite care, meals on wheels, and congregate housing. Physicians, nurses, and therapists must act together harmoniously with the patient and his or her family. There may be several physicians, e.g, the primary physician, a neurologist, and a surgeon, as well as nurse specialists and others. All contribute to the patient's goal of becoming well and all are important; the continuity of care coordinator brings together their various inputs and channels them in the patient's interests.

If the patient/client enters the health care system through the acute hospital, he or she must have an acute illness and require care that can be provided only in such a setting. On entering such a facility, the patient is immediately approved for that care and assigned a length of stay through the utilization review process. When he or she no longer needs acute care as defined by criteria imposed by Medicare, Medicaid, or private insurers, further reimbursement will not occur, and the hospital needs to move the patient to another setting if further care is still needed. The decision as to what setting is appropriate can be made easier with the help of a professional who assists other caretakers to work with the patient and family and can provide guidance on the regulations and the choices.

Continuity of care coordinators are frequently social workers or nurses who have developed both knowledge of the health care reimbursement and insurance system and skill in working with families and a number of health care providers and other services. It is an interdisciplinary and multidisciplinary effort;[4] in my hospital, the Continuing Care Unit uses the professional services of a social worker and a community health nurse.

The process must start early in the patient's hospital stay and should include a careful assessment to determine the level of care that the patient requires, the extent of family support, and the community resources that are available. Alternatives must be considered to assure the use of the least costly and least restrictive setting to provide the necessary care.

THE FRIGHTFUL SCENARIO

Patients and families ordinarily have limited knowledge of health care and what is covered by their insurance. During the crisis of an illness, they have difficulty understanding why Mother cannot go to a skilled nursing facility (SNF) when she requires only intermediate care, and why Medicare will not cover all costs. Often they say to themselves, "Well, if Medicare won't pay, Mother has Blue Cross and that covers everything!" Then, the family starts looking at nursing homes, only to find there are no beds available in the large multilevel facility two streets from their home, and to be told that they must take the bed in the less pretentious facility ten miles away. Medicare benefits are now terminated in the hospital, and if Mother is not transferred tomorrow (after the legally mandated 24-hour notice) the hospital will send a bill to the family. Thus, the stage is set for what can be a disastrous experience for patient and family.

The problems are compounded by the regulations that affect reimbursement, the fact that the nursing home industry is largely for-profit (while the acute care settings are largely nonprofit), the stringent regulations governing long-term care, and (in many areas) the lack of nursing home beds. A major fault of the Medicare benefit system is that it covers acute care (hospital stay, short-term SNF, and short-term home care), even though the elderly are more likely to have chronic illnesses requiring long-term care which is not provided for. The system was designed to meet acute needs and is therefore more responsive to the 50-year-old person who comes to the hospital with gallbladder disease than the elder with painful, physically limiting degenerative joint disease. The Medicare regulations regarding skilled nursing facility level of care, as promulgated by the Health Care Financing Administration (HCFA) have become so stringently interpreted by fiscal intermediaries that reimbursement is limited to extremely heavy care patients.[5] For example, the patient with tube feedings or a wound that requires frequent, extensive, sterile dressing changes will be paid for. However, the person who has a healing wound that needs a simple dressing but requires frequent supportive care to maintain or prevent deterioration will not be considered a skilled nursing care patient. The need for providers to document very specifically to validate an unstable condition frequently denies benefits to qualified recipients. Even though the physician may order daily physical therapy (another skilled service that qualifies for Medicare reimbursement in skilled nursing facility), if the physical therapist's documentation does not show specific treatments required, goals identified, and continued progress towards these goals, the payment will be denied. With these things in mind, the anxiety that is produced by the thought of retrospective denial of payment is one of the factors that strongly leads nursing homes to seek only private-paying patients.

Probably the most significant barrier to the timely transfer from acute to long-term care is finances. If private financing is not available, Medicaid must be applied for—a cumbersome, time-consuming, and often humiliating process. Nursing homes want assurance that everything is in place prior to transfer, and payment is the major factor.

In the face of this dilemma, how do hospitals manage to help patients and families? By developing credibility and being knowledgeable about nursing homes' specific resources, hospitals can improve relationships with homes so they are more receptive to that hospital's patients. Hospitals and long-term care facilities can work together to increase awareness of the problems of long-term care. Practitioners in long-term care settings have special skills that health professionals in acute hospitals need to practice when caring for the elderly; nursing home personnel need to learn skills from hospital clinicians as they increasingly care for patients with special needs, such as hyperalimentation.

Additional barriers to orderly progress through the system include such problems as physician coverage and the absence of family. The patient's primary physician may not be willing or able to continue to care for the patient in the long-term care setting, and transfer may be delayed and continuity interrupted while arranging physician coverage. This problem may be traumatic for the patient, especially if there had been a long relationship with the physician. If there is no immediate family, it may be necessary to go through the process of having a guardian appointed, which often causes a delay in transfer.

THE CONTINUING CARE COORDINATOR'S ROLE

The many factors involved in the placement process put stress on acting together harmoniously, and the continuing care coordinator is often in the middle of a situation where an angry physician just "wants the patient out," a distraught family has no money, and a long-term care system has no beds for patients with limited funds. When this occurs, it is necessary for all parties to reexamine their roles in the process and to try new approaches. Perhaps the physician can take another look at the treatments he or she has prescribed and revise them to help in the management of the patient. Perhaps the family needs to be encouraged to participate more actively in the search for a bed. Perhaps more pressure must be put on the welfare system to process the Medicaid application. At this time, someone could remind a nursing home of the several private patients it is caring for and urge it to take on a Medicaid patient.

When plans are ready for transfer of a patient from a hospital to a long-term care facility, the attempt to assure continuity begins. The system should include a written care plan encompassing physician's orders and discharge summary, nursing care plan, therapist's plan, and social worker's summary. The plan should accompany the patient when transferred so there is no break in continuity. It must state the level of care which the patient requires and the care plan must validate the level of care which the patient is actually receiving. The physician is responsible for documenting the appropriate level of care. In some demonstration projects done by professional standards review organizations in the past, this responsibility was given to continuing care coordinators. As a participant in the Charles River PSRO long-term care demonstration project, I realized that at the time I affixed my name to the level of care certificate I could be held liable if third-party payment were denied. Charles River PSRO had one of several long-term care demonstration projects which developed a system for binding certification of level of care determination and initial length of stay (with limitation) in SNF prior to admission. This assured the SNF of payment under Medicare/Medicaid for the initial length of stay. The continuing care coordinators in their member hospitals were authorized, after passing an initial monitoring period, to certify the level of care and length of stay.

I believe that, regardless of payment, quality of care is maintained only by assuring a mechanism for continuity of care. In health care, "quality assurance" is the catch phrase, and a mechanism for continuity of care must be effective if quality is to be assured during the transfer process from one care setting to another.

THE FUTURE OF LONG-TERM CARE

What is the future of the hospital/nursing home interface? In this era of cost-containment efforts amid rising health care costs, the appropriate use of health care becomes even more important. In Massachusetts the new health care financing law, Chapter 372, has set the stage by changing the retrospective reimbursement formula to a prospective pricing system which limits the amount paid to a hospital based on a complicated formula. The diagnosis related group, a national prospective pricing program, has been implemented in most other states. This system also sets the price in advance, but on the basis of diagnosis. The impact of both of these systems is to tightly restrict hospitals to provide inpatient care for only the most acutely ill patients. Any unnecessary days become a major financial burden to the hospital.

Whether it be Chapter 372 or some other prospective pricing program, discharge planning and continuity of care are vital to the health care industry and to hospitals particularly. Coordinating multidisciplinary professionals, resolving patient/family issues, arranging for appropriate care, and implementing the necessary financial resources must be accomplished in an effective, efficient, and timely manner. Hospital administrators must recognize the crucial role of continuing care personnel in helping to maintain a viable financial picture. The physician, who is the authority figure from the patient's perspective, must be intimately involved in the process. But, as with other supportive services, the physician's understanding and timely use of continuing care personnel will assist him or her and expedite patient care. Hospitals, therefore, must continue to provide an environment that allows for the development and implementation of coordinated continuing care.

The alternatives to institutional care must be actively researched. There are many resources available to help people remain in their homes. These include home health care (visiting nurses, home health aides, physical and occupational therapists, social workers, and medical equipment, etc.) and other home care supports (such as homemakers, meals on wheels, transportation, personal emergency response system, friendly visitors, and foster care). Hospice care is a very special program which offers an alternative for the terminally ill patient and his or her family. Hospice programs should be a vital part of any community's health care and must be developed where voids exist. The future promises more elderly in our society, especially those 80 years of age and older, who are the most intensive users of health care. Families must be encouraged and given the support—both service and financial—to care for their loved ones. Long-term care facilities should be working to get patients back to community settings.

Continuing care professionals' skills are especially needed to coordinate the multiple services which are necessary for the successful home care plan. As society and the health care industry recognize the place of home care in health care cost containment, the role of continuing care will be emphasized. Coordinating home care plans is as important as coordinating nursing home transfers.

CONCLUSION

Bridging the gaps between various health care settings—acute hospitals, nursing homes, rehabilitation hospitals, home care—in a cost-effective, timely, efficient, professional, and humane manner is a vital task. This task is increasing in intensity due to changes in population with a shift to the elderly, the financial crunch of the health care system, and the limited availability of physical resources. Continuing care discharge planning is a specialty with its own body of knowledge and organizations developing standards of practice. Continuing care professionals assure quality care for patients moving through the health care system, provide assistance to the physician and other care providers, and assist hospitals to maintain financial viability—certainly a valuable component of health care in the 1980s.

NOTES

1. These are found in Medicare (Title XVIII) regulations as promulgated by the Health Care Financing Administration and interpreted and managed by fiscal intermediaries. Various state health departments have incorporated regulations for discharge planning, *e.g.*, MASS. ADMIN. CODE tit. 105, §150.003 (E)(2)(1978).
2. ACCREDITATION MANUAL FOR HOSPITALS, 1983 EDITION (Joint Commission on Accreditation of Hospitals, Chicago, Ill.) (1982) at 194.
3. American Association for the Continuity of Care, 1101 Connecticut Avenue, N.W., Suite 700, Washington, D.C. 20036.
4. K.M. MCKEEHAN, CONTINUING CARE: A MULTIDISCIPLINARY APPROACH TO DISCHARGE PLANNING (Mosby, St. Louis, Mo.) (1981).
5. 42 U.S.C. §1395x(j) (Supp. 1976).

5

The Dilemma of Long-Term Care: An Industry View

Ralph E. Hazelbaker, M.B.A.

The mid-1980s are critical years for the long-term care profession. Budget deficits at the federal and state levels exert heavy pressure on both Medicare and Medicaid funding. The prospect of burgeoning future needs brings into question the entire concept of entitlement. Should government—we the people—fund and pay for all indigent medical need? Or should government pay for only that portion of need that we as taxpayers believe we can comfortably fund?

THE PRESENT STATUS

In discussing this whole area of reimbursement for long-term care, it is helpful to examine the industry. Statistically, we have providers that now operate approximately 1.5 million beds in the United States.[1] Approximately 75 percent are owned and operated by proprietary interests. Average per patient day rates range from $35 for intermediate care (ICF) patients to $45 for skilled nursing facility (SNF) patients. The total annual revenue for the long-term care industry was approximately $26 billion in 1982.

Medicaid (Title XIX) funding accounts for approximately 50 percent of annual industry revenues—and 60 percent of bed usage. Medicare (Title XVIII) funding accounts for approximately 2 percent of revenue. Private-paying individuals account for 35 percent, and other sources, such as Veterans Administration and private insurers, for 3 percent.

In terms of patient makeup, the median age of nursing home patients was 81 in 1982. Some 70 percent of these residents are over 70 years of age. At any given time, 5 percent of the over-65 population reside in nursing homes, and approximately 20 percent of the over-65 population will reside in nursing homes at some time during their lives. More than 20 percent of persons over age 85 currently are nursing home residents. In total, the industry now serves more than 1.4 million patients and experiences an average occupancy rate in excess of 95 percent of total certified capacity.[2]

AREAS OF CONCERN

With such a large portion of our population involved as patients, and with such huge sums of public monies being expended each year, it is only natural that there is significant public concern about the industry. In the past these concerns have been amply voiced in public forums and disseminated through the broadcast and print media. Principally, such concerns have involved charges of less-than-adequate care, sometimes including substandard physical facilities and poor living conditions or food services. Often the charges focused on the industry's supposed lack of attention to the human and physical needs of the aged resident. But the long-term care profession has come a long way since Mary Adelaide Mendelson published her infamous book, *Tender Loving Greed,* in 1975.[3] Consumer activists and the public at large have influenced our legislative bodies to enact more stringent regulatory standards for buildings and for physical operations, to increase surveillance by state departments of health and federal agencies, and to introduce such sophisticated techniques as patient assessment and computerized quality assurance to aid in controlling and upgrading daily care.

In their turn, industry leaders have influenced their professional peers to institute self-regulation through state and local peer review groups, through programs of national organizations, such as the American Health Care Association's Quest for Quality, and through simple peer pressure at all levels. Gradually, legislators and regulators have come to recognize the cause and effect relationship between adequate payments for services and the delivery of quality care. As a consequence, over the immediate past many states have provided significant increases in funding to support higher quality care.

The result of these efforts is evident in information released to the public by the Health Care Financing Administration. HCFA studied both ICF and SNF nursing homes to determine those which meet the essential requirements for achieving a status which permitted them to be surveyed at much less frequent intervals. More than 26 percent of the homes in each category of certification achieved this status.[4]

46

FUTURE NEEDS

Now, we find ourselves at a point of decision. The elderly population is growing in absolute numbers and as a percentage of our total population. At present those individuals age 65 and over constitute 25 million, or 11 percent of the population, and 1983 was the first year that grandparents outnumbered teenagers.

In the immediate future we will probably experience a greater influx of veterans into proprietary nursing homes. As the huge cohort of World War II veterans passes ages 65, the Veterans Administration is simultaneously cutting back its construction programs and attempting to reduce its operating expenditures. This trend is augmented by the likely impact of the newly enacted diagnosis related group provision for hospital reimbursements, i.e., earlier release of patients to lesser care settings.

By the year 2000 the population age 65 or over will amount to approximately 35 million, or 12 percent of the total population.[5] Moreover, increasing longevity (females now have an average life expectancy of 86 years), coupled with changing family and social patterns, portend less family-provided home care and greater long-term care utilization rates. It is estimated that, by the year 2000, 50 percent of nursing home patients will be age 85 or older.[6]

While studies indicate that in the future we will experience more intensified utilization of long-term care facilities than we do now, long-term care facilities are currently operating at or near effective capacity, at rates in excess of 95 percent. The industry's effective capacity is estimated at approximately 98 percent, due to the frictional movement of residents in and out of facilities.[7] This is an important challenge that our society must soon act upon.

Due to these factors, demand for long-term care beds will force new construction for expansion and for replacement of obsolete facilities at a greater rate than the present 1 to 2 percent annual increase in industry capacity. Some present estimates now project a valid need for as many as 75,000 new long-term care beds each year over the next decade.[8]

Construction cost estimates range upward from the present approximate $22,000 per bed to amounts that can only be determined by the timing of the construction, the rate of inflation, and building costs at the time. If this need is met, projected construction costs alone could approach or exceed $2 billion per year. Prognosticators speculate that total annual nursing home expenditures may increase to $80 billion by the 1990s.[9] Such estimates cause the industry to ask significant questions. What will be the source of funding for this construction? What will be its cost? What kind of payment devices can we develop to ensure repayment of construction costs? What of the daily operating costs of these facilities?

Will the government become the payer of last resort? Can we meet these challenges?

CONDITIONS FOR ACTION

The answer from proprietary providers is positive: we can do all these things that need to be done. But that affirmation requires that we inject rationality into the processes by which future long-term care operating standards and reimbursement policies are made. Unless we acknowledge and accommodate the legitimate concerns of all parties in the long-term care environment, any policies or programs bear the seeds of their own destruction.

We must recognize the role of each of the characters in this play:

— The patient or resident who needs the service, but who is the actual payer in only a minority of cases

— That vast body of the populace representing the interests of the resident—family, friends, interested consumer groups, and the public at large

— Those individuals in government who have the ultimate responsibility for setting the standards and for determining the payment policies

— The providers of the needed care who are, in essence, only intermediaries in this system (We, as providers, necessarily respond to the needs of the patient or resident group within the framework and conditions imposed by the regulatory and payer groups.)

Of course, the argument can be made that the nation does not need, or at least that the government cannot afford, to provide all the health care services which will be needed or desired by the increasing numbers of the elderly. In a time of budget crisis, limitations on resources are essential. In fact, through health planning and restrictive certificate-of-need policies, several states are attempting to forestall nursing home bed growth and to impose limits on the amount and types of care they will support. Such efforts conflict with the consumerists' cry for unlimited and unconstrained access. They also conflict with the entitlement concept—where government provides for the specific, as well as the general, welfare of its citizens.

Based on past trends, it is likely that proprietary groups will be asked to supply the bulk of the expansion capital and the operating capabilities for the future growth of the nursing home industry. Given this presumption, I think it is important that we note some ever-present economic and social fundamentals:

1. *Capital flows to its optimum return.* If capital funding in the magnitude of $2 billion per year is to be accomplished, a market rate of return must be paid for that capital. The cost of this interest is a significant problem.

   In the immediate past, the principal source of funding for nursing home development and construction has been industrial bonds (IDBs). Such relatively low-return, tax-free issues have been sufficiently attractive to investors in an otherwise excessively costly market. In one of those strange crosscurrents of Washington politics, these bonds have become the target of legislation aimed to remove tax shelters.[10] If eventually successful, such a law would effectively remove IDBs as a source of funding for most long-term care providers, with devastating effects for nursing home construction and renovation. While the ostensible purpose of this legislation is to close another abusive tax loophole, is such a blanket prohibition good public policy if it eliminates a main source of industry funds and no substitute is provided?

   Moreover, what of reimbursement policies that pay essentially all costs of debt funding but place severe limits on payment of returns to equity capital? Is it rational to discourage equity investment, which is vitally needed, and simultaneously to encourage debt funding, which is less desirable?

2. *Management and labor act in their own self-interest.* Just as capital must receive its appropriate return, management and labor must be paid market rates for their services. The very nature of historical mechanisms for cost reimbursement severely limits the ability of a provider to realize incentive payments for managment efficiency and, perhaps most important, to pay more than the minimum wage to most of the provider's work force. Dedication to their profession alone motivates most employees to give of themselves to deliver quality services. This cannot be counted on to continue.

3. *Arbitrary constraints often, if not always, lead to unintended consequences.* There are many well-meant prohibitions which may or may not accomplish their original purpose but which, in the process, create far-reaching disruptions in the environment of long-term care. The pros and cons of health planning in long-term care are a singular example. The certificate-of-need process has generated inefficiencies, needless expense, and time delays causing cost additions at least equivalent to its presumed savings. Meanwhile, obsolete facilities continue to enjoy monopoly status in communities that urgently need new, modern beds.

Similarly, restrictive or even archaic cost reporting, surveillance, and payment procedures discourage thousands of providers from participating in Medicare. Meanwhile the federal government pays millions annually for high-cost patient days in hospitals while patients await nursing home placement.[11]

AN ACTION AGENDA

In conclusion, let me suggest an outline for the type of environment that will satisfy our long-term care needs.

1. Rational health planning which recognizes and accommodates the increasing need for beds throughout the country
2. Maintenance of present capital funding mechanisms, such as IDBs, until satisfactory alternatives evolve in the marketplace
3. Returns on reimbursed equity at 1.5 times the Hospital Insurance Trust Fund rate in both Medicare and Medicaid
4. Reimbursement in both Titles XVIII and XIX of *all* reasonable costs in a prospective reimbursement system that is based on valid statistical principles and will allow or accommodate merit increases and wage upgrades for employees
5. Incentives or returns for managerial efficiency
6. Patient assessment or quality assurance programs based on self-assessment and surveillance through the exception principle
7. The capability to innovate with care plans, personnel deployment, and computerization in patient care and reporting, so that providers may operate more effectively in both institutional and noninstitutional settings
8. A change in the bureaucratic mentality which defines cost containment as a zero-sum game where the only acceptable cost-saving methodology for government is to fail or refuse to reimburse the *reasonable* costs of providers
9. The development of multilateral approaches and sources in the private sector for payments for services, such as reverse annuities, private pensions, long-term care insurance, block time, and similar risk-sharing alternatives

Our objectives can be obtained, given sincere desire and effort by all the participants in the long-term care community. The various groups must acknowledge the interests of others, accept a rational analysis of reasonable alternatives, and demonstrate faith in cooperative decision making.

Meanwhile, our 1,200,000 employees and associates continue to provide professional medical and nursing care, professional physical and functional therapies, complete dietary and nutritional services, housekeeping and laundry services, daily transportation and activities, and social services counseling to residents and their families. All in all, we provide tender, loving concern for more than 1.4 million residents nationwide, 24 hours a day, seven days a week, more than 500 million patient days per year.

We provide these services at a daily average cost of less than $40 per day—less than the cost of a single motel room in almost any American city. Long-term care is the most efficient and cost effective segment of our health care continuum. It is the best buy in health care today. And we, the proprietary providers, want to maintain it as such in the future.

NOTES

1. *See generally* CONGRESSIONAL CONFERENCE, NURSING HOME FACTS AND TRENDS (American Health Care Association, Washington, D.C.) (May 1983); NURSING HOME FACTS IN BRIEF (National Council of Health Centers, Washington, D.C.) (1982) at 21 [hereinafter cited as NURSING HOME FACTS AND TRENDS].
2. NURSING HOME FACTS IN BRIEF, *supra* note 1, at 1.
3. M. MENDELSON, TENDER LOVING GREED (Vintage Books, New York) (1975).
4. *See* NURSING HOME FACTS AND TRENDS, *supra* note 1, at 20. DHHS regulations allowing greater flexibility in the survey and certification of long-term care facilities were never put into effect. *See* Hamme, J.M., ch. 12 of this text. *See also* Brown, L., *The Regulatory Assault,* JOURNAL OF HEALTH POLITICS, POLICY AND LAW 7:772(1982).
5. Montgomery Securities, The American Nursing Home Industry: Introduction to a Changing Industry (unpublished manuscript) (May, 1983) at 18 [hereinafter cited as The American Nursing Home Industry].
6. NURSING HOME FACTS AND TRENDS, *supra* note 1.
7. The American Nursing Home Industry, *supra* note 5, at 40.
8. La Violette, S., *Nursing Home Chains Scramble for More Private-Paying Patients,* MODERN HEALTHCARE 13(5):138 (May 1983); *see also* Cohen, E., ch. 16 of this text.
9. The American Nursing Home Industry, *supra* note 5, at 2.
10. CONGRESSIONAL RECORD (February 24, 1983) at H636–38.
11. *See* Leavitt, C., ch. 4 of this text.

6

Vertical Integration in the Health Care Industry: Where Do Services to the Elderly Fit?

Scott A. Mason, D.P.A.

INTRODUCTION

Vertical integration is becoming a viable concept in the health care industry. It is not clear, however, to what extent services to the elderly are being brought into corporate strategy in diversified health care organizations. The purpose of this chapter is to describe vertical integration in the health care industry; attempt to provide a historical perspective on key trends; and discuss how trends toward vertical integration may increase in the future and what these trends suggest for physicians, administrators, and patients.

HISTORICAL PERSPECTIVE

It should be recognized that the concept of vertical integration is not new to the health care industry. Just as important is the fact that different segments of the industry in the United States have historically evolved separately. Beginning in the late 1800s with the advent of the modern hospital at Johns Hopkins University, the acute care facility was established and developed independently of other types. Facilities that provided psychiatric care and services to the aging evolved quite separately from acute care institutions. Moreover, a particularly distinguishing characteristic about the American health care industry is that public health has evolved entirely apart from either of these care segments and has come to be seen as a purely governmental responsibility. Given the diverse segmentation within the industry and the varied development of

each segment, it is little wonder that vertical integration is being touted
by some as an important strategy that may represent significant improvements in the U.S. health care system.

While not a new concept to the hospital industry, little vertical integration has taken place thus far. Several multihospital systems, such as
National Medical Enterprises, Rush Presbyterian–St. Luke's Medical
Center in Chicago, and the Greenville Hospital System in Greenville,
South Carolina, have successfully diversified along different levels of
care. It is doubtful that the originators of this concept relating to the
development of regional systems of health care in England in the 1920s
envisioned this application of vertical integration—where a single corporate entity owns all resources.[1] In the American health care system, however, vertical integration probably could not have arisen in any other way.
Clearly, the growth of private enterprises, largely through the development of the for-profit hospital chains beginning in the late 1960s, has
spurred some of these developments.

Historically, vertical integration has caught on slowly in the health
industry, perhaps for several reasons. Obviously, the historical separation
and "parochialism" among different segments of the health industry
played some part. Possibly more important, the sources of reimbursement for different services are almost entirely unrelated to the recipient.
The growth in health insurance in the United States began with basic
hospital and surgical coverage in the early twentieth century,[2] and has
since extended to include such things as catastrophic illness, dental care,
hearing aids, and eye glasses. The interface between payment to hospitals
and to long-term care facilities was essentially created by the enactment of
Medicare and Medicaid legislation in 1965.[3] Nonetheless, the specific
reimbursement regulations relating to acute care evolved separately from
regulations for long-term care segments.[4] Another factor inhibiting the
growth in vertical integration has been legal barriers. In particular, antitrust laws[5] and the inability of nonprofit hospitals to operate profit-making facilities under a single hospital structure[6] have retarded this trend.
The recent advent of corporate reorganization and diversification within
the hospital industry has probably eliminated this latter barrier.[7] Finally, a
market for the expansion of long-term care services simply did not exist
until recently. Due in large part to the technological successes of the acute
care segment of the industry, the long-term care segment has become a
much more attractive market in the past decade. The ability of people to
live longer, though possibly with some chronic (versus episodic) disease,
has resulted in the development of an attractive elderly marketplace.
While the integration between long-term care services and other segments of the health industry has historically been lacking, it is likely that
there will be a much stronger connection in the future.

Key Trends Likely to Increase Future Vertical Integration

Certainly one of the more important trends toward a continuing integration of services to the elderly with other segments of the health care industry is the growth and differentiation of multiinstitutional arrangements among hospitals. These arrangements (often referred to as networking) include anything from informal shared services to single corporate ownership of multiple entities. They are, according to a recent American Hospital Association survey, currently estimated to involve more than a third of the hospital industry.[8] They take all forms, including for-profit, nonprofit, and a combination of the two. Most capital available to the industry appears to be flowing into these hospital systems to the exclusion of smaller (and riskier) independent facilities which are finding access to capital through the investment community limited. These hospital systems increasingly develop aggressive diversification strategies that take them into additional levels of care, in some cases including long-term care and services to the elderly.

A second trend is the general diversification taking place within the hospital industry itself. Hospitals are diversifying, partially in response to changing federal postures (such as DRG-based payment systems) that appear to make acute care hospitals more vulnerable to financial distress. Hospitals are also responding to a growing public recognition of health care as an industry broader than merely acute care.[9] Much of this diversification is moving toward less costly ambulatory care or related services that promise a quick return on investment. Unfortunately, some of this diversification is taking place without consideration for the effect that it may have on the existing business. This may explain why hospitals have been reluctant to diversify into long-term care services. Historically, the long-term care industry is one of the few segments of the health care industry that has been reimbursed as poorly as, if not worse than, the hospital industry.[10] Hospitals looking for alternative revenue sources to offset federal reimbursement cutbacks in acute care have been reluctant to take on a business that appears equally capital poor.

Implications of Current Trends

Nonetheless, these trends have a number of implications for physicians, long-term care facility administrators, patients, and the general public. For physicians, these trends suggest the following:

— Greater competition from corporate partnerships involving hospitals and multiinstitutional arrangements

— Increased attractiveness of long-term care as a practice setting due to closing of hospital medical staffs, anticipated oversupply of physicians, and growing elderly population
— Increased variety of marketplace economic relationships, including more full-time salaried positions as opposed to fee-for-service practice

To long-term care facility administrators the implications are numerous, perhaps including the following:

— The need to interact more closely with their hospital counterparts
— The need to diversify away from inpatient services to a fuller spectrum of services to the aged
— The need for strong marketing emphasis, enabling the organization to attract patients beyond those who are covered by public programs
— The need for a greater orientation toward strategic business planning

Ultimately these trends must be interpreted with respect to their impact on the patient, although there may be potential drawbacks—less autonomy among providers or decisions made on financial, impersonal factors. Yet, to many, vertical integration of services to the elderly can be viewed as only positive from the standpoint of the consumer. Specific implications include:

— Improved coordination among services
— Enhanced ability to "shop" for care
— The existence of more options in the marketplace, which perhaps has the negative effect of more confusion but which has the positive benefit of better buys for services as well as better packaging of services

Clearly, services to the elderly do fit within the trend toward vertical integration that is slowly emerging within the health care industry. The consumer will only benefit from a furtherance of this trend. Those of us employed in different segments of the industry should do all that we can to enhance this trend, recognizing the long-term benefits to all concerned.

NOTES

1. *See generally* R.E. MACSTRAVIC, MARKETING OBJECTIVES FOR HOSPITALS (Aspen Systems Corp., Germantown, Md.) (1980).
2. *See generally* P. STARR, THE SOCIAL TRANSFORMATION OF AMERICAN MEDICINE (Basic Books, New York) (1982) at 235–98.
3. Social Security Amendments of 1965, 42 U.S.C. §1396(a)(13)(A)(1965).
4. *See generally* D.M. KINZER, HEALTH CONTROLS OUT OF CONTROL: WARNINGS TO THE NATION FROM MASSACHUSETTS (Teach'em, Inc., Chicago) (1977) at 30–45.
5. Sherman Antitrust Act, 15 U.S.C. §1 (1976); Clayton Act §7, 15 U.S.C. 18 (1914); Federal Trade Commission Act §5,15 U.S.C. §45 (1914).
6. *See generally Health Planning; Corporation Reorganization,* in HOSPITAL LAW MANUAL (Aspen Systems Corp., Germantown, Md.) (1983) at ¶6–2 and ¶4–1.
7. Rosenfeld, R.H., *Market Forces Set Off Skyrocketing Interests in Hospital-Doctor Ventures,* MODERN HEALTHCARE 14(6):70–74 (May 1, 1984).
8. American Hospital Association Survey, unpublished data, 1983–84.
9. Social Security Amendments of 1983, 42 U.S.C.A. §1305 (West) (1983).
10. Ting, H.M., *New Directions in Nursing Home and Home Healthcare Markets,* HEALTHCARE FINANCIAL MANAGEMENT 14(5):62 (May 1984).

7

The Federal Role in
Health Care Financing

David A. Winston, M.A.

To begin, I would like to put into perspective some of the major initiatives now under way that affect health issues. The issues are complex
and multifaceted, and I would not presume to be expert in most of those
areas; I have, however, had the privilege of working on some of these
issues and initiatives.

WHAT WAS BEHIND THE
PROSPECTIVE PAYMENT SYSTEM

First, what happened in health care financing in 1983 was nothing short
of astonishing. The Reagan administration came forward with a comprehensive program of prospective payment: an idea that has been around
for at least 15 years. For the last 8 years, Congress in one form or another
had suggested that the Department of Health and Human Services develop a proposal on prospective payment. Nothing came of these efforts.
But in 1982, less than three months after receiving the Administration's
report, Congress passed the prospective payment system and it was
signed into law.[1]

Why did that happen? I think that the word "cost" sums up the
dominant public policy concern about health care in this country today.
The prospective payment legislation passed because we reached a crisis of
confidence in our ability to contain and control health costs. Once Congress concluded that it had to act, the question was what it should do. The
concern about costs was a bipartisan concern, and this commitment resulted in Congress's ability to do something about it.

At least two administrations previous to President Reagan's had
tried to restrict the growth of health care costs. Under President Nixon's

Cost of Living Council, the Subcommittee on Health Care wielded more regulatory control over the health industry than did any of the other elements of the Council. When I came to Washington under the Carter administration, the Senate Subcommittee on Health and Scientific Affairs went to Georgetown University for a hearing. Senator Edward Kennedy started by castigating the health care industry and specifically pinpointing hospitals as the villains. Joseph Califano, then Secretary of HEW, in a very effective presentation, pronounced the health care industry full of avarice and greed, and incapable of being competitive. At that time, health care costs were 8.5 percent of the gross national product,[2] a fact which Secretary Califano found totally unacceptable. "Something had to be done," he said, and his solution was to impose revenue controls over hospitals.

When I was asked by the Reagan White House to assist in developing some initiatives on health care, my first question was: "Why has it taken you two years to get around to it? We thought you were going to do it in the first year." At the time, I knew of the proposal that had been developed by Secretary Richard Schweiker and his staff and sent to the White House. I thought it was very good, but nothing concrete happened. When the people in the White House received the proposal, they did what good politicians do—they talked to those who would be affected, and they discovered that almost everything proposed would irritate somebody or some group. That is not very good politics, so the idea was killed.

What changed? Why did prospective payment fly through Congress in 1983? At that time the budget estimate was $54.5 billion for Medicare alone; by 1987 that figure was estimated to reach somewhere between $98 and $105 billion. Health care has also been the fastest growing component in the federal budget. If we are worried about deficits, taxes, and the economy, we simply cannot allow such growth to continue. That crisis finally resulted in action.

I wanted to be sure that all of this work would be given an interested response by those who make the decisions in the White House, so I arranged to provide materials to the President himself. These are some of the figures that we included in our briefing to the President. In 1950 we spent $12 billion for health care in this country, which was 4.5 percent of the gross national product. The government's share of these costs was 25 percent. By 1965, just one year before Medicaid, we were spending $35 billion for health care—5.6 percent of the gross national product—and the federal share of it was still 25 percent. In 1980, 15 years after Medicare, we spent $240 billion for health care, or about 9.2 percent of the gross national product. But now the federal portion of the total was 42 percent. In 1990 health care costs are estimated to be $798 billion, or

10.8 percent of the gross national product. The federal share of the total would be 46 percent. In this rising percentage lies the reason for all the concern. We would not hear so much about health care costs if not for the fact that there is no other segment of the economy in which the federal government is such a major purchaser.

We must recognize that one of the primary causes of this growth has clearly been government reimbursement policies, some of which, one hopes, are now on the way to correction. The other cause has been a tax policy that encouraged the purchase of more and more health insurance coverage for employees. We created a reimbursement system that insured most individuals from any concern about health care costs. More people got first dollar coverage, and, to both the consumer and provider, cost consciousness seemed unnecessary because a third party paid health costs. Demand and technology were also major causes of the growth in health care costs at a rate three times the rate of inflation for the rest of the economy.

It is clear that the government has taken a new tack with reference to cost control. Having decided to become a more prudent buyer of health care services, it will figure out a reasonable cost from its perspective, rather than that of the health industry, and will base payments on those calculations. The government won't concern itself with cost at an individual hospital; rather, the hospital will have to live within the established rate. In the next few years, the government will be focusing on the issues surrounding reimbursement for costs associated with capital, capital formation, and equity.

OPTIONS FOR FEDERAL PROGRAMS

After the Reagan administration took office, changes in health care policy increased. All of the current innovations had one purpose: to restrain the government's share of health care costs, and to cap the growth of Medicaid and Medicare expenditures. One can readily see that the options of federal programs are limited. For a public program which must contain costs, the options are reduction of benefits, meaning payment for fewer services, which is not popular with people who are used to receiving them; reduction of the number of people eligible to draw the benefits, which is again hardly a popular target of reform (Medicare eligibility, for example, is tied to Social Security eligibility); or restriction of payment. We see this last option in the administration's proposal for copayments, by which individuals would pay a greater share and the government a lesser share of personal health care costs. This policy has two objectives: cost saving, and restriction of demand.

In the long term, the Reagan administration is clearly interested in what many call the "competitive" theory. I hardly ever use that term, because I think it is confusing. I prefer to talk about injecting market incentives into the health care system, as illustrated by this story. There was a woman whose child had chicken pox, and during the course of the illness her pediatrician saw this child three times. (I am told by pediatricians that this is overutilization, but that is not the point.) Something very unusual happened; she got a bill. Something even more unusual occurred; she objected to the charge. She went back to the pediatrician and said she thought it was too high. His response was very predictable; he was outraged that she should challenge his professional judgment. With some umbrage he said, "I think you must understand, madam, that I did see your child three times during the course of his illness." "Yes, that's true," she said, "and I certainly think you ought to be reimbursed for your time." "But," she added, "I think you must understand that it was my child who infected the school. Now, what's that worth to you?" That is a woman who understood value for services rendered, and that is what we are talking about. How can we maximize value for services rendered? The question is not whether we are going to have competition, or whether we are going to have regulation, but rather, what is the appropriate mix. I think that is the crux of the public policy decision that is before us today. Will we provide a system that injects market oriented incentives to achieve more effective service delivery, limiting the amount of health insurance that one can purchase and requiring prospective payment for hospital and physician services? Or will we take the other route, returning to controls over the hospitals and, ultimately, over other providers as well?

I have always taken the view, and I think the Reagan administration shares it, that no single element of the health care system got us into this situation. The hospitals are not the bad guys; the nursing homes are not the bad guys. We got into trouble because of our ability to provide more and better health care due to the new technology, more manpower, and other factors. Accordingly, we all ought to be a part of the solution. We are entering a period in which the health care system will use money more slowly than it did previously.[3] The health-related percentage of the gross national product will continue to grow, although at a slower rate; we will all have to make adjustments.

PRIVATE DEVELOPMENTS IN HEALTH CARE DELIVERY AND PAYMENT

The Reagan administration is very interested in an approach that would encourage private developments. I am very encouraged by the way the private sector is adapting to a more cost sensitive environment. We see the development of preferred provider organizations (PPOs)—a tremendous change in our perception of health insurance. For over 40 years, we have been used to the idea that once insured, either publicly or privately, one was free to go to any provider and that provider could use whatever facility seemed preferable. The alternative offered by PPOs is for health care purchasers to negotiate specific contracts at given rates with specific providers. The terms usually require, or strongly encourage, through financial incentives, that patients covered by the purchaser use a specific facility. This is a tremendous shift in our attitude about how health care should be paid for and delivered in this country. Similarly, the health maintenance organization (HMO) is now one of the hottest items on the financial side of health care, and a number of plans are being converted from not-for-profit HMOs to for-profit—clearly demonstrating that there is private money to invest in alternative delivery systems.

These changes are exciting because they demonstrate initiatives for change in the private sector at a much faster rate than is possible at the governmental level. Consider, for example, changes in reimbursement procedures for health insurance. At Blyth Eastman Paine Webber, a wholly-owned subsidiary of Paine Webber, the chairman of the board sent around a message reporting that the company's health care costs had increased 35 percent over the previous year. Finding this totally unacceptable, Paine Webber, unlike the government, did not take very long to act. Only two weeks later its health insurance program was redesigned. Now, surgery done on an outpatient basis is reimbursed. If a patient is admitted to the hospital, he or she pays the first day's room and board charges, without reference to the deductible, and is reimbursed only 80 percent of the remaining cost. I think we are going to see this approach to employee health insurance coverage more and more as the emphasis is placed upon new modes of delivery of health care. That is exciting, and I do not think we ought to be afraid of it at all.

As we look at a changing health delivery environment, we also must change our perception of education, both for those who provide the services and for those who use them. For years, graduate schools have offered specialized health care administration or hospital administration programs. Now, as we look around the country, hospitals are increasingly interested in hiring M.B.A.s because they want the business orientation. Our educators must bring this sophistication to those who will work in the health care industry.

Finally, one of the least noticed, but ultimately one of the most enduring, changes in the health care industry over the last 15 years has been the dramatic shift away from traditional forms of providing capital, particularly for hospitals. Fifteen years ago, the majority of hospitals financed their capital projects through community fund raising and other kinds of charitable activity. Now well over 90 percent of them go to the debt market. My firm is a banking firm providing those funds. When we look at a potential issue, we most want to know not that it is a community service or that it is well-entrenched in the community, but whether we will get our money back. A hospital, as far as we and the bondholders are concerned, is a business and must act like a business. That attitude is a tremendous change. More training is needed to prepare our administrators to handle what are becoming very large and complex businesses.

FUTURE TRENDS

It is important that we realize that both the actual number and the percentage of elderly in our population is growing. This population requires lots of health care, so health care is going to continue to be a growth industry. There is no way around it. Millions of people across the country are employed in providing a very important life-giving service. I do not think any of us ought to be browbeaten into accepting the idea that 10.8 percent of the gross national product is too much to pay for health care. Why should we spend more for recreation or entertainment than for health care? That said, we have to be more realistic and recognize that the future growth must be more gradual than it has been.

Because of this growth, the need for long-term care services is going to increase dramatically. I must admit that I don't know how long-term care should be structured. But I can point out some of the difficult problems facing the government: how to determine who is eligible, how to determine which level of government ought to be involved, and how to bring the insurance industry into it. These are very knotty problems, which need to be addressed because we all recognize they will not go away. In the negotiations on the federalization of Medicaid, one problem got much closer to a solution than I thought it would. Both sides agreed early that federalization would not include long-term care, which would be left to the states. I was once in charge of the Medicaid program in California, and I know what a headache it is for the states, with negotiated rates, the problems that go along with licensure, and all of the other problems in the facilities. Somehow we have to find a way to develop the continuum of care from acute to chronic to residential. Nobody has done that very well yet. Even as we try to develop life care centers, or residential care centers, there is still a great deal to be learned. Certainly my firm is learning, with some sense of pain, that we do not have all the answers on their development. I think one of the challenges that all of us have to be concerned with is how we develop that continuum of care over the next few years.

Conclusion

I frequently hear that we are at a crossroad in health care. I do not know whether that is true or not, since you never really know whether you are at the crossroad until you have passed it. We are, however, in a very elastic environment. The one thing—the absolute that we all have to deal with— is that health care costs are large, they are growing, and the government's willingness and/or ability to pay for its share is becoming increasingly less certain. As we try to do something about those costs, I hope we can avoid some of the polarization that I see occurring between the deliverers of health care and the purchasers of health care. There are those in the health delivery system who say they do not want to be regulated any more than anyone else, and suggest that we explore some of the market-oriented alternatives. On the other hand, many purchasers—including some of the commercial insurers, Blue Cross plans, unions, and a substantial part of the business community—are saying that they are not a part of the problem. According to them, the providers are the bad guys. The purchasers' suggested solution is to impose revenue controls over all the providers in each state. Having some experience with regulation, I do not think that is a very good idea. It would keep the attorneys busy, because when the government formulates a regulation, someone has to figure a way to get around it. I do not think this is good for the health care industry. We have an opportunity now, if we will seize it, to give serious thought to what kind of delivery system, payment system, and health care we want as we all grow older.

Notes

1. Social Security Act Amendments of 1983, 42 U.S.C. §1305 (1983).
2. *See generally* Freeland, M.S., Schendler, C.E., *National Health Expenditure Growth in the 1980's: An Aging Population, New Technologies, and Increasing Competition,* Healthcare Financing Review 4(3):1 (March 1983).
3. *Id.*

Section II

Reimbursing Long-Term Health Care

8

Medicare and Medicaid Update

Larry A. Oday, J.D.

Expenditures for the Medicare and Medicaid programs have been increasing at an alarming rate.[1] Federal spending for these programs is
now 600 percent greater than it was in 1970, and in 1983 Medicare and
Medicaid spent as much every month as they did during the entire year of
1966 (their first full year of operation).[2] The rising costs of these programs reflect general increases in the cost of health care. These increases
are so large that they could soon threaten the quality of health care and
the access of some Americans to this care.

Controlling the costs of Medicare and Medicaid clearly must be an
objective of paramount importance in the 1980s. The urgency of this task
has been enhanced by the expectation that within two years expenditures
from the Medicare Hospital Insurance Trust Fund will exceed its income.
Both the Reagan administration and Congress have been keenly aware of
this urgency; in the last few years, they have been intensely active in
resolving the growing fiscal problems of Medicare and Medicaid. As a
result of the joint efforts of Congress and the Department of Health and
Human Services (DHHS), four pieces of legislation with a major impact
on Medicare and Medicaid were enacted during the period 1981–83.[3]
These new laws contain some short term attempts to solve major problems. Many of their provisions, however, reflect the conviction of both
Congress and the administration that they offer ultimate solutions to
these major problems.

Perhaps the most important is the prospective payment system introduced by the 1983 Social Security amendments.[4] This chapter begins
with an outline of some of the more significant aspects of this drastic
change in the approach to Medicare reimbursement for inpatient hospital services. It then briefly discusses the study of prospective payment for
skilled nursing facilities now underway in DHHS. This is followed by
some observations about Medicaid reimbursement and the alternative

reimbursement systems that some state Medicaid programs have established. After discussing Medicaid "home- and community-based" waivers, the chapter ends with some significant extensions of Medicare coverage made in the last several years.

MOVING TOWARD PROSPECTIVE PAYMENT FOR HOSPITALS

In 1982 Congress undertook the most significant Medicare initiative in recent years by passing the Tax Equity and Fiscal Responsibility Act (TEFRA), which made changes in Medicare reimbursement. Until TEFRA, Medicare reimbursement for institutional care and other services covered by Part A had always been based on actual incurred costs.[5] Although not all costs were recognized, most were allowed if they were determined to be "reasonable" by Medicare, and such amounts were paid in full. As expenditures rose, so did Medicare payments. This retrospective payment system provided no inducement for providers to contain their costs because they knew that Medicare would pay all the costs.

TEFRA ultimately resulted in the enactment early in 1983 of the prospective payment provisions of the Social Security amendments of 1983, making these major changes in Medicare reimbursement for most acute care hospitals:

1. It modified the cost limits that had existed since 1972 by introducing a case mix measure into the formula for calculating the limits, substituted a per discharge limit for the per day limit, and subjected all of a hospital's costs to the cost limits (except medical education and capital).

2. It provided for constraints on the annual rate of growth in hospital expenditures per discharge.

3. It offered, for the first time, an incentive for hospitals to operate efficiently.[6]

In addition to making these changes, in TEFRA Congress directed the Secretary of Health and Human Services to develop a legislative proposal for prospective Medicare payment to hospitals, skilled nursing facilities, and, to the extent feasible, other providers.[7] In December 1982, DHHS submitted a report which included a prospective payment plan for hospitals. The hospital prospective plan was included in the Health Incentives Reform package sent to Congress on February 28, 1983. The bill, H.R. 1900, moved rapidly through Congress, and on April 20, 1983, President Reagan signed it.[8]

MEDICARE PROSPECTIVE PAYMENT FOR HOSPITALS

Under the new prospective payment system (effective October 1, 1983), Medicare reimbursement to hospitals is related to each patient's diagnosis, treatment, and certain other differences among patients. All patients are categorized into 467 different diagnosis related groups (DRGs) for which payment can be made. Rates are determined in advance for each of these groups, and hospital payments are based upon its patients' DRGs. Generally speaking, the more complex the case, the higher the payment.

The Department published interim final regulations that set different rates for urban and rural hospitals.[9] As required by the law, the regulations initially set different rates for nine separate regions of the country. After three years, when the system has been completely phased in, all hospitals will be paid under a national rate system. In atypical cases, involving uncommon lengths of stay or extraordinarily costly treatment ("outliers"), the law permits the Secretary of DHHS to authorize additional payments.

Several kinds of hospitals, such as long-term, psychiatric, rehabilitation, and pediatric hospitals, are excluded from the prospective payment system because available DRG data is not appropriate. Once experience with the program is gathered, several other kinds of hospitals will be permitted to request exceptions.

The prospective payment system was enacted when government and other actuaries were predicting insolvency of the Medicare Trust Funds if patterns of expenditures continued. While an important goal of prospective payment is to slow the rate of growth in Medicare spending, the expectation is that this will be accomplished without adverse fiscal impact upon hospitals or other providers. Prospective payment is designed to reverse the effects of retrospective reimbursement, which encouraged providers to spend, fully confident that the more they spent the more they would get from Medicare. Prospective payment offers rewards for provider efficiency, and greater efficiency usually means lower costs. The new system reduces the cost-reporting and regulatory burden upon hospitals and so should favorably affect their administrative costs. It will be relatively easy to understand and administer, and will assure hospitals of reliably predictable payment for their services.

To mitigate the effects of a sudden change in the Medicare method of payment, both the law and the regulations provided for a three-year transition to a fully national prospective payment system. This provided that, in the first year, 75 percent of prospective payment was based on each hospital's own rate and 25 percent on regional rates. By the third year, 25 percent of payment was to be related to a hospital's own historic experience, 37.5 percent to regional rates, and 37.5 percent to national rates. Payment rates were to be published every September 1 for the following fiscal year, providing the predictability mentioned earlier.

PROSPECTIVE PAYMENT FOR
SKILLED NURSING FACILITIES

The same concerns that motivated enactment of the prospective payment system for hospitals prompted Congress in the Social Security amendments of 1983 to direct the Secretary to study "the impact on skilled nursing facilities of hospital prospective copayment systems."[10] That provision required the Secretary to submit a report to Congress before December 31, 1983 that both analyzed the impact and made recommendations concerning payment for skilled nursing facilities.

The fundamental issues regarding skilled nursing facility (SNF) reimbursement are the same types that were addressed in developing a prospective payment system for hospitals. Prospective payment systems for all facilities share several objectives. The system should be simple to administer, capable of quick implementation, and easy to understand. It should promote predictability of government expenditures, establish the government as a prudent buyer of services, and create incentives to be efficient. Within these broad objectives, it is necessary to develop an analytical framework by which various prospective payment methodologies can be tested.

The prospective payment system for skilled nursing facilities must have two fundamental characteristics: a unit of payment and a price-setting mechanism. The unit of payment can be per diem, per unit of service, per admission or discharge, per capita, or (as we chose for hospitals) per case. Under the price-setting mechanism, cost finding could be continued as it is in the retrospective cost reimbursement system. An alternative is the prospective budgeting many states use for their alternative Medicaid hospital reimbursement systems. There could also be negotiated rates or some sort of competitive bidding system. A final possibility is a formula approach like that imposed on hospitals, where a base and index are set and trended forward.

What kind of methodology DHHS ultimately will recommend for paying SNFs prospectively under Medicare is still far from clear. Yet, the mere fact that Congress chose to pay hospitals one way under Medicare does not mean that DHHS will recommend, or that the Congress will adopt, a similar system for paying SNFs. SNFs are not hospitals, an obvious but important distinction. The institutions themselves are very different, and the benefits that Medicare provides for services in those institutions vary markedly. What the government pays for those services need not be comparable.

In its study of the related, but different, issues of SNF reimbursement, DHHS is using the same rigorous analysis that characterized its examination of hospital reimbursement. One of the big issues is whether there can or should be a case-mix measure for SNF, and if so, what it should be. For hospitals, case mix clearly matters. That is why the DRG system, based on 467 different kinds of diagnoses, was chosen. Nothing like DRGs exists for SNFs. Perhaps we should try to develop a series of diagnoses that classify patients and measure resource consumption in an SNF. At the moment, however, these are only ideas about how this might work. Yale University, which developed the DRGs for hospitals, has developed something similar for SNFs called resource utilization groups (RUGs). They must be tested by DHHS researchers. The issue still remains: does case mix matter in an SNF, and if so, how is it measured?

SIGNIFICANT MEDICAID REIMBURSEMENT CHANGES

One significant development in Medicaid and long-term care was the enactment of the Boren amendment a few years ago.[11] The Boren amendment gave states great flexibility in enacting their own alternative reimbursement systems, first, in 1980 with respect to intensive care facilities and SNFs, and again in 1981 with respect to hospitals.[12] Thirty-eight states now have some sort of prospective payment system for long-term care facilities.[13] These states have adopted four general categories of rate-setting methodologies. Some still use the old retrospective facility-specific rate system, a full cost reimbursement method subject to year-end retroactive adjustment to reflect a facility's actual incurred allowable cost. Others use a prospective facility-specific system wherein the rate is set in advance of a fiscal year by adjusting a prior year base period by an economic index or allowance for inflation. Some states have a uniform class rate system in which an established rate is set for all facilities in the same class. Finally, some states have a hybrid of the facility-specific and class rate systems.

Within these categories, and aside from adjusting the definitions of allowable costs, states use a variety of means to control nursing home expenditures. Some states make classifications based on the level of care, e.g., a skilled nursing facility (SNF), an intermediate care facility (ICF), or an intermediate care facility/mentally retarded (ICF/MR). Some states make distinctions based on whether the facility is freestanding or hospital based, on the geographic location of the facility, or on its number of beds. Some states impose payment limitations based on such factors as minimum occupancy, maximum profit allowances, and so on. There was already a great diversity in the Medicaid program and the Boren amendment has fostered even more. It is consistent, however, with the goal of the Reagan administration to give the states the kind of flexibility that they say they need in managing their Medicaid program.

DEINSTITUTIONALIZATION OF MEDICAID PATIENTS

Certain eligibility requirements in the Medicaid law have encouraged patients who want to return to their homes, and who are medically able to do so, to remain in institutions. The celebrated case of Katie Beckett and its ad hoc solution brought this anomaly into the limelight.[14] The 1981 Omnibus Reconciliation Act provided an interim generic solution to this problem by authorizing states to request "home- and community-based" waivers under which they could design home health care programs for Medicaid reimbursement in lieu of institutionalization.[15] Any state requesting such a waiver must demonstrate that the alternate programs of care in the home or community setting will cost no more than the institutional care would have cost. Those who are covered by such a waiver need not be institutionalized, but the state must certify that they would require care in an intensive care facility or SNF were services not available under the waiver. Many states' waiver programs target specific groups of Medicaid eligibles, for example, the mentally retarded, the developmentally disabled, or aged persons. Home- and community-based waivers may continue for three years. They may be extended for three-year periods thereafter at the state's request. As of August 31, 1983, 48 home- and community-based waivers had been approved in 36 states. States have responded openly to this program, and it seems to be working well.

WAIVER OF THE THREE-DAY PRIOR HOSPITALIZATION REQUIREMENT FOR SKILLED NURSING SERVICES

TEFRA also permits waiver of the requirement that Medicare can pay for a stay in an SNF only if it is preceded by at least a three-day hospital stay.[16] Two further requirements, however, introduce a serious complication. First, the Health Care Financing Administration (HCFA) may waive the three-day prior hospitalization requirement only if it does not compromise the acute care nature of the SNF benefit. Second, waivers may not result in increased Medicare payments. These are important and significant preconditions and HCFA and the rest of DHHS are concerned about implementing the waivers which this provision authorizes without compromising them completely. Among other things, the federal government is considering what kinds of medical conditions might be appropriate for grants of waivers, and they will be advised by a HCFA panel of physicians and the Public Health Service.

CONCLUSION

Beset with money problems, the Medicare and Medicaid programs nevertheless continue to provide needed help to aged, disabled, and low-income people in meeting the costs of their medical care. Since they were enacted in 1965, both programs have undergone considerable change, and there is no doubt that further change is inevitable. Much of the change has been desirable and beneficial; some has not been very successful. Many of the changes of the last few years, however, hold the promise of benefitting not just Medicare and Medicaid and their beneficiaries, but the entire health care system.

NOTES

1. Social Security Act, 42 U.S.C.§301 et seq. (1970).
2. *See generally* Scanlon and Feder, *The Long Term Care Market Place: An Overview,* HEALTHCARE FINANCIAL MANAGEMENT 14(1):18, 28 (January 1984).
3. Medicaid and Medicare Amendments of 1981, 42 U.S.C. §1305 (1982): Omnibus Budget Reconciliation Act of 1981, Pub. L. No. 97–35, 95 Stat. 357; The Tax Equity and Fiscal Responsibility Act of 1982 (TEFRA), Title I, Subtitle A, Part I, Pub. L. No. 97–248; 96 Stat. 324; Social Security Act Amendments of 1983, 42 U.S.C. §1395 (1983).
4. Social Security Act Amendments of 1983, 42 U.S.C. §1395ww (1983).
5. Social Security Act, 42 U.S.C. §1395c et seq. (1972). [Part A Hospital Insurance Benefits for Aged and Disabled].
6. TEFRA, 42 U.S.C. §1395ww (1982).
7. TEFRA, 42 U.S.C. §1320b–5 (1982).
8. Social Security Act Amendments of 1983, 42 U.S.C. §1305 (1983).
9. 42 C.F.R. §§405, 409, 489 (1983).
10. Social Security Act Amendments of 1983, 42 U.S.C. §1395x (1983).
11. 42 U.S.C. §1396a(a)(13) (1982).
12. Omnibus Reconciliation Act of 1981, 42 U.S.C. §1396a (1981). *See also* 42 C.F.R. 447.250–.272 (1981).
13. Woolhandler, S., and Himmelstein, D.U., *Terms of Endowment: Prospective Hospital Reimbursement in Massachusetts,* HEALTH PAC BULLETIN 15(2):13 (March–April 1984).
14. Katie Beckett was a child dependent on a ventilator. President Reagan waived

Medicaid rules to allow Katie to return home, *see generally "Tax Dollars Wasted" Charges Respiratory Therapy Association,* LAW, MEDICINE & HEALTH CARE 12(2):82 (April 1984).

15. Omnibus Reconciliation Act of 1981, 42 U.S.C. §1396n (1981).
16. TEFRA, 42 U.S.C. §1395x (1982).

9

Alternative Methods of Financing Long-Term Care

Stanley S. Wallack, Ph.D.

The long-term care system today is fragmented, largely because its financing systems are uncoordinated. We cannot achieve an integrated delivery system until we bring about an integrated financing system.

In addition to overcoming fragmentation, we have a larger political and philosophical question to address: how to create a large enough flow of dollars to finance long-term care in this country. The problem of inadequate funding was well-illustrated in a *New York Times* story of May 4, 1983.[1] The article was about Mr. Joseph Brill, formerly a middle-class person. Mr. Brill is now relegated to living in a camper while trying to support his wife, who has been in an institution for a long time. The story describes how Mr. Brill has become impoverished by paying for his wife's care and how Medicaid is trying to extract Mr. Brill's last few dollars. Mr. Brill's tragedy is not an uncommon story.

As many people know, the largest cause of catastrophic, out-of-pocket expenditures for older people today is long-term care services. Until we change the financing system for long-term care, we will not be able to solve most of these problems. Public expenditures for long-term care are attached to a welfare program, namely Medicaid, and there is no way that a welfare program in the 1980s is going to pay for good long-term care, the high-quality care that we would want as middle-class people. Therefore we have to implement major changes that will overcome both fragmentation and inadequate financing.

It is imperative to look for solutions in large concepts rather than in inexpensive Band-Aid remedies. In this chapter, I focus on one such solution, the "social/HMO". I also describe other solutions that I believe may solve our major financing problems, and in particular the continuing care retirement community.

How Much Is Enough?

Let me begin by asking two questions. The first is whether the $30 billion spent annually on long-term care would be adequate if we learned to use it more efficiently.[2] I think the answer is no, because there are too many elderly and the number is growing too rapidly for $30 billion to respond to their needs. Between the years 1980 and 2030 the total U.S. population will grow by 40 percent, but the over-85 population will increase threefold.[3] These are the individuals who need long-term care. They need assistance in performing such basic tasks as bathing and dressing, and these needs are greater than those of 65-year-old people. Therefore it is clear that we will need to allocate more resources to the care of the aged.

The second question is how to finance the greater dollar level. Will it be financed the way it has been thus far, through a growing share of public dollars? Can we look to the federal and state governments to increase their expenditures for long-term care? Again, I think the answer is no. For now the federal government will have a hard time even maintaining such programs as Medicare and Social Security.

Unless something is done to prevent it, the Medicare trust fund will be depleted within a few years. The size of the problem is dramatic, and to illustrate, contrast the Social Security program's difficulties with Medicare's. The problem for Social Security is that the program is 10 percent out of balance. The Medicare trust fund program, on the other hand, is a 70 percent problem in that the annual deficit is expected to approach the annual income of the fund by the mid-1990s.[4] Clearly, major alterations in these programs will have to occur in this decade. If we decide that we want to maintain the public proportion of the costs, then a substantial increase in taxes for the Medicare program will be necessary for the federal government to increase its funding for the aged's health care.

What about states? Although public expenditures accounted for 56 percent of nursing home costs in 1981, the vast majority of that percentage (about 45 percent) was spent by Medicaid.[5] Nursing home costs for many years have exceeded one-third of medical expenditures. Many states are in worse financial shape than the federal government and are scrutinizing their budgets with extreme care.[6] Understandably, states have been trying to control long-term care expenditures for nursing homes. Even though they are third-party payers of nursing homes, many states can limit the number of nursing home beds directly through certificate-of-need requirements, or through their rules on reimbursement, allowance of depreciation, and return on capital.[7] This level of control does not extend to actually determining the number of nursing home beds created or maintained. In a number of states, there are no nursing homes being built today.[8] I believe that the recent trends will continue and that there may be a further decrease in the growth rate of nursing home beds so long as the states are the major payers. Therefore I do not think that we can look toward the government for financing as we did a few years ago. Instead we will have to rely on private financing.

There are two ways to encourage the private sector to finance more long-term care. The first is to provide higher retirement incomes for the elderly. Currently, a major part of the elderly's replacement income is from Social Security. Further, the methods employed for determining Social Security pensions result in lower payments to 75- or 85-year-olds than to 65- or 70-year-olds. This is because the Social Security Administration ties one's retirement payment to one's wage history. Therefore those retirees who are oldest receive the smallest incomes. In 1980, the median family income for those aged 65–67 was $12,400 while the median family income for those aged 73–79 was $8,450.[9] A major reason for this difference is the Social Security system. As we think about how to increase the incomes of the elderly, we must be particularly concerned about the incomes of people when they are 75 and 85 years old, as these persons need more dollars to pay for long-term care.

There are four ways in which we could increase the income of the elderly. One is through private pensions; a useful technique is to turn a life insurance benefit into a pension annuity. A second way, which is unlikely to occur, is for the government to reorganize Social Security and tie benefits to needs by redefining Social Security as a needs-based program. Since people's needs usually grow with age, they should receive higher payments as they grow older. The third way is for the government to develop a new, tax-exempt savings program, such as the one for individual retirement accounts, dedicated to long-term care. This would encourage people to save money for their long-term care. The fourth way is to establish "reverse mortgages." This idea is creating a lot of excitement today because 70 to 75 percent of the elderly own their own homes, most of them outright.[10] Homes are the largest asset for most elderly people. If this asset could be turned into an annuity payment, it could be an important way to pay for long-term care in the future.

Clearly there are ways to increase the income of the elderly, and some of them will be implemented. However, I do not think an income strategy is the best direction to take. I think a preferable approach is an insurance strategy of some sort because of today's distribution of long-term care expenditures. We find that a very small percentage of the people consumes the bulk of medical care expenditures. A Congressional Budget Office study of the nonpoor, nonelderly found that in 1978, 1 percent of the families accounted for 22 percent of expenditures and 5 percent for 49 percent of expenditures. For major corporations, we sometimes find that a small percentage of their employees consumes up to 40 or 50 percent of the health care dollars.[11] When we look at Medicaid data, we find that 5 percent of the population consumes 81 percent of Medicaid's total of inpatient hospital days. Finally, 8.8 percent of the population consumes 70 percent or more of Medicare expenditures.[12]

While there does not exist a comprehensive set of data on utilization and costs with which to determine the unevenness of the distribution, it seems reasonable to hypothesize that 10 to 15 percent of the elderly account for 90 percent or so of expenditures. The disproportionate distribution of Medicare acute expenditures is partially because 5 percent of the consumers are in nursing homes. Most of the remaining dollars go for the very disabled who live in the community. Undoubtedly there is a very uneven distribution of long-term care expenditures. Even if we were to increase income for all of the elderly, it would not solve the problem, unless it were a tremendous increase. Therefore an insurance concept, involving the pooling of funds, should be considered. If we could spread the cost for every elderly person among the whole population, it would not be a catastrophic expenditure for any one individual.

One approach is a social insurance program similar to a federal financing strategy. The Congressional Budget Office once studied this suggestion, but determined that it would be too costly to set up a long-term care fund.[13] Since the mid-1970s, interest in the social insurance approach has waned.

Alternatively, large private insurance companies could offer a long-term care option. Thus far, insurance companies have been reluctant to enter the arena. Many of these companies are headed by actuaries who insist on "solid" estimates; they have a great deal of trouble predicting the cost of long-term care in 20 years. If they sell a policy to a 40-year-old, they are looking at costs 20, 30, or 40 years in the future. These costs are very difficult to predict. Furthermore, they do not know what to sell; they are concerned that tastes will be different in 20 or 30 years. There are also the problems of marketing the policy. In general, it seems that 40-year-olds do not wish to purchase long-term care insurance. They do not believe that they are going to need it, as the likelihood is far in the future. Therefore insurance companies feel it would be very hard to sell.

Another problem with selling long-term care insurance is the possibility of adverse selection. Basically the question is who will purchase insurance. If it is only sick individuals, the insurance companies are in trouble; they would not be spreading the risk, and premiums could be consistently too low as the least sick leave the insurance program. So insurance companies would have to develop ways to avoid adverse selection, and most companies are fearful that they cannot do so.

Finally, another reason for not developing an insurance policy is that there is really no demand for such a policy from the insurance companies' customers, the corporate benefit managers. Employers are worried about today's health care costs and the disability benefits of their current work force. They are not demanding that insurance companies develop a long-term care benefit package. Therefore insurance companies are not thinking about it seriously. For all of the foregoing reasons, I do not think that insurance companies will move into the long-term care arena.

VIABLE MEANS OF POOLING FUNDS

There are some ways in which we can start to move toward better financing of long-term care. Insurance arrangements are possible, but one has to guard against adverse selection. If insurance is provided on an individual basis, this requires funding before the onset of the chronic illness. We can also avoid adverse selection by enrolling all individuals or even all of those belonging to particular groups, e.g., teachers or lawyers.

Another way of avoiding adverse selection is to include in the policy a set of benefits that will be attractive to all older persons. It could be housing, such as retirement communities, or it could be medical care, because all of the elderly are fearful of very high medical expenditures. The point is that there are ways of packaging long-term care that will make it attractive to everybody, thereby avoiding adverse selection.

As we start to think through what the new insurance policy should include, it is important that we develop a policy that has a wide scope of services. We do not want just a nursing home benefit. We want a comprehensive set of covered services in order to get the right kinds of service substitutions. However, a wide benefit package can become very expensive. Policy makers worry a great deal about offering such an extensive package to everybody. The private insurance companies would prefer to sell only skilled nursing home benefits, because they think they can control utilization in these facilities.

Given that a wide set of benefits is preferable, but very expensive, we have to establish some limits in costs. We need—in current jargon—a prospectively budgeted system. That is, we need a firm idea of what the system will cost. A prospectively budgeted system can be adopted on one of two bases: an individual basis with each individual having a set of benefits, or a group basis, for an enrolled population. The enrolled population can be a group of individuals or only those enrolled with a particular provider. I prefer an enrolled population model since the provider has incentives not to overutilize services and to deliver the services in an efficient manner. So what we need to develop is a private financing mechanism that pays for a comprehensive set of long-term care services on a prospective budget basis. Furthermore, once we do this we need to link together the financing and delivery systems.

There are two models that fit the criteria I have been talking about. There is the continuing care retirement community (or life care community), and there is the system we have developed at Brandeis University, the social/HMO.

THE CONTINUING CARE RETIREMENT COMMUNITY

Continuing care retirement communities are a fast-growing part of long-term care. They basically accomplish two things: provide a very broad set of services such as social services, nursing home services, and food to people who enter the community, and they provide housing through a campus-based approach. In general, people who join these communities do so when they are healthy, although once they enroll, health care services are provided as needed.

The chief attraction of such life care communities is that they spread the financial risk among those needing care. Although there are more than 300 continuing care retirement communities today, they all have similar financial arrangements. They all require payment of a significant front-end premium and monthly premiums. Some argue that the communities are too expensive; they are not cheap, but they are not so expensive that they are accessible only to the very wealthy. The University of Pennsylvania recently completed a study of continuing care retirement communities. The study found that 75 percent of the communities had front-end fees—entry fees—of less than $50,000 and monthly fees of less than $750 in 1981, with the average being $35,000 and $560, respectively.[14]

These continuing care communities also vary in the amount of long-term care insurance they provide. In some of these communities, individuals pay the same monthly rate regardless of whether they live in a residence or in a nursing home where they use many more resources. In others, the people that need to be in the nursing home share the costs. I know of a few communities that have been going on for 15 years or more, have an average age between 82 and 84, have 20 percent of their residents in the nursing home, and, interestingly enough, have never taken a cent of Medicaid.[15] This has occurred because they have effective insurance mechanisms operating in these communities. Since everybody spends the same amount, nobody has to go broke. They have, in effect, created a self-insured program and have given a lot of people a lot of financial protection.

In quality of care, many of these communities are excellent—perhaps because the nursing home is part of the community. People who live in the community know that the nursing home at some time may be their home. Therefore they are very concerned about what that nursing home looks like and how it is run.

These communities, then, have some very attractive aspects with regard to financing and quality of care. There are obviously some potential problems, and there are some legal issues that may have to be resolved. For instance, individuals pay significant amounts of money to join the communities. These individuals are at risk, for if the community goes bankrupt, tremendous hardships may result. We need to develop appropriate financial protection for those who enroll. In nine states, comprehensive laws have been enacted to regulate continuing care communities. Other states need to develop rules governing these organizations because the communities in fact are operating an insurance program and need to be regulated to an extent.

The principal drawback of these communities is that access to them is limited, in part because they require sizeable front-end fees. Unfortunately these fees are rising due to the increasing expense of building continuing care communities. We are trying to develop lower-cost alternatives to the communities, including zones that do not require people to live on campus.

The important point to note is that with continuing care communities, we do have in place a system that is privately financed, gives people protection, and provides good long-term care.

THE SOCIAL/HMO: AN INTEGRATED DELIVERY SYSTEM

The second significant model that is about to become operational is the social/HMO. With the support of the federal Health Care Financing Administration and several private foundations, the Heller School of Brandeis University has taken this idea from the blackboard to the point of actually starting four social/HMOs around the country. The social/HMO is an innovative model of financing and delivery of care. Simply stated, it is trying to take the model of the health maintenance organization and attach to it a set of long-term care and social services. Its appeal and marketability, to a large extent, are based on the premise that all elderly want more financial protection from medical care costs. By including medical care dollars and medical care services in the benefit package, we may be able to substitute ambulatory and home services for expensive hospital and nursing home care. Once this is done, the sizeable dollar savings derived from reductions in hospital care will be used for long-term care services.

There are four sites in which social/HMOs are being developed. By design, they have very different orientations to medical or long-term care services. One site is the Kaiser system in Portland, Oregon. Currently an active HMO, based on a medical model, it will expand into long-term care. Another organization, in New York, is the Metropolitan Jewish Geriatric Center. This is a large rehabilitation facility, but it has been providing only long-term care services. A third site is in Minneapolis. This project, Senior Plus, is a joint venture between Ebenezer Society, a large, established organization providing a wide array of long-term care services, and Group Health, the largest HMO in Minneapolis. The fourth site is a community-based case management agency called SCAN (Senior Care Action Network), in Long Beach, California.

All four groups plan to enroll an over-65 population that resembles the community in terms of age, health status, and entitlements (that is, Medicare and Medicaid). The goal is to include a cross section of the elderly population. To put this model in place, we had to secure a series of very complicated waivers involving the major payers—Medicaid and Medicare. Some private premiums will be instituted to pay for the expensive long-term services. We will also use public dollars. In order to minimize adverse selection—where only individuals in need of expensive care join—the private premium will be only $20–45. That means we cannot include all of the long-term care benefits that we would want. The benefit package, for example, will have limited nursing home benefits, although it is still better than what now exists under Medicare. The Medicaid individuals, who receive state payments, will have unlimited nursing home benefits. The social/HMO model provides an integrated set of services, and should include all of the desired medical and long-term services.

By including a broad scope of services, we think we will deliver a more appropriate set of services. There will be one responsible provider; that provider will have a prospective budget and will be the one eventually at financial risk. The provider has an incentive to use the least expensive and most appropriate services. This model should spread the cost of catastrophic expenditures, since people will have much more insurance coverage for long-term care. In theory, people will not be faced with huge out-of-pocket expenses, and fewer people will go through the unfortunate experience of becoming eligible for Medicaid by "spending down" to the necessary income level because of high medical expenditures.

The importance of the latter point should be highlighted. To maintain the commitment to long-term care, states can keep more people off welfare by dropping the requirement to spend down. The only way they can do that is with more private insurance or private financing up front.

Finally, we think the social/HMO has the potential to provide tremendous savings in total costs by keeping the elderly out of costly institutions—either hospitals or nursing homes. In our preliminary studies we have estimated reductions in hospital care by about 25 percent.[16] Some of the researchers working on the social/HMO project think the estimate is a little high; I think it is low. In fact, there are HMO sites serving the elderly that are already claiming hospital reductions of slightly greater than 25 percent.[17] In any case, the potential dollar savings from reduced hospitalization is significant, as per capita hospital costs for the elderly are well over $1,000 annually. With the savings, we want social/HMOs to provide a wide and more appropriate set of long-term care services. This would, we believe, give more people financial protection.

Conclusion

In facing the issue of long-term care, we currently have some adequate programs in place, although we need to keep unfolding and developing new alternatives. We clearly have a lot to learn, but we can start to move forward. We must move forward now because of the growing number of frail elderly. It is up to the providers to be innovative, to develop delivery systems that the public and its officials trust and are willing to put money into. Because of the financing difficulties of present systems, providers have an incentive to develop new systems soon. It is not surprising that the hospital community originally designed medical insurance; thus far, the continuing care communities have developed the only comprehensive insurance for long-term care. The providers of long-term care must find innovative and appropriate solutions to our current long-term care financing dilemmas. I hope this essay has provided a framework for the developing solutions.

Notes

1. *Elderly Enlist Lawyers to Gain Social Services,* New York Times, May 4, 1983, at B4, col. 1.
2. J.L. Callahan, S.S. Wallack, Reforming the Long-Term Care System (Lexington Books, Lexington, Mass.) (1981) at chapter 1.
3. Bureau of the Census, U.S. Dept. of Commerce, 1970 Census of the Population (U.S. Gov't Printing Office, Washington, D.C.) (1973).
4. *Prospects for Medicare's Hospital Insurance Trust Fund: An Information Paper, Special Committee on Aging of the United States Senate,* 98th Cong., 2nd Sess. (March 1983) Table 1 at 2.
5. Waldo, D., Gibson, R., *National Health Expenditures, 1981,* Health Care Financing Review 4(1):1 (September 1982).
6. *See generally* Morris, R., Youket, P., *The Long-Term Care Issues: Identifying the Problems and Potential Solutions,* in Reforming the Long-Term-Care System, *supra* note 2, at 19.

7. *See, e.g.*, E. WICKS, J. LEURHRS, DEVELOPING STATE POLICY ON HEALTH CARE COSTS: GOVERNOR'S TASK FORCE INITIATIVES (National Governors Association, Washington, D.C.) (1984); Feder, J., Scanlon, W., *Regulating the Bed Supply in Nursing Homes*, MILBANK MEMORIAL FUND QUARTERLY 58:1 (Winter 1980) [hereinafter cited as *Regulating Bed Supply*]; Baldwin, C., Bishop, C., *Return to Nursing Home Investment: Issues for Public Policy*, HEALTH CARE FINANCING REVIEW 5(4):43, 44 (Summer 1984).

8. *Regulating Bed Supply, supra* note 7.

9. SOCIAL SECURITY ADMINISTRATION, U.S. DEPT. OF HEALTH AND HUMAN SERVICES, INCOME OF THE POPULATION 55 AND OVER, 1980 (U.S. Gov't Printing Office, Washington, D.C.) (1983) at Table 10.

10. U.S. GENERAL ACCOUNTING OFFICE, DEMOGRAPHIC AND ECONOMIC CHARACTERISTICS OF SOCIAL SECURITY RETIREE FAMILIES (U.S. Gov't Printing Office, Washington, D.C.) (1982).

11. *See* CONGRESSIONAL BUDGET OFFICE, CATASTROPHIC MEDICAL EXPENDITURES: PATTERNS IN THE NON-ELDERLY, NON-POOR POPULATION (U.S. Gov't Printing Office, Washington, D.C.) (1982); Rosenbloom, D., Gertman, P., *An Intervention Strategy for Controlling Costly Care*, BUSINESS AND HEALTH 1(8):6 (July/August 1984).

12. Dobson, A., Scharff, J., Corder, L., *Six Months of Medicaid Data: A Summary from the National Medical Care Utilization and Expenditures Survey*, HEALTH CARE FINANCING REVIEW 4(3):115 (March 1983).

13. CONGRESSIONAL BUDGET OFFICE, LONG-TERM CARE FOR THE ELDERLY AND DISABLED (U.S. Gov't Printing Office, Washington, D.C.) (1977).

14. H.E. WINKLEVOSS, A.V. POWELL, CONTINUING CARE RETIREMENT COMMUNITIES: AN EMPIRICAL, FINANCIAL AND LEGAL ANALYSIS (R.D. Irwin, Inc., Homewood, Ill.) (1984).

15. Personal communication with Donald Moon, Executive Director, Foulkeways at Gwynedd, Gwynedd, Pa., and Lloyd Lewis, Executive Director, Kendal at Longwood, Kennett Sq., Pa.

16. Diamond, L., Gruenberg, L., Morris, R., *Elder Care for the 1980's: Health and Social Services in One Prepaid Health Maintenance System*, THE GERONTOLOGIST 23(2):148–54 (1983).

17. See Health Maintenance Organization Risk Contracting under Medicare, Grants and Contract Report to Health Care Financing Administration (September 1984) at 69.

10

The Ties That Bind: Life Care Contracts and Nursing Homes

Lawrence R. Leonard, J.D.

INTRODUCTION

The nursing home business in the United States is a growth industry.[1] Approximately 1.3 million people[2] live in 26,000 nursing homes.[3] These homes provide a necessary service for those persons who seek to enter a facility for the elderly but require greater medical attention than is available at boarding homes.[4] Those who must choose nursing home life, however, often are not in a good position to evaluate the alternatives before them. The average age of nursing home residents is 82.[5] Most are widowed; only 10 percent have a living spouse.[6] Most are alone; half have no close relatives.[7] Most are mentally impaired.[8] Two-thirds of all residents come to the nursing home from their own homes; few of them will ever leave.[9] The average stay is 2.4 years.[10]

One of the most important decisions these people must make is determining how to finance their stay. The cost of maintaining a person in a nursing home is likely to be over $12,000 a year.[11] While Medicaid and Medicare pay more than half of this cost,[12] nursing home residents and their families bear the remainder.[13] One method by which a resident may pay for care is through a life care contract. These contracts require applicants to pay a certain entrance fee and to transfer to the home part or all of their property in consideration for the home's promise to provide care for the remainder of the applicant's life.

Applicants may encounter serious problems when entering into life care contracts with nursing homes. First, they may bind themselves to unfavorable living conditions. Many nursing homes are substandard.[14]

Reprinted with permission of the American Society of Law & Medicine from AMERICAN JOURNAL OF LAW & MEDICINE 8(2):153–73 (Summer 1982).

Substandard conditions include sanitary violations, fire hazards, abuse
by employees, neglect, unnecessary use of physical restraints, inadequate
control of drugs, poor food or poor food preparation, misappropriation
and theft, assaults on human dignity, and lack of proper physical care.[15]
Having exchanged much, if not all, of his or her property to obtain the
life care contract, the resident may have little means by which to escape
an unhealthy or dangerous environment. Second, a nursing home may
be financially unsound, and in the event of bankruptcy, what had formerly been the resident's assets would be carried into insolvency. Third,
the life care contract may be patently unfair if it does not include clauses
which allow the resident to live at the home during an initial probationary
period, and subsequently terminate the contract for good cause. Because
the unique position of the life care resident makes a thorough understanding of these problems necessary, individuals should enter into life
care contracts only after having had the opportunity to experience life in
the nursing home.

   This chapter examines the problems life care contracts can pose for
nursing home residents. The chapter then reviews applicable case law,
statutes, and regulations concerning life care contracts. The chapter con-
cludes by delineating guidelines for constructing life care contracts.

PROBLEMS WITH LIFE CARE CONTRACTS
AND NURSING HOMES

BINDING NATURE OF LIFE CARE CONTRACTS

The most important characteristic of a life care contract is that it effectively binds the nursing home resident to the home for the remainder of
his or her life. Although the amount of property exchanged varies with
the age and health of each applicant,[16] the relative cost is usually great
enough to leave the resident with little means of support outside the
home.

   The binding nature of life care contracts raises ethical considerations. After the parties sign the contract, the home has no financial
incentive to provide satisfactory care. The home can increase its profits by
spending as little money as possible on the life care resident. Additionally
the financial incentives are different for life care residents than pay-by-
the-month or medical residents. For the latter, the home receives a regular fee to provide care, which may increase due to increased costs. However, life care residents have paid an initial fixed rate. The longer the
resident lives, the more it costs the home to care for the resident, and

ultimately the home realizes less profit. If the life care resident dies after living at the home for only a short period of time, the home will have earned a substantial profit. These considerations should be borne in mind by the potential life care resident, underlining the necessity for contracting with a reputable, quality nursing home.

SUBSTANDARD HOMES

Evidence indicates that patient abuse in nursing homes is rampant.[17] Many nursing homes contain health deficiencies such as unhygienic handling of food, medicine and laundry; filthy hallways, kitchens, bathrooms, and bedrooms; incontinent patients left in their own waste; urine and feces covering floors; and the presence of scabies.[18] Many homes also contain fire hazards. In 1976 there were 9,000 nursing home fires, resulting in an estimated 540 deaths and property damage of $6 million.[19] Other deficiencies include poor food or poor food preparation,[20] and misappropriation or theft.[21]

In many homes, patients are abused by employees. This abuse includes deliberate physical violence and intimidation.[22] Residents may suffer from staff negligence, leading not only to poor care, but also to injury and death.[23] Nursing home staffs may fail to treat injuries or ailments, to change bedding, dressings, or catheters, to give proper medication or physical treatment, or to oversee residents' activities.[24] Residents may be victims of assaults on their human dignity, as when they are unnecessarily restrained, bathed without privacy, given tattered clothing, insulted, or harassed.[25] They may be subject to reprisals from the nursing home staff for complaining about the home's conditions.[26]

Problems may occur in the medical treatment of residents. Visits by physicians are often few and far between.[27] If a physician does visit a nursing home, his examinations of the residents may be only cursory. As a result, the nurses or untrained staff must provide the medical care.[28] There also may be insufficient dental care, psychiatric care, and podiatry care.[29] Drug misuse and abuse in nursing homes has been called "a kind of pharmaceutical Russian roulette."[30] According to a six-state study conducted by the General Accounting Office, 82 percent of the drugs administered in nursing homes were given with insufficient consideration of their appropriateness or possible synergystic effects.[31] Some nursing home staffs have given drugs intended for one resident to another, used outdated drugs, and used drugs to control residents for the staff's convenience.[32]

The executive director of the National Citizens' Coalition for Nursing Home Reform summarized the problems in the nursing home system in testimony in 1979:

We are clear on the fact that America's nursing home system works only for the people who profit from it. It does not work for nursing home residents and their families.

Thousands of citizens in nursing homes are suffering isolation, neglect, insult and abuse, and inadequate, even criminally negligent care at this very moment. Sadly, their suffering is not new, nor is it unknown. It is a blight on this society which has been well documented for nearly fifteen years.[33]

Government efforts to control abuse through regulation have been inadequate.[34] The current regulatory system is in need of improvement.[35] A Connecticut nursing home ombudsman testified before Congress that Connecticut's and the federal government's requirements "deal very little with the patient and his or her needs. . . . [Additionally] it is my opinion that neither the State nor the Federal Government takes necessary action when violations occur."[36] The vice-chairman of the Ways and Means Committee of the Washington State Senate testified that his state was doing "a lousy job" of regulating its nursing homes.[37] The director for public policy of the American Association of Homes for the Aging testified that "the fragmentation of agency responsibility has contributed greatly to the inefficiency of the current regulatory program."[38] A spokesperson for the nursing home industry, however, testified that there was too much regulation, and that the combination of local, state, and federal regulations was duplicative, inefficient, and confusing.[39] Moreover, the witness stated that the regulatory system plays a major role in increasing nursing home costs.[40] Despite their different perspectives, all sides—consumers, government, and the nursing home industry—agree that nursing home regulation is inefficient.

FINANCIALLY UNSTABLE HOMES

When a nursing home enters into a life care arrangement, it promises to care for the resident for life. This support obligation assumes that the home will continue operating at least for the life of the resident, and that the quality of care will not deteriorate beyond the parties' expectations. Problems may arise, however, if the home, due to financial instability, cannot complete its performance owed to the resident. The life care resident may face grave difficulties should the nursing home file for bankruptcy.

When a debtor files for bankruptcy, it is granted an automatic stay with respect to its creditors.[41] The stay prevents creditors from reaching the assets of the debtor until a repayment plan has been devised. In the case of a life care resident, the stay would prevent the resident, as a creditor, from recovering on the contract he or she signed with the home. Because the terms of the life care contract passed all of the resident's property to the home, that property is considered the debtor's. Although the debtor/nursing home would have breached its agreement with the resident, settlement of the contract must await the bankruptcy court's approval of a repayment plan.[42]

Once a stay is granted, the life care resident has no means of support. The resident is forced to depend on other means, such as public assistance, in order to live. Moreover, the resident loses the ready access to medical care that was probably an important factor in the original decision to move into the home.

In determining the claims against the debtor/nursing home, the creditors are repaid according to an order of priority established in the Bankruptcy Code. Creditors who have a security interest in some property of the debtor—a lien on some specific property, created by an agreement[43]—are repaid first.[44] The next class of creditors to be repaid is the priority unsecured creditors.[45] Of this group, the life care resident would stand fifth in line to receive payment[46] of up to $900.[47] Since all higher priority claims must be repaid first, and since in any event the maximum repayment allowed under the Bankruptcy Code is only $900, life care residents whose homes go bankrupt lose practically their whole investment—which in many cases is all the property they owned.

The accompanying psychological and emotional problems can be devastating to the resident. One documented psychological effect, known as transfer trauma, arises from "abrupt and involuntary transfer of elderly residents from one home to another."[48] Transfer trauma can occur when there is a loss of a familiar physical environment or changes in neighbors, staff, and routine. Elderly residents may suffer from transfer trauma when separated from friends in the nursing home, or moved to homes located in areas that visitors may find hard to reach. Numerous studies have shown that such forced movement almost always causes depression or regressive behavior, and may even result in the resident's death.[49]

PROBATIONARY AND TERMINATION CLAUSES

A life care contract should include both a probationary period and a termination clause. A probationary period usually lasts between one and six months,[50] and gives the home and the resident an opportunity to determine whether they will be satisfied with each other. On an initial visit, an applicant may be given a one-sided view of the home. If the applicant has an opportunity to live there on a probationary basis, however, the home might not be able to maintain a false front. During the probationary period, the applicant has the right to cancel the contract and withdraw from the home if he or she is not satisfied, and the home has the right to refuse to admit the applicant as a permanent resident.[51] If either event occurs, the applicant is entitled to the return of his or her property, minus an amount to cover the cost of his or her care while he or she lived there.[52]

A termination clause allows the resident to cancel the life care contract after giving the home sufficient notice of his or her intention to leave.[53] After the notice period expires, the resident is entitled to the return of his or her property, less the cost of his or her care while he or she lived in the home. An unduly long notice period may prevent the resident from recovering his or her property. Since the average stay in a nursing home is less than two and one-half years,[54] the resident may die prior to the termination of the contract, permitting the home to retain the resident's assigned property.[55] The termination clause protects the resident from subsequent deterioration of the home without the necessity of suing to rescind the contract.

Problems may arise in the disposition of property when the resident dies either during the probationary period or after giving notice of termination. Where the contract fails to provide for disposition of the resident's property in these situations the matter may be resolved in court. Rules of contract law in different jurisdictions vary as to when contracts become binding and when they have been terminated.[56]

The last problem occurs when the resident seeks to invoke the termination clause after the value of the property exchanged has been spent for his or her care. If he or she terminates the contract, the home is no longer required to provide for his or her care, since both obligations are canceled. If he or she does not terminate the contract, the substandard care that may have motivated him or her to seek recision will likely continue. His or her only alternative then would be to sue to improve the quality of care.

PAST CHALLENGES AND PRESENT LAWS

In the past, life care residents and their heirs have questioned the legal validity of life care contracts and their provisions. For the most part, these attacks have failed. Nevertheless, they may have publicized these contracts in a manner that has caused some states either to regulate or abolish them. Additionally, state and federal regulation of nursing homes has a direct impact on the life care resident. This section discusses past challenges and present laws regarding nursing home and life care contracts to establish the foundation upon which a framework for proper life care contracts may be devised.

PAST CHALLENGES TO LIFE CARE CONTRACTS

Life care residents, representatives of their estates, and disappointed heirs have challenged the validity of life care contracts and the enforceability of certain provisions within the contracts. Where the resident died shortly after signing over all of his or her property, challengers have alleged that the contract was unconscionable and against public policy, and that the home was unjustly enriched. Where the resident died during the probationary period, plaintiffs have sought to compel the home to return the resident's assets. Some residents have tried to cancel their contracts on the ground that there was lack of mutuality when the contract was signed.[57] Assignments of future-acquired property have also been challenged.[58] A review of these cases indicates that life care contracts are generally enforced.

Adequacy of Consideration and Benefit of the Bargain

The courts have seldom annulled life care contracts because of inadequacy of consideration or because one party benefited from the bargain.[59] A Nebraska case enunciated the basic rule that the adequacy of consideration is determined at the time the contract is made, not at the death of the resident.[60] In that case the resident paid $13,354 for a life care contract, based on the resident's life expectancy multiplied by a $900 annual charge. The court found the fee paid to be a reasonable reflection of the cost of services for the care to be provided over the resident's expected lifetime.[61] Most courts have upheld life care contracts even though the home realized the benefit of its bargain when the resident died prior to the nursing home's expenditure of significant costs for her care.[62] Similarly, where the resident has required services in excess of what was compensated for by the property transfer, courts have held the parties to their bargains and required the nursing home to continue providing the necessary care.[63]

Lack of Mutuality

Life care contracts generally do not fail for lack of mutuality. In a California case, a resident who voluntarily left a home after seven months sued for a refund of her entrance fee,[64] claiming that the life care contract was void due to lack of mutuality of obligation. The court refused to invalidate the contract, however, stating that the home was always able and willing to perform, and therefore was obligated under the contract.[65] On the other hand, a court may find lack of mutual obligation where a resident wishes to withdraw during the probationary period. In a New York case,[66] where the resident died one month after entering the home, the court reasoned that since payment was conditioned on the resident remaining at the home, there was no mutuality of obligation until the two-month probationary period expired.[67]

Death During Probationary Period

Disposition of a resident's property when he or she dies during the contractual probationary period is determined by the parties' intent.[68] Where the contract expressly provides for disposition of the resident's property if he or she dies during the probationary period, courts will generally uphold the terms of the contract.[69]

Where the contract is silent as to the disposition of his or her property in this event, courts generally allow the resident's estate to recover property paid to the home.[70] However, where the resident has manifested an intent to be bound by a permanent life care arrangement, the nursing home will be allowed to retain all fees paid.[71] For example, in *Caldwell v. Basler, Inc.,*[72] the resident lived in the home under a month-to-month agreement, then signed a permanent agreement for life care. The contract provided for a 90 day probationary period, but the resident died after six weeks. The resident's estate sued to have the property returned, but the court ruled that the home was entitled to retain the property. The court reasoned that under California's strict regulation of life care contracts,[73] the resident should have been considered a life care resident as of the day the contract was signed.[74]

In *Gold v. Salem Lutheran Home Association of the Bay Cities,*[75] the resident moved in the home August 1 for a two-month probationary period. On September 25 he signed a life care contract with the home and paid the home $8,500. The contract was to commence October 1, at the expiration of the two-month probationary period. The resident died on September 28. The court held that although the contract was not to commence until October 1, it was enforceable as of September 26 and thus the home was entitled to retain the $8,500.[76] An important factor in the case, although unstated by the court, was that the intent of the parties to finalize the life care agreement was apparent. Since the resident wanted to stay at the home, the last few days of the probationary period were not necessary to provide the resident with an opportunity to evaluate the home.[77]

Assignment of Future-Acquired Property

In some early cases, life care contracts were challenged on the ground that the assignment of future-acquired property was unlawful. Under general principles of contract law, one cannot sell what one does not have,[78] nor can one assign a mere possibility of receiving something.[79] In a New Jersey case, a nursing home resident inherited $30,000 just before her death.[80] Her nieces claimed the inheritance, contending that the resident's assignment to the home did not include the possibility of a legacy, and that a contract to assign all future-acquired property was contrary to public policy. The court upheld the contract, stating that expectancy by inheritance, although not assignable at law, is assignable in equity for valuable consideration.[81] The home's agreement to care for the resident constituted such consideration. Other courts have followed the rule that assignments of future-acquired property are permissible if supported by valuable consideration.[82]

Termination of the Contract

Many courts require a resident seeking to terminate a life care contract to show good cause, such as substantial breach of the contract by the home.[83] Generally, transfer of a resident to a hospital, where medically necessary, will not constitute a substantial breach.[84] Deviations from the contract, such as substitution of self-insurance for coverage through an insurance carrier, or an increase in the monthly medical fee, have been found not to constitute substantial breach of the contract.[85] However, a resident seeking to terminate during a probationary period may be entitled to cancel the contract for any reason or no reason at all.[86]

Some life care contracts contain termination clauses. A resident wishing to terminate a life care contract may have to rely upon particular grounds stated in the clause.[87] The contract may also delineate certain procedures which the resident must follow to formally terminate the contract.[88]

In summary, courts have found that life care contracts are enforceable agreements that do not suffer from lack of mutuality. A home's promise to care for the resident for life is adequate consideration for a transfer of the resident's property. Future-acquired property may be lawfully assigned to the home for a valuable consideration. Further, if the resident desires to cancel the agreement based on a breach of contract by the home, he or she must show that the breach was substantial.

LAWS AND REGULATIONS AFFECTING LIFE CARE CONTRACTS

Both the federal government and the states regulate nursing homes. Many of these regulations bear indirectly on life care contracts. For instance, the Secretary of the Department of Health and Human Services (DHHS) is empowered to make all necessary rules and regulations for nursing homes that receive federal aid.[89] To this end, DHHS has promulgated a nursing home "Residents' Bill of Rights."[90] Additionally, some states have promulgated their own "patients' bills of rights."[91] Adequate protection of all nursing home residents assures protection of life care residents who, by the nature of their permanent contracts, are most vulnerable to abuse. Additionally, some states affect life care contracts directly, either by close regulation or total prohibition.[92]

Federal Regulation

Nursing homes that wish to participate in the Medicare[93] and Medicaid[94] programs—as most do[95]—must conform to all applicable federal regulations.[96] Included in these regulations is a set of Standards for Payment for Skilled Nursing and Intermediate Care Facilities.[97] The "bill of rights"[98] within these standards was designed to ensure the health and protection of all nursing home residents. Every nursing home must have written policies and procedures to ensure that each resident has the right to be informed,[99] to receive medical attention and treatment,[100] to be protected from arbitrary transfer and discharge,[101] to be able to exercise individual rights,[102] to manage personal financial affairs,[103] to be free from abuse and restraints,[104] to be treated with dignity and to have his or her privacy respected,[105] to not be compelled to work for the home,[106] to correspond and associate with others,[107] to participate in activities,[108] and to retain and use personal possessions.[109] Additionally, the DHHS regulations delineate standards for nursing homes regarding safety,[110] environment and sanitation,[111] meal service,[112] medication,[113] health,[114] and other services.[115]

State Regulation

Since the states directly participate in the Medicaid program, they are empowered to regulate nursing homes.[116] Additionally, states regulate and set standards for nursing homes under their police power. Generally, the states' departments of health or human resources license nursing homes and promulgate appropriate regulations.[117] The offices of the attorneys general assist in drafting the regulations and are responsible for their enforcement.[118] These state authorities are responsible for ensuring that nursing homes provide quality care and meet all state and federal requirements for reimbursement. Some states have promulgated patients' "bills of rights" for nursing home residents,[119] usually similar to those established by DHHS. These regulations, where properly enforced, protect life care residents from substandard homes.

Some states regulate life care contracts directly.[120] For instance, both California and Colorado require that nursing homes obtain certificates of approval before offering life care contracts and continue to monitor life care programs after approval has been granted.[121] California has appointed a board to oversee the operations of the life care facilities.[122] Colorado places responsibility for regulating these contracts with the commissioner of insurance.[123] In both of these states, homes that offer life care contracts must maintain reserves that cover their obligations.[124]

If the home goes bankrupt, life care contract holders are given preferred claims against the assets of the home.[125]

A few states have abolished life care contracts.[126] In New York, any money advanced on a contract for admission to a nursing home "as security for performance of the contract . . . or to be applied to payments upon such contract . . . when due" remains the resident's money and is held in trust by the home.[127] The home may not mingle the resident's money with its own and must keep it in a separate interest-bearing account. Since this provision cannot be waived,[128] any attempt to create a life care contract will fail. Pennsylvania directly abolished life care contracts, stating simply that "Skilled Nursing and Intermediate Care Facilities shall not require or permit a patient to assign his assets to the facility in return for a life care guarantee."[129] These states have decided that the problems associated with life care contracts outweigh their benefits.

For some elderly individuals, however, the benefits of life care contracts—knowing that care will be provided as long as they live—may make entering into one worthwhile. Once the applicable federal and state laws and regulations are understood, the framework for constructing a life care agreement can be delineated. With proper guidelines, the risks associated with life care contracts can be minimized and the nursing home resident protected.

FRAMEWORK FOR CONSTRUCTING A LIFE CARE CONTRACT

CHOOSING THE NURSING HOME

The most important step for a potential life care resident is choosing the right nursing home. There are several sources to which a resident may turn to seek information about this process.[130] Generally, the potential resident's physician should recommend whether the resident requires skilled or intermediate care. Intermediate care facilities are less expensive than skilled facilities, but do not provide intensive medical or nursing care.[131]

The individual should visit each prospective nursing home unannounced, preferably during a meal time in order to determine the quality of the food. The prospective resident should also notice the number of nurses and staff available.[132] By examining the facility, speaking with residents and noticing the general atmosphere, the individual will be better able to determine whether the home would meet his or her expectations.

PREPARING THE CONTRACT

Once a suitable home has been found, the applicant's attorney should prepare a life care agreement with the nursing home that incorporates by reference all applicable state and federal laws regarding standards of care and patients' rights.[133] Failure to maintain the appropriate standards should be considered sufficient basis to rescind the contract.[134] In this manner, many of the problems of trying to prove substantial breach may be alleviated.[135]

The contract should provide for a probationary period to give both the resident and the home an opportunity to determine if the arrangement will be satisfactory.[136] The home may insist on requiring specific grounds for termination during the probationary period.[137] These grounds, however, if required, should recognize an individual's good faith preferences that may not be easily categorized in advance.

Disposition of the resident's property if the resident dies during the probationary period should be made clear in the contract. Should the resident die or leave during this period, the home will be entitled to retain a fee commensurate with the care provided while the resident lived there. This fee should be stated in the contract, based on an appropriate per day rate.

The contract should also include a termination clause to allow the resident to cancel the contract after the probationary period. A termination clause will give the resident some leverage over the treatment he or she receives. The clause should include a reasonable notice period to allow the home to rectify any problems. Additionally, a notice period protects the home by preventing the resident from terminating the contract on his or her deathbed, depriving the home of the benefit of its bargain. The termination clause may contain a statement of the grounds upon which the contract may be canceled, such as failure to provide satisfactory care, or failure to maintain state or federal standards.[138]

INSURING FINANCIAL STABILITY

In a state that requires a nursing home to maintain monetary reserves covering the obligations assumed under life care contracts and give life care residents preferred claims against the assets of the home,[139] a life care resident is protected should the home become insolvent. In other states, a life care resident's property is vulnerable to the possibility of disastrous financial loss.[140] To protect against this danger, the resident's attorney should provide for some degree of financial security. The attorney could have the home post a bond guaranteeing its performance, the value of which should be the estimated cost of caring for the resident for the rest of his or her life.[141] The nursing home would contract with a bonding company designating the life care resident as the third party beneficiary. Thus, if the home breaches the life care contract, the bonding company pays the resident the full value of the bond. If the home fulfills its obligation, it cancels the bond at the resident's death.

Alternatively, the attorney could perfect a security interest in some property of the home to secure the home's performance of its obligation. With a perfected security interest, the resident is protected should the home go bankrupt since the resident would have first priority in that particular asset.[142] If the proceeds from sale of this asset are insufficient to provide for the cost of caring for the resident for the rest of his or her life, remaining claims against the home would be unsecured.[143]

OMBUDSMAN SERVICE

Under DHHS's Grants for State and Community Programs on Aging, each state is empowered to establish and operate a statewide long-term care ombudsman program.[144] The nursing home ombudsman investigates and resolves complaints made by or on behalf of elderly residents that may adversely affect their health, safety, welfare, or rights.[145] The ombudsman monitors the development and implementation of all federal and state laws and regulations pertaining to the nursing homes,[146] and is given complete access to all facilities and residents.[147] The resident can turn to the ombudsman when the nursing home fails to respond to his or her concerns or needs.

CONCLUSION

Despite the increasingly important role of Medicare and Medicaid, life care contracts are still a significant means of financing the costs of nursing home care. Elderly individuals contemplating life care agreements should bear several considerations in mind. Because the life care resident will receive nursing home care for the rest of his or her life, the resident generally must assign everything he or she owns to the home in exchange for that care. Once the individual becomes a resident, the chances of leaving are reduced by the permanent nature of the contract. After the expiration of the probationary period, the resident can afford to leave the home only if the contract contains a termination clause or if the resident can prove that the home substantially breached its contractual obligations.

Many nursing homes have substandard conditions. Some are financially unstable. The risks caused by these conditions should be considered before entering into a life care contract. If the potential life care applicant finds a suitable home that offers quality care, many of the problems associated with life care contracts can be avoided.

Life care contracts are generally enforced and cannot be rescinded absent proof of substantial breach. State and federal laws, which are designed to protect nursing home residents and insure that they are properly cared for, should negate the need for residents to resort to the court. If the contract includes probationary and termination clauses, and the home is willing to guarantee its performance by a bond or security interest, then the life care contract can benefit the nursing home resident. In this event, the tie that binds can be advantageous.

NOTES

1. F. Moss, V. Halamandaris, Too Old, Too Sick, Too Bad 74 (1977). Between 1960 and 1978, nursing home revenues increased 3,000 percent from $500 million to $15.5 billion. *Special Problems in Long-Term Care: Hearing Before the Subcommittee on Health & Long-Term Care of the House Select Committee on Aging*, 96th Cong., 1st Sess. 2 (1979) [hereinafter cited as *Special Problems in Long-Term Care*].
2. *Special Problems in Long-Term Care, supra* note 1, at 1.
3. *Developments in Aging: 1980: A Report of the Special Senate Committee on Aging*, 97th Cong., 1st Sess. 77 (1981) [hereinafter cited as *Developments in Aging: 1980*].
4. Two types of nursing homes offer nursing care. The Skilled Nursing Facility (SNF) has a minimum of one registered nurse in charge of nursing on the day shift, eight hours a day, seven days a week. In addition, at least one licensed practical nurse must be in charge of nursing on the 3:00 p.m. to 11:00 p.m. shift and on the 11:00 p.m. to 7:00 a.m. shift. The Intermediate Care Facility (ICF) has one licensed practical nurse in charge of nursing on the morning shift, seven days a week. Also, ICFs make arrangements for consultation with a registered nurse at least four hours per week. H. Rowland, The Nurse's Almanac 413–14 (1978). References in this Chapter to "nursing home" and "home" include both SNFs and ICFs unless otherwise indicated.

    SNFs and ICFs should be distinguished from boarding homes. Unlike nursing homes, boarding homes do not provide medical attention, and the standards that they must meet are far less strict. *Fraud and Abuse in Boarding Homes: Hearing Before the House Select Comm. on Aging*, 97th Cong., 1st Sess. 4 (1981). [hereinafter cited as *Fraud and Abuse in Boarding Homes*]. There are approximately 100,000 boarding homes in the United States housing approximately a million people, but standards for these homes are minimal and enforcement lax in most states. *Id.* at 2. (*See also* Beyer, J., Bulkley, J., Hopkins, P., *A Model Act Regulating Board and Care Homes: Guidelines for States*, Mental and Physical Disability Law Reporter 8(2):150–251 (March-April 1984).) This Chapter does not include boarding homes in its discussion of nursing homes and life care contracts.
5. *Special Problems in Long-Term Care, supra* note 1, at 3; H. Rowland, *supra* note 4, at 428.

6. *Id.*
7. *Id.*
8. H. ROWLAND, *supra* note 4, at 430.
9. Only 20% of those who enter a nursing home ever return home. *Special Problems in Long-Term Health Care, supra* note 1, at 3.
10. *Id.*
11. If, in 1978, the nursing home industry received revenues of $15.5 billion to care for 1.3 million residents, the cost averages to approximately $12,000 per resident per year. Accounting for inflation and other costs, this amount may now be significantly higher. *See supra* note 1 and accompanying text.
12. H. ROWLAND, *supra* note 4, at 412.
13. *Id.*
14. MOSS & HALAMANDARIS, *supra* note 1, at 127.
15. *Special Problems in Long-Term Care, supra* note 1, at 650 (incorporating AFL-CIO EXECUTIVE STATEMENT & REPORT, NURSING HOMES & THE NATION'S ELDERLY (1977)).
16. Much in the way that insurance companies use actuarial tables in determining annuities, nursing homes determine each applicant's life expectancy to arrive at a minimum property value which it would consider before offering a contract to an applicant.
17. *See, e.g., Special Problems in Long-Term Health Care, supra* note 1; *Developments in Aging: 1980, supra* note 3; *Fraud and Abuse in Boarding Homes, supra* note 4; *Drug Abuse in Nursing Homes: Hearing Before the House Select Comm. on Aging,* 96th Cong., 2d Sess. (1980); MOSS & HALAMANDARIS, *supra* note 1, at 15–131.
18. MOSS & HALAMANDARIS, *supra* note 1, at 26–27; *Special Problems in Long-Term Care, supra* note 1, at 196–222 (incorporating testimony of Daphne H. Krause, President, Minneapolis Age and Opportunity Center, Inc., and the M.A.O. National Institute on Aging, Minneapolis, Minn. [hereinafter cited as D. Krause Testimony]. The testimony includes extracts from the Minnesota Department of Health files). The House Select Committee on Aging reported that 11 percent of the intermediate care facilities in the United States suffer from sanitary violations. *Special Problems in Long-Term Care, supra* note 1, at 524.
19. MOSS & HALAMANDARIS, *supra* note 1, at 59. Seventy-two percent of United States' nursing homes have one or more major fire hazards. *Special Problems in Long-Term Care, supra* note 1, at 120.
20. *Special Problems in Long-Term Care, supra* note 1, at 227 (incorporating D. Krause Testimony, *supra* note 17).
21. *Id.* at 410–11; MOSS & HALAMANDARIS, *supra* note 1, at 29–30.
22. *Special Problems in Long-Term Care, supra* note 1, at 288–306 (incorporating D. Krause Testimony, *supra* note 17); MOSS & HALAMANDARIS, *supra* note 1, at 15–26.
23. *Special Problems in Long-Term Care, supra* note 1, at 160 (incorporating D. Krause Testimony, *supra* note 17).
24. *Id.* at 160–95; MOSS & HALAMANDARIS, *supra* note 1, at 25.
25. *Special Problems in Long-Term Care, supra* note 1, at 331–39 (incorporating D.

Krause Testimony, *supra* note 17); Moss & HALAMANDARIS, *supra* note 1, at 32–33, 36–37.

26. *Special Problems in Long-Term Care, supra* note 1, at 414 (incorporating D. Krause Testimony, *supra* note 17); Moss & HALAMANDARIS, *supra* note 1, at 33–34.

27. *Special Problems in Long-Term Care, supra* note 1, at 391–93 (incoporating D. Krause Testimony, *supra* note 17); Moss & HALAMANDARIS, *supra* note 1, at 171–84.

28. *Special Problems in Long-Term Care, supra* note 1, at 391 (incorporating D. Krause Testimony, *supra* note 17).

29. *Id.* at 407–8.

30. Moss & HALAMANDARIS, *supra* note 1, at 39.

31. *Drug Abuse in Nursing Homes: Hearings Before the House Select Committee on Aging, supra* note 17, at 40–56 (1980).

32. *Special Problems in Long-Term Care, supra* note 1, at 412–13 (incorporating D. Krause Testimony, *supra* note 17); Moss & HALAMANDARIS, *supra* note 1, at 30–31.

33. *Special Problems in Long-Term Care, supra* note 1, at 5–6 (statement of Elma Griesel, Executive Director, National Citizens' Coalition for Nursing Home Reform).

> The coalition's information comes from several sources: Our 62 member groups' day-to-day experience in nursing homes and with regulatory agencies; letters and telephone calls from family members and current and former nursing home employees; a growing library of State and Federal legislative and regulatory studies; newspaper investigations; our field experiences as we travel around the country training local nursing ombudsman and volunteer advocates; and our contacts and work with the growing number of legal services programs which handle nursing home cases.

34. *See id.*

35. Griesel evaluated the system in this manner:

> The regulatory system is understaffed, disorganized, misdirected, and too often desensitized to the problems I have cited. How do we know?
>
> We have turned to it for assistance and have closely monitored its activities or failure to act. We have had it turn away from our information, our questions and pleas for change, while at the same time, individual employee advocates within that system have turned to us, the consumers, for the answers and support they need to resolve the problems.
>
> The regulatory system is in a state of disarray, often totally unaccountable to the public it was intended to serve.
>
> Regulatory agencies suffer from staff shortages and lack of qualified staff to survey and enforce standards. Indeed, in many ways—the regulatory system has been guided by the frequent presence and influence of industry spokesmen. No one else is there to give them support or to assist them in any attempt to go in the right direction. No wonder that their loyalties are directed to the providers instead of to the public. The inspection system, in spite of universal acknowledgment that it does not work, still looks only at the facilities' capacity to deliver care instead of the actual care delivery. It is still a paper compliance system. Even when deficiencies are found, regulatory agencies frequently lack appropriate authority to insure immediate correction of serious life and health threatening conditions.

Many agencies and health programs struggle daily with this complicated structure. Among the most important are health systems agencies,
which continually bend to the persuasions of the industry and feel they must
approve new nursing homes for providers who have flagrantly violated established, however minimal, standards. Or health systems agencies which promulgate long-term care plans, favorable to nursing home investment interests,
at the expense of the development of less traditional, emphatically needed
alternatives to institutionalized care.

Also included are the State nursing home ombudsman programs
which have been given a mandate to handle all the thousands of complaints
across the country, with virtually pennies for program development and staff.

On top of all that, we, the taxpayers, are forced to pay billions to
perpetuate this distorted and inhumane system.

Accountability for taxpayers' moneys supplied to facilities is often minimal. Antifraud and abuse programs have only begun to create suitable mechanisms to uncover the numerous frauds in this field. These new units are
confronted by a system in which records are scarce, or gaining accessibility to
records can be laborious and frequently impossible.

Id. at 7–8 (statement of Elma Griesel).

36. *Id.* at 40 (statement of Jacqueline C. Walker, State Nursing Home Ombudsman, Dept. of Aging, Hartford, Conn.).

37. *Id.* at 48 (statement of Jim McDermott, Chairman, Educ. Comm., Vice
Chairman, Ways & Means Committee, Wash. State Senate).

38. *Id.* at 78 (statement of Laurence F. Lane, Director for Public Policy, American Ass'n of Homes for the Aging).

39. *Id.* at 87 (statement of Jack A. MacDonald, Executive Vice President, Nat'l
Council of Health Care Serv.).

40. *Id.*

41. 11 U.S.C. §362 (Supp. IV 1980).

42. *Id.* §1129.

43. *Id.* §101 (37).

44. *Id.* §725.

45. *Id.* §507.

46. *Id.* §507(a)(5).

47. *Id.* Specifically, the Code provides:

(5) Fifth, allowed unsecured claims of individuals, to the extent of $900 for
each such individual, arising from the deposit, before the commencement of
the case, of money in connection with the purchase, lease, or rental of property, or the purchase of services, for the personal, family, or household use of
such individuals, that were not delivered or provided.

48. CAL. HEALTH & SAFETY CODE §1770.5 (West 1979) (legislative findings).

49. Blenkner, *Environmental Change & the Aging,* 7 THE GERONTOLOGIST 101
(1967).

50. NURSING HOME LAW MANUAL, FINANCIAL MANAGEMENT 1 (Aspen Systems
Co., Rockville, Md.) (1971) [hereinafter cited as ASPEN SYSTEMS CORP.].

51. *Id.*

52. If this amount is not specified in the contract, the resident may be charged
much more than the actual cost of care, and more than he or she expected.

53. ASPEN SYSTEMS CORP., *supra* note 50, at 27.

54. *See supra* note 10 and accompanying text.
55. Nicolaysen v. Pacific Home, 151 P.2d 567 (Cal. Dist. Ct. App. 1944).
56. *See infra* notes 66–77 and accompanying text.
57. "'Mutuality of contract' means that obligation rests on each party to do or permit doing of something in consideration of other party's act or promise; neither party being bound unless both are bound." BLACK'S LAW DICTIONARY 920 (rev. 5th ed. 1979).
58. Mere or future expectancies cannot be assigned at law but may be assigned in equity. *See infra* notes 78–82 and accompanying text.
59. *See, e.g.,* Wilson v. Dexter, 192 N.E.2d 469 (Ind. 1963); Dalton v. Florence Home for the Aged, 49 N.W.2d 595 (Neb. 1951).
60. Dalton, *supra* note 59, at 599.
61. *Id.*
62. *See, e.g.,* Gold v. Salem Lutheran Home Ass'n of the Bay Cities, 347 P.2d 687 (Cal. 1959); Stoddard v. Gabriel, 234 Iowa 1366, 14 N.W.2d 737 (1944).
63. Bruner v. Oregon Baptist Retirement Home, 302 P.2d 558 (Or. 1956). The court stated that since the home would have profited financially by the resident's early death, the resident may profit from the benefit of his bargain. *Id.* at 560.
64. Inderkum v. German Old People's Home, 74 P.2d 83 (Cal. Dist. Ct. App. 1937).
65. *Id.* at 83–84. Additionally, the court held the contract valid even though performance could not be specifically enforced.
66. Kirkpatrick Home for Childless Women v. Kenyon, 196 N.Y.S. 250 (Sup. Ct. 1922), *aff'd* 199 N.Y.S. 351 (1923).
67. Kirkpatrick, 196 N.Y.S. at 253.
68. *See* Caldwell v. Basler, Inc., 37 Cal. Rptr. 307 (Dist. Ct. App. 1964); Gold, *supra* note 62, at 687.
69. *See, e.g.,* Bower v. The Estaugh, 369 A.2d 20 (N.J. App. Div. 1977) (resident paid $16,750 entrance fee and died one month later).
70. *See, e.g.,* Riemenschneider v. Fritz Reuter Altenheim, 369 A.2d 24 (N.J. App. Div. 1977); Smith v. Eliza Jennings Home, 199 N.E.2d 733 (Ohio 1964).
72. Caldwell, *supra* note 68, at 307.
73. CAL. HEALTH & SAFETY CODE §§1770–1791.6 (West 1979 & Supp. 1982).
74. Caldwell, *supra* note 68, at 309.
75. Gold, *supra* note 62, at 687.
76. *Id.* at 689.
77. *Id.* The court ruled the doctrine of frustration inapplicable because the resident's death was reasonably forseeable, and hence the terms of the contract were enforced. *Id.*
78. *See* Taylor v. Barton Child Co., 117 N.E. 43 (Mass. 1917); *see generally* J. CALAMARI & J. PERILLO, THE LAW OF CONTRACTS 659 (1977).
79. *See* Eagan v. Luby, 133 Mass. 543 (1882).
80. Fidelity Union Trust Co. v. Reeves, 125 A. 582 (N.J. 1924), *aff'd* 129 A. 922 (N.J. 1925).
81. Reeves, 125 A. at 583.

82. Connelly v. Methodist Home of D.C., 190 A.2d 550 (D.C. 1963); Newburyport Soc'y for Relief of Aged Women v. Noyes, 192 N.E. 54 (Mass. 1934); Ressler's Estate, 18 Pa. D. & C. 393 (1933).
83. *See* Van Valkenburg v. Retirement Homes of the Detroit Annual Conference of the Methodist Church, 151 N.W.2d 197 (Mich. 1967); Pickard v. Oregon Senior Citizens, Inc., 395 P.2d 168 (Or. 1964).
84. *See, e.g.,* Connelly, *supra* note 82, at 550 (D.C. 1963); Stiegelmeier v. West Side Deutscher Frauen Verein, 178 N.E.2d 516 (Ohio 1961). *But see* Stocking by Monteiro v. Hall, 100 A.2d 408 (R.I. 1953).
85. Pickard, *supra* note 83, at 168 (1964).
86. *See* Baltimore Humane Impartial Soc'y & Aged Women's & Aged Men's Homes v. Marley, 144 A. 521 (Md. 1929).
87. *Id.* at 522.
88. Van Valkenberg, *supra* note 83, at 197.
89. 42 U.S.C. §1302 (1976 & Supp. III 1979).
90. 12 C.F.R. §442.311 (1980).
91. *See, e.g.,* COLO. REV. STAT. §25-1-120 (1973 & Supp. 1981); N.C. GEN. STAT. §§130–264 to 266 (1981).
92. *See infra* notes 120–29 and accompanying text.
93. 42 U.S.C. §§1395-1395s (1976 & Supp. 1979).
94. *Id.* §§1396-1396k.
95. Almost 20,000 nursing homes voluntarily participate in Medicare and/or Medicaid programs. *Developments in Aging: 1980, supra* note 3, at 77.
96. 42 U.S.C. §§1396-1396k (1976 & Supp. III 1979).
97. 42 C.F.R. §§442.1-442.516 (1980).
98. *Id.* §§442.311 (1980). The Resident's Bill of Rights provides:

The ICF must have written policies and procedures that insure the following rights for each resident:

(a) *Information.* (1) Each resident must be fully informed, before or at the time of admission, of his rights and responsibilities and of all rules governing resident conduct.

(2) If the ICF amends its policies on residents' rights and responsibilities and rules of conduct, each resident in the ICF at that time must be informed.

(3) Each resident must acknowledge in writing receipt of the information and any amendments to it.

(4) Each resident must be fully informed in writing of all services available in the ICF and of the charges for these services including any charges for services not paid for by Medicaid or not included in the ICF's basic rate per day. The ICF must provide this information either before or at the time of admission and on a continuing basis as changes occur in services or charges during the resident's stay.

(b) *Medical condition and treatment.* (1) Each resident must—

(i) Be fully informed by a physician of his health and medical condition unless the physician decides that informing the resident is medically contraindicated;

(ii) Be given the opportunity to participate in planning his total care and medical treatment;

(iii) Be given the opportunity to refuse treatment; and

(iv) Give informed, written consent before participating in experimental research.

(2) If the physician decides that informing the resident of his health and medical condition is medically contraindicated, the physician must document this decision in the resident's record.

(c) *Transfer and discharge.* Each resident must be transferred or discharged only for—

(1) Medical reasons;

(2) His welfare or that of the other residents; or

(3) Nonpayment except as prohibited by the Medicaid program.

(d) *Exercising rights.* Each resident must be—

(1) Encouraged and assisted to exercise his rights as a resident of the ICF and as a citizen; and

(2) Allowed to submit complaints or recommendations concerning the policies and services of the ICF to staff or to outside representatives of the resident's choice or both, free from restraint, interference, coercion, discrimination, or reprisal.

(e) *Financial affairs.* Each resident must be allowed to manage his personal financial affairs. If a resident requests assistance from the ICF in managing his personal financial affairs—

(1) The request must be in writing; and

(2) The ICF must comply with the recordkeeping requirements of §442.320.

(f) *Freedom from abuse and restraints.* (1) Each resident must be free from mental and physical abuse.

(2) Each resident must be free from chemical and physical restraints unless the restraints are—

(i) Authorized by a physician in writing for a specified period of time; or

(ii) Used in an emergency under the following conditions:

(A) The use is necessary to protect the resident from injuring himself or others.

(B) The use is authorized by a professional staff member identified in the written policies and procedures of the facility as having the authority to do so.

(C) The use is reported promptly to the resident's physician by that staff member.

(g) *Privacy.* (1) Each resident must be treated with consideration, respect, and full recognition of his or her dignity and individuality.

(2) Each resident must be given privacy during treatment and care of personal needs.

(3) Each resident's records, including information in an automatic data bank, must be treated confidentially.

(4) Each resident must give written consent before the ICF may release information from his record to someone not otherwise authorized by the law to receive it.

(5) A married resident must be given privacy during visits by his spouse.

(6) If both husband and wife are residents of the ICF, they must be permitted to share a room.

(h) *Work.* No resident may be required to perform services for the ICF.

(i) *Freedom of association and correspondence.* Each resident must be allowed to—

(1) Communicate, associate, and meet privately with individuals of his choice, unless this infringes on the rights of another resident; and

(2) Send and receive personal mail unopened.

(j) *Activities.* Each resident must be allowed to participate in social, religious, and community group activities.

(k) *Personal possessions.* Each resident must be allowed to retain and use his personal possessions and clothing as space permits.

99. *Id.* §442.311(a).
100. *Id.* §442.311(b).
101. *Id.* §442.311(c).
102. *Id.* §442.311(d).
103. *Id.* §442.311(e).
104. *Id.* §442.311(f).
105. *Id.* §442.311(g).
106. *Id.* §442.311(h).
107. *Id.* §442.311(i).
108. *Id.* §442.311(j).
109. *Id.* §442.311(k).
110. *Id.* §§442.321-442.323.
111. *Id.* §§442.324-442.330.
112. *Id.* §§442.331-442.332.
113. *Id.* §§442.333-442.337.
114. *Id.* §§442.338-442.342.
115. *Id.* §§442.343-442.346. In July 1980, DHHS proposed a general revision of the current regulations establishing the conditions which nursing homes must meet to participate in Medicare and Medicaid. 45 Fed. Reg. 47368-85 (1980). The proposed revision was designed to "simplify and clarify the regulations, to focus on patient care, to promote cost containment while maintaining quality care, and to achieve more effective compliance." *Id.* at 47368. In January 1981, however, the proposed regulations were withdrawn because their economic impact had not been determined. 46 Fed. Reg. 7408 (1981) (proposal withdrawn). The Reagan administration is now reviewing the conditions of participation for nursing homes as part of its "regulatory effort," and the proposed revision is under review. Semiannual Regulations Agenda and Review List, 46 Fed. Reg. 55621 (1981). Currently, DHHS is awaiting the results of a special study it has commissioned on nursing home regulatory issues from the Institute of Medicine of the National Academy of Sciences. *See* Hamme, J.M., chapter 12 of this text.
116. 42 U.S.C. §1396a (1974 & Supp. 1982).
117. *See, e.g.,* Alaska Stat. §18.20.060 (1974); Conn. Gen. Stat. §19-580 (Supp. 1982); Hawaii Rev. Stat. §321-11(10) (Supp. 1981); Ky. Rev. Stat. Ann. §216 A.070 (Bobbs-Merrill 1977) (licensing of nursing home administrators); Miss. Ann. Stat. §43-11-13 (Vernon 1972); S.D. Codified Laws Ann. §34-12-13 (Supp. 1981); Va. Code §32.1-127 (1979); Wash. Rev. Code Ann. §18.51.070 (Supp. 1982).

118. *See generally* COMMITTEE ON THE OFFICE OF ATTORNEY GENERAL, NAT'L ASS'N OF ATTORNEYS GENERAL, ENFORCING QUALITY CARE IN NURSING HOMES (1978), *reprinted in Special Problems in Long-Term Care, supra* note 1, at 553–628.
119. *See supra* note 91.
120. CAL. HEALTH & SAFETY CODE §§1770-1791.6 (West 1979 & Supp. 1982); COLO. REV. STAT. §§12-13-101 to -199 (1978 & Cum. Supp. 1981); *see also* MO. ANN. STAT. §§376.900-376.950 (Vernon Supp. 1982).
121. CAL. HEALTH & SAFETY CODE §§1771.2, 1771.3 (West 1979 & Supp. 1982); COLO. REV. STAT. §§12-13-102, 12-13-103 (Cum. Supp. 1981).
122. CAL. HEALTH & SAFETY CODE §§1791-1791.6 (West 1979).
123. COLO. REV. STAT. §§12-13-102, 12-13-103 (Cum. Supp. 1981).
124. CAL. HEALTH & SAFETY CODE §1775 (WEST 1979); COLO. REV. STAT. §12-13-107 (Cum. Supp. 1981).
125. CAL. HEALTH & SAFETY CODE §1777 (West 1979); COLO. REV. STAT. §12-13-106(7) (Cum. Supp. 1981).
126. N.Y. PUB. HEALTH LAW §2805-f (Consol. Supp. 1982); 28 PA. ADMIN. CODE §201.38 (1979).
127. *Id.* §2805-f(1).
128. *Id.* §2805-f(3).
129. 28 PA. ADMIN. CODE §201.38 (1979).
130. For instance, Moss & Halamandaris devote a chapter in their book to the proper steps to follow in choosing a nursing home. MOSS & HALAMANDARIS, *supra* note 1, at 219–32. They also provide a list of organizations and other professional groups interested in long-term care that may be of help. *Id.* at 300–304.
131. Moss & Halamandaris suggest that the potential resident visit the home either between seven and eight o'clock in the morning or between eleven and one, when she can observe the noon meal. *Id.* at 223. They also recommend returning to the facility late at night. *Id.*
132. *Id.* at 227.
133. *See supra* notes 90–129 and accompanying text.
134. "Failure to maintain" should mean more than just the commission of a single violation. Rather, it should mean the commission of repeated violations or failure to rectify same.
135. *See supra* notes 83–88 and accompanying text.
136. Most last one to six months. *See, e.g.,* MO. ANN. STAT. §376.925 (Vernon Supp. 1982) (providing minimum one week period). Ideally, the period should be longer. ASPEN SYSTEMS CORP., *supra* note 50, at 1.
137. *Id.* at 26.
138. *See* Van Valkenberg, *supra* note 83, at 197; *see also* ASPEN SYSTEMS CORP., *supra* note 50, at 26.
139. *See supra* notes 120–25 and accompanying text.
140. *See generally supra* notes 42–47 and accompanying text.
141. *See generally* 4 A. CORBIN, CORBIN ON CONTRACTS, §799 (1951). The bond is similar to an insurance contract. The home pays a fee equivalent to a pre-

mium, and the bonding company establishes a bond guaranteeing the performance of the home.

142. 11 U.S.C. §506 (1976 & Supp. IV 1980).
143. *See supra* notes 41–47 and accompanying text.
144. 45 C.F.R. §1321.43 (1980).
145. *Id.* §1321.43(c)(1).
146. *Id.* §1321.43(c)(2).
147. *Id.* §1321.43(d).

Section III

Legal Issues Facing Long-Term Care Providers

11

Antitrust Law for Long-Term Health Care Providers

Phillip A. Proger, J.D.*

The delivery of long-term health care in the United States occurs within a complex system of services in which free market competition has played, and continues to play, a significant role. Recognition of the role of competition in health care, however, is a relatively recent phenomenon in American society, particularly within the legal system. It was not until 1975, for example, that the United States Supreme Court in *Goldfarb v. Virginia State Bar*[1] held that learned professions involve activities over which the federal antitrust laws may have jurisdiction. Since the *Goldfarb* decision, many practices involving the delivery of health care have been challenged and evaluated under the antitrust laws.[2] The practical implication of these decisions is that the courts now recognize that health care is subject to competition and that such competition is governed by the rules of antitrust.

BASIC PRINCIPLES

The nature of the antitrust laws as applied to the health care delivery system is, as with any business, analogous to the role assumed by the referee of a game. Although the antitrust laws are similar to the many other regulatory laws—created by statute and subsequently interpreted by the courts—they are somewhat different in that, like a referee, they assume a detached role. For example, federal securities laws are active, because they require certain businesses to take affirmative steps, such as filing information with the Securities and Exchange Commission. In

*The author wishes to thank Kenneth L. Klothen, an associate with the firm of Baker & Hostetler in Cleveland, Ohio, for his assistance in the preparation of this chapter.

contrast, the antitrust laws rarely require such positive action. As long as a business plays the game of competition fairly, the antitrust laws do not interfere with the daily operations of that business. Just as a football referee interferes with a football game only when a rule of the game has been broken, the antitrust laws interfere with business operations only when competition has been unfairly conducted.

The substantive rules of antitrust in the United States rely on the premise that competition in the American economic system is based on price, quality, and service. The basic rule of antitrust prevents unfair competition in price, quality, and service by prohibiting anticompetitive acts or agreements among competitors, among buyers and sellers, or among other parties participating in the free market system. The distinction between proper competition based on price, quality, and service, on the one hand, and unfair competition, as defined by the antitrust laws, on the other, may be illustrated by the following example.

International Widget and American Widget both sell widgets in the United States. If International Widget unilaterally decided to stop selling widgets east of the Mississippi because it was in the company's economic best interest to do so, and American Widget unilaterally decided to stop selling widgets west of the Mississippi because it was in the company's economic best interest to do so, neither company would violate the antitrust laws. If, on the other hand, International Widget and American Widget *agreed* to allocate the widget market according to this scheme, each company would violate the antitrust laws by making an agreement that would artificially interfere with competition. Among other things, such an agreement would be unfair to consumers. A consumer living east of the Mississippi, for instance, would be denied the right to buy an International Widget product unless he were willing to travel to some locality west of the Mississippi, and denied the benefit of competition between International Widget and American Widget on the variables of price, quality, and service.

STATUTORY FRAMEWORK

There are three major antitrust statutes in the United States that aim to prohibit such artificial interference with free market competition. The most significant statute for health care professionals is the Sherman Act, which was passed in 1890 to stop the aggregation of economic interests, particularly among the post–Civil War railroads and mine-holding interests. Section 1 of the Sherman Act prohibits every contract, conspiracy, or combination in restraint of trade.[3] Based on this broad prohibition, and recognizing that *all* agreements must in some sense restrain the activities of the parties to such agreements, the courts have developed a concept called the "Rule of Reason," which requires that agreements affecting competition must be reasonable. The courts have determined whether an agreement is reasonable by making two inquiries. The first inquiry concerns the purpose of the agreement. If an agreement has the purpose of restraining competition, it is automatically unlawful. In the second example concerning International Widget and American Widget, the companies' agreement to allocate their markets is unlawful because its purpose is to stop competition between them.

The second inquiry which courts pursue under the Rule of Reason evaluates the effects of the agreement at issue. If the agreement restrains competition, it must not only have a legitimate business purpose (that is, one which is not anticompetitive), but it must also be the least restrictive means of achieving that business purpose. If there is another way to effectuate that business purpose which restrains competition less severely, the parties must attempt to implement that alternative before implementing their more anticompetitive agreement. Finally, as an adjunct to the Rule of Reason, the courts have developed the "per se" rule under Section 1 of the Sherman Act. Under the per se rule, any agreement among competitors that affects price is per se unreasonable and therefore always unlawful, regardless of legitimate purpose or lack of reasonable alternatives.

In 1914 Congress added two more antitrust statutes by enacting the Federal Trade Commission Act and the Clayton Act. The Clayton Act deals with certain practices that previously fell within the Rule of Reason analysis under the Sherman Act. More specifically, the Clayton Act prohibits exclusive dealing arrangements (whereby parties agree not to deal with the competitors of one or both) and certain "tying" arrangements (whereby the availability of one product is conditioned on the purchase of another product) that substantially lessen competition, and establishes a private right of action for particular plaintiffs.[4] The Clayton Act also prohibits certain mergers where the effects of the merger would be to lessen competition. The Federal Trade Commission Act created the Federal Trade Commission, a government body expert in economics and competition, and broadly prohibits unfair methods of competition as well as unfair and deceptive business acts or practices.[5] Finally, Congress amended the Clayton Act in 1936 by enacting the Robinson-Patman Act, which prohibits sellers from offering competing buyers different prices when such discrimination may lessen competition.[6]

One of the most significant aspects of the Clayton and Robinson-Patman Acts for health care professionals is that these statutes do *not* apply to the sale of services.[7] Since most health care fits within the definition of "services," the Sherman Act is generally the only antitrust statute that applies to the delivery of health care. One caveat to this generalization is that long-term health care institutions are entitled to a competitive price under the Robinson-Patman Act when acting as purchasers of goods required to run those institutions.[8]

THE HEALTH CARE CONTEXT

As noted earlier, the interaction of the Sherman Act with the delivery of health care services is a relatively recent phenomenon. Until the mid-1970s, the "learned profession exemption" excluded health care from the prohibitions of the antitrust laws. According to the learned profession doctrine, the practices of certain professionals were not commerce and therefore could not be regulated by the federal government under the Commerce Clause of the U.S. Constitution. Since the antitrust laws depend on the Commerce Clause for their jurisdiction and therefore regulate only those activities that are in or affect interstate commerce, there was no antitrust jurisdiction over health care. In *Goldfarb,* the U.S. Supreme Court rejected the learned profession exemption[9] and, subsequently, found that health care was within the jurisdiction of the antitrust laws.[10]

Antitrust issues in the delivery of long-term health care have arisen in the context of daily business operations and have resembled the antitrust issues in the operation of any business. For example, the Department of Justice viewed a recent nursing home merger in Los Angeles as raising a traditional Clayton Act merger issue and asked whether the merger tended to lessen competition. Finding that the merger did have this effect, the Justice Department worked out an agreement with the acquiring nursing home in order to reduce its market share and to eliminate the anticompetitive aspects of the merger. The sale of certain assets and the development of a leasing arrangement solved the antitrust problems.

Other antitrust issues have emerged in the context of contracting, particularly among competing health care providers. As the earlier widget example illustrates, agreements among competitors are always the most suspect under the antitrust laws because they can have the most negative effect on competition. In this vein, the Department of Justice's Antitrust Division has challenged nursing homes in South Carolina and Montana that formed group bargaining positions and agreements, through their state nursing home associations, to use in negotiating with their respective state governments about participation in Medicaid.[11] The agreements among the nursing homes to negotiate particular rates in a certain way were among purported competitors, and therefore they were agreements to restrain competition. As such, they resembled the hypothetical agreement between International Widget and American Widget to allocate markets. The Department of Justice required the nursing homes to stop their agreed practices and to sign consent decrees.[12]

Exclusive dealing issues also have arisen in the context of health care delivery. For example, the legality of referral agreements between hospitals and particular groups of physicians have been examined under an exclusive dealing analysis. The legality of a referral agreement essentially depends on the extent to which the agreement denies other competitors access to the relevant market. If a hospital has an exclusive referral agreement with one group of physicians, the agreement may be legal if there are many hospitals in the relevant geographic market and the hospital at issue represents a small percentage of the relevant referral base in the market. If, on the other hand, the hospital is the only one in the community and the contracting physician group is the only group of its type with referral rights at the hospital, serious antitrust concerns arise. In general, the greater the contracting hospital's percentage of the market and the longer the time provided for the exclusive arrangement, the more likely it may be that an exclusive referral agreement will raise antitrust problems.

The U.S. Supreme Court recently addressed the exclusive referral issue in *Hyde v. Jefferson Parish Hospital District No. 2.*[13] The U.S. Court of Appeals for the Fifth Circuit had struck down an exclusive contract between a hospital and a group of anesthesiologists.[14] According to the court of appeals, the relevant hospital market was limited to the single defendant hospital, and the agreement therefore excluded anesthesiologists outside of the group from 100 percent of that market. The Supreme Court, however, reversed after reviewing the relevant market and determining that the defendant hospital competed in a much larger geographic market and therefore had considerably less ability to force patients to accept its anesthesiologists. Patients who did not wish to employ the services of the hospital's anesthesiologists, the Supreme Court reasoned, would go to other hospitals in the area for their surgery. Thus, anesthesiologists excluded from the defendant hospital could still compete for these patients by obtaining staff privileges at other hospitals, and the impact of the exclusive arrangement on competition was not substantial enough to be held per se illegal.

Agreements and concerted activity that affect the relationship of allied health professionals to health care institutions are also bound to raise antitrust issues similar to those under the exclusive dealing analysis. In general, the right of allied health professionals to compete in the delivery of health care services will be protected by the antitrust laws. The antitrust laws are designed to allow such innovation and creativity and to preserve for everyone with a product or service the opportunity to compete in the market. Many physicians and institutional providers have expressed concern that the antitrust laws may thus operate to interfere with decisions regarding the quality of care. This is a legitimate concern, but will not necessarily be the case. If, for example, an institution decides not to permit members of an allied health profession to practice on its patients, *and* if it can demonstrate that the decision was made solely to maintain the quality of care at the institution and not to insulate the institution's physicians from competition by allied health professionals, the antitrust laws will not necessarily intervene. This is an area of considerable controversy, however, and must be approached with particular caution.

Whenever an agreement among competitors or among buyers and sellers in the health care delivery system is made, the purpose and effect of the agreement should be examined to ensure that the agreement is not anticompetitive. Two questions that should be asked in making any such agreement are, first, what is the purpose of this agreement, and second, who may be hurt by it. If the agreement has a legitimate business purpose and provides the least restrictive means of implementing that purpose, it will likely be sustained under a Rule of Reason analysis.

In addition, any agreements among competitors concerning the purchase, leasing, price, or use of durable medical equipment are made in the context of the antitrust laws. Parties should avoid agreements that affect the price of medical equipment, since they will likely be carefully scrutinized under the per se rule that the courts have developed as an adjunct to the Rule of Reason.[15]

Another major area of antitrust concern which may become relevant for health care institutions is that of merger law. Mergers of two facilities may violate Section 7 of the Clayton Act if their effect "may be substantially to lessen competition, or to tend to create a monopoly."[16] Mergers may also violate Section 1 of the Sherman Act if they constitute a "contract, combination . . . or conspiracy in restraint of trade." The Department of Justice has recently revised its Merger Guidelines, which set forth the Department's position concerning the circumstances under which a merger would violate one or both of those statutes.[17]

Merger analysis involves complex issues of market definition, market share, the difficulty of entry into the market, and measurement of efficiencies to be gained.[18] Those issues are too involved for treatment here. However, at its core merger analysis now involves a measurement of the increase in concentration in the market occupied by the merging firms. This increase is measured by the Herfindahl-Hirschman Index (HHI), which is calculated by adding together the squares of the individual market shares of all the firms in the market. Markets with an HHI of 1,000 are considered unconcentrated, those with an HHI of 1,000 to

1,800 are considered moderately concentrated, and those with an HHI above 1,800 are considered highly concentrated.

Generally, if the postmerger HHI will be below 1,000 the merger will not be viewed as anticompetitive. Where the postmerger HHI falls within the moderately concentrated range of 1,000–1,800, mergers producing an *increase* in the HHI of more than 100 points will be viewed with suspicion. Where the postmerger market is highly concentrated (HHI over 1,800), mergers resulting in an HHI increase of more than 50 points will be presumed anticompetitive.

Assume that four skilled nursing facilities, A, B, C, and D operate in a geographic market. A's market share is 50 percent, B's is 25 percent, C's is 15 percent, and D's is 10 percent. The premerger HHI is $(50)^2 + (25)^2 + (15)^2 + (10)^2$, or 3,450. The market is highly concentrated. If C and D seek to merge, the HHI of the postmerger market would be $(50)^2 + (25)^2 + (25)^2$, or 3,750—an HHI increase of 300 points. Absent other circumstances which would tend to show that the proposed merger was procompetitive, the Justice Department would be likely to challenge the merger of C and D.

CONCLUSION

The antitrust laws should not be viewed as an obstacle to providing health care services. They are detached laws that are designed to enhance competition, and the courts have, in general, not sought to turn them into a regulatory structure which would further burden the health care sector of the economy. As long as providers of health care keep in mind the general prohibition against anticompetitive practices whenever they enter into any agreement, whether it is an exclusive referral contract or a contract for the purchase of medical equipment, the antitrust laws should serve to help providers deliver innovative and profitable forms of health care services in the United States.

NOTES

1. Goldfarb v. Virginia State Bar, 421 U.S. 773 (1975) [hereinafter referred to as Goldfarb].
2. *See, e.g,* Arizona v. Maricopa County Medical Soc'y, 457 U.S. 332 (1982); Blue Shield of Virginia v. McCready, 457 U.S. 465 (1982).
3. 15 U.S.C. §1.
4. *Id.* §14.
5. *Id.* §45.
6. *Id.* §13.

7. *Id. See* Baum v. Investors Diversified Services, 409 F.2d 872 (7th Cir. 1969) ("commodity" as used in Clayton Act is restricted to products, merchandise, or other tangible goods).

8. 15 U.S.C. §13(c).

9. Goldfarb, *supra* note 1, at 786–88.

10. Hospital Building Co. v. Trustees of Rex Hosp., 425 U.S. 738 (1976).

11. United States v. Montana Nursing Home Ass'n, 1982–2 Trade Cas. (CCH) ¶ 64,852 (D. Mont. July 1, 1982) (consent decree); United States v. South Carolina Health Care Ass'n, 1980–2 Trade Cas. (CCH) ¶ 64,316 (D.S.C. April 11, 1980) (consent decree).

12. *Id.*

13. 104 S. Ct. 1551 (1984).

14. 686 F.2d 286 (5th Cir. 1982).

15. *See* HOSPITAL LAW MANUAL VOL. IIA ¶ 5-4, ¶ 5-9 (Aspen Systems Corp., Rockville, Md.) (1984).

16. 15 U.S.C. §18.

17. *Justice Department Merger Guidelines, reprinted in* ANTITRUST AND TRADE REGULATION REPORT, No. 1169 (June 14, 1984) (special supplement).

18. Joint ventures are also generally subject to the same standards. *See, e.g.,* United States v. Penn-Ohio Chemical Co., 378 U.S. 158 (1964).

12

Quality Control of Long-Term Care through Accreditation, Licensure, and Standards

Joel M. Hamme, J.D.

Assuring quality control of long-term health care for the elderly raises legal and policy issues which may be placed into three broad categories: describing what the law currently is, deciding what the law should be, and discussing what the law may become. This chapter will touch on all three of these topics associated with controlling the quality of long-term care.

The significance of the quality control issue is readily apparent in both human and monetary terms. A study conducted in 1977 showed that there were approximately 14,500 long-term care facilities for the elderly in the United States and over 1.1 million residents—most of them over age 65—in these facilities.[1] Ethically, these residents are entitled to receive dignified care and proper medical treatment. The establishment and enforcement of health care standards for licensure and, if the facility desires, Medicare and/or Medicaid certification, are designed to guarantee this right. Licensure and certification are also aimed at ensuring that the vast amounts of money spent on long-term care are well spent, and that needed services are delivered. It has been estimated, for example, that in 1981 long-term care cost more than $24 billion nationally. Of this amount, about $4 billion was for Medicaid skilled nursing care services and approximately $4.5 billion for intermediate care for Medicaid beneficiaries.[2] The assurance of quality control is important, particularly in light of the number of facilities and residents that may be affected by poor quality of services, and in terms of the vast amounts of money, both public and private, that are spent.

Health care for the elderly extends beyond long-term care in general and the Medicaid program in particular. For the sake of simplicity and brevity, however, this chapter will concentrate on quality control in

nursing homes participating in the Medicaid program. This particular
model illustrates the types of problems, concerns, and policy dilemmas
which arise in developing health care standards for the elderly.

Government enforcement mechanisms trigger several basic levels of
quality care assurance. Among them are the states' licensure and the
federal certification processes for facilities that wish to participate in the
Medicare, Medicaid, or Veterans Administration programs. This chapter
examines the conditions that long-term care facilities must meet in order
to participate in the Medicaid programs, the existing legal procedures
that govern quality care standards among Medicaid long-term care facilities, and the various mechanisms by which these standards are enforced.

Before we examine the current law, it is important to review the
controversy of the past several years over the Medicare and Medicaid
conditions of participation for long-term care facilities. That controversy
highlights varying views of what the standards should be and how they
should be enforced, and it underscores some of the strengths and weaknesses of the current system.

THE CARTER ADMINISTRATION PROPOSALS: POLICY DEBATE OVER MEDICARE AND MEDICAID CONDITIONS OF PARTICIPATION

The Carter administration's efforts to change the Medicare and Medicaid
conditions of participation for long-term care facilities were motivated by
a number of considerations. These included a desire to revise the regulations to make them clearer and more readable; a belief that regulations
predicated on patient assessment would better allow for planning and
integrating the patient's care; and a perception that existing regulations
should be altered to account for changing technology and developments
in gerontology.[3]

When it sought to make these revisions, the Carter administration
spent a number of years and considerable effort in obtaining comments
from the public and the industry. This public input was sought not only
to comply with the Federal Administrative Procedure Act[4] but also to
enhance the quality of the rulemaking process. Comments were obtained
following publication of a general notice suggesting possible changes[5]
and a specific proposed rule.[6] In addition, hearings were held throughout the country.[7] Although it was widely recognized that conditions in the
nation's nursing homes had markedly improved since the late 1960s and
early 1970s, public comment suggested that too much of the survey
process was paperwork oriented and too little time was accorded to measuring patient care.[8]

Specifically, in July 1980 the Carter administration proposed to shift the survey and certification process for facilities from a "facility oriented" to a "patient oriented" one.[9] For better or worse, the Carter administration proposal would have increased the number of requirements for federal certification and the amount of federal oversight. This proposal never became final because in late 1980, after Ronald Reagan's election as president, Congress passed an appropriations measure prohibiting finalization until the Department of Health and Human Services (DHHS) received revised cost estimates and an impact evaluation from the Office of Management and Budget.[10] In the last days of the Carter administration, the patients' rights portion of the proposal was approved by the Secretary of DHHS, but that approval was withdrawn several days later when President Reagan came into office.[11]

It was widely expected that the Reagan administration would go in the opposite direction from the Carter administration and deregulate the Medicare and Medicaid certification process; in fact, it attempted to do so. Federal funding for survey efforts was curtailed, and in May 1982, DHHS proposed new regulations that, among other things, would have created a more flexible survey cycle and allowed deemed certification status[12] for long-term care facilities accredited by the Joint Commission on the Accreditation of Hospitals.[13] The Reagan administration claimed that longer certification periods for, and fewer surveys of, facilities with good survey compliance records would permit surveyors to focus on problem facilities. Critics of the proposal argued that it would weaken both enforcement of the conditions of participation and protection of long-term care facility residents.

The Reagan administration's initial efforts were stymied in September 1982, when Congress enacted a six-month moratorium on any change in procedures for certification and in requirements for Medicare and Medicaid long-term care facilities.[14] This moratorium was later extended for another four months.[15]

In 1983 legislation was introduced in the House of Representatives to extend the moratorium even further. One bill—entitled the "National Nursing Home Standards Act of 1983"[16]—would have established a 13-member National Commission on the Regulation of Nursing Homes. The Commission would have been composed of members of the Institute of Medicine of the National Academy of Sciences, representatives of nursing home residents, long-term care providers, and state officials with responsibilities in this area. The Commission would have been empowered to study the necessity and adequacy of current survey and certification procedures, to review alternative regulatory approaches, and to make specific recommendations for changes and improvements. Under the proposed legislation, these recommendations would have been due no later than September 30, 1984, and the moratorium would have extended for six months beyond the time that the Commission submitted its recommendations.[17] Ultimately, supporters of this legislation reached an agreement with DHHS in which the bill was dropped and DHHS funded an independent study of these issues by the Institute of Medicine.

The details of the proposals which have been debated over the past four years are not, in and of themselves, significant. Despite widespread criticism of the existing survey and certification procedures (including criticism from both the nursing home industry and residents' rights groups), the significant point is that, while no group or point of view has yet been able to muster the political consensus needed to make any changes, each group has been able to block changes proposed by others.

LITIGATION

While these policy debates raged, efforts were made to forge changes in Medicaid survey and certification standards through litigation. In 1975 two nursing home residents in Colorado filed a class action in federal court against the facility in which they resided, and against federal and state officials responsible for enforcement of the Medicaid Act.[18] In *Estate of Smith v. O'Halloran*,[19] the plaintiffs alleged that government officials at both the federal and state levels had failed to discharge their legal duties to ensure that long-term care facilities furnished high quality care to Medicaid beneficiaries. The plaintiffs further claimed that these failings had culminated in poor care, which violated constitutional, statutory, regulatory, and contractual rights of the plaintiff class to optimal care.

In 1978 the case took a strange twist when the state officials switched sides. This occurred when the plaintiffs dropped their charges against the Colorado officials, who in turn filed a complaint against DHHS, alleging that DHHS was responsible for any problems in the Medicaid certification and survey process. Both the plaintiffs and the state officials claimed that, in order to fulfill its duties (including its statutory responsibility to ensure compliance with the state's approved Medicaid plan), DHHS should be required to revamp that process to focus upon patients and their needs through the use of resident assessments.[20] In addition, the plaintiffs and state officials contended that the existing system failed to achieve quality care because it concentrated upon facilities rather than patients.

Proceedings in *Estate of Smith v. O'Halloran* were stayed in 1980 when it appeared that the Carter administration's proposal paralleled what the plaintiffs were seeking. When that proposal was not adopted, however, the case resumed and a trial was held.

In a decision filed February 8, 1983,[21] the federal district court found that a patient care management system, such as that advocated by the plaintiffs, was feasible. The court noted, however, that the legal issue was not whether such a system was possible or desirable but whether DHHS was required by law to implement such a system. The court ruled that DHHS did *not* have such a duty. In reaching this conclusion, the court found that states have important roles in licensing, certification, and reimbursement of Medicaid providers. Under the Medicaid statute, in fact, the federal government's primary tool for ensuring compliance with statutory requirements is to withhold Medicaid funds from any state which fails to meet or enforce those standards.[22] In the court's view, the plaintiffs were seeking to change the Medicaid program from a joint federal-state effort, in which the states have frontline responsibility, to a national health care program. The court emphasized in this regard that Colorado officials recognized the state's power to change matters but simply lacked either the resolve or the resources to make such changes. Finally, the court noted that it was not determining the responsibilities of state officials or of the long-term care facilities that had become involved in the case. The plaintiffs' claims against the facilities were separated from the claims against the federal defendants and were to be tried separately.[23]

The district court's decision was overruled in October 1984.[24] The United States Court of Appeals for the Tenth Circuit held that the Secretary of Health and Human Services has a duty to establish a system adequately informing the Secretary as to whether those facilities receiving federal assistance satisfy the requirements of the Act, including the provision of high quality patient care. The court further stated that the Secretary's failure to promulgate regulations allowing the Secretary to remain informed regarding a facility's compliance would constitute "an abdication of the Secretary's duty." Furthermore the court held that where the plaintiffs can show this, an appropriate remedy lies in an injunction whereby the court can compel performance, thus effecting the congressional intent. Thus the federal appeals court identified DHHS, not the states, as the entity for ensuring facilities' compliance with statutory requirements, and held that DHHS should examine the facilities' actual compliance, not their theoretical ability to comply, with the requirement of providing high quality patient care.

At the least, the complexities of *Estate of Smith v. O'Halloran* demonstrate that the courts, DHHS, and Congress have all become involved in deciding what types of survey and certification standards should exist.

The first portion of this chapter has examined the policy questions surrounding survey and certification standards. In summary, there seems to be general agreement that the current standards should be changed, but there is little agreement as to how they should be amended. We now examine the current Medicaid survey and certification process and discuss the nature of that process.

Existing Medicaid Survey and Certification Procedures: The Conditions of Participation

There are 18 conditions for participation by skilled nursing facilities in the Medicare or Medicaid programs.[25] These conditions are designed to ensure the availability of needed services, quality of care, correct levels of care, a safe physical environment, and enhancement of patient living experiences and activities. There are 88 separate standards within the 18 conditions of participation for skilled nursing facilities.[26]

For Medicaid intermediate care facilities, there are seven general areas covered by the certification regulations and 46 specific regulatory directives within these seven areas.[27] In many respects, these regulations are identical or similar to the conditions and standards of participation for skilled nursing facilities.

Under federal regulations, each Medicaid facility must be surveyed at least once every year to determine whether it meets the conditions of program participation.[28] One problem with this procedure is that determinations of compliance or noncompliance with many of the regulatory requirements are highly subjective. For example, it is difficult to determine how many or what percentage of patient care plans have to be missing, or judged inadequate, to find that the facility does not comply with that standard. What constitutes an "inadequate" patient care plan? Many of these decisions are simply judgment calls; there are no objective or easily applied criteria which allow the standards to be marked clearly.

Worse yet, there are no well-defined or objective guidelines which govern the larger and more important certification decisions. For example, it is difficult to determine how many standards must be found out of compliance in order for the condition of participation to be considered violated. It is also difficult to determine when a facility is "certifiable." Instead of determining certification standards by a verifiable yardstick, surveyors are basically required to decide certification issues by using a broad formulation that is easy to state but difficult to apply. That formulation decides whether the facility provides adequate care to its patients or whether its practices endanger the health, safety, and welfare of its residents. Despite numerous regulations, the surveyors' task essentially boils down to an exercise similar to the Supreme Court's review of cases involving obscenity. As one Supreme Court justice lamented, "Perhaps I could never succeed in intelligibly [defining hard-core pornography]. . . . But I know it when I see it. . . ."[29] In the current survey process, the regulations do not pinpoint noncertifiable facilities, but surveyors are expected to know them when they see them.

There is no way to escape the fact that many judgments about patient care needs, and a facility's ability and willingness to meet those needs, are inherently subjective. No one would be well served if we ignored this fact, or simply designed a new system and pretended that the new system were objective. Any system will contain some subjectivity. Nonetheless, the current system is too subjective, and this is unfair to surveyors, facilities, residents, the government, and the public.

ENFORCEMENT MECHANISMS AND SANCTIONS

For a long time, much of this unfairness related to a lack of flexibility or variety in enforcement mechanisms. Originally the survey process led to one of three conclusions: either the facility was not certifiable and could not participate in the Medicaid program; the facility was in full compliance with program requirements, and was entitled to unconditional certification; or the facility had deficiencies but still warranted certification.[30] In the last instance, the facility was still unrestricted in its ability to admit and care for Medicaid patients. It was simply required to correct deficiencies and have its correction plan approved. In addition, a review had to occur within a limited period of time to ensure that the plan had been implemented.

This system recognized very little gradation among facilities and had particularly draconian consequences for the facility and its patients if an incorrect determination were made. Essentially, the certification process was an all or nothing proposition. Indeed, program decertification was the only sanction available. This sanction was so severe that there was a reluctance to use it. Better means had to be developed to provide both sufficient incentives and disincentives for the identification and correction of relatively minor (albeit important) problems.

The most tangible gains that we have seen over the past few years have been in the area of developing new and flexible sanctions. These sanctions do not erase the subjectivity of the current survey and certification process, but by increasing the options available to surveyors, they reduce subjectivity and allow the sanctions to fit more closely and appropriately with the deficiencies that they seek to correct.

Two of these new and more flexible enforcement mechanisms include intermediate sanctions and civil money penalties.

In the Omnibus Reconciliation Act of 1980,[31] Congress empowered the Secretary of DHHS and the state Medicaid agencies to use what are called "intermediate sanctions," either in conjunction with or in lieu of facility decertifications under the Medicare or Medicaid program.[32] The intermediate sanction consists of the withholding of payments for any program beneficiaries admitted after a specified date. For all practical purposes, this is a freeze on the admission of program patients. In short, where there is a determination that the facility has significant deficiencies that do not jeopardize patients, the intermediate sanction provision permits a facility to continue to care for and be reimbursed for program patients who already reside there; however, the sanction does bar the facility from reimbursement for more program beneficiaries.

Unfortunately, there has been no federal experience with the intermediate sanction because the Secretary of DHHS as of mid–1985 had yet to issue proposed regulations implementing the agency's authority in this area. Proposed regulations are expected to be published shortly. The Secretary of DHHS has taken the position, however, that the absence of regulations does not preclude single state Medicaid agencies from imposing intermediate sanctions.

In 1981 Congress enacted a provision which permits DHHS to impose, through the administrative process, civil monetary penalties for fraudulent or abusive claims submitted by Medicare or Medicaid providers.[33] Under the statute, a civil monetary penalty of up to $2,000 may be levied for each item or service falsely or improperly claimed. In addition, an assessment of up to twice the amount claimed may be imposed. DHHS has issued final regulations to implement the civil money penalties provisions.[34]

CONCLUSION

The survey and certification process can and should be more objective and should be focused less on paperwork and more on the quality of care actually furnished to patients. No system, however, will entirely eliminate subjective evaluations of the adequacy of patient care. The last few years of political debate over the Medicare and Medicaid conditions of participation have not achieved consensus but have only resulted in a stalemate under which the current conditions of participation—criticized from all sides for different and inconsistent reasons—remain in effect. Public concern over past perceived and actual abuses in the long-term care industry may foreclose governmental deregulation despite the current popularity of that concept. Moreover, the judiciary, which frequently acts when the executive and legislative branches are deadlocked, has demonstrated a reluctance—as exemplified by *Estate of Smith v. O'Halloran*—to resolve this controversy. Under these circumstances, change has been confined to the nature of the penalties for inadequate care, rather than a redefinition of what constitutes adequate care. In the long run, this may be the easier, and perhaps the wiser, approach. By creating new and more flexible types of sanctions, we can reduce many of the worst and most undesirable aspects of the current process while constructing a system that better encourages and ensures adequate long-term care for the elderly.

NOTES

1. U.S. DEPT. OF HEALTH & HUMAN SERVICES, HEALTH, UNITED STATES: 1982 (U.S. Gov't Printing Office, Washington, D.C.) (1983) Table 62 at 127, Tables 46 and 47 at 106–8.
2. *Id.* Table 83 at 154; *All about Medicaid* (Carson Communications, Washington, D.C.) (May 2, 1983) p. 2.
3. *See* 45 Fed. Reg. 47368 (1980) (never codified).
4. Administrative Procedure Act, 5 U.S.C. §§551–557 (1977).
5. 43 Fed. Reg. 24873 (1978).
6. Conditions of Participation for Skilled Nursing and Intermediate Care Facilities, 45 Fed. Reg. 47368 (1980) (never codified).
7. *See* 45 Fed. Reg. 47368 (1980) and 50373 (1980).
8. *See* 45 Fed. Reg. 47368 (1980).
9. 45 Fed. Reg. 47368 (1980).
10. Making further appropriations for fiscal year 1981, Pub. L. No. 96–536, Section 119, 94 Stat. 3166, 3172 (1980).
11. 46 Fed. Reg. 7408 (1981).
12. By law, hospitals accredited by the Joint Commission on Accreditation of Hospitals are "deemed" to meet program certification requirements. *See* 42 U.S.C. §1395x(e) (1982); 42 C.F.R. §405.1901(d) (1983).
13. Medicare and Medicaid: Survey and Certification of Health Care Facilities, 47 Fed. Reg. 23404 (1982) (to be codified at 42 C.F.R. pts. 405, 431, 442, 489, and 490) (proposed May 27, 1982).
14. Six-Month Moratorium on Deregulation of Skilled Nursing and Intermediate Care Facilities, Pub. L. No. 97–248, §135, 96 Stat. 375 (1982).
15. Continuing Appropriation for Fiscal Year 1983, Pub. L. No. 97–276, §146, 96 Stat. 1186, 1199 (1982).
16. H.R. 2997, 98th Cong., 2d Sess. (1983).
17. *Id.*
18. The Medicaid Act is contained at 43 U.S.C. §1396 (1976).
19. Estate of Smith v. O'Halloran, 557 F. Supp. 289 (D. Colo. 1983), reported in CCH MEDICARE & MEDICAID GUIDE ¶ 32,445 (1983-1 Transfer Binder). One of the plaintiffs, Smith, died after suit was filed but before a decision was reached.
20. A system of resident assessments involves surveys focused on patient care in which enforcement would assure, as a condition of program participation,

that long-term care facilities are furnishing high quality rehabilitative, nursing, psychosocial, and mental care to ensure that residents are able to maintain or attain their independence and ability to care for themselves. *See* Estate of Smith v. O'Halloran, *supra* note 19, at 293.

21. Estate of Smith v. O'Halloran, *supra* note 19.
22. 42 U.S.C. §1396c (1976).
23. Much of this discussion is taken from Hamme, J., *Deciding Medicaid Major Policy Issues,* CONTEMPORARY ADMINISTRATOR FOR LONG TERM CARE, (May 1983) at 8.
24. Estate of Smith v. O'Halloran, 747 F.2d 583 (10th Cir. October 29, 1984).
25. *See* Public Health, 42 C.F.R. §§405.1120-405.1137 and 442.202(c)(1982). The conditions of participation include areas such as medical direction, nursing services, and dietetic services.
26. *Id.* The standards are simply the components of each condition. For example, the dietetic services condition of participation involves seven standards—staffing, menus and nutritional adequacy, therapeutic diets, frequency of meals, preparation and service of food, hygiene of staff, and sanitary conditions. *See* Public Health, 42 C.F.R. §405.1125 (1982).
27. *See* 42 C.F.R. §422.300-422.346.
28. 42 C.F.R. §442.110 (1981).
29. Jacobellis v. Ohio, 378 U.S. 184, 197 (1964) (Stewart, J. concurring).
30. *See* 42 C.F.R. §§431.151-431.154 and 442.100-442.115 (1982).
31. Omnibus Reconciliation Act of 1980, Pub. L. No. 96-499, 94 Stat. 2599 (1980).
32. Omnibus Reconciliation Act of 1980, Pub. L. No. 96-499, §§916(a), (b) (1) (A), and (b)(2), 94 Stat. 2599, 2623, 2624 (1980); Public Health, 42 U.S.C. §§1395cc(f), 1396a(i), and 13961(c)(1982).
33. Omnibus Budget Reconciliation Act of 1981, Pub. L. No. 97-35, §2105, 95 Stat. 357, 789–92 (1981); Civil Monetary Penalties, 42 U.S.C. §§1320a-7a (1982).
34. 45 C.F.R. Part 101.

13

Decreasing the Nursing Home's Exposure to Liability: A Concern for All

Alan S. Goldberg, J.D.

INTRODUCTION

Owners and operators of nursing homes are finding that they must increasingly be alert to the possibility of having to defend themselves against various charges of legal liability.

Identification of areas of liability exposure in long-term care facilities or other institutional settings for the elderly requires digging below the surface. Unfortunately, these areas do not usually come to one's attention until an explosive event has already occurred. Thereafter, people become more sensitive and astute, and thus able to prevent and deal with similar situations.

Problems linked to malpractice provide one example of this phenomenon. In the long-term care setting, it is tempting to think that physicians provide only visitation or recertification services, and do not perform operations and other invasive procedures of the type which usually increase their exposure to malpractice claims. However, if one looks more carefully at the kinds of problematic situations that can arise in long-term care facilities, one can see that the basis for malpractice suits is certainly there. For example, inappropriate placement, changes in levels of care, the right or the absence of the right to be treated with medication, and the so-called "pull-the-plug" decisions all create circumstances in which decisions can be challenged on the grounds of malpractice.

Supervisors and administrators in long-term care facilities may be even more concerned about the possibility of vicarious liability. Those who are not directly involved in an alleged malpractice can face liability, either of a monetary or of a criminal nature, for the acts of others for whom they are responsible.

The right of privacy is still another area of concern, the most subtle and problematic. More and more people are discovering this right, and they are willing to spend their time and money to preserve it, even in cases where the person for whom the right is asserted may have already expired.

The purpose of this chapter is to discuss these three interrelated areas in which litigation is increasing, so that persons involved in the operation of nursing homes may be better prepared to take preventive measures. Some implications of state and local law, insurance company disclaimers, and contractual agreements are also discussed.

MALPRACTICE AND VICARIOUS LIABILITY

Malpractice refers to the failure of a person providing professional services to act in accordance with the prevailing standard in the community for someone of the same profession, so that some harm results.

Anyone employed in a nursing home may be found to have committed an action or to have omitted to take an action that may involve him or her in an allegation of malpractice. Nurses and physicians, as well as allied health professionals such as physicians' assistants, physical therapists, and aides, are all susceptible to claims against them for the failure to perform their duties and responsibilities in a manner equivalent to that which might normally be expected.

When a judgment is made against a nursing home employee for malpractice who bears the monetary responsibility? The responsibility or liability for malpractice may be individual or vicarious, since separate levels of liability exist. Personal liability means being directly responsible for one's own actions and the consequences thereof. Vicarious liability means liability for the actions of others for whom one is responsible. For example, supervisory nurses or health care administrators may not only be susceptible to the claim of malpractice for their individual actions, but also be held responsible for the actions of any staff working under their direction. Vicarious liability is especially frightening in the context of the nursing home or similar types of health care institutions because it can be imposed even on the owners.

Other areas of liability are somewhat like vicarious liability, such as the responsibility to exercise appropriate care in selecting those people who act in the nursing home. This is a responsibility, often called corporate liability, which is ordinarily thought of as occurring in a hospital rather than a nursing home. Yet, cases have been brought against nursing homes; the law today supports the proposition that not only might a physician face individual liability for malpractice, but that the institution itself and the individuals who chose or should have chosen that individual physician to render services in the facility might also face liability.

These sorts of situations may involve not only monetary judgments but also criminal complaints. We are in an age when states are seeking to impose criminal liability upon the persons or even corporations that own or are responsible for the operation of health care facilities such as nursing homes. A nonprofessional might not immediately think of a criminal complaint being brought against a corporation, but such complaints certainly can be filed and a criminal penalty in the nature of a fine can be assessed. Corporations cannot be locked up, but individuals related to the corporation can be.

Having set out all of these serious and troublesome issues, let us consider how they may be faced by those who work in, operate, or own nursing homes, and even by individuals who simply know patients or deal with them regularly. Experience teaches that, although the perspectives may differ, the goals of all involved in long-term care facilities are the same: good care for the patient, proper running of the facility, and a reasonable measure of profit in order to function. Careful attention to organization, the development of appropriate policies and procedures, and periodic reviews and evaluations can enable a facility both to meet these goals and to protect itself against legal claims.

Owners and operators can reduce the risk of liability first of all by becoming better informed. Prosecutors in various states repeatedly complain that many involved in nursing homes or similar institutions have absolutely no idea of, nor the slightest sensitivity to, their own rights, their own responsibilities, and the harm that can befall them in certain situations, even ones in which they do not actively participate. Continuing familiarity with federal, state, and local statutes, regulations, ordinances, codes, and licensing requirements is needed. Frequently, professional associations provide educational opportunities for their members to enable them to stay abreast of changes in the law and of developing trends in enforcement. Administrators are also well-advised to provide training and information to their staffs, to inform them of their own legal rights and responsibilities, and to familiarize them with applicable laws concerning the rights of patients.

Administrators need to be adequately informed as well about what is taking place within their own facilities. I recommend that a program be established in every location to monitor situations that may involve exposure to liability. Organization structure and bylaws, as well as job descriptions of responsibilities, merit periodic review. Policies, operational procedures, and physical conditions likewise require regular evaluation.

Insurance protection agreements, contracts made for admission and care, and record-keeping systems must be reassessed periodically for adequacy.

The administrator is also advised to establish systematic review of the medical and personal status of each resident of the facility to monitor the sufficiency of care being given. Attention must be paid that patients are informed of their rights and given the opportunity to air complaints and grievances. Care must be taken to account for residents' funds. Opportunities for staff to communicate with family members are advised.

Finally, procedures are needed for speedy and thorough investigations of any allegations of improper conduct by staff members.

THE RIGHT OF PRIVACY

Suppose someone comes into or even calls a facility and casually requests information, giving little in the way of identification and less in the way of evidence of authority. Most people would answer quickly, casually, and accurately, without checking whether that person is targeting them or the facility for a criminal or civil investigation. A casual response in such a situation could breach the right of privacy.

The legal right of privacy protects one's choice to be left alone and to be free of undesired and unwarranted publicity. It is important for nursing home personnel to be aware of this right and to be unafraid to exercise it on behalf of themselves, the institution, and its residents.

Simply refusing to speak to someone does not mean that one is guilty or responsible or liable. We all have the right not to talk to other people, except when the legal process forces us to do otherwise. In investigatory situations, whether criminally or civilly based, disclosure of information about a facility and its patients without proper evidence of the need and of the authority of the individual seeking that information, creates a risk of liability because that disclosure may breach the right to privacy.

The bases for many criminal and civil cases are the many statutes of our legal system, which can be used to bring almost any kind of suit. More difficult to deal with, though, than this large body of law is a body of law—common law—which is somewhat hidden. From the common law are derived the right of privacy and other related rights. In other words, there are rights and liabilities that are not covered by statutes and legislation but ensue from the common law—the results of efforts of courts to define and determine various rights and liabilities of people over a period of time. The right of privacy is a classic example of a right which did not exist in written form, and which is not found overtly in the U.S. Constitution, but which was recognized many years ago in a Supreme Court decision, and is now effective in both federal and state law.

One area of particular interest today with respect to the right of privacy concerns situations in which decisions are made to withhold or terminate life-sustaining mechanisms. A patient's right to give or withhold consent for treatment has been recognized as an aspect of the right to privacy, to be free of bodily invasion. To protect themselves from complaints by patients, family members, or guardians, nursing homes must take care to inform the patient and interested persons fully of the patient's condition and treatment choices, to obtain written consent for any treatment or decision not to use certain measures, and to document carefully in the patient's record, the steps taken. In unusual or ambiguous situations, court guidance may be necessary.

In addition to establishing some type of program within a facility to protect those who work there, a similar program should be established for patients. Persons who own or are responsible for operating long-term care nursing facilities or similar types of institutions must be reminded that they have an active responsibility to protect the rights of their patients. The institution or corporation must also protect its own rights. People sometimes look with disfavor at institutions or corporations protecting the rights which they themselves say individuals have. For example, in courtrooms, patients giving testimony are often seen in a more positive light than are owners and operators giving testimony. It is important to remember that in cases raising legal and ethical issues in long-term care, both patients and owners or operators need to be protected. Neither one nor the other is entitled to better representation. In fact, we can serve the best interests of both, appropriately and ethically.

STATE LAW

Another area of law which many in the long-term care field do not properly emphasize is state law and regulation. People sometimes will ignore the responsibilities mandated by their state, since federal laws seem so much more profound and all-encompassing. Yet, the constitutions of the states protect rights of privacy and other individual rights. One does not have to look to the federal Constitution for these rights. State laws, as well as the ordinances that cities and towns enact, are likely to become more important in the future. This will be the case particularly if more creative ways of furnishing health care to the elderly are implemented.

INSURANCE

While health care facilities usually have health care and liability insurance available as protection in the event of a judgment against them, this insurance may not always be effective. There are some situations in which insurance is simply unavailable, or may be lost because the facility has taken certain actions that have prejudiced the rights of the insurance company. Prejudicing an insurance company's rights is dangerous because an insurance company may disclaim liability. To return to the previous example, if one has thoughtlessly revealed information that should not have been told in the best interests of the facility and even of oneself, the insurance company has no responsibility to pay under the insurance policies, because its rights were prejudiced.

CONTRACT LAW

One other component of the nursing home's exposure to liability is the contract. To gain entry to a nursing facility or a hospital, a patient generally signs an agreement, which is of course critical to employers, employees, and patients concerned about liability. Most people in health care, particularly in long-term care, do not pay enough attention to contractual relationships, and do not realize that contractual liability can be much more extensive in certain cases than noncontractual liability. For example, the statute of limitations, which governs the amount of time beyond which one may not assert a claim, is generally much longer for the assertion of claims in actions involving contracts or agreements than in "tort" actions, such as for negligence or malpractice. Therefore, although the period of time for a tort action may have expired, the contractual liability may remain open for a much longer period. To eliminate this problem, and to minimize similar problems, a contract can be drawn with appropriate terms to address these issues. For example, the parties can agree upon a specific, more limited statute of limitations within the contract. Although there are certain aspects of liability which may not be disclaimed, including liability for negligent actions, the extent or duration of liability may be limited within the terms of the contract.

Patients, or their families or guardians, are advised to read the language of contracts and agreements carefully at the time that they are signed. When agreements are carefully written and all parties are fully informed as to their terms and meaning, future difficulties can often be avoided.

CONCLUSION

Persons responsible for the administration and operation of nursing homes need to be as informed as possible about the risks of liability that exist for the facility itself and all those associated with it. However, an awareness of the risks, the development of procedures for monitoring activity within the facility and for the protection of the rights of employees and patients, and care in making contractual agreements can help considerably to minimize these risks.

14

Nursing Homes as Teaching Institutions: Legal Issues

Marshall B. Kapp, J.D., M.P.H.

The difficulty in attracting competent physicians (Mitchell, 1982), nurses (AHCA, 1982), and allied health professionals into nursing homes and the consequent deficiencies in the quality of medical care rendered to the residents of such institutions (Federated Council, 1981; Rabin, 1981) have been widely lamented. One approach that is increasingly advocated as a means of encouraging health professional involvement and commitment and bringing appropriate clinical skills, judgment, and standards to the nursing home population is to establish linkages between health professions, educational programs, and long-term patient care and, specifically, to begin utilizing nursing homes as clinical geriatric training sites (R. Butler, 1981; Foley & Libow, 1980; Hagan, 1980; Holden, 1982; Libow, 1982; Pawlson, 1982; Robbins & Beck, 1982; Schwartz, 1982), much as acute care hospitals have been employed for teaching purposes over the past half century. Development of this concept has been slow but steady (R. Butler, 1979; Collins, 1981). The strong impetus in this direction is evidenced by the joint creation and substantial funding in 1982 of a demonstration Teaching Nursing Home Program by the Robert Wood Johnson Foundation and the American Academy of Nursing (American Medical News, 1982).

There is every reason to suspect that the development of nursing homes as teaching institutions will have a salutary effect on patients, students, practitioners, nursing homes, and the community. However, it has been observed (Mehlferber, 1982) that:

Based on a presentation at the 35th Annual Scientific Meeting of the Gerontological Society of America, Boston, November 21, 1982. Reprinted by permission of THE GERONTOLOGIST, Vol. 24, No. 1, 1984.

As the teaching nursing home concept becomes a reality and affiliations with [health professions schools] continue to develop, it is important at the outset of program development to determine who will be responsible for the program in your facility. Issues such as defining the obligations of all parties involved, confidentiality and privacy of the resident, liability, supervision, evaluation, philosophy, ethics and legal responsibilities of research components, must be carefully analyzed and jointly decided upon (p. 15).

More particularly, our society, based on a commitment to the human dignity and well-being of all health care consumers, has placed significant limitations on the clinical activities in which a student may engage. The law views students as essentially no different than unlicensed lay persons. Under state practice acts, students may not diagnose, prescribe, or administer treatment except under the supervision and control of an appropriate licensed or certified professional.

Providing the student with the direction mandated by the law (and good clinical and educational principles) is one of the most difficult challenges confronting the administrator and professional staff of a teaching nursing home. This chapter examines the legal implications raised by the supervisory function and explicates potential liabilities associated with the undertaking of such responsibilities. Many of the issues and implications discussed will be relevant to nonteaching nursing homes as well as those engaged in formal educational activities.

LIABILITY: GENERAL CONSIDERATIONS

Although most attention has focused thus far on governmental action to vindicate resident rights (Caldwell & Kapp, 1981; Kapp, 1981), there is an increasing tendency to consider and implement private enforcement actions, in the form of individual malpractice lawsuits, on behalf of nursing home residents who believe that they have been injured by the acts or omissions of their facility (P. Butler, 1979a; National Senior Citizens Law Center, 1981; Wilson, 1978). Legal theories on which such claims have been based include the nursing home's common law duty to provide adequate care and to refrain from intentional or negligent conduct that proximately causes reasonably foreseeable harm to the resident, violation of resident care provisions contained in the admission contract, and the resident's status as an express or implied intended third-party beneficiary of federal and state statutes and regulations governing the operation of nursing homes (Brown, 1979; P. Butler, 1979b; Miller, 1980; National Association of Attorneys General, 1978).

When a patient is damaged while under care in which a student has been involved, the student, the clinical professional charged with supervising the student, the school in which the student is enrolled, and the affiliated nursing home in which the alleged injury arose are all likely defendants in a civil lawsuit initiated by the patient. This may occur in a variety of contexts.

INFORMED CONSENT

It is common practice for medical students to be introduced, or to introduce themselves, to health care recipients in teaching institutions as "young doctors" or simply as "doctors." This practice offends deeply held ethical principles based on respect for the resident's individual autonomy and fundamental right to self-determination in medical decision making. It undermines the trust that should be the underlying bond in the provider/resident relationship and unjustifiably interferes with the resident's ability to make free and informed treatment choices (Basson, 1982).

This practice of misleading residents about the educational status of their care givers is also fraught with potential legal pitfalls, both for the student and for those responsible for the student's supervision. Failure to accurately inform a resident that the person with whom the resident is asked to deal is a student may expose that student, the supervisors, the school, and the affiliated nursing home to possible lawsuits alleging claims of fraud, deceit, misrepresentation, invasion of privacy, and lack of informed consent (Alton, 1977; Annas, 1980; Hirsh, 1978).

A number of forces encourage efforts to eliminate residents' misunderstanding regarding the identity and role of students who may be involved in their care. Standards of the Joint Commission on Accreditation of Hospitals concerning Patient/Resident Rights and Responsibilities (JCAH, 1980) provide that a nursing home must have a written policy that includes the resident's right to "be informed of the nature and purpose of any technical procedures that are going to be performed, as well as know by whom such procedures are going to be carried out" (p. 52). Federal regulations governing skilled nursing facilities (SNFs)[1] and intermediate care facilities (ICFs)[2] participating in the Medicare and Medicaid programs ensure the resident's right to be fully informed of health status and to participate in the planning of medical treatment. The official organs of the nursing home industry are firmly on record in support of the resident's prerogative to knowledgeably approve or refuse proffered health care (AHCA, 1981; Harris, 1982).

It is the common law (judge-made) doctrine of informed consent that gives greatest thrust both to the requirement that all residents have fully disclosed to them the qualifications and status of those treating them and to the resident's opportunity to reject treatment by a student or anyone else by whom he or she does not wish to be treated. Failure to explicitly identify the student status of one who is or may be participating in the resident's care vitiates the resident's consent and constitutes a fraud. Trespassing on a resident's physical or mental integrity without express or implied permission may expose the student, supervisors, school, and nursing home to civil tort charges of battery or negligence. Where a resident is physically or mentally incompetent to make treatment decisions, a surrogate decision maker will be acting on the resident's behalf (Jost, 1981), and that person should be told the educational status of any student who may be participating in the resident's care.

As a practical matter, legal research reveals no actual cases in which anyone has been sued successfully for failure to disclose training status. Further, with the exception of one 1932 case[3] involving the outrageous conduct of 12 medical students separately performing pelvic and rectal examinations on a pregnant woman over her strenuous objection, no reported cases have been discovered that were grounded on the clinical participation of a student in the face of patient refusal. Nevertheless, the theoretical basis for these types of lawsuits is solid, and the growing litigiousness and consumers' rights consciousness of the American populace (Lieberman, 1981) make lawsuits of this nature a distinct possibility for the future. Students and their supervisors who ignore their duty to make the status of each member of the care-giving team unambiguously known to the resident do so at their own serious peril.

SUBSTANDARD CARE

Even though a resident or surrogate may effectively consent to the clinical participation of a person who is correctly comprehended to be a student, no consent is given to be injured as a result of the care that is rendered. The nursing home owes its residents a duty of due care and may be held civilly liable for a breach of the standard defining that duty.

A nursing home must generally adhere to a duty of reasonable care to avoid foreseeable injury, which must include recognition of the specific resident's age and mental and physical condition as it is known or reasonably should be known to the facility. JCAH standards and state licensing and federal certification regulations are often accepted by the courts as defining this tort standard of reasonable care to which nursing home residents are entitled (Hackler, 1977). For example, violation of the federal mandate that each SNF resident must have an individualized plan of medical care that must be adhered to[4] may be considered negligence per se, thereby eliminating the need to adduce independent expert testimony to establish the appropriate standard of care.

A professional staff member responsible for supervising students placed in the facility encounters potential direct legal liability to an injured resident based upon that professional's own erroneous acts or omissions, even where the injury actually occurs at the hands of the student being supervised. Where the supervising clinician writes an improper prescription or gives an inappropriate order and the student carries it out to the resident's detriment, direct liability may attach to the professional's own conduct (Dooley, 1977; Southwick, 1978). The supervising clinician is also exposed to direct liability when acting as a resident's responsible caretaker and failing to listen to and consider student remarks that merit consideration in the decision-making process on a case (Gots & Kaufman, 1978). The student may especially have something noteworthy to offer in circumstances in which the resident or resident's family is endeavoring to utilize the student as an informational conduit to the professional in charge. Additionally, a resident may impose direct liability on a clinical professional who is responsible for supervising a student under whose care the injury occurred on the theory that the professional was negligent in delegating a task to a student whom the professional knew or should have known to be inadequately trained for the task or otherwise incapable of executing it (King, 1977; Southwick, 1978). A supervisory clinician is expected to have a reasonable grasp of the abilities of specific students and to assign functions accordingly. Finally, direct liability of the professional may be predicated on general negligent dereliction of supervisory duties (King, 1977).

In addition to claims that may arise from the supervisor's own conduct, legal peril for both the staff member and the nursing home itself may also encompass vicarious liability for the negligent conduct of students. Under the principles of agency, which comprise the part of contract law that embodies the concept of employer ("master") and employee ("servant"), an employer is civilly liable for injuries to the person or property of third persons occasioned by the tortious negligence of an employee which occurred within the scope of employment (Pegalis & Wachsman, 1980; VanBiervliet & Sheldon-Wildgen, 1981). This doctrine is referred to as *"respondeat superior,"* which is translated from the Latin as "Let the master answer." (This doctrine also applies to intentional as well as negligent wrongdoing of the subordinate in those situations where the superior should reasonably have foreseen the intentional misdeed.)

Several arguments have traditionally been proposed to justify the imposition of liability upon an employer who is personally innocent of misconduct (Frankel, 1981; Prosser, 1955; Waltz & Inbau, 1971). *Respondeat superior* is often defended as a form of enterprise liability, in which the business entity that profits from the activity of a subordinate is considered the more just risk taker or loss bearer. Also frequently cited is the "deep pocket" theory; an injured person should have the right to seek compensation from an economically solvent defendant, who is more likely to be the employer than the employee. In addition, the employer is in a better posture than the employee to approximate future damages and to treat them as an operating expense, thereby spreading the risk among all those who do business with the employer. In other words, an employer is able to purchase liability insurance coverage to guard against the contingency of being held vicariously liable for an employee's negligent actions. Finally, since an employer has the power to select the employee and to control job-related behavior, the *respondeat superior* doctrine would seem to promote the desirable social policy of encouraging greater care in the selection of employees and in the supervision of their work.

Three elements are necessary for the creation of an agency relationship on which imposition of vicarious liability based on the *respondeat superior* doctrine may be supported (James & Sherrard, 1980). First, the parties must voluntarily consent to enter into an arrangement whereby the agent will act for the benefit and under the direction and control of the principal. Second, the agent must be acting within the scope of employment. Most vital, the principal must possess the general power to control the agent's work.

Each of these elements is normally present in the teaching nursing home context. First, all parties voluntarily consent to enter into a relationship whereby the student acts for the benefit (in helping to care for residents and in financially contributing to the staff members and facility through the payment of tuition and fees) and under the direction (in order both to learn from the practicum experience and to receive a favorable evaluation) of the clinician and nursing home. There need not be an express contract between the parties or even a conscious realization that the agency relationship has been created. It is irrelevant that the student is not financially compensated for fulfilling the agent's part of the bargain or, in the situation of voluntary teaching and service by full-time practicing care givers with or without clinical appointments in academic programs, that the clinical supervision is rendered free of charge (Cavenar et al., 1980).

Second, the student restricts resident-related activities to those tasks assigned or permitted by the supervisor and facility. Finally, the practicing professional and the nursing home, by virtue of position, have the power to directly control the student's performance. Whether that control is actually exercised in any particular case is immaterial. It is only important legally that they have the right to exert such control if they choose to do so (Frankel, 1981; Southwick, 1978). Whether the supervisor in effect "treats" the resident through the student or offers only occasional comments to the student is of no consequence; that is, the supervisor's actual degree of involvement in the management of a resident's care makes no significant difference from a legal standpoint.

There is also a strong policy rationale for courts to rely on in characterizing students as agents for liability analysis purposes (Kraus, 1980). In the long-term health care area, the resident entrusts total personal welfare to a specific institutional service provider and its professional staff, and that provider and those individual staff members who have accepted that trust should bear the burden of ultimate responsibility for the quality of care delivered.

Respondeat superior is not exclusively a form of strict or absolute liability since some substandard conduct by the subordinate is requisite in order to activate the liability of the supervisor or facility. Specifically, a supervising care giver or affiliated institution may not be held legally liable for the conduct of a student unless the student rendered negligent care that proximately caused a resident to suffer compensable injuries. The standard of care against which a student's performance is to be legally evaluated varies among jurisdictions. The prevailing rule is that, when an individual undertakes to provide a clinical service, that individual will be held answerable to the same standard of care as a certified or licensed, experienced professional performing the same task rather than to what could reasonably be expected from one possessing less training and skill.[5] Under the majority of relevant judicial opinions, supervisors and affiliated health facilities may not delegate tasks to students without having them held to a practitioner's standards. In contrast, at least some cases have held that medical postgraduate trainees are required to possess only such skill and exercise such diligence as other postgraduate trainees regularly possess and exercise under similar circumstances.[6]

As already noted, the supervising clinician is not the only superior who shoulders potential vicarious liability for resident injuries negligently inflicted by a student. A health care facility is civilly accountable for damages caused when a student from an affiliated educational institution negligently injures a patient in the course of fulfilling a clinical practicum at the facility. The doctrines of vicarious liability and corporate responsibility apply with full force to nursing homes that undertake the role of clinical teaching site (Hackler, 1977). It is feasible, however, for the facility to shift liability away from itself and exclusively to the school or student by clearly stating that intention in the affiliation contract executed between the institution and the educational program. Disclaimer clauses are a common practice in the business world (Kraus, 1980).

Likewise, the school in which the student is enrolled may be held vicariously liable for the student's negligent resident care (Kraus, 1980). The school receives an economic benefit from students through payment of tuition and fees and in return promises to provide teaching, including direct supervision during clinical clerkships. Moreover, the affiliation agreement negotiated between a health care institution and a school ordinarily calls for students to be supervised by paid or voluntary members of the school's faculty. A health professions school also owes a duty to exercise reasonable care to the public to whom it offers its health care services.[7]

Of some consolation to supervising clinicians, schools, and affiliated nursing homes held vicariously liable for the negligence of students is the possibility, at least theoretically, of recovering those amounts that they are forced to pay as damages from the erring student under the principle of indemnification (Morris, 1981). Every wrongdoer is personally liable for the harm suffered by another as a result of the wrongdoer's negligent (or intentional, for that matter) misdeeds. When liability for the negligence of a student attaches to the supervisor or institution, they have a legal cause of action against the student who was personally at fault. This claim may be asserted by way of cross-compliant in the same litigation brought by the resident against the supervisor or facility or by an independent action commenced directly against the negligent student. This right of indemnification exists, of course, only when the superior itself is free from personal wrongdoing in causing the resident's injury. The promise of indemnification in this context is probably more ephemeral than real, however, given the impecunious condition of most students and the standard practice of educational institutions and affiliated health care facilities to themselves provide the liability insurance coverage for their students.

CONFIDENTIALITY

The situation is likely to arise in which a resident, either verbally or by submitting to examination or treatment, reveals certain personal information to a student that is then shared with the clinical supervisor or vice versa. At first blush, this dissemination of personal resident data may seem to run afoul of the general legal and ethical precepts of privacy and confidentiality.

This type of sharing of information, however, is vital for both pedagogical and resident care purposes. This factor has been recognized in the general rule of law (Annas et al., 1981) that, when an individual is being served in a health care facility, he or she impliedly consents to the viewing of relevant records and the discussion of his or her case by all those who are directly concerned with providing care. This informational privilege that health care providers enjoy to know the facts regarding those consumers for whom they are responsible includes students and their supervisors. This practice is a matter of custom and may take place without the patient being made aware of it, although an abundance of legal caution and favorable provider/resident relations suggest that the resident should be informed that the facts relating to his or her care may be shared between students and supervisors (Cavenar et al., 1980).

RECOMMENDATIONS

The discussion presented above is in no way intended to intimidate nursing home administrators, professional staff members, or educators or to impede the essential process of hands-on clinical training of future health care practitioners. Nevertheless, the real potential for legal liability, direct or vicarious, flowing from resident care rendered by health professions trainees must be kept firmly in mind as educational programs and affiliation agreements are devised and operationalized. A few specific recommendations are offered:

1. All nursing home personnel should wear name tags identifying them by name and title or position. In particular, supervising clinicians, schools, and nursing homes should make certain that all students wear name tags visibly identifying themselves as such and indicating their school connection and should ensure that students are verbally introduced to residents and families according to their correct designations.

2. Every nursing home and affiliated school should provide training sessions devoted to ethical considerations and obligations owed by students to the nursing home residents whom they serve.

3. Principals should devote substantial attention to quality control of their agents and should exercise their powers concerning acceptance, retention, evaluation, and discipline of students in their facilities as conscientiously as possible.

4. Clinical professionals and nursing homes should exercise diligence and enthusiasm in fulfilling supervisory responsibilities. With the prestige of a faculty appointment and educational affiliation comes potential legal liability. Professionals and institutions should supervise students in a manner that is careful and complete enough to be consonant with the legal obligations that accompany the supervisory powers.

5. Closely connected to the previous point, discretion as to whether a student under one's tutelage should be assigned or permitted to perform a particular task must be exercised judiciously by each clinician and facility. The supervisor is expected

to know a student's capabilities and not assign tasks that the student is not able to handle. Although it is the obligation of the educator to provide practical experiences from which learning may take place, it must be remembered that students should be regarded as trainees and as extensions of the resident care activities of the nursing home and its staff, not as substitutes who can make decisions and take actions that are rightfully within the exclusive province of the responsible professional and health facility (Alton, 1977). Nursing homes must resist the temptation to utilize students only as an attractive source of free labor to compensate for shortcomings in the recruitment of qualified physicians (Mitchell, 1982) and nurses (AHCA, 1982).

6. When a student has taken part in a resident's care, the nursing home's clinical records should clearly indicate the degree of faculty supervision to which the student was subjected. An accurate and complete record documenting who did what concerning the resident's treatment is both ethically proper and practically advantageous to a supervisor's or nursing home's defense in the event of subsequent allegations of malpractice (Alton, 1977).

7. Health professions schools and their affiliated nursing homes should assiduously review their affiliation contracts to make certain that these agreements correctly reflect their respective wishes and understandings concerning the distribution of supervisory responsibility and the allocation of ultimate financial responsibility for resident injuries negligently (or intentionally) inflicted by students. Necessary amendments to the affiliation agreements should be negotiated and signed.

8. Every nursing home should incorporate into its standard admission contract a clause relating to the possibility that some resident care may be rendered by students. This contingency should be fully explained to and understood by entering residents and their families.

9. Every nursing home should have a provision in its policy and procedure manual that clearly delineates how administration and professional staff are to delegate authority to and exercise supervisory control over subordinates (Coggeshall, 1973), including students who are assigned to the facility as part of a clinical practicum.

10. Every clinical department in an educational institution sponsoring placed students should draft and enforce guidelines concerning supervisory expectations of paid and voluntary faculty

members. These should be explicitly accepted by each faculty
member as a condition of faculty appointment and distributed
to each student as a practicum sponsored by that department is
begun. Affiliated nursing homes should insist upon this practice as a condition of affiliation.

CONCLUSION

Implementation of these suggestions need not unduly inhibit either the
educational process or delivery of resident care. As a realistic matter,
identification of an individual as a student will rarely inspire a resident or
his or her family to refuse the student's participation or to lose confidence in the student's ability to contribute to resident care (Alton, 1977;
Hirsh, 1978). A policy of honesty will not substantially deprive students
of the "real life" experiences that their proper training requires. Further,
in the overwhelming percentage of cases where the student performs
appropriately assigned functions in a nonnegligent manner under adequate clinical supervision, no danger of legal liability exists.[8] The experience thus far of American health professions schools and their affiliated
health care facilities shows that it is indeed possible to successfully combine legitimate educational goals, quality care, and the fulfillment of legal
responsibilities. This positive experience can and should be translated to
the sphere of teaching nursing homes.

NOTES

1. 42 C.F.R. §405.1121(k)(3)(1981).
2. 42 C.F.R. §449.12(a)(1)(ii)(B)(3)(1981).
3. Inderbitzen v. Lane Hospital, 12 P.2d 744 (Cal. 1932).
4. 42 C.F.R. §405.1124(d)(1981).
5. McBride v. United States, 462 F.d 72 (9th Cir. 1972).
6. Rush v. Akron Hospital, 171 N.E.2d 378 (Ohio App. 1957).
7. Emory University v. Porubiansky, 282 S.E.2d 903 (Ga. 1981).
8. Levy v. Vaughan, 42 App. D.C. 146 (1914).

REFERENCES

Alton, W. *Malpractice*. Little, Brown & Co., Boston, 1977.
American Health Care Association. Policy statement: Patients' rights. *American Health Care Association Journal*, 1981, 7, 55–60.
American Health Care Association. Public policy issues: AHCA's views on long-term care matters. *American Health Care Association Journal*, 1982, 8, 9–17.

American Medical News. Nursing homes, RNs to collaborate on foundation-sponsored project. *American Medical News,* March 12, 1982, *25,* 9.

Annas, G. The care of private patients in teaching hospitals: Legal implications. *Bulletin of New York Academy of Medicine,* 1980, *56,* 403–11.

Annas, G., Glantz, L., and Katz. B. *The rights of doctors, nurses, and allied health professionals.* Avon, New York, 1981.

Basson, M. Case study: The "student doctor" and a wary patient. *Hastings Center Report,* 1982, *12,* 27–28.

Brown, R. *The rights of older persons.* Avon, New York, 1979.

Butler, P. Assuring the quality of care and life in nursing homes: The dilemma of enforcement. *North Carolina Law Review,* 1979, *58,* 1317–82. (a)

Butler, P. *Nursing home quality of care enforcement: Part I—Litigation by private parties.* Legal Services Corporation, Washington, D.C., 1979. (b)

Butler, R. Geriatrics and internal medicine. *Annals of Internal Medicine,* 1979, *91,* 903–8.

Butler, R. The teaching nursing home. *Journal of the American Medical Association,* 1981, *245,* 1435–37.

Caldwell, J., and Kapp, M. The rights of nursing home patients: Possibilities and limitations of federal regulation. *Journal of Health Politics, Policy and Law,* 1981, *6,* 40–48.

Cavenar, J., Rhoads, E., and Sullivan, J. Ethical and legal aspects of supervision. *Bulletin of the Menniger Clinic,* 1980, *44,* 15–22.

Coggeshall, J. *Management of retirement homes and long-term care facilities.* Mosby, St. Louis, 1973.

Collins, J. Nursing homes and medical schools: The growing link. *Geriatrics,* 1981, *8,* 135–38.

Dooley, J. *Modern tort law: Liability and litigation* (Vol. 2). Callaghan, and Company, Chicago, 1977.

Federated Council for Internal Medicine. Geriatric medicine. *Annals of Internal Medicine,* 1981, *95,* 372–76.

Foley, C., and Libow, L. Fellowship and residency training in geriatric medicine: The nursing home experience. In American College of Physicians, *Proceedings of the conference on the changing needs of nursing home care.* American College of Physicians, Washington, D.C., 1980.

Frankel, C. *Lawyers' medical cyclopedia of personal injuries and allied specialties* (3rd ed., Vol. 1). Allen Smith Company, Indianapolis, 1981.

Gots, R., and Kaufman, A. *The people's hospital book.* Avon, New York, 1978.

Hackler, E. Expansion of health providers' liability: An application of *Darling* to long-term health care facilities. *Connecticut Law Review,* 1977, *9,* 462–81.

Hagan, D. Nursing homes as a training site for LPNs/LVNs. *Journal of Long-Term Care Administration,* 1980, *8,* 1–12.

Harris, S. Protecting residents' rights. *American Health Care Association Journal,* 1982, *8,* 3–7.

Hirsh, H. Which physicians are students? The patient has a right to know. *Hospital Medical Staff,* 1978, *7,* 11–14.

Holden, C. Butler leaving Institute on Aging. *Science,* 1982, *217,* 616–17.

James, A., Jr., and Sherrard, T. Agency. In A. James, Jr. (ed.), *Legal medicine: With special reference to diagnostic imaging.* Urban and Schwarzenberg, Baltimore, Md., 1980.

Joint Commission on Accreditation of Hospitals. *Accreditation manual for long-term care facilities* (3rd ed.). Joint Commission on Accreditation of Hospitals, Chicago, 1980.

Jost, D. The problem of consent for placement, care, and treatment of the incompetent nursing home resident. *St. Louis University Law Review,* 1981, *26,* 63–104.

Kapp, M. Protecting the rights of nursing home patients: Using federal law. *Florida Bar Journal,* 1981, *56,* 212–15.

King, J., Jr. *The law of medical malpractice.* West Publishing Company, St. Paul, Minn., 1977.

Kraus, G. Legal forum. *Radiology Management,* 1980, *2,* 44–45.

Libow, L. Geriatric medicine and the nursing home: A mechanism for mutual excellence. *The Gerontologist,* 1982, *22,* 134–41.

Lieberman, J. *The litigious society.* Basic Books, New York, 1981.

Mehlferber, K. The teaching nursing home: A review of two models proposed. *American Health Care Association Journal,* 1982, *8,* 13–15.

Miller, J. An evaluation of regulatory standards and enforcement devices in the nursing home industry. *Akron Law Review,* 1980, *13,* 715–29.

Mitchell, J. Physician visits to nursing homes. *The Gerontologist, 1982, 22,* 45–48.

Morris, W. The negligent nurse—The physician and the hospital. *Baylor Law Review,* 1981, *33,* 109–43.

National Association of Attorneys General. *Enforcing quality of care in nursing homes.* National Association of Attorneys General Foundation, Raleigh, N.C., 1978.

National Senior Citizens Law Center. Tort actions: A potential tool for nursing home advocates. *Clearinghouse Review,* 1981, *14,* 1260–63.

Pawison, L. Clinical medical education in the nursing home: Opportunities and limits. *Journal of Medical Education,* 1982, *57,* 787–91.

Pegalis, S., and Wachsman, H. *American law of medical malpractice* (Vol. 1). Lawyers Cooperative Publishing Company, Rochester, N.Y., 1980.

Prosser, W. *Law of torts* (2nd ed.). West Publishing Company, St. Paul, Minn., 1955.

Rabin, D. Physician care in nursing homes. *Annals of Internal Medicine,* 1981, *94,* 126–28.

Robbins, A., and Beck, J. Guidelines for graduate medical education in geriatrics. *Journal of Medical Education,* 1982, *57,* 762–68.

Schwartz, T. For fun and profit: How to install a first-rate doctor in a third-rate nursing home. *New England Journal of Medicine,* 1982, *306,* 743–44.

Southwick, A. *The law of hospital and health care administration.* Health Administration Press, Ann Arbor, Mich., 1978.

VanBiervliet, A., and Sheldon-Wildgen, J. *Liability issues in community-based programs: Legal principles, problem areas, and recommendations.* Paul H. Brookes Publishing Company, Baltimore, Md., 1981.

Waltz, J., and Inbau, F. *Medical jurisprudence.* Macmillan Publishing Company, New York, 1971.

Wilson, S. Nursing home patients' rights: Are they enforceable? *The Gerontologist,* 1978, *18,* 255–61.

Section IV

Rights of Long-Term Care Residents

15

Nursing Home Residents' Rights: An Overview and Brief Assessment

Robert N. Brown, J.D., LL.M.

Over a decade has passed since the U.S. government adopted regulations establishing a bill of rights for nursing home residents. These regulations (and those of the states which are patterned after them) require nursing homes to treat residents with basic human decency. When most people (even health professionals) think of nursing home patients' rights, it is the federal requirements they have in mind. In my view, the field of residents' rights is much broader—residents can claim rights from sources beyond the specific residents' rights provisions of state and federal law and have rights against persons and entities other than the facility in which they reside.

The Constitution, Social Security Act, state protective services provisions, common law, and a rich body of ethical literature are all important to nursing home residents. Protections for these individuals against third-party payers, other health care providers, and family members can be as important to nursing home residents as rights against the nursing home.

I also believe that exploration of how rights are to be enforced is as important as the enumeration of rights themselves. To a great extent, nursing home residents suffer not because they lack rights, but because we lack effective means to ensure that their rights are respected. We must give much more attention to this complex topic than we have in the past. As we do so, we should remember that in many areas voluntary cooperation between nursing home residents and the facilities in which they reside is likely to benefit both.

An Overview of Nursing Homes

Approximately 25 million persons in the United States are 65 or older.[1] While many older persons (particularly the younger elderly) are quite healthy, the health of many persons 75 and older is quite poor. Many of these individuals suffer multiple chronic illnesses and require assistance with daily life. The assistance required by most of those persons is non-medical and unskilled in character: supervision and assistance with eating, toileting, bathing, dressing, walking, and meal preparation are the primary needs of persons requiring long-term care.[2] Of the approximately 8 million persons (elderly, physically disabled, mentally ill, or developmentally disabled) who require some form of long-term care, only approximately 1.5 million reside in nursing homes at any one time. The remainder reside at home (alone or with relatives) or they reside in nonmedical residential care facilities.[3] Nursing homes thus are one part of a larger system of long-term care.

There are approximately 19 thousand nursing homes in the United States, providing varied levels of services and accepting different forms of reimbursement.[4] Skilled nursing facilities offer 24-hour nursing care under the supervision of a registered nurse and are used primarily by persons leaving hospitals for recuperative care lasting less than a month.[5] Reimbursement for such care is provided by both Medicare and Medicaid.[6] Intermediate care facilities provide health-related care services to individuals requiring long-term care but at a less medically intensive level. Public reimbursement for such care is available only through Medicaid.[7] Many facilities provide both skilled and intermediate care.

Nearly 75 percent of all nursing homes are private, proprietary facilities. Slightly over 15 percent are private nonprofit facilities, with the balance operated by various levels of government.[8] Within the proprietary segment of the nursing home industry, there is an increasing movement toward centralization of ownership. National corporations are purchasing a large number of facilities throughout the country and increasingly are entering other aspects of the long-term care market. In this respect the nursing home industry may be a prototype of the health care industry of the future.[9]

The average nursing home resident is 81 years old and suffers from several chronic conditions. Over half of nursing home residents have some degree of mental impairment, more than half are unable to walk without assistance, and more than half have no close family or friends. Most require assistance with bathing, dressing, toileting, and other aspects of daily life.[10] Nursing home residents thus are very old, frail, and isolated. These characteristics are important in the design and implementation of a system of rights. It is very important to protect such a frail and dependent population, yet difficult for these individuals to assert rights without assistance.

REGULATION AND FINANCING OF NURSING HOMES

Nursing homes are regulated by the states in which they are located. In addition, facilities which have sought certification for participation in Medicare or Medicaid must also satisfy federal Conditions of Participation authorized by Congress and promulgated by the Department of Health and Human Services (DHHS). Primary responsibility for determining compliance with both state and federal requirements rests with the states.[11]

Financing of nursing home care is divided about equally between public and private sources. Of the approximately $24 billion spent on nursing homes in 1981, more than $10 billion was paid by patients or their families, while not quite $14 billion came from public sources. About 90 percent of the public reimbursement for nursing home care came from Medicaid. Medicare and private health insurance together pay less than 4 percent of the costs of nursing home care.[12]

Responsibility for nursing home regulation and financing is fragmented—public and private, state and federal actors all are involved. Achieving the right balance is an important policy issue for the future.

OVERVIEW OF NURSING HOME RESIDENTS' RIGHTS

The subject of rights has always been an important topic in philosophy. For centuries philosophers have debated questions concerning the existence and definition of rights.[13] In the last three decades we have seen the rise of widespread rights movements. The civil rights efforts on behalf of blacks led to rights movements in other contexts.[14] The rights of institutionalized persons have been the focus of efforts for at least 20 years—prisoners,[15] mental patients,[16] the developmentally disabled;[17] all have been the subjects of campaigns for the recognition of rights. Hospital patients also have been the beneficiaries of this rights movement.[18]

The rights movement came to nursing homes in the early 1970s. Borrowing from the efforts begun on behalf of others, nursing home advocates urged the adoption of rights for residents of nursing homes. This movement led in the mid-1970s to the adoption by DHHS of a bill of rights for nursing home residents.[19] This movement has continued in the states, with many adopting a bill of rights for their nursing home residents.[20]

As used in this chapter, the term "right" refers both to a legally enforceable entitlement to receive something of value (such as treatment consistent with state or federal requirements) and to the liberty to do certain things (such as receive visitors or to send mail) without interference from others. Occasionally in this chapter I will use the term "right" more broadly, to include interests not yet regarded as legally enforceable, but which are deserving of legal protection.

The existence of residents' rights imposes duties on others, (nursing homes and their employees, state and federal agencies, family members) either to provide that which a patient has a claim or entitlement to receive or to refrain from interfering with a liberty that a patient possesses. The meaning or scope of a right often is unclear. Patient rights evolve as the Constitution is interpreted by the courts, as statutes and regulations are adopted and interpreted, and as contractual and common law duties are defined. Thus legislatures, administrative agencies, courts, and the interested parties themselves all have a role in defining patient rights.

The existence of a right assumes the availability of a remedy if that right is violated. Normally, legal rights are enforced by the person possessing the right or by somebody, such as a guardian, selected or appointed to act on the right holder's behalf. Occasionally rights are enforced by others, for example by administrative agencies. Most legal rights are enforceable in court (state, federal, or both), but occasionally other entities, such as administrative agencies, have authority to interpret and enforce rights.

Nursing home rights may be enforced in many ways. In some cases the rights are enforceable by the resident in court. Other times, the resident must go to an administrative agency (at least initially). Still other times, a right is enforced exclusively by an administrative agency. The existence of effective remedies for violation of resident rights is an important issue for nursing home residents. Often the problem nursing home residents face is not that they lack rights. Rather, it is that the remedies available to enforce their rights are inadequate. This problem has been the subject of considerable attention in recent years, and many states have adopted laws designed to improve remedies for resident right violations.

FEDERAL RIGHTS

When one speaks of rights, the first source that comes to mind is the U.S. Constitution, and particularly the Bill of Rights found in the first ten amendments to the Constitution, made applicable to the states by the 14th Amendment to the Constitution. The protections against restrictions on speech, religion, assembly, and privacy, the prohibition against deprivation of life, liberty, and property without due process of law, and the prohibition against denying any person the equal protection of the laws are all founded expressly or implicitly on the Bill of Rights, and have been important to civil rights advocates in other areas.[21]

The Constitution has been an important source of rights for nursing homes in their disputes with federal and state governments over licensure, certification for participation in Medicare and Medicaid, and payments.[22] For example, nursing homes have argued successfully that they could not be decertified from participation in Medicaid without adequate notice and an opportunity to contest the government's allegations upon which a decision to decertify was based.[23]

Nursing home residents also have used the U.S. Constitution, but with less success than one might expect. The best known of the constitutional cases involving nursing home residents is *O'Bannon v. Town Court Nursing Center,*[24] a suit in which a nursing home and its residents challenged a decertification decision that would have led to the nonconsensual transfer of the residents. An argument was made on behalf of the residents that they enjoyed a property interest in their continued placement in that specific home stemming from the free choice of provider portion of the Social Security Act, certain provisions of the patients' bill of rights, and the Medicaid fair hearing regulations. These provisions, it was argued, entitled the residents to stay in the facility until a hearing was held, in which the residents could participate, concerning the desirability of decertifying the facility.[25] The lower courts agreed with these contentions, but on appeal the Supreme Court disagreed.

The Court concluded that none of the provisions of the Social Security Act or DHHS regulations cited by the residents entitled them to a hearing prior to transfer. The Court concluded further that there was insufficient evidence of harm caused by a transfer to justify the holding of a hearing prior to transfer.[26] It viewed the dispute primarily as between the state and the facility, with the residents only indirectly affected.[27] The Court likened the residents to tenants in an apartment building in which the landlord had a dispute with the utility company. It stated that the tenants would not be entitled to a hearing prior to termination of utilities to the building and concluded that, likewise, nursing home residents were not entitled to a hearing prior to decertification of the facility.[28] Other courts since *O'Bannon* have reached similar conclusions with respect to a resident's right to participate in decisions affecting the closure of a nursing home in which he or she resides.[29]

Another problem reducing the value of the Constitution as a source of residents' rights is the issue of whether the Constitution even applies to decisions adversely affecting nursing home residents. The Constitution primarily protects us against actions by the government. It provides no direct protection against activities by private individuals and entities. Because most nursing homes are private (either profit or nonprofit), there are serious doubts about whether the Constitution imposes any limits on a nursing home's freedom of activity, even when that activity is harmful to residents. The requirement that there be state action to invoke constitutional protection is satisfied in homes owned and operated by a governmental unit, such as county homes and Veterans Administration homes. In such facilities, residents may assert constitutional rights. In the more common situation of a resident in a private facility, the requirement of state action is difficult to surmount. The U.S. Supreme Court occasionally has ruled that a private entity is performing a public function or is so closely involved with the government that its action becomes state action for purposes of invoking constitutional protections. More often, however, the Court has declined to find a relationship sufficient to find the state action necessary to make the Constitution applicable.[30]

In *Blum v. Yaretsky,*[31] a suit challenging New York's utilization review process, the Supreme Court considered whether nursing home or physician decisions to transfer Medicaid patients from a nursing home constitute state action. The trial court enjoined the utilization review process because of procedural deficiencies and concluded that decisions by facilities to transfer patients, where the decisions were part of the utilization review process, were actions of the state to which the Constitution applied. During the course of litigation, a consent agreement was reached concerning most aspects of the utilization review process. The portion of the case that reached the Supreme Court involved decisions by nursing homes and private physicians outside of the normal utilization review process. The Court concluded that these decisions were private in character and could not be attributed to the state. Therefore, the due process protections of the 14th Amendment did not constrain the process by which the decisions and transfers were carried out.[32] Two dissenting justices argued that these actions were intimately tied to the Medicaid cost containment provisions of the Social Security Act and were therefore actions of the state to which the due process clause applied.[33]

The *O'Bannon* and *Blum* cases illustrate the complexities of defining resident rights through constitutional adjudication. The residents' claims for due process were based on earlier interpretations of the due process clause by the Supreme Court. In *Goldberg v. Kelly,*[34] a landmark case decided in 1970, the Court ruled that welfare benefits could not be terminated without prior notice and a hearing. Since then the Supreme Court and lower federal and state courts have been asked to rule on the application of *Goldberg* to benefits under Social Security, unemployment compensation, housing, and other social programs.[35] The Court's response to these claims has been inconsistent. In recent years the Court has ruled with increasing frequency that governmental decisions may be made without requiring prior notice and a hearing.[36] As *O'Bannon* and *Blum* illustrate, extensive litigation often is necessary before one can obtain a definitive ruling on whether residents possess a particular constitutional right. And even a decision by the Supreme Court is not fully definitive, since a slightly different factual situation can lead to a different result.

Despite the losses suffered in these important cases, nursing home residents are likely to continue to try to rely upon the Constitution to protect their interests against governmental actions affecting them directly.

The most visible sources of federal rights for residents of nursing homes are the bills of rights promulgated by DHHS as part of the federal regulatory requirements imposed upon nursing homes participating in Medicare and Medicaid.[37]

A skilled nursing facility (SNF) is required to have a written residents' rights policy which is made available to residents and their families or guardians at the time of admission. The nursing home is also required to train its staff on the implementation of this residents' rights policy.[38] The facility's policy must include the following protections.

— At the time of admission the resident must be informed of his or her rights and of services available at the facility and charges for these services.

— The resident must be fully informed of his or her medical condition.

— The resident must not be transferred involuntarily except for medical reasons, for nonpayment, or for protection of other residents. Except in an emergency, when a nonconsensual transfer occurs, advance notice must be given.

— The resident should be encouraged to exercise his or her rights and to express grievances about the facility to the facility's staff and to outsiders. No discrimination or reprisal may occur as a result of these complaints.

— The resident must be free from mental and physical abuse and from chemical and physical restraints except as authorized by a physician or to protect the resident or other patients from injury.

— The resident must be assured confidentiality with respect to his or her personal and medical records and is empowered to authorize their release to others.

— The resident must be treated with consideration, respect, and dignity and must be accorded privacy in treatment and in care for personal needs.

— A resident cannot be required to perform services for the facility except in limited circumstances.

— The resident is authorized to associate and communicate privately with others in person or by mail.

— A resident may participate in social, religious, and community activities and, with some limitations, may retain and use personal clothing.

— The resident is authorized to meet privately with his or her spouse and, with some exceptions, to share a room with that spouse if both are residents of the facility.

— A resident may manage his or her personal financial affairs. The facility is required to account quarterly for financial transactions made on behalf of the resident if the facility has been authorized by the resident to handle money.

This list is a summary of the residents' rights applicable for skilled nursing facilities. A slightly different list exists for residents of intermediate care facilities and for residents of ICFs for the mentally retarded.

Thus, many fundamentally important aspects of a resident's life are protected explicitly by these federally imposed obligations. To the extent that a facility honors these obligations, the quality of life of a nursing home resident is enhanced. Most requirements of resident bills of rights can be followed easily by the staffs of well-managed facilities.[39] Unfortunately, not all facilities implement the bill of rights adequately. Frequently cited violations of residents' rights include improper patient care, failure to respect patient privacy, and the use of improper restraints.[40]

DEFICIENCIES IN FEDERAL RIGHTS

The effectiveness of the federal resident bill of rights as a protective measure has been reduced by several deficiencies. One problem is the vague quality of the rights conferred by these federal regulations. For example, the requirement that a patient be treated with "consideration, respect, and full recognition of dignity and individuality, including privacy in treatment and care for his personal needs"[41] provides little guidance to the relatively untrained staffs of nursing homes. It is not surprising that failures to respect residents' dignity and privacy are frequently cited.

Another problem with these provisions is that they allow certain rights to be overridden at the direction of a physician. Thus, a physician can abrogate the requirement of being told one's medical condition, as well as the rights to associate and communicate with others, to participate in social, religious, and community activities, to retain personal property, and to share a room with one's spouse.[42]

The restraint measure illustrates anothers problem with these provisions. It prohibits the use of restraints except as authorized by a physician or when necessary to protect the resident or others from injury.[43] The protection against excessive restraints is undercut by the exceptions. Further, common law rules make a facility potentially liable for unconsented-to restraints upon an individual's physical liberty, for inadequate supervision of restrained patients, and for injury to residents who are permitted to wander under circumstances in which the facility should be able to reasonably forsee a potential danger. Thus, neither the staff nor the resident is given satisfactory guidance by these provisions.[44]

Another deficiency with the federal resident rights is that provisions are inadequate for the complex ethical and legal questions that surround medical decision making in nursing homes. Although nursing home residents are less likely than patients in acute care facilities to experience an acute medical crisis, important health care decisions must be made. What diagnostic tests should be used? What modes of treatment should be begun or continued? Should a patient be transferred to an acute care setting? Should pain-reducing but possibly life-shortening medications be used? A growing body of ethical literature and much common law and constitutional doctrine exist to guide nursing homes and physicians with respect to these decisions.[45] Residents, their families, and nursing homes must look to these bodies of ethical and legal doctrine rather than simply to the residents' bill of rights to resolve these questions.

Closely related are problems of medical experimentation. Although the residents' bill of rights authorizes a resident to decline to participate in medical research,[46] the ethical and legal problems associated with medical research in nursing homes are more complex than the regulations suggest.[47]

These provisions also fail to consider adequately the pervasive problem in nursing homes of the resident with diminished capacity for decision making. About 50 percent of nursing home residents have some diminished decision-making capacity.[48] However, few of these individuals have been declared incompetent by judicial process. The bill of rights allows the resident's guardian, next of kin, or other entity to exercise rights of persons who have been either formally adjudicated incompetent, or found by a physician to be medically incapable of understanding their rights or of communicating about them.[49] These broad delegations of power to physicians and of rights to third parties are troublesome. In addition, the rules are of little help to residents or staff in deciding how to carry out the broad range of decision making involved in nursing home life—from routine matters of what to wear, what to eat, and whether to participate in an activity, to more important medical decisions and decisions involving transfers to and from the facility.[50]

Recognizing these and other deficiencies, the Carter administration proposed amendments to the federal bill of rights as part of its larger attempt to improve the federal regulatory mechanism for nursing homes. It proposed that a unified set of regulations be established for intermediate and skilled nursing facilities, that the bill of rights be upgraded from a standard to a condition of participation, and that many of the ambiguities existing in the current regulations be eliminated.[51] Although DHHS Secretary Patricia Harris signed the resident rights regulations in the last days of the Carter administration, they were rescinded by the Reagan administration shortly after taking office, and have never gone into effect.[52]

DHHS is also responsible for implementing the Social Security Act which establishes both the Medicare (Title 18) and Medicaid (Title 19) programs. DHHS does this by issuing regulations that impose quality care obligations on nursing homes. Residents of nursing homes have a right to receive treatment that is consistent with the requirements imposed by the Social Security Act and the regulations issued by DHHS. The content of these regulations and the methods by which they should be enforced have been subject to considerable controversy.[53] In an effort to end this controversy, the Carter administration proposed to overhaul the entire set of DHHS nursing home regulations, but early in the Reagan administration these proposed changes were rescinded. The Reagan administration itself proposed changes in federal regulations governing nursing homes as part of a general deregulation effort. One proposal would have permitted automatic, or "deemed," federal certification of facilities accredited by the Joint Commission on Accreditation of Hospitals; others sought to alter the cycle in which nursing homes are inspected, or make changes in the enforcement mechanism. These proposals were sufficiently controversial that their implementation has been blocked by Congress. A study by the national Institute of Medicine of nursing home standards and enforcement was commissioned by DHHS and is nearing completion.[54] This study explored such questions as what standards should govern nursing homes, who will enforce these standards, how frequently should homes be inspected, what resources should be available to the states to assist with enforcement, and what sanctions should be applied to noncomplying facilities. Resolution of these issues is critical to nursing home residents.

In addition to the Social Security Act, a number of other federal acts and regulations are sources of rights for nursing home residents.

Examples include the Civil Rights Act of 1964, which prohibits discrimination on the basis of race, color, or national origin in any program receiving federal assistance;[55] the Age Discrimination Act of 1975, prohibiting discrimination on the basis of age in programs receiving federal financial assistance;[56] and the Rehabilitation Act of 1973, prohibiting discrimination on the basis of handicap.[57]

STATE RIGHTS

The inadequacies of the federal nursing home rights have led many states in recent years to promulgate their own bills of rights. In general, these parallel the federal rights provisions, but frequently provide more detail, have fewer exceptions, and in some instances provide rights not found in the federal standards.[58] State rights provisions typically provide more direction concerning the use of restraints, and are more explicit about residents' privacy and about rights concerning medical decision making.[59] In addition, the rather general federal protections against involuntary transfers from nursing homes have been expanded by several states to restrict transfers much more explicitly and to provide more elaborate procedural protections before transfers can occur.[60]

The states, in regulating nursing homes, frequently create or specify rights for the residents of those facilities. Residents or their proxies who are dissatisfied with facility compliance generally can request the state to enforce these requirements. In addition, these rights can be the basis for private law suits.[61]

In addition to state social service and health statutes, their primary sources of rights, nursing home residents can look to state human or civil rights laws regulating discrimination on the basis of race, sex, age, and handicap, as well as state consumer protection laws and other similar provisions. In addition, state guardianship, conservatorship, and probate laws are important to nursing home residents because so many are mentally impaired. These laws regulate personal and financial decision making by and for impaired persons. Nursing home personnel often assume that they or relatives of nursing home residents are empowered to make decisions for impaired residents. While this sometimes is true, often it is not. Guardianship and related laws determine when and within what limits surrogate decision making is lawful, indicate who may act for another, and dictate the procedures that must be followed before a surrogate can be appointed.[62]

Other important surrogate decision-making devices available in some states include the Living Will or Natural Death Acts, which regulate decision making for terminally ill individuals,[63] and durable power of attorney provisions.[64] These latter instruments authorize an individual to designate another to make decisions for that individual if disability or impairment prevents making decisions on his or her own.

COMMON LAW RIGHTS

In addition to the constitutional, statutory, and regulatory sources of resident rights discussed thus far, one should be aware that nursing homes are subject to common law obligations imposed by the courts. Of most relevance to nursing homes are judicial decisions involving various tort claims. A nursing home undertakes to provide care and medical services to its residents. If it fails to do so or does so negligently, and a patient is injured as a direct result, the home may be held liable. Similarly, the home may be liable for injuries intentionally caused to residents of the home by employees. Nursing home recognition of the potential for liability should lead to careful supervision of employees and enhancement of the quality of care.[65]

Another tort doctrine of considerable importance to nursing home residents is the body of cases imposing liability on health care providers for treatment without consent. In general, a physician may not provide treatment except in an emergency without the voluntary, informed, and competent consent of the patient or an authorized substitute. This body of law has recently been of great importance in several well-known cases involving termination of care to comatose or terminally ill patients. In the future, it is likely to be of considerable importance in nursing homes.[66]

Ordinarily, a contractual relationship exists between a nursing home and its residents. Nursing homes enter into contracts with the state and federal governments. These contractual provisions can directly or indirectly confer rights upon residents of nursing homes, and private litigation to enforce these contractually agreed upon obligations can be commenced by nursing home residents.[67]

ENFORCEMENT

The obligation to respect the rights outlined above lies principally with the facility. It is in a facility's own interest to honor resident rights, to be sensitive to resident needs, to keep informed of developments, and to train its staff (including unlicensed personnel) to respect residents' rights. Doing so is both good human relations policy and good business. Failing to do so may expose the facility to considerable financial and legal risk. Many of the most commonly cited violations of nursing home resident rights, such as failure to respect privacy, failure to consult residents prior to making decisions affecting them, and the imposition of improper restraints, are problems that a well-run facility with a sensitive and well-trained staff can avoid.

Enforcement of resident rights, particularly those derived from state and federal statutory and regulatory sources, rests with the states and, to a lesser degree, with DHHS. Annual inspections can reveal violations of rights. In addition, complaints can be filed with the state regulatory agencies by residents, their families, and others. Increasingly, states have enacted formal complaint resolution mechanisms and are obligated under state law to investigate promptly and act on complaints. In addition, the states have ombudsman programs designed to work with nursing homes and their residents to ensure that nursing home residents' rights are respected. These state agencies vary substantially in their organization, size, and effectiveness of operation. In addition, outside volunteers ranging from church groups to consumer and legal advocacy organizations frequently visit facilities to assist residents. In some states these groups have formal, recognized rights of access, while in others they do not. States are experimenting with other devices to ensure compliance with federal and state regulatory standards concerning resident rights. For example, some states require employees of facilities to report rights violations to the administrator of the home or to a state regulatory agency.[68]

As noted earlier, the principal problem of nursing home residents is not the lack of rights theoretically available to protect them but the lack of effective means by which to ensure that these rights are respected. The primary enforcement device available to the federal government is decertification from Medicare or Medicaid when facilities do not comply with federal Conditions of Participation. States may withdraw or revoke the license of a facility which is seriously deficient and/or decertify the facility from Medicaid participation. In addition, many states are experimenting with a range of financial and other intermediate sanctions to induce compliance with quality of care standards and respect for the rights of nursing home residents. Civil fines, reduction in licensed capacity, the authority to withdraw or reduce the number of Medicaid residents, the use of receiverships, and negative reimbursement adjustments are all examples of recent state initiatives.[69]

Thus far, little is known about the effectiveness of these devices in enforcing quality of care standards and inducing compliance with nursing home residents' rights. A careful study should be undertaken.

Another area worthy of study is the use of private dispute resolution mechanisms for disputes concerning resident treatment decisions and violations of residents' rights. In the consumer and labor areas, for example, we are increasingly relying on alternative dispute resolution mechanisms. Some experimentation with devices of this kind in the nursing home area might be fruitful.

As mentioned previously, residents can claim rights under private contract and tort doctrines. Typically, a privately brought suit is the vehicle by which the existence of these rights is confirmed and sanctions are imposed for violations of rights.

In addition, private litigation by nursing home residents can be used as an enforcement device for rights conferred by federal or state laws and regulations. Some states have explicitly authorized private suits by patients as a means of enforcing the rights provisions found in state law.[70] Private actions can enforce federally created standards as well. For example, a federal court of appeals ruled recently in a Colorado class action suit that the Medicaid sections of the Social Security Act require DHHS to assure itself that nursing home residents actually receive adequate care.[71]

RIGHTS OF ACCESS TO NURSING HOMES

In many geographic areas nursing homes enjoy high occupancy rates. These high rates permit nursing homes to be selective in their choice of residents. Medicaid recipients, persons whose conditions require special attention, and minority group members frequently experience difficulty in obtaining access to nursing homes.[72]

Although Medicaid reimbursement is important to the nursing home industry, Medicaid-eligible persons frequently have more difficulty entering nursing homes than do private-pay patients.[73] Medicaid reimbursement rates often are lower than the rates nursing homes charge for private-pay residents; consequently, nursing homes prefer to fill beds with private-pay residents whenever possible. In addition, some nursing homes require that all residents initially enter the facility as private-pay patients. Only after a period as a private-pay patient will the facility permit the individual to apply for Medicaid and convert to Medicaid status. Several states have responded to this problem. New Jersey has imposed a requirement that nursing homes accept Medicaid residents as a condition of licensure.[74] Minnesota prohibits nursing homes participating in Medicaid from charging private-pay residents a rate higher than that paid by the state for Medicaid patients.[75] This law is intended to reduce the economic incentive to prefer private-pay over Medicaid residents. The private-pay duration-of-stay agreements arguably violate federal law and have been the subject of several state initiatives recently.[76]

To reduce the reluctance of nursing homes to accept Medicaid residents because of inadequate reimbursement levels, nursing home residents and their advocates can profitably join with the nursing home industry to seek adequate reimbursement from the state legislatures.

"Heavy-care residents" have difficulty in obtaining access to nursing homes due primarily to state reimbursement rates that provide few economic inducements. As a consequence, nursing homes are reluctant to take such persons because of the higher costs of providing services to them. The result is that those most in need of nursing home care frequently are unable to obtain it. A few states have begun to address this problem by revising their Medicaid reimbursement rate to reward facilities caring for heavy-care residents.[77]

Minority group members tend to be underrepresented in the nursing home population. The reasons for this are not clear. However, if this is the product of discrimination based upon race, such discrimination is unlawful under the Civil Rights Act of 1964 and under state civil rights statutes.[78]

TRANSFERS

Nursing homes are part of a continuum of care. Residents come to nursing homes from their own homes, from hospitals, and from other settings. Nursing home residents have a legitimate concern about their treatment by the health care system.[79] Frequently, the decision to send a person to a nursing home is not initiated by that person. Family members unable to provide home-based care or hospitals concerned about the unavailability of reimbursement or the need to fill hospital beds with new patients may initiate the transfer of a patient to a nursing home. Our present structure does not fully protect persons from unwanted or inappropriate placement in a nursing home. Nursing homes should be careful to ensure that competent residents referred to them truly consent to admission to the facility. Further, the facility should accept only those residents for whom it is capable of caring.

LEVEL OF CARE TRANSFERS

Residents whose care is reimbursed by public sources, either Medicaid or Medicare, often are transferred from one facility to another, or from one section of a facility to another section, or from a facility back into the community, because a utilization review committee or similar entity determines that the patient no longer needs a certain level of care. Since transfers can affect patient health adversely, protection against abrupt and unwanted transfers to, from, and within facilities is important to nursing home residents. In recent years several states have supplemented the federal protections against unwanted transfer by imposing additional requirements that must be satisfied prior to transfer of a resident. In addition, litigation has been commenced to enhance the protections available in such situations.[80]

HEALTH CARE COSTS

The dramatic rise in Medicaid expenditures in recent years has prompted concern about the cost of financing long-term care. In some states, nursing home reimbursement constitutes well over 50 percent of the state Medicaid budget. As a result, the federal government and many state legislatures and Medicaid agencies desire to tighten eligibility requirements and to take other measures to reduce long-term health care costs.[81]

An example of the rising concern over the high cost of long-term care is the recent effort to revive relative responsibility requirements. A traditional feature of public welfare law is the attempt to require families to share a portion of the cost of public assistance provided to family members. This concept, termed "relative responsibility", conditions payment of public assistance upon the willingness of spouses, parents, and children to bear a portion of the financial burden of caring for the family member needing care. The issue of greatest present concern is whether adult children should be required to pay a portion of the cost of caring for their elderly parents. DHHS has indicated that the Social Security Act does not bar states from imposing financial responsibility upon adult children to care for their elderly parents. This represents a reversal of prior policy by DHHS. Substantial questions surround the lawfulness of this policy change. Although most states have not yet begun to impose upon family members the cost of caring for elderly parents, several states have indicated an interest in so doing.[82]

Barriers to Medicaid eligibility, adverse level of care decisions, and reimbursement formula alterations all affect ability to obtain nursing home care and to ensure that care received is of decent quality. Persons concerned about nursing home residents can join with the nursing home industry to ensure that cost control decisions are not made in such a way as to harm individuals needing nursing home care.

Although most persons requiring long-term care receive such care at home, state payment mechanisms for long-term care reward institutional care in nursing homes rather than home-based care. As a result, some nursing home patients could receive care at home, if financing for such care were available. States have begun to provide some financing for home-based long-term care. Important policy questions are how to organize and finance such care, who should be authorized to provide care, and how acceptable quality can be assured.[83]

RIGHTS WITHIN FAMILIES

Disputes frequently arise within families over how an elderly family member should be cared for, whether to transfer an elderly person to a nursing home, how to pay for nursing home care, and other aspects of medical or financial care of an older relative. Facilities should be sensitive to such issues. Often there is no easy resolution of these disputes. Older persons' interests frequently are ignored or sacrificed by their families. Rights advocates and public policy planners must devote substantial attention to questions of rights and responsibilities within the family.

CONCLUSION

As the nursing home rights movement enters its second decade, its focus will shift from the establishment of basic human rights for residents of homes to issues of enforcement and to the broad and complex systemic issues outlined in this chapter. It is likely that new strategies will be needed and new alliances will be formed. While I believe that progress will continue, I do not underestimate the difficulty of the task. We need to examine the reforms just instituted to see which hold the most promise. I also urge that we look to the reform efforts in related fields, such as mental health. There is much to learn.

NOTES

1. Scanlon, W.J., Feder, J.M., *The Long Term Care Market Place: An Overview,* HEALTHCARE FINANCIAL MANAGEMENT 14(1):18–30 (January 1984) [hereinafter cited as Scanlon and Feder].
2. *Id.* at 19.
3. *Id.* at 18–19.
4. P.L. GRIMALDI, MEDICAID REIMBURSEMENT OF NURSING HOME CARE (American Enterprise Institute for Public Policy Research, Washington, D.C.) (1982) at 7. *See also* NATIONAL SENIOR CITIZENS LAW CENTER, NURSING HOME LAW: A LEGAL SERVICES MANUAL (Office of Program Support, Legal Services Corp., Washington, D.C.) (1982) at 2 [hereinafter cited as NURSING HOME LAW].
5. GRIMALDI, *supra* note 4, at 7.
6. R.N. BROWN, THE RIGHTS OF OLDER PERSONS (Avon Books, New York) (1979) at 242 [hereinafter referred to as RIGHTS OF OLDER PERSONS].

7. *Id.* at 244. A third kind of nursing home is an intermediate care facility for the mentally retarded. Not included in my discussion are board and care homes providing nonmedical custodial assistance with daily life. These facilities, which exist in most areas of the country, frequently are used for housing former state mental hospital patients. Medicare and Medicaid reimbursement is unavailable for care in these facilities and they are governed, if at all, by regulatory standards and agencies different from those responsible for nursing homes. Although the problems experienced by residents of these facilities are similar to those experienced by nursing home residents, until recently little attention has been paid to these problems. The ABA Commissions on Legal Problems of the Elderly and on the Mentally Disabled conducted a major study which culminated in a model act regulating board and care homes. *See* Beyer, J., Bulkley, J., Hopkins, P., *A Model Act Regulating Board and Care Homes: Guidelines for States*, MENTAL AND PHYSICAL DISABILITY LAW REPORTER 8(2):150–251 (March–April 1984).

8. U.S. National Center for Health Statistics, *The National Nursing Home Survey: 1977 Summary for the United States* in VITAL AND HEALTH STATISTICS, SERIES 13 No. 43 (U.S. Gov't Printing Office, Washington, D.C.) (1979).

9. Scanlon and Feder, *supra* note 1, at 25–26.

10. *Id.* at 18.

11. Brown, R.N., *An Appraisal of the Nursing Home Enforcement Process*, ARIZONA LAW REVIEW 17(2):304, 313 (1975) [hereinafter referred to as *Nursing Home Enforcement*].

12. Scanlon and Feder, *supra* note 1, at 25–26.

13. *See* D. LYONS, RIGHTS (Madsworth Publishing Co., Inc., Los Angeles, Ca.) (1979); Martin, R., Nickel, J.W., *Recent Work on the Concept of Rights*, AMERICAN PHILOSOPHICAL QUARTERLY 17(3):165–80 (July 1980).

14. *See* R. KLUGER, SIMPLE JUSTICE: THE HISTORY OF BROWN V. BOARD OF EDUCATION & BLACK AMERICA'S STRUGGLE FOR EQUALITY (Vintage Trade Books, New York) (2d ed. 1977).

15. *See* D. RUDOVSKY, A.J. BRONSTEIN, E.I. KOREN, THE RIGHTS OF PRISONERS (Avon Books, New York) (2d ed. 1977).

16. *See* Lyon, M.A., Levine, M.L., Zusman, J., *Patient's Bill of Rights: A Survey of State Statutes*, MENTAL DISABILITY LAW REPORTER 6(3):178–201 (May-June 1982); Brown, P., *Public Policy and the Rights of Mental Patients*, MENTAL DISABILITY LAW REPORTER 6(1):55 (January/February 1982); Paschall, N., Eichler, A., *Rights Promotion in the 1980s*, MENTAL DISABILITY LAW REPORTER 6(2):116 (March/April 1982). *See generally* S.S. HERR, S. ARONS, R. WALLACE, LEGAL RIGHTS AND MENTAL-HEALTH CARE (Lexington Books, Lexington, Mass.) (1983).

17. *See* S.S. HERR, RIGHTS AND ADVOCACY FOR RETARDED PEOPLE (Lexington Books, Lexington, Mass.) (1983); P.R. FRIEDMAN, THE RIGHTS OF MENTALLY RETARDED PERSONS (Avon Books, New York) (1976); Garvey, J.H., *Freedom and Choice in Constitutional Law*, HARVARD LAW REVIEW 94(7):1756–94 (May 1981).

18. *See* G.J. ANNAS, THE RIGHTS OF HOSPITAL PATIENTS (Avon Books, New York) (1975).

19. *Nursing Home Enforcement, supra* note 11, at 317.
20. *Nursing Home Enforcement, supra* note 11, at 313–14; NURSING HOME LAW, *supra* note 4, at 4. *See generally* Butler, P.A., *Assuring the Quality of Care and Life in Nursing Homes: The Dilemma of Enforcement,* NORTH CAROLINA LAW REVIEW 57(5):1317–80 (June 1979) [hereinafter referred to as *Assuring Quality Care*].
21. *See generally* RIGHTS AND ADVOCACY FOR RETARDED PEOPLE, *supra* note 17; LEGAL RIGHTS AND MENTAL-HEALTH CARE, *supra* note 16.
22. *See Nursing Home Enforcement, supra* note 11, at 333.
23. Jones, N.E., *Termination of Skilled Nursing Facility Medicaid Provider Agreements: Procedural Due Process Requirements,* AMERICAN JOURNAL OF LAW & MEDICINE 6(4):451–96 (Winter 1981).
24. 447 U.S. 773 (1980).
25. *Id.* at 781.
26. *Id.* at 785–86.
27. *Id.* at 787–88.
28. *Id.* at 788–89.
29. *See* Bumpus v. Clark, 681 F.2d 679 (9th Cir. 1982); Punikaia v. Clark, 720 F.2d 564 (9th Cir. 1983).
30. *See generally* J.E. NOWAK, R.D. ROTUNDA, J.N. YOUNG, CONSTITUTIONAL LAW (West Publishing Co., St. Paul, Minn.) (2d ed. 1983) at ch. 14.
31. 457 U.S. 991 (1982).
32. *Id.* at 1012.
33. *Id.* at 1027–28. Other courts have considered whether a nursing home is sufficiently public to invoke constitutional protection. *See* Hoyt v. St. Mary's Rehabilitation Center, 711 F.2d 864 (8th Cir. 1983); Cape Cod Nursing Home v. Rambling Rose Rest Home, 667 F.2d 238 (1st Cir. 1981); Wagner v. Sheltz, 471 F.Supp. 903 (D. Conn. 1979); Fuzie v. Manor Care Inc., 461 F. Supp. 689 (N.D. Ohio 1977); Stitt v. Manor Care Inc., Medicare and Medicaid Guide (CCH) ¶29,409 (N.D. Ohio 1978).
34. 397 U.S. 254 (1970).
35. *See generally* S. BREYER, R. STEWART, ADMINISTRATIVE LAW AND REGULATORY POLICY (Little, Brown & Co., Boston) (1979) at ch. 7.
36. *See, e.g,* Connecticut Board of Pardons v. Dumschat, 452 U.S. 458 (1981); Hewitt v. Helms, 103 S.Ct. 864 (1983); Olim v. Wakinekona, 103 S.Ct. 1741 (1983).
37. *See, e.g.,* Skilled Nursing Facilities, 42 C.F.R. §405.1121(k) (1982); Standards for Intermediate Care Facilities for the Mentally Retarded, 42 C.F.R. §§442.402–406 (1982).
38. The list of rights presented in the text is a summary of the provisions of 42 C.F.R. §405.1121(k) (1982). More detailed information on these rights can be found in Brown, R.N., *A Bill of Rights for Nursing Home Patients,* TRIAL 13(5):22–28 (May 1977); Wilson, S.H., *Nursing Home Patients' Rights: Are They Enforceable?* THE GERONTOLOGIST 18(3):255–61 (June 1978) [hereinafter cited as Wilson].
39. Soskis, C.W., *Teaching Nursing Home Staff About Patients' Rights,* THE GERONTOLOGIST 21(4):424–30 (August 1981) [hereinafter cited as Soskis]; Harris,

S., *Protecting Residents' Rights,* AMERICAN HEALTH CARE ASSOCIATION JOURNAL 8(1):3 (January 1982).

40. *See generally* B.C. VLADECK, UNLOVING CARE (Basic Books, Inc., New York) (1980); RIGHTS OF OLDER PERSONS, *supra* note 6, at ch. 8.

41. 42 C.F.R. §405.1122(k)(9); *see* Soskis, *supra* note 39. The vagueness of the bill of rights is partially alleviated by the interpretive guidelines issued by DHHS which help nursing home residents, their families, facilities, and state surveyors better understand the content of the rights policies. *See* Wilson, *supra* note 38, at 255–61.

42. Skilled Nursing Facilities, 42 C.F.R. §405.1121(k)(3), (11), (12), (13), (14).

43. *Id.* §405.1121(k)(7); *see generally* RIGHTS OF OLDER PERSONS, *supra* note 6; Kapp, M.B, *Legal and Ethical Issues in Resident Independence,* AMERICAN HEALTH CARE ASSOCIATION JOURNAL 9(2):22–25 (March 1983) [hereinafter cited as *Legal and Ethical Issues in Resident Independence*].

44. *See generally Legal and Ethical Issues in Resident Independence, supra* note 43.

45. See PRESIDENT'S COMMISSION FOR THE STUDY OF ETHICAL PROBLEMS IN MEDICINE AND BIOMEDICAL AND BEHAVIORAL RESEARCH, MAKING HEALTH CARE DECISIONS (U.S. Gov't Printing Office, Washington, D.C.) (1982); PRESIDENT'S COMMISSION FOR THE STUDY OF ETHICAL PROBLEMS IN MEDICINE AND BIOMEDICAL AND BEHAVIORAL RESEARCH, DECIDING TO FOREGO LIFE-SUSTAINING TREATMENT (U.S. Gov't Printing Office, Washington, D.C.) (1983); LEGAL AND ETHICAL ASPECTS OF TREATING CRITICALLY AND TERMINALLY ILL PATIENTS (Doudera, A.E., Peters, J.D., eds.) (AUPHA Press, Ann Arbor, Mich.) (1982); Kapp, M.B., *Nursing Homes as Teaching Institutions: Legal Issues,* THE GERONTOLOGIST 24(1):55–60 (February 1984), reprinted in chapter 14 of this text.

46. 42 C.F.R. §405.1121(k)(3).

47. *See, e.g.,* Ratzan, R.M., *Being Old Makes You Different: The Ethics of Research with Elderly Subjects,* HASTINGS CENTER REPORT 10(5):32–42 (October 1980).

48. AMERICAN HEALTH CARE ASSOCIATION, QUESTIONABLY COMPETENT LONG TERM CARE RESIDENTS: PROBLEMS AND POSSIBLE SOLUTIONS (American Health Care Association, Washington, D.C.) (1982) at 2 [hereinafter cited as AMERICAN HEALTH CARE ASSOCIATION].

49. 42 C.F.R. §405.1121(k).

50. AMERICAN HEALTH CARE ASSOCIATION, *supra* note 48; Jost, D.T., *The Problem of Consent for Placement, Care and Treatment of the Incompetent Nursing Home Resident,* ST. LOUIS UNIVERSITY LAW JOURNAL 26(1):63–104 (December 1981).

51. CALDWELL, J.M., KAPP, M.B., *The Rights of Nursing Home Patients: Possibilities and Limitations of Federal Regulation,* JOURNAL OF HEALTH POLITICS, POLICY AND LAW 6(1):40–48 (Spring 1981); Kapp, M.B., *Protecting the Rights of Nursing Home Patients: Using Federal Law,* FLORIDA BAR JOURNAL 55:212–15 (March 1981).

52. 46 Fed. Reg. 7408 (January 23, 1981). In a separate undertaking, DHHS issued a final rule concerning the protection of nursing home patients' personal funds. 45 Fed. Reg. 49,440 (July 24, 1980) (to be codified at 42 C.F.R.

§§405,442,447.) These regulations required the final approval of the Office of Management and Budget to become effective, which approval has never been received.

53. 42 C.F.R. §§405.1109–.1137; *Assuring Quality Care, supra* note 20, at 1330.
54. *See generally* NATIONAL CITIZENS' COALITION FOR NURSING HOME REFORM, CONSUMER STATEMENT OF PRINCIPLES FOR THE NURSING HOME REGULATORY SYSTEM—STATE LICENSURE AND FEDERAL CERTIFICATION PROGRAMS (N.C.C.N.H.R., Washington, D.C.) (1983).
55. 42 U.S.C. §2000(d) (1982).
56. *Id.* §6101.
57. 29 U.S.C. §794 (1982).
58. *See, e.g.,* FLA. STATE. ANN. §400.022 (West Supp. 1983); ILL. ANN. STAT. ch. 111 ½ (1977); MICH. COMP. LAWS ANN. §333.20201 (1980); OHIO REV. CODE ANN. §§3721.10–.99 (1980).
59. *Id.*
60. *See, e.g.,* MICH. COMP. LAWS ANN. §§333.21773–76 (1980).
61. *See Assuring Quality Care, supra* note 20, at 1372.
62. Kapp, M.B., *Adult Protective Services: Convincing the Patient to Consent,* LAW, MEDICINE & HEALTH CARE 11(4):163–67 (September 1983) reprinted in chapter 20 of this text.
63. *See* RIGHTS OF OLDER PERSONS, *supra* note 6, at ch. 10; J.A. ROBERTSON, THE RIGHTS OF THE CRITICALLY ILL (Ballinger Publishing Co., Boston) (1983).
64. *See* Note, *Appointing an Agent to Make Medical Treatment Choices,* COLUMBIA LAW REVIEW 84(4):985–1031 (May 1984).
65. *Nursing Home Enforcement, supra* note 11, at 346; *Assuring Quality Care, supra* note 20, at 1369.
66. RIGHTS OF OLDER PERSONS, *supra* note 6, ch. 10.
67. *Nursing Home Enforcement, supra* note 11, at 349.
68. *See generally* Regan, J.J., *When Nursing Home Patients Complain: The Ombudsman or the Patient Advocate,* GEORGETOWN LAW JOURNAL 65(3):691–738 (February 1977); COMMISSION ON LEGAL PROBLEMS OF THE ELDERLY, AMERICAN BAR ASSOCIATION, MODEL RECOMMENDATION: INTERMEDIATE SANCTIONS FOR ENFORCEMENT OF QUALITY OF CARE IN NURSING HOMES (American Bar Association, Chicago) (1981).
69. *Assuring Quality Care, supra* note 20, at 1347–76.
70. *Assuring Quality Care, supra* note 20, at 1369–76.
71. *In re* Estate of Smith, 747 F.2d 583 (10th Cir. 1984); *see also Assuring Quality Care, supra* note 20, at 1373.
72. RIGHTS OF OLDER PERSONS, *supra* note 6.
73. *Id. See* NURSING HOME LAW, *supra* note 4, at ch. 6.
74. New Jersey Association of Health Care Facilities v. Finley, Medicare and Medicaid Guide (CCH) TT 30,535 (N.D. New Jersey 1980).
75. Minnesota Association of Health Care Facilities, Inc. v. Minnesota Department of Public Welfare, 742 F.2d 442 (8th Cir. 1984).
76. 42 U.S.C. §1396 h(d)(2)(A) (1984); Glengariff v. Snook, Medicare and Medicaid (CCH) TT 33,605 (N.D.N.Y. 1984); Bellotti v. Kimwell Nursing Home,

Civ. Act. No. 124745 (Mass. June 23, 1978); *see also* National Senior Citizens Law Center, NURSING HOME LAW LETTER, issue 76 (August 1983).

77. *See generally* J. HOLAHAN, STATE RATE SETTING AND THE EFFECTS OF NURS-ING HOME COSTS (Urban Institute, Washington, D.C.) (1983).
78. 42 U.S.C. §2000(d) (1984).
79. Donahue, W.T., *What About Our Responsibility Toward the Abandoned Elderly?* THE GERONTOLOGIST 18(2):102–11 (April 1978).
80. *See, e.g.,* MICH. COMP. LAWS ANN. §§333.21773–75 (West 1980).
81. National Health Law Program, *Health Care for the Poor During 1983: A Time of Reassessment and Transition,* CLEARINGHOUSE REVIEW 17(9):976–88 (January 1984); C. ESTES, *et al.,* FISCAL AUSTERITY AND AGING: SHIFTING GOVERN-MENTAL RESPONSIBILITY FOR THE ELDERLY (Sage Publishers, New York) (1983).
82. *See generally* Scanlon and Feder, *supra* note 1; NURSING HOME LAW LETTER, 66–69, 80–81 (National Senior Citizens Law Center, Washington, D.C.) (1982–84).
83. *See generally* Scanlon and Feder, *supra* note 1.

16

Nursing Homes and the Least-Restrictive Environment Doctrine

Elias S. Cohen, M.P.A., J.D.

This chapter addresses the rights of a group of elderly persons who need ongoing long-term care and have few choices. Frequently, these elderly persons are mentally impaired, poor, and dependent upon public financial support. More often than not, they are confronted with a lack of choice that is psychologically tantamount to coercion. This lack of choice produces inordinately acquiescent behavior that places these elderly persons in a life situation that impairs their normal exercise of liberty. Those of us concerned with the well-being of the elderly must focus on the nature of the "liberty" to which frail, mentally impaired old people are entitled, and on the nature of developments in law, medicine, and social services, the new technologies of service delivery, and the new definitions which have been applied to those who are impaired.

THE INHABITANTS OF NURSING HOMES

Tonight about 1.3 million elderly people will be put to bed in America's nursing homes—a number that is about 40 to 50 percent greater than those of all ages who will bed down in general hospitals.[1] About 55 percent of nursing home residents rely on Medicaid payments to support their stay in the home.[2]

The average age at admission is just above 80,[3] and the median age of the residents is over 80 years.[4] About three-fourths of all residents in nursing homes are women.[5] The vast majority of them, men and women, are widowed and alone.[6] Only about 15 percent were never married.[7] It is estimated that about one-third of those in nursing homes are without immediate families and virtually alone; about half have no one nearby.[8] Nursing home residents *are* disabled—physically and mentally. Indeed, nursing homes may be termed the new mental hospitals of America. Moreover, there are studies which suggest that for every impaired nursing home resident, there are between 1 and 2.5 similarly impaired persons living in the community.[9]

If one lives to be 80, it is likely that he or she will spend some time in a nursing home, and the chances are about 1 in 4.5 that death will occur there.[10] The average length of stay is nearly three years.[11]

FUTURE GROWTH AND PAST TRANS-INSTITUTIONALIZATION

The numbers involved are huge and will grow. To give some idea of the volume we are confronting, consider that between now and the year 2010 the population 85 and over is expected to double.[12] Since it is the very old who primarily use nursing homes, if we continue to admit patients to nursing homes without introducing some very radical procedural and programmatic changes, it will be necessary for public, profit, and non-profit resources to create an additional 1,000 beds for America's nursing home stock every week between now and the end of the century.

It is not necessary to recite here the statistics on the growth of the nursing home industry. However, it is useful to consider the demographic shifts that have occurred as a result of what has been inaccurately termed "deinstitutionalization" from mental hospitals, as well as from the closing of mental hospital doors to those elderly who had been admitted in the past.

In 1952 I served as Assistant Superintendent at Manteno State Hospital in Manteno, Illinois. That was 1952 B.T. (Before Thorazine). Manteno was not the largest such facility, but it was, unfortunately, not unusual considering the number of mental hospitals in America with more than 1,000 patients. Manteno was not as big as Pilgrim State in New York, which had 13,000 patients, nor as large as Milledgeville in Georgia with 12,000 patients. It was a little bit bigger than Byberry in Philadelphia which had only 6,000 and was nearly matched by other behemoths like Chicago State Hospital and Elgin State Hospital, both in Illinois, and Rockland State Hospital in New York of *Snakepit* fame. In a commendable fit of revulsion, combined with a variety of other professional and sociological factors, state mental hospitals of America, which once housed about 560,000 patients, began in the 1950s the long process of closing their wards, dumping their patients into communities which were not prepared with supportive services, and closing their doors to those who did not fit the new and stringent criteria for admission. The development of psychotropic drugs made patient management an easier affair in smaller institutions staffed largely by nonprofessional nursing personnel without any psychiatric training, much less psychiatric supervision.

Wilma Donahue, in her 1978 Kent lecture delivered to the Gerontological Society of America,[13] spelled out in painful detail and effectively analyzed the obstacles which thwarted efforts to achieve real deinstitutionalization. She highlighted the ineffective and inadequate fiscal planning that attended the shifts in locus of service, the impact of decisions like *O'Connor v. Donaldson*[14] and *Wyatt v. Stickney,*[15] the failure of community mental health centers, the pressures from the profit-making sector, and negative community attitudes. Furthermore, she noted that the availability of federal Medicaid dollars created an enormous pressure to shift patients from the sole fiscal responsibility of the states to become the joint responsibility of state and federal governments.

In the mid-1950s, about 160,000 of the 560,000 patients in public mental hospitals were 65 and older.[16] Recently, that figure had dropped to about 42,000.[17] Obviously, in the generation since 1955, hundreds of thousands of elderly people have been shunted to other types of facilities and arrangements.

None of this suggests that the monstrous mental hospitals of the 1950s should not have been emptied. It does suggest, however, that we have created some new entities for a very frail and vulnerable group for whom few protections, legal or ethical, exist.

The Admissions Process

How do patients get into nursing homes? How many patients give voluntary, competent informed consent to their admission to a nursing home? How many patients (and this may sound very strange) enjoy the benefits of a commitment proceeding, the assistance of counsel, and other due process rights concerning their "incarceration" in a nursing home? Under what circumstances and conditions are decisions made regarding admission of a patient to a nursing home?

The scenarios are all too familiar. Let me indicate a few examples, taking into account the characteristics of the older people that I have mentioned above. First, consider Mary Jones, an 80-year-old, white female living alone on Supplemental Security Income (SSI) on the second floor of a walk-up apartment in a run-down section of the city, who falls and suffers a hip fracture. The open reduction of her fracture is successful, and her recovery from the surgery is uncomplicated. While in the hospital, she is diagnosed as having some cardiac decompensation, anemia, and arthritis in her hands and elbows. After 14 days of hospitalization, the utilization review committee finds she is no longer in need of hospital care. Upon notification, the hospital social service staff makes 38 frantic phone calls before locating a nursing home which will care for Ms. Jones. No provision is made to investigate the potential for rehabilitation, housing rearrangements, home health services, or chore services, any of which might have enabled her to return to her home or another community setting. Mary is presented the "opportunity" to enter the nursing home, which will provide good care for her until she is able to return to her own home. Neither the hospital nor the Medicaid agency, nor for that matter the nursing home or anyone else, will undertake the case management function necessary to seek the community services which might make it possible for her to avoid nursing home care altogether or to return home in a short time following a full course of successful rehabilitation. To add to the drama, we learn that Mary's stay in the nursing home exceeds 60 days, a period beyond which her SSI cannot continue, and so she loses her apartment in the community. Mary's "opportunities" dwindle, and she faces life in a nursing home for the rest of her days.

Then, consider the case of John Smith, who lives alone and is becoming increasingly impaired as a result of Alzheimer's disease. He is increasingly bewildered, frequently lost within just a few blocks of home, and unable to carry out his shopping, laundry, and other basic requirements of daily living. One day he trips on the curb, falls, cuts his head, and is taken to the local hospital emergency room. He is treated, but he is unable to tell anyone where he lives. He is placed temporarily in an urban shelter or some similar facility which can accommodate him for only 48 to 72 hours. During this time, arrangements are made to place Mr. Smith in an intermediate care facility where he will be assured of a decent place to sleep, three square meals a day, and an oak chair in front of a television set. There is no formal commitment proceeding, no case management effort, and no arrangement for community services which might have made possible his remaining in the community.

Last, we have Rebecca Williams, an 83-year-old, frail, mildly forgetful, white female, who falls ill with influenza that keeps her in bed a good bit of the time in her modest urban apartment. She has a Social Security income of $295 a month. During her illness, her neighbors attempt to shop for her and arrange an occasional meal. She deteriorates and develops complete urinary incontinence. When informed, the visiting nurse society arranges for home visits. Ms. Williams continues to deteriorate and is admitted to a general hospital. After three days, the utilization review committee finds that she is no longer in need of acute care, although her incontinence has continued. Arrangements are made for nursing home care, and the scenario proceeds as with Mary Jones.

None of these examples is novel or unique; variations of these tragic situations occur repeatedly in communities and hospitals all over America. Thus far, to my knowledge, no lawsuits have been brought against hospitals for their failure to make appropriate arrangements in accordance with community standards and state-of-the-art knowledge of social services, case management, or adequate rehabilitation. Nor has anyone been sued for damages stemming from an involuntary incarceration in an inherently coercive environment.

How is it that so much deprivation of freedom, so much intrusion on the rights of older people, can occur without litigation on their behalf?

How is it that so many health and social agencies, physicians, nurses, and social workers—the helping professions—have participated in the wholesale deprivation of liberty and rights of impaired older people?

The answers are complex, and lie in our historical notions about how rights are vindicated, our historical fictions concerning vendor payments and unrestricted grants, and our historical notions about the definitions of liberty.

THE CLAIM-BASED SOCIETY

A benevolent Congress, politically responsive state and local legislatures, and a relatively affluent society have conferred a wide array of benefits upon America's elderly population.[18] In varying degrees, benefits have been conferred upon the elderly who are poor, disabled, unemployed, or mentally ill. Additionally, Medicare and the Social Security Old Age Program brings benefits and services to all—regardless of need or disability.

However, benefits and entitlements in our country are not self-executing. This is true of public and private benefits. To take advantage of commercial warranties and guarantees one must file a claim. Similarly, individuals must press their own cases for Social Security benefits, food stamps, health services, social services, or similar bounties. Even where there is no possible basis for *requiring* a claim to be filed (as opposed to mandating an automatic delivery of a benefit), we require applications to be made. For example, Social Security Old Age (Title 2) benefits are available to persons 72 and over, and no earned income limitation applies.[19] Why doesn't the Social Security Administration just send the money, particularly when they have an address for a previously employed worker? In all instances, a claim must be filed. We live in what I have termed a claim-based society.

A claim-based approach to benefits makes certain presumptions about claimants: they must be independent, motivated, and knowledge-able about their rights and have some means of access to legal services or accounting services. An impaired old person, while not incompetent or in need of a conservator or a representative payee, will likely not function in accordance with these presumptions, and as a result may be penalized. Frequently, the very old are alone, frail, and dependent economically, physically and psychologically. They are often tired and have low physical and psychological reserves. Here a presumption that an assertive claim-ant will protest when his or her rights are invaded, denied, or withheld is unrealistic. As a result, society is failing to protect the rights of those older adults who are not able to protect themselves.

This presumption discriminates viciously against those members of society who are reticent to file claims, ignorant of their own entitlements, physically immobile, or unable to comprehend the complex world of public benefit systems. Those who have family or friends to assist them in asserting their claims may manage reasonably well. They have the advan-tage, not only of knowing what they want, but of having someone who can give effect to their decisions.

THE TORTUOUS PATH TO THE LEAST-RESTRICTIVE ENVIRONMENT

The least-restrictive environment doctrine is part of a time honored tra-dition in American jurisprudence.[20] It has an attractive logic on its face. The logic, however, springs from an eighteenth century characterization of the relationship between citizen and government, where government had the power to fetter the individual for the good of many, but only as much as was absolutely essential.

In the nursing home context, the analysis is not limited to a "re-strictive environment" composed in terms of locked wards versus un-locked wards, leave provisions, or even institutional routines.[21] The issue has to do with restrictions on autonomy which translate into restrictions on the entire array of choices that people make in their daily lives. This concept may include decisions about what shirt to wear, whether to have eggs or cereal or baked beans for breakfast, whether to watch channel 10 or channel 6 on the television, whether to go out and walk in the rain or stay in, whether to keep the house at 64 degrees or 72 degrees, whether to go away for the weekend or go to the park for the day, and whether to spend time with a friend or alone.

The procedures surrounding nursing home placement may indi-cate the extent to which a patient's decision to enter a home is voluntary. What level of participation did the patient engage in, what information was he or she given, what assistance was he or she given in assessing the proper claims for community services, what case management services might he or she have been assured of, and what legal assistance was provided? One might also ask: Under what circumstances were the facts explained? Was he or she surrounded by a gaggle of white-coated physicians, nurses, social workers, and others, all of whom were assuring the patient that their only interest was in him or her? Was the patient importuned by professionals or family "to do it for me"? Was the patient presented a picture of no alternatives and utter unavailability of community services? In other words, was the environment an inherently coercive one, where the patient was surrounded by people all wearing the badges of authority and on whom the patient was dependent (or perceived that he or she was dependent)?

Getting to the question of the least-restrictive environment requires some definition of the competing interests. First, there are conflicting interests within the hospital itself. The hospital has a clear interest in minimizing unreimbursed care caused by "excessive days." The hospital's fiscal interest may be in conflict with the hospital's interest in carrying out its traditional duty to provide the patient with proper care that will positively affect his or her recovery. The interest in avoiding excess days may overwhelm other interests, or at least give them a somewhat lower priority.

Second, there are the patient's interests and his or her perception of them. Those interests range from survival to achieving the highest possible quality of life measured by the reasonable exercise of autonomy, enjoyment, and sense of self-worth. Finally, the state has an interest in those patients who rely on Medicaid. It is a trifurcated interest balancing cost, administrative convenience, and patient care. This balance must be struck in accordance with the professional state of the art which requires the inclusion of case management and health and social services in the community as well as acute medical care delivered on an inpatient basis.

In terms of a least-restrictive environment analysis, at some point the everyday components of life in the nursing home must be considered. Nursing home patients are to a certain extent incarcerated individuals subject to considerable regulation of their freedom and considerable limitation on their choices. The restrictions may include limitations on the freedom to associate or to travel and on residents' expectations of privacy. The absence of any due process in the deprivation of these freedoms is combined with the total regulation of the patient's life by the physician who, according to the Patient's Bill of Rights promulgated in the Code of Federal Regulations,[22] has the power to interdict the Constitution of the United States—a power generally denied to everybody else.

As a threshold hypothesis, one might assert that nursing home patients, mentally impaired or otherwise, are subjected to de facto commitment that confines them against their will or, at the very least, under circumstances that are other than voluntary. This de facto commitment is indistinguishable from a de jure commitment, except for the absence of due process. That suggests that patients entering nursing homes, and who are thus subject to very considerable loss of freedoms, should be entitled to at least the same due process protections that apply to involuntary mental hospital patients.

However, the analogy between nursing homes and mental hospitals is imperfect. The court decisions on mental hospitals have established a right to be released in the absence of treatment.[23] The "fix-up" cases, *Wyatt v. Stickney*[24] and *Willowbrook*,[25] are better analogized to the prison cases,[26] in that the courts were reflecting the public conscience over gross filth, gross neglect, gross overcrowding, and gross understaffing, rather than enunciating a clear and unmistakable finding of a right to treatment. Perhaps the closest we have come thus far is the Third Circuit's ruling in the *Pennhurst* case,[27] which asserts a right to habilitation for the mentally retarded and defines habilitation in explicit terms of community services rather than institutional confinement.

The field of mental retardation seems to have embedded in its very ethos some ethical rights which have become incorporated into rights provided by law.[28] The reasons for the advances in retardation (as opposed to mental health or aging) are related, it seems to me, to a long history—honored in the breach—of children's right to education, recently applied to and vindicated for the retarded in many states. There is a somewhat shorter experience with the Rehabilitation Act of 1973 and the Developmentally Disabled Assistance and Bill of Rights Act of the mid-70s,[29] the U.S. Supreme Court's holding in *Pennhurst* notwithstanding.[30] The Rehabilitation Act's and the DD Act's declarations of Congressional intent have had a significant impact beyond anything comparable for the frail elderly with whom we are concerned here. The Education of All Handicapped Children Act has also been important. A built-in advocacy group of parents of retarded children have in the last 20 years stepped forward and sought the legislative support necessary to advance the notion of a right to habilitation. On these legislative and, in some cases, constitutional, provisions have been engrafted procedural elements that have risen to the level of right. These include such things as individual habilitation plans and explicit kinds of special education particularly suited to the needs of retarded persons.

The elderly in nursing homes are denied such elements of fundamental justice as procedural due process upon prospective incarceration, the right to a multidisciplinary assessment that makes possible differential diagnosis in accordance with the state of the art, the right to case management and periodic review of the plan developed pursuant to the assessment, and finally, the right to less restrictive alternatives to institutional care.

While it is impossible to determine whether the nursing home is the least-restrictive alternative in the absence of some very particular other remedies, it is probably not.

REMEDIES

The remedies are simply stated. First, admission procedures for nursing homes must be amended to assure due process for those in danger of incarceration. This alteration may occur by statute, by common practice, or by common law. There is, at this time, nothing on the horizon either by way of litigation, model statutes, or proposed bills to suggest alterations that would provide for genuine due process protections.

A somewhat more advanced remedy is the alteration of assessment procedures for prospective long-term care patients. An increasing number of states either are experimenting with, or have established by statute, procedures for mandatory preadmission assessments.[31] Furthermore, for several years the federal government has conducted at ten sites around the country a demonstration project known as the channelling program. This program is designed to undertake patient assessments and follow them with case management and application of good community services. The objective is to avoid unnecessary placement in nursing homes.[32] In addition there is currently an effort in one state to establish through litigation the right to assessment, good case management, and delivery of community services for frail elderly persons.[33]

New assessment standards, in my opinion, are more apt to develop through a Medicaid requirement than through case law. However, an assessment process is subject to conversion from a patient care device to an eligibility determination process or a classification scheme governing payments, as we have seen in the case of DRGs. Thus it must be coupled with additional rights. The first of these is the right to case management geared to the needs of frail elderly long-term care patients. Case management is most apt to find its way into practice through requirements set forth in regulations governing Medicaid and subsequently transported to other non-Medicaid patients. Case management, however, is effective only where there are services to be requisitioned on behalf of particular patients. Thus, the right corresponding to assessment and case management is the right to gain access to particular services in the community, or in institutions such as day hospitals, day rehabilitation centers, patient rehabilitation centers, senior center programs, visiting nurse programs, home medical and home social services, and other service settings.

Finally, a warning is offered. In the development of these associated rights, there is a great hazard that they will be applied primarily, if not solely, to patients who are eligible for Medicaid or Medicare. In fact, these rights are needed by *all* patients—private paying or otherwise. It is a sad fact of our times that, while independent wealth is helpful, it is no guarantor of the least-restrictive alternative. This issue is a real challenge to long-term health care providers.

CONCLUSION

The needs for due process in admission to nursing homes, for state-of-the-art assessment to assure accurate identification of problems and solutions for case management to guide the patient through the benefit maze to arrive at the proper treatment, and for the right to claim the treatment of choice (and particularly a range of community services) suggest the need for a combination of ethical, economic, judicial, and legislative solutions. Fundamental to the changes that would adequately respond to the new techonologies of care giving and the growing numbers of the frail is a transformation in the ethics of medicine, nursing, and social work toward treatments and environments in which frail elderly will flourish. This is different from a purely legalistic "least-restrictive alternative" approach.

Furthermore, if this ethical change occurs, the formal due process issues will diminish. However, until it does, there must be some judicial determination on how much process is due the frail elderly being incarcerated in nursing homes. Finally, financial imperatives may drive legislators to amend current statutes, for example, those that favor institutional care over community services.

It appears that while the least-restrictive alternative doctrine was useful in the first generation of cases concerned with mental retardation, mental illness, and even aging, there are new complexities today that leave it somewhat unfulfilling. Similarly, judicial and legislative remedies, while necessary, are not entirely sufficient to fulfill the needs of the elderly.

NOTES

1. U.S. National Center for Health Statistics, *Characteristics of Nursing Home Residents, Health Status and Care Received: National Nursing Home Survey,* in VITAL AND HEALTH STATISTICS SERIES 13 No. 51 (U.S. Gov't Printing Office,

Washington, D.C.) (1981) at 1–29 [hereinafter cited as *National Nursing Home Survey*].

2. Freeland, M.S., Schendler, C., *National Health Expenditure Growth in the 1980's: An Aging Population, New Technology, and Increasing Competition,* HEALTH CARE FINANCING REVIEW 4(3):1 (1983). *See also* R.J. BUCHANAN, HEALTH CARE FINANCE (Lexington Books, Lexington, Mass.) (1981) at 5–6.

3. U.S. GENERAL ACCOUNTING OFFICE, PRELIMINARY FINDINGS ON PATIENT CHARACTERISTICS AND STATE MEDICAID EXPENDITURES FOR NURSING HOME CARE. Publication IPE-82-4 (General Accounting Office, Washington, D.C.) (July 15, 1982).

4. *National Nursing Home Survey, supra* note 1, at 3.

5. *Id.*

6. *Id.*

7. *Id.*

8. U.S. SENATE COMMITTEE ON AGING, NURSING HOME CARE IN THE UNITED STATES: FAILURE IN PUBLIC POLICY, INTRODUCTORY REPORT (U.S. Gov't Printing Office, Washington, D.C.) (1974) at 16.

9. B. VLADECK, UNLOVING CARE (Basic Books, New York) (1980) at 15. *See also* Department of Health and Human Services, Office of the Assistant Secretary for Planning and Evaluation, WORKING PAPERS ON LONG-TERM CARE (U.S. Gov't Printing Office, Washington, D.C.) (1981) at 17.

10. Kastenbaum, R., Candy, S., *The 4% Fallacy: A Methodological and Empirical Critique of Extended Care Facility Population Statistics,* INTERNATIONAL JOURNAL OF AGING AND HUMAN DEVELOPMENT 4(1):15–21 (1973). *See also* Ingram, D., Barry, J.R., *National Statistics on Death in Nursing Homes: Interpretations and Implications,* THE GERONTOLOGIST 17(4):303–8 (August 1977).

11. *National Nursing Home Survey, supra* note 1, at 10.

12. C. ALLAN, H. BROTMAN, CHARTBOOK ON AGING IN AMERICA (White House Conference on Aging, Washington, D.C.) (1981) at 6.

13. Donahue, W., *What About Our Responsibility Toward the Abandoned Elderly?* THE GERONTOLOGIST 18(2):102, 103–5 (1978).

14. O'Connor v. Donaldson, 422 U.S. 563 (1975).

15. Wyatt v. Stickney, 344 F. Supp. 373 (M.D. Ala. 1972).

16. Sherwood, S., Mor, V., *Mental Health Institutions and the Elderly,* in HANDBOOK OF MENTAL HEALTH AND AGING (Prentice-Hall, Englewood Cliffs, N.J.) (1980) at 857.

17. National Institute of Mental Health, Division of Biometry and Epidemiology, unpublished data, 1978.

18. Clark, R.L., Menefee, J.A., *Federal Expenditures for the Elderly: Past and Future,* THE GERONTOLOGIST 21(2):132–37 (1981). *See also* S. CRYSTAL, AMERICA'S OLD AGE CRISIS: PUBLIC POLICY AND THE TWO WORLDS OF AGING (Basic Books, New York) (1982).

19. Social Security Act, 42 U.S.C. §1395f (1970) [(a) Requirements of requests and certifications].

20. *See* Chambers, D.L., *Alternatives to Civil Commitment of the Mentally Ill: Practical Guides and Constitutional Imperatives,* MICHIGAN LAW REVIEW 70:1108, 1145–67 (May 1972).

21. *See* Covington v. Harris, 419 F.2d 617 (D.C. Cir. 1969).

22. 42 C.F.R. §405.1121(k)(1–14) and (1).

23. *See* O'Connor, *supra* note 14, at 563.

24. Wyatt, *supra* note 15, at 373.

25. New York State Association for Retarded Children v. Carcy, 393 F. Supp. 715 (E.D.N.Y. 1975).

26. Holt v. Sarver, 309 F. Supp. 362 (E.D. Ark. 1970).

27. Halderman v. Pennhurst State School and Hospital, 612 F.2d 84 (3d Cir. 1979), *rev'd on other grounds and remanded,* 451 U.S. 1, *on remand,* 673 F.2d 647 (3d Cir. 1982).

28. *See generally* S.S. HERR, RIGHTS AND ADVOCACY FOR RETARDED PEOPLE (Lexington Books, Lexington, Mass.) (1983).

29. Rehabilitation Act of 1973, 29 U.S.C. §701 (1973).

30. Pennhurst State School and Hospital v. Halderman, 451 U.S. 1 (1981).

31. *See* Knowlton, J., Clouser, S., Fatula, J., *Nursing Home Pre-admission Screening: A Review of State Programs,* HEALTH CARE FINANCING REVIEW 3(3):75–87 (1982).

32. SELECT COMMITTEE ON AGING, SUBCOMMITTEE ON HEALTH AND LONG-TERM CARE, LONG-TERM CARE FOR THE 1980's: CHANNELING DEMONSTRATIONS AND OTHER INITIATIVES (U.S. Government Printing Office, Washington, D.C.) (1980).

33. Linden v. King, CA 79-862T (D. Mass. 1979). *See also* Abraham v. Winter, CA J790388R (S.D. Miss. 1979).

17

Protecting the Rights of Questionably Competent Long-Term Care Facility Residents

Susan Harris, M.P.H., J.D.

In discussing the protection of long-term care residents, it is useful first to identify the rights that are commonly ennumerated in applicable statutes and regulations. They are stated in a variety of ways, but can be categorized as follows:

— contract rights
— rights of association and communication
— rights related to admission, transfer, and discharge
— property-related rights
— rights of autonomy or choice
— privacy rights
— rights related to physical security
— procedural rights
— retention of civil rights
— affirmation of human dignity as a foundation of other rights

While residents' rights are fairly easy to identify, it is difficult to devise mechanisms that will assure their protection. One reason for this is that most rights must be asserted by the individual concerned. The mere statement that a right exists has little meaning; it is only when an individual makes and communicates a choice that this right takes on genuine meaning.

A second reason for this difficulty in actuating rights is that an estimated 50 percent of long-term care residents have significant, either permanent or intermittent, mental impairment. Although the manifestation of impairment varies significantly in time, many residents appear mentally disabled on admission to a facility. In fact, one of the major reasons for admission is that the family is unable to cope with an individual who must be closely supervised 24 hours a day. Most impaired residents require some assistance in decision making.

Third, for a variety of reasons, to date few mentally impaired residents have been formally adjudicated incompetent. Moreover, many recognize that traditional notions of guardianship may create as many problems as they solve. It is often stated that the law assumes competency; however, for this population, such a simplistic assumption may not be ethically adequate.

Fourth, facilities have varied responsibilities in addition to protecting the rights of individual residents. These duties include providing care to individual residents and protecting collective rights, as well as obligations to families, visitors, staff, and the community.

Fifth, very often the primary role and function of a long-term care facility are unclear. Residents may stay in facilities for long periods of time; the resulting obligation to provide both social and health care often creates conflicts that are not easily resolved. Further, the beneficent or paternalistic obligation to provide care and protection, while at the same time encouraging autonomy and freedom of movement, creates an additional tension.

Finally, many other individuals and groups besides those within the facility are involved in and concerned about protection of long-term care residents and their rights. In addition to family interests, there are the interests of legal and protective services, state survey and licensing agencies, and the state and local ombudsman programs. Very often, these actors differ from facility staff in their perceptions of appropriate actions and priorities in protecting the rights of long-term care residents.

TYPES OF DECISIONS

Because assertion of rights requires continual decision making, and because it is inappropriate to seek judicial review of all decisions, it becomes both convenient and practical to consider protection of residents' rights in terms of the types of decisions that are made. Although specific decisions may vary in significance, decision making is a regular occurrence. Some decisions are simple and routine, with little consequence or impact, others are more significant. Some decisions must be made promptly, others recur on a regular basis. Clearly, some form and amount of substitute decision making becomes necessary for residents whose mental faculties are impaired and who cannot or will not make or communicate their own decisions.

Often, decisions appear to be made on an ad hoc basis, relying more on expediency than on thoughtful analysis. In situations where the decision does not necessarily involve immediate life or death questions, where all concerned individuals agree, where they believe that they can accurately identify the wishes of the individual affected, and where there does not appear to be an imminent threat of litigation, most frequently decisions are made and implemented informally. The danger in this approach is that individual rights are often ignored in the interests of simplicity and avoidance of lengthy and expensive public processes.

Informal substitute decision making requires scrutiny. That is, the substitute decision maker must be authorized, individual due process rights must be honored, and some external oversight should be supplied. Some time ago the American Health Care Association (AHCA) developed an ad hoc committee to investigate these problems.[1] The committee developed a classification system for decision making. Several other systems have been suggested in the literature. Regardless of which particular system one prefers, some type of classification system is useful in organizing thinking, in avoiding unnecessary infringement upon resident rights and interference with individual autonomy, and in developing a logical approach to the problem and its resolution.

The classification system devised by the AHCA Committee recognizes five types of decisions:

1. *Decisions with immediate, relatively insignificant effects.* These include daily choices about matters such as selection of clothing or food items and participation in regular activities. The primary concern presented here is preservation of dignity; relatively little protection is required. In most cases, training of staff members and increasing their sensitivity to the issues will be adequate.

2. *Decisions with long-range effects but of relatively little significance.* These include decisions regarding purchase of routine, low value items such as clothing; nonintrusive treatments, including most medications; and participation in major outings or activities. Basic civil liberties may be at issue; moderate protection, particularly authorization and oversight, is required.

3. *Major decisions with long-term effects.* These include decisions on most surgical procedures, medications with potential for major effects on mental and physical condition (for example, psychotropic medications), sale of property or making of investments, and the use of physical restraints. Concerns here include personal and civil liberties and property rights; a fairly high degree of protection is required.

4. *Decisions on admission to and discharge from a long-term care health*

facility and on surrogate appointment and authority. Because these
decisions can limit or otherwise affect decisions in other categories, and because a high potential for conflicts of interest exists,
more protection is required than for decisions in the third
category.

5. *Decisions with life and death implications.* These include decisions
regarding high risk, intrusive, or irreversible medical procedures
such as amputation, certain medications such as chemotherapy
for malignancies, and the initiation and discontinuation of life
support systems. The highest degree of protection is required.

There are some treatments, common in long-term care facilities, to
which no clear categorization or standard is easily applied. Use of alternative nutrition systems, such as tube or intravenous feedings, and administration of antibiotics for major infections frequently fall into this
ambiguous category. While these treatments appear to be simple and
common, they often have life and death implications. In a recent decision,
a New Jersey court rejected application of the "ordinary/extraordinary"
dichotomy in deciding that a nasogastric tube could be removed from a
comatose patient exhibiting no cognitive or volitional function.[2] The
court indicated that the condition and prognosis of the patient as well as
previously expressed or implied patient preferences, are the most critical
factors to be applied in medical decision making for incompetent
patients.

DECISION-MAKING PROCESSES:
CRITERIA FOR EVALUATION

After some categorization of decisions and the amount of protection they
require has been agreed upon, it is useful to next consider criteria for
evaluating different systems for making these decisions. The following is
a list of criteria developed by the AHCA's task force:

— *Manifestation of individual opinion.* Does the alternative system
result in the manifestation of the individual's opinion or decision? Does it do so directly (through his or her own words or
writing, such as a living will) or indirectly (as where the individual has designated a substitute decision maker, using a durable power of attorney)?

— *Finances.* How costly is the alternative system to the individual,
the individual's family, the facility, and the public funding agencies? Cost should be defined in terms of measurable units of
service, in order to make adequate comparisons. Further, actual

and theoretical availability of funds should be considered. For example, a system that is theoretically open to all but requires minimum out-of-pocket costs of $1,000 is actually open only to those who can afford it.

— *Family concerns.* Is the alternative system sensitive to the wishes of the individual's family or close friends?

— *Resolution of differences.* Does the alternative system accommodate differing opinions among members of the individual's family, and does it provide a means to resolve differences? Does it consider the degree of responsibility and interest of those involved? When medical decisions are being made, what effect does the physician's opinion have?

— *Prompt decision making.* Does the alternative system permit decision making in an expeditious manner? Can the decision maker react promptly when making a specific decision?

— *Minimal restriction.* If the alternative system employs substitute decision making, is it the least-restrictive limitation of the resident's basic rights and freedom? Does it permit the individual to continue to be involved with or actually to make decisions as much as possible?

— *Constitutional adequacy.* Does the alternative system provide protection for constitutional rights, for example, due process rights to notice or a hearing?

— *Broad applicability.* Can the alternative system easily be applied to numerous individuals (within the facility), or is it by its nature limited to a relatively small percentage of individuals? Is it applicable to noninstitutionalized individuals?

— *Conflict of interest.* Does the alternative system provide for identification and resolution of conflict of interest issues? Does it also recognize different value systems (e.g., those of physician, attorney, or guardian) that affect individual approaches and actions?

— *System response.* Does the alternative system permit prompt activation of surrogate functions when the individual becomes incapacitated, or does it involve protracted initial formal proceedings? Can someone with authority to make decisions do so shortly after the need arises?

— *Availability of appeal.* Does the alternative system offer judicial review or other recourse for appeal of specific adverse decisions?

— *Relationship to original decision.* Is there a reasonable relationship, in terms of time and scope, between an earlier decision (to delegate authority for a particular course of action) manifested by the individual or his or her substitute and its application at a subsequent point in time? For example, if an individual indicated 20 years previously that he did not want "heroic measures" taken, what weight should be given to that decision today? How should "heroic" be defined, given changes in medical technology?

DECISION-MAKING PROCESSES: ALTERNATIVE SYSTEMS

In general, systems that protect individual rights are a composite of elements. That is, there are very few pure systems. However, the general approaches of these systems can be divided into five basic categories.

The first type is the individual control system under which an individual executes documents that have future effect, such as a durable power of attorney,[3] or a "living will."[4] The problem with such a system is that its use may be limited by statutory or judicial constraints, as well as by the individual's unwillingness to execute such documents in anticipation of future incompetence. Additionally, most concepts applied in this type of system are relatively new and untested. Time will tell whether this system will gain in acceptance and usefulness.

The second type, the admission contract system, is used now to some extent by most health care providers. At its extreme, it would delegate to specified others significant amounts of authority to make health care decisions and would identify and empower surrogate decision makers. One practical question often raised is whether a facility should or may require the appointment of a guardian prior to admission if an individual is obviously disoriented or otherwise impaired at the time admission is sought.

The third method, private damage litigation, involves expansion and application of existing tort law. Limitations on this system include the finite capacity of courts and the ability and willingness of individuals to litigate their often personal grievances. Additionally, legal principles regarding the measure of damages may as a practical matter limit the ability both to litigate and to recover adequate financial compensation.

The fourth system, the existing guardianship process, requires judicial determination of incompetence.[5] In some states, limited guardianships that can be applied only as needed have been authorized; but courts appear reluctant to extend or expand this mechanism absent statutory authority. Other problems include family reluctance, cost, lack of interested or qualified persons to serve as guardians, inadequate judicial oversight, limited or inadequate representation during judicial proceedings, and the broad effects of the determination of incompetency. The representative payee system, authorized by federal law, permits bypassing guardianship procedures for certain financial decisions for recipients of specified federal funds. Because the authorized procedures provide minimal protection for the individual concerned, several recommendations for legislative reform have been proposed and it appears that modifications would be desirable and practical.

The last system that we identified includes an assortment of alternatives with a social service emphasis. For example, adult protective services and long-term care ombudsman programs provide varying degrees of protection and assistance in problem solving. In general, the client must be able to participate in the process and have some degree of mental competency. A positive aspect of many of these programs has been the experimental use of volunteers to serve as surrogates or to assist individuals in decision making. The effects of this approach should be monitored and evaluated to determine its value for all protective systems.

AHCA's ad hoc committee developed suggestions for a new, innovative decision-making system. While the committee did not recommend the system, they believed that some of the concepts it embodied should be carefully considered by policymakers when reviewing existing systems. Basic concepts included: use of volunteer surrogates selected by the client; use of administrative agency proceedings and oversight for lower level, uncontested decisions; provision for some degree of judicial oversight and review; and retention of maximal authority and autonomy by the client. Major changes in common public and professional perceptions and attitudes, as well as in current state laws, would be required. Adequate funding would be a major problem; however, cost per client served might compare favorably to existing systems. Figures 1 and 2 describe such a system.

IMPLEMENTING DECISION-MAKING SYSTEMS

Decisions about the development of appropriate systems cannot be made without considering other peripheral, yet important, factors. As a matter of economic reality, one must assess the relative costs and benefits of any system, including the availability of needed resources. Other considerations include social factors such as the effects of "ageism" upon values and decisions, the tensions between professional services and "volunteerism," and the varying perspectives and values of different generations and social classes. Demographic changes indicate that our population is aging; as a result, larger amounts of a wide variety of services will be required. Interests and priorities of legal and consumer advocacy groups will continue to be important. Changes in long-term care facilities, such as increased sensitivity of staff members to resident autonomy, movement away from the medical model of care, high occupancy rates, and increased community involvement in monitoring the quality of resident care will also affect decisions.

Last, all those involved in evaluating and selecting appropriate systems and making policy decisions will follow one of three basic approaches. One approach, a compromise position, recognizes that absolutes may be incapable of implementation. Another, more reactive position, tends to favor the use of absolutes to correct real or perceived problems. This approach often leads to "overkill"—the development of a system that creates more problems than it solves. The last, and, I believe, least desirable position would advocate minimal or no change, insisting that the problem does not exist. This would result in actual backward movement, diminishing the rights of those individuals in long-term care facilities who most need protection.

There are additional basic questions that appear to affect both policy makers and individuals involved in surrogate decision-making issues. First is whether the fact of institutionalization legitimately should determine the type of system used. That is, should public agencies be more concerned about or involved in decision-making systems that affect institutionalized individuals than in systems affecting individuals residing in private homes, either their own or those of others? Another problem concerns whether the time factor involved should make a difference. Should an individual's short life expectancy, due to terminal disease, permit decision making to be less protected? Still another quandary is whether a system should apply to all individuals with impaired decision making or only to those in specific situations. Consider, for example, whether a single process would be appropriate in all the following situations: (1) disagreement exists among those involved; (2) alternative choices vary significantly in their practicality; (3) the issues at stake are perceived to be of high value (e.g., a large estate or a life-and-death treatment choice); and (4) no close family member is involved. Finally, should the ability or inability to identify or agree upon the best interests of the individual affected be an influential factor?

It is increasingly important that society address these problems, focusing on the rights of institutionalized individuals whose decision-making capacity is impaired, while developing a system that will be applicable in most, if not all, surrogate decision-making situations. Narrowly focusing upon the theory of "rights protection," so that it becomes an abstraction, can result in losing sight of practical considerations. However, it is important to give adequate consideration to important principles of self-determination while attempting to develop a system that will be both practical and effective.

Figure 1: Decision-making Oversight

Category of Decision	Functional Impairment Classification		
	Financial/Business	Self-Protection & Daily Living	Medical Care
1. Daily choice	Individual/provider of care within limits set by surrogate*	Individual/provider of care within limits set by surrogate*	Individual/provider of care within limits set by surrogate*
2. Long-range low impact	Individual/provider of care with surrogate consultation or review*	Individual/provider of care with surrogate consultation or review*	Individual/provider of care with surrogate consultation or review*
3. Major financial and treatment	Surrogate with minimal oversight	Surrogate with minimal oversight	Surrogate with minimal oversight
4. Admission,† discharge and assumption of authority‡	Surrogate initiation. Provider assessment of individual. Oversight required.	N/A	Surrogate initiation. Provider assessment of individual. Oversight required.
5. Life and death	N/A	N/A	Existing judicial (or other) mechanism as defined by state law

Reprinted from AHCA report, *Questionably Competent Long Term Care Residents: Problems and Possible Solutions* (1982).

*The degree of surrogate review and consultation should be agreed upon by the provider of care and surrogate and clearly stated in writing. In most instances, the surrogate would wish to be consulted for many category 2 decisions. At a minimum, the surrogate should be consulted whenever written authority would be required or if the provider of care questions the individual's comprehension about a specific matter.

†The long term care provider has the responsibility, on admission, to ascertain the voluntariness of the individual's admission and his/her competency. If either is questionable, the oversight agency must be contacted. Its function will depend on the alternative selected by the state.

‡After a designated surrogate and provider file appropriate notice with the individual and the proper oversight organization, agency, or court, the surrogate may automatically assume authority for all category 1 and 2 decisions. Formal authorization must be given before the surrogate is permitted to make other decisions.

178 JOB B0174-0172-05 FIG.2/SURROGATE
REV:08-16 EXP:06-25 MV SIZ: 59.10

Figure 2: Surrogate Decision-making Process

I. On Admission

Provider assesses individual for competency and voluntariness of admission

If admission is voluntary and individual appears competent, he is given opportunity to designate a surrogate.

Admission procedure includes description of surrogate functions, procedures for initiating surrogate's assumption of authority, and implications of designation and nondesignation.

If individual does not appoint a surrogate, when he demonstrates a disability, provider can notify oversight entity to investigate competency and appoint* surrogate, if necessary.

If individual appoints surrogate,

If either is questionable, oversight agency is contacted to:

1. Investigate propriety of admission and make decision,* and/or
2. Investigate competency and appoint* surrogate, if necessary. If resident is competent, assist him in appointing surrogate. (Alternative: agency investigates and makes recommendations to court)

If surrogate has been appointed and must assume authority, follow assumption of authority procedures.

II. After Admission

Competent individual makes own decisions. Provider performs ongoing assessment and requests assumption of authority when individual demonstrates need for surrogate to act.

For individual determined to be incompetent, follow assumption of authority procedures.

III. Assumption of Authority

When individual demonstrates need for surrogate decision-making, provider and surrogate file notice with agency. Surrogate makes category 1 and 2 decisions immediately. If surrogate is unable or unwilling to serve, provider requests entity to investigate and appoint surrogate, as if no surrogate had been appointed.

If surrogate assumption of authority was approved on admission, go to next step.

Agency investigates and approves assumption of authority. (Alternative: agency makes recommendation to court)

Provider and surrogate enter into written agreement as to category 1 and 2 decision making. Surrogate makes retained (and final) 1 and 2 and all category 3 decisions, consulting with individual as much as possible.

Any person with standing (as defined in statute) may request agency review of surrogate decisions. Agency investigates and makes decisions.* (Alternative: reports and refers to court)

Surrogate files annual reports with agency as required. Surrogate requests agency review and recommendations for discharge and problem decisions.

Surrogate refers category 5 decisions to agency for appropriate action according to state law.

Reprinted from AHCA report, *Questionably Competent Long Term Care Residents: Problems and Possible Solutions* (1982).
*Judicial review is available for all agency decisions.

The rights of long-term care residents are real and worthy of protection, and no existing mechanism adequately protects those rights by authorizing appropriate decision-making processes. Significant changes are required in order to attain adequate protection of the rights of our most impaired and vulnerable long-term care facility residents.

NOTES

1. The report of the committee, *Questionably Competent Long Term Care Residents: Problems and Possible Solutions* (AHCA, Washington, D.C.) (1982), used as the basis for much of this chapter, is available from AHCA, 1200 15th Street, NW, Washington, D.C. 20005.
2. *In re* Conroy, 457 A.2d 1232 (N.J. Super. Ch. 1983), *rev'd*, 464 A.2d 303 (N.J. Super. A.D. 1983). The court considered the state's interest in preserving life and invasion of the patient's right to privacy and still rejected the ordinary/extraordinary distinction. The intermediate appellate court reversed the lower court's decision that removal of the nasogastric tube was proper in Conroy's medical condition (comatose but still responding to external stimuli), and held that withholding nutrition was analogous to mercy killing if the patient was able to eat with manual assistance. The New Jersey Supreme Court reversed the intermediate appellate decision and held that removal of the feeding tube was proper if certain procedural safeguards were met. 486 A.2d 1209 (1985). *See generally* Childress, J., Lynn, J., *Must Patients Always Be Given Food and Water?* HASTINGS CENTER REPORT 13(5):17 (October 1983); Micetich, K.C., Steinecker, P.H., Thomasma, D.C., *Are Intravenous Fluids Morally Required for a Dying Patient?* ARCHIVES OF INTERNAL MEDICINE 143:975 (May 1983). *See also* Dresser, R., Boisaubin, E., *Ethics, Law, and Nutritional Support,* ARCHIVES OF INTERNAL MEDICINE 145:122 (January 1985); Siegler, M., Weisbard, A., *Against the Emerging Stream: Should Fluids and Nutritional Support Be Discontinued?* ARCHIVES OF INTERNAL MEDICINE 145:129 (January 1985); Paris, J., Reardon, F. *Court Responses to Withholding or Withdrawing Artificial Nutrition and Fluids,* JOURNAL OF THE AMERICAN MEDICAL ASSOCIATION 253:15 (April 19, 1985); Annas, G., *Fashion and Freedom: When Artificial Feeding Should Be Withdrawn,* AMERICAN JOURNAL OF PUBLIC HEALTH 75:685 (June 1985).
3. The durable power of attorney allows a competent individual to appoint an agent to make or carry out his or her health care decisions when the individual becomes incompetent. The document must include some version of the phrase, "This power of attorney shall become effective upon the disability or incapacity of the principal." In most states, it is not yet clear whether health care decision making is a permissible use of durable power of attorney. *See* PRESIDENT'S COMMISSION REPORT, *infra* note 4, at 145.
4. The language of living wills varies. Most, however, mention "life-sustaining procedures which would serve only to artificially prolong the dying process." *See* PRESIDENT'S COMMISSION FOR THE STUDY OF ETHICAL PROBLEMS IN MEDI-

CAL AND BIOMEDICAL AND BEHAVIORAL RESEARCH, DECIDING TO FOREGO LIFE-SUSTAINING TREATMENT: ETHICAL, MEDICAL, AND LEGAL IMPLICATIONS FOR HEALTH CARE DECISION MAKING (U.S. Gov't Printing Office, Washington, D.C.) (March, 1983) at 139.

5. *E.g.,* 21 OHIO REV. CODE ANN. §2111.01(D) (Page Supp. 1983).

18

Guardianship: Public and Private

Winsor C. Schmidt, Jr., J.D.

Guardianship is "the office, duty, or authority of a guardian," and the relation between guardian and ward.[1] A guardian manages the person and property of another, the "ward," who is considered incapable of self-administration.[2] Guardianship in Florida, for example, is governed by the Florida Guardianship Law.[3] The historical purpose of guardianship is care of another, but closer examination reveals an alternative function:

> Recognize guardianship for what it really is: the most intrusive, non-interest serving, impersonal legal device known and available to us and as such, one which minimizes personal autonomy and respect for the individual, has a high potential for doing harm and raises at best a questionable benefit/burden ratio. As such, it is a device to be studiously avoided.[4]

Guardianship is avoided, statistically. A recent study of six states (Deleware, Minnesota, North Carolina, Ohio, Washington and Wisconsin), with a total population of 29 million, found that only 17,000 guardianship petitions were filed in one year.[5] This filing rate of .059 percent (one of every 1,706) corresponds interestingly with the filing rate of .056 percent (one of every 1,785) for Florida in 1977 (4,724 guardianships opened of a population of 8,432,927).[6] Involuntary civil commitment for mental treatment and for alcohol treatment are more frequent events. However, this data does not reflect the growing and potential impact of guardianship especially from the perspective of individual wards.

Older persons are an at-risk group according to both the legal[7] and functional criteria for guardianship. Guardianship law emphasizes mental incapacity in justifying the adjudication of incompetence, with the

Reprinted with permission of the Florida Bar Association from THE FLORIDA BAR JOURNAL, March 1981, pp. 189–92.

consequence that "anyone, especially an older person, who needs a guardian is popularly assumed to be mentally ill. The aged person with a few of the symptoms of chronic brain syndrome, such as forgetfulness, is more likely to be judged mentally ill and therefore to be declared incompetent."[8] The aging of the population may bring proportionately increased numbers of persons into the guardianship process.

There is also evidence that as deinstitutionalization proceeds, and where involuntary civil commitment criteria and procedures become more restrictive, use of guardianship increases.[9] This tendency may combine with a growing number of poor people to verify one commentator's conclusion: "When examined in the larger context of social programming through which we purport to help the less advantaged, involuntary guardianship emerges as an official initiation rite for the entry of the poor and the inept into the managed society."[10]

Furthermore, annual per capita filing rates do not take into consideration the net annual addition to guardianship rolls (1,400 to 1,500 in Florida[11]—guardianships opened, minus guardianships closed through death, exhaustion of the estate, and restoration of legal competence), the number of people who could be adjudicated incompetent but are not,[12] and the number of people for whom some alternative, or moral equivalent of guardianship, suffices. Guardianship is much more frequent than judicial utterances of acquittal by reason of insanity (an event "rarer than the annual incidence of poisonous snake bites in Manhattan"[13]), yet scholarly and case law attention to guardianship does not even approach the mountain of literature and litigation on the insanity defense.

PERSONAL CONSEQUENCES

The personal consequences of guardianship are substantial. The subject of guardianship "may be subject to greater control of his or her life than one convicted of a crime."[14] In Florida, for example, a person adjudicated incompetent is statutorily "presumed to be incapable of managing his own affairs or of making any gift, contract, or instrument in writing that is binding on him or his estate."[15] In most states, a finding of legal incompetence restricts or takes away "the right to: make contracts; sell, purchase, mortgage, or lease property; make gifts; travel, or decide where to live; vote, or hold elected office; initiate or defend against suits; make a will, or revoke one; engage in certain professions; lend or borrow money; appoint agents; divorce, or marry; refuse medical treatment; keep and care for children; serve on a jury; be a witness to any legal document; drive a car; pay or collect debts; manage or run a business."[16] The loss of any one of these rights can have a disastrous result, but taken together, their effect is to reduce the status of an individual to that of a child, or a nonperson.

These consequences might be mitigated, at least on a *quid pro quo* basis, if guardianship services were beneficial. Unfortunately, there is evidence that guardianship is beneficial only to persons other than the ward. In their landmark study of over 400 guardianships, Alexander and Lewin found that wards ended up worse in every case:[17]

> Under the present system of "Estate Management by Preemption" we divest the incompetent of control of his property upon the finding of the existence of serious mental illness whenever divestiture is in the interest of some third person or institution. The theory of incompetency is to protect the debilitated from their own financial foolishness or from the fraud of others who would prey upon their mental weaknesses. In practice, however, we seek to protect the interests of others. The state hospital commences incompetency proceedings to facilitate reimbursement for costs incurred in the care, treatment and maintenance of its patients. Dependents institute proceedings to secure their needs. Co-owners of property find incompetency proceedings convenient ways to secure the sale of realty. Heirs institute actions to preserve their dwindling inheritances. Beneficiaries of trusts or estates seek incompetency as an expedient method of removing as trustee one who is managing the trust or estate in a manner adverse to their interests. All of these motives may be honest and without any intent to cheat the aged, but none of the proceedings are commenced to assist the debilitated.[18]

Or, as a psychiatrist more succinctly put it, "'for every $100,000 in a given estate a lawyer shows up, for every $25,000 a family member shows up.'"[19]

Another study illustrating the high risks of intervention involved a quasi-experimental design carried out by Blenkner and associates through the Benjamin Rose Institute in Cleveland.[20] The provision of enriched, protective services (including guardianships) to the experimental group not only failed to prevent or slow deterioration or death, but the experimental group actually had a higher rate of institutionalization and death than did the control group who received referral services or nothing.

Guardianship is sometimes used for an individual who is "likely to . . . inflict harm on himself,"[21] despite some other evidence that involuntary treatment for dangerousness to self may increase the rate of suicide.[22] Thus, empirical questions about guardianship elicit suggestions that guardianship serves third party interests, fails to make the ward better off than before appointment of a guardian, increases the chances of institutionalization and probably of death, results in more negative outcomes as the time of the guardianship relationship increases, and constitutes a most restrictive alternative that is inevitably overutilized.

ALTERNATIVES TO GUARDIANSHIP

There are less restrictive[23] alternatives to guardianship. Appropriate utilization of such alternatives should make guardianship even more of a last resort. These alternatives[24] include: power of attorney; durable family power of attorney ("living wills");[25] appointment of an agent; single transaction court ratification of a particular action; joint tenancy; inter vivos transfers of property; deeds of guardianship;[26] trusts; substitute or representative payee;[27] protective services;[28] and civil commitment.

When the less restrictive alternatives are exhausted, the last resort of guardianship can be considered. Important concerns at this time are the criteria and procedures for guardianship.

An important study undertaken by the National Law Center of George Washington University indicated that statutory definitions for incompetence are vague and contribute to an erroneous belief that individual capabilities are well reflected in generalizations about age, mental or physical health, and the like.[29] Attorneys and physicians who participated frequently in guardianship cases could not agree on the meaning of such criteria, frequently with such observations as "has no psychiatric meaning," or "ambiguous as hell."[30]

A reform alternative to such criteria as Florida's[31] would restrict guardianship eligibility to "gravely disabled"[32] persons who lack the capacity to make informed decisions about proposed care, treatment, or management services.[33] "Gravely disabled" is adopted from the California conservatorship law[34] that, along with New York's, has been commended as a model.[35] "Gravely disabled" would be defined as "unable to meet essential requirements for one's physical health or safety or to manage one's financial resources as a result of a severe mental disorder."[36]

"Severe mental disorder," in turn, would be defined as "a severe impairment of emotional processes, ability to exercise conscious control of one's actions, or ability to perceive reality or to reason or understand, which impairment is manifested by instances of grossly disturbed behavior."[37] This definition includes the emotional, volitional, and cognitive components of mental functioning in terms understandable to physicians, attorneys, judges, and laypersons alike. Persons suffering from such causal or categorical generalities as "advanced age," epilepsy, mental retardation, and acute addiction or alcoholism would qualify if the disability produced a functionally severe mental disorder.

Current guardianship procedures nationally do not seem to decrease the risk of erroneous deprivation of the liberty and property interests noted above. Presence of the proposed ward at the incompetency hearing is frequently waived,[38] often on the ironic ground that presence at one's own hearing will be harmful.[39] Other due process issues include inadequate notice;[40] the absence of counsel or essentially symbolic rather than aggressive representation in all but a very few cases;[41] the absence of court review;[42] the fact that appeals are nonexistent or usually waived;[43] that the vague legal standard is arbitrarily applied;[44] that dismissals of petitions are rare;[45] and that hearings are cursory, with most only taking several minutes.[46] Given the importance of counsel for the exercise of procedural rights, any ineffective assistance of counsel is a particularly disturbing development. More than one commentator has noted that counsel in such mental disability cases as guardianship functioned "'as no more than a clerk, ratifying the events that transpire[d], rather than influencing them.'"[47] There is reason to believe that such procedural practices also occur in Florida.[48]

STATUTORY REMEDIES

In addition to the Uniform Probate Code,[49] suggested statutory remedies to procedural, and substantive, guardianship deficiencies abound.[50] A recently suggested Model Public Guardianship Statute contains guardianship procedure and criteria that attempt to combine the best of all the suggestions, in addition to reflecting a recent survey of the guardianship statutes in the 50 states.[51]

Highlights of the reform proposal include: functional, rather than causal or categorical, eligibility; partial or limited guardianship;[52] specified purpose of restoration or development of capacity; monitoring of private guardianships by public guardians; voluntary guardianship; determinant guardianship terms of no more than one year per term; precondition of the availability of beneficial services; "clear, unequivocal, and convincing" as the standard of proof; required presence of the proposed ward at the hearing except when medically incapable; right to counsel including minimum required duties; right to jury trial;[53] right to independent medical and psychological evaluation; qualified right to remain silent at any evaluation;[54] right to present evidence and confront and cross-examine witnesses; applicability of formal civil rules of evidence; qualified prohibition of opinion testimony regarding diagnosis;[55] right to instruction of jury or court regarding the influence of any psychotropic medication on the proposed ward; right to appeal and appellate counsel; required application of the least-restrictive alternative principle; physician immunity for emergency treatment without consent, instead of temporary guardianship, emergency guardianship, and the like; qualified right to services; and, provision for public guardianship.

THE SUPPLY OF GUARDIANS

Public guardianship is an aspect of the area of guardianship most in need of reform—the supply of guardians.[56] An incompetent with a sizeable estate, or with willing and responsible family members or friends, has little difficulty in having someone serve as guardian. A proposed ward without such resources,[57] however, has a very different situation.

In April 1977, Florida's Office of Aging and Adult Services found in a statewide survey of its social workers that 2,700 identifiable people (1,700 were over age 60) had an unsatisfied need for a guardian. Almost 1,000 of these had been adjudicated incompetent, but no guardian appointed.[58] The balance needed to be adjudicated incompetent and have a guardian appointed, in the opinion of the social workers, but for most of them no guardian was available. The addition of other eligible population groups (mental health and developmental disabilities clients—but not nursing homes) yields a more recent estimate of 11,147 persons in need of a guardian in Florida.[59]

Another vacuum in the provision of guardianship services exists for institutionalized persons, especially the elderly in nursing facilities and the state mental hospitals. At Florida's largest mental institution, Florida State Hospital, for example, there are at least 600 patients who are legally incompetent, without guardians, but classified as "voluntary" patients.[60] Most are elderly people who were institutionalized under the pre–Baker Act civil commitment statute with criteria of mental incompetence, never appointed a guardian,[61] and statutorily grandfathered away from the protections allowed involuntaries under the Baker Act. A proportionate number of incompetent "voluntaries" without guardians (almost one-third of the resident population) probably exists at Florida's other mental institutions.

The consequences of guardianship may be serious, but the effect of legal incompetence without a guardian, or of functional incapacity without guardianship assistance, is total lack of protection. In 34 other states, there is some statutory provision for public guardianship to address the need for guardians.

PROBLEMS OF PUBLIC GUARDIANSHIP

Public guardianship, the appointment and responsibility of a public official to serve as legal guardian, is not without its own problems. In Los Angeles the public guardian has been sued for inappropriate institutionalization of wards, and in Chicago the former public guardian was found to have looted estates of personal property, failed to seek entitlements, consented to experimental medical treatment on mental patients, and noted visits to wards who in fact were dead at the time of the alleged visits.[62] However, the public guardian experience in Arizona and Delaware is generally favorable: nonintrusive professional guardianship service that assists persons without family, friends, or resources to secure access to rights, benefits, and entitlements.

The success of public guardianship is dependent upon several clear considerations. The public guardian must be independent of any service providing agency (no conflict of interest), and the public guardian must not be responsible for both serving as guardian, and petitioning for adjudication of incompetence (no self-aggrandizement). The public guardian must be adequately staffed and funded to the extent that no office is responsible for more than 500 wards, and each professional in the office is responsible for no more than 30 wards.[63] A public guardian is also only as good as the guardianship statute[64] governing adjudication of incompetence and appointment. Failure in any of these considerations will tip the benefit/burden ratio against the individual ward, and the ward would be better off with no guardian at all.

FLORIDA'S APPROACHES

Florida, like approximately two dozen other states, has several approaches to the need for guardians that is met in 34 states by public guardianship. These approaches include: benign neglect; informal guardianship by neighbors, nursing homes, and the like without legal process or authority; civil commitment to a mental institution ("poor man's guardianship"); private attorneys on a pro bono or nominal fee basis (sometimes with dozens of wards each); banks or trust companies (for modest estates);[65] nonprofit corporations,[66] usually with a religious affiliation; county social service programs utilizing volunteers; citizen groups serving as guardian banks;[67] and Florida's newly appropriated Public Guardianship Pilot Project in the Office of the State Courts' Administrator.

These approaches are not meeting Florida's needs, but the best alternatives to public guardianship may be dramatic enhancement of the last four. The Cathedral Foundation in Jacksonville, for example, seems to be performing an excellent service. The keys to such approaches are willingness to work oneself out of a job; resistance to the social service starvation that sees any service, even guardianship, as better than none; and avoidance of being both guardian and applicant for adjudication of incompetence.

Guardianship is a comparatively unheralded device that can be expected to grow in use as the country, and state, population's average age increases. The purpose of guardianship is assistance, the *parens patriae* responsibilities of the state made manifest. Unfortunately, more than cursory consideration of guardianship in practice yields fairly negative results.

The literature relating to guardianship contains little that endorses general guardianship practice or argues forcefully for guardianship.[68] Numerous individual professionals cite a large need for guardianship, but positive results for individual wards are so far no more than anecdotal at best, and disappointing in the aggregate.

There are less restrictive, and more appropriate, alternatives to guardianship. Several models now exist for guardianship criteria, procedures, public guardianship, and alternatives to public guardianship. Guardianship should presume an exhaustion of all alternatives. Guardianship in any event may reflect individual, professional, and social service bankruptcy.

The need for guardianship reform seems great, and should proceed.

NOTES

1. BLACK'S LAW DICTIONARY (5th ed. 1979) at 636.
2. *Id.* at 635.
3. FLA. STAT. ANN. 744 (West Supp. 1980). For detailed information on the law, see FLORIDA BAR CONTINUING LEGAL EDUCATION SECTION, FLORIDA GUARDIANSHIP PRACTICE (1978); FLORIDA JUSTICE INSTITUTE, FLORIDA BAR, OLDER FLORIDIANS HANDBOOK: LAWS AND PROGRAMS AFFECTING OLDER FLORIDIANS (1980); GUARDIANSHIP MANUAL (Model Legal Services, Florida State Hospital, Chattahoochee, Fla.) (1980).
4. Cohen, E.S., Protective Services and Public Guardianship: A Dissenting View (address at 31st Annual Meeting of the Gerontological Society, Dallas, Texas) (November 20, 1978).
5. Axilbund, M., *Exercising Judgment for the Disabled: Report of an Inquiry into Limited Guardianship, Public Guardianship and Adult Protective Services in Six States* (Executive Summary) (American Bar Association Commission on the Mentally Disabled, Washington, D.C.) (1979) at 21.
6. W. SCHMIDT, *et. al.*, PUBLIC GUARDIANSHIP AND THE ELDERLY (Ballinger Publishing Co., Cambridge, Mass.) (1981) at 148; U.S. DEPARTMENT OF HEALTH, EDUCATION, AND WELFARE, OLDER AMERICANS, 1977 (U.S. Gov't Printing Office, Washington, D.C.) (1978).
7. *E.g.,* "senility is a triggering criterion in Florida," FLA. STAT. §744.102(5) (1980). *But see In re* Brown, 7 N.W. 899 (Mich. 1881) (mere allegation of age or senility is insufficient to support guardianship petition); McGuigan's Estate, 37 A2d. 717 (Pa. 1944).

8. Regan, J., Springer, G., Protective Services for the Elderly, a working paper prepared for the Special Committee on Aging, United States Senate (1977) at 36, *citing* Lehman, L., *Guardianship,* in SOCIAL WELFARE OF THE AGING (J. Kaplan and G.J. Aldridge, eds.) (1962) at 312. *See also* Cohen, E.S., *Old Age and the Law,* WOMEN'S LAW JOURNAL 53(3):96 (Summer 1967).

9. *See* W. SCHMIDT, *et al., supra* note 6 (California, Maryland, and Missouri are three states where this phenomenon is allegedly occurring). This may be part of a larger social control continuum whereby decriminalization of alcohol and drug offenses in the criminal justice system leads to enhanced use of civil commitment, at which point "criminalization" of civil commitment (tightening criteria and procedures) leads to enhanced use of guardianship. I predict that reform of guardianship (tightening criteria and procedures) will increase the use of adult protective services. Society tolerates only a certain amount of deviance before calling into play certain incapacitative devices, usually in the name of "rehabilitation," benevolence, and paternalism. *See generally* N. KITTRIE, THE RIGHT TO BE DIFFERENT: DEVIANCE AND ENFORCED THERAPY (John Hopkins University Press, Baltimore, Md.) (1971).

10. Mitchell, A.M., *Involuntary Guardianship for Incompetents: A Strategy for Legal Services Advocates,* CLEARINGHOUSE REVIEW 12(8):451, 466 (December 1978).

11. SCHMIDT, *et al., supra* note 6, at 148.

12. State social workers in Florida in 1977 claimed that 2,700 people, 1,700 age 60 and over, identified by name and address, needed to be adjudicated legally incompetent and have a guardian appointed. Memorandum from the Aging and Adult Services Program Office, Department of Health and Rehabilitative Services, Tallahassee (1977), table reprinted in SCHMIDT, *et al., supra* note 6, at 147. A more recent Florida needs assessment, adding counts from public and private mental health receiving facilities and community mental health centers and clinics, indicates that 4,430 people are functionally but not legally incompetent. Schmidt, W., Peters, R., Legal Incompetents' Need for Guardians in Florida (1983) (unpublished study).

13. A. STONE, MENTAL HEALTH AND LAW: A SYSTEM IN TRANSITION (Jason Aronson, Inc., New York) (1975) at 218, *citing* Cohen, E.S., Book Review, CONTEMPORARY PSYCHIATRY 13:386 (1968) (reviewing A. GOLDSTEIN, INSANITY DEFENSE).

14. Heap v. Roulet, 590 P.2d 1, 3 (Cal. 1979).

15. FLA. STAT. §744.331(8) (1979).

16. R. BROWN, THE RIGHTS OF OLDER PERSONS (Avon Books, New York) (1979) at 286. *But see* Rogers v. Commissioner of Mental Health, 458 N.E. 2d 308 (Mass. 1983).

17. G. ALEXANDER, T. LEWIN, THE AGED AND THE NEED FOR SURROGATE MANAGEMENT (Syracuse University Press, Syracuse, N.Y.) (1972) at 136.

18. *Id.* at 135.

19. SCHMIDT, *et al., supra* note 6, at 109.

20. M. BLENKNER, *et. al.,* PROTECTIVE SERVICES FOR OLDER PEOPLE: FINAL REPORT (Benjamin Rose Institute, Cleveland, Ohio) (1974); Blenkner, M., Bloom, M., Nielson, M., *A Research and Demonstration Project of Protective Services* SOCIAL CASEWORK 52:483 (1971).

C

21. FLA. STAT. §744.331(1) (1979).
22. Greenberg, D.F., *Involuntary Psychiatric Commitments to Prevent Suicide,* NEW YORK UNIVERSITY LAW REVIEW 49 (2 & 3):227, 236, 250, 256–59 (1974). In analogous areas, a long-term major delinquency program found no significant difference between treatment and control groups; in fact, the longer and more intense the treatment, the more negative were eventual outcomes. *See* McCord, J., *A Thirty-Year Follow-Up of Treatment Effects,* AMERICAN PSYCHOLOGIST 33:284 (1978); McCord, J., McCord, W., *A Follow-Up Report on the Cambridge Somerville Youth Study,* ANNALS OF AMERICAN ACADEMY OF POLITICAL & SOCIAL SCIENCE 322:89 (1959); McCord, J., Consideration of Some Effects of a Counseling Program (unpublished manuscript) (1979).

    A study of mental patients released from Alabama mental institutions by court order concluded that "family members adjusted expectations and accepted the patient home" when the state did not provide the alternative of a mental hospital. Leaf, A., *Patients Released after "Wyatt": Where Did They Go?,* HOSPITAL AND COMMUNITY PSYCHIATRY 28:366 (1977).
23. *See, e.g.,* Shelton v. Tucker, 364 U.S. 479, 488 (1960). "In a series of decisions this Court has held that, even though the governmental purpose be legitimate and substantial, that purpose cannot be narrowly pursued by means that broadly stifle personal liberties when the end can be more narrowly achieved. The breadth of legislative abridgment must be reviewed in the light of less drastic means for achieving the same basic purpose."
24. *See generally* BROWN, *supra* note 16, at 343–47; Regan, Springer, *supra* note 8, at 42–46; SCHMIDT, *et al., supra* note 6, at 182; Horstman, P.M., *Protective Services for the Elderly: The Limits of Parens Patriae,* MISSOURI LAW REVIEW 40(2):215 (Spring 1975); Regan, J., *Protective Services for the Elderly: Commitment, Guardianship and Alternatives,* WILLIAM & MARY LAW REVIEW 13(3):569 (Spring 1972).
25. *See* FLA. STAT. §709.08 (1983); Alexander, G.J., *Premature Probate: A Different Perspective on Guardianship for the Elderly,* STANFORD LAW REVIEW 31:1003 (July 1979); *Legal Problems of the Aged and Infirm—The Durable Power of Attorney—Planned Protective Services and the Living Will,* REAL PROPERTY PROBATE & TRUST JOURNAL 13(1):1–67 (Spring 1978).
26. *See, e.g.,* Schlesinger, *Deeds of Guardianship,* PROBATE & PROPERTY 8:4 (1978).
27. Recipients of funds from several government agencies (Civil Service, Department of Defense, Railroad Retirement Board, Social Security Administration, Veterans Administration) can have substitute payees appointed if the individual meets a test of incapacity that varies from agency to agency. *See* Regan, *supra* note 24, at 612–13.
28. *See, e.g.,* ALA. CODE §38-9-1 *et seq* (Supp. 1982).
29. R. ALLEN, E. FERSTER, H. WEIHOFEN, MENTAL IMPAIRMENT AND LEGAL INCOMPETENCY (Prentice-Hall, Englewood Cliffs, N.J.) (1968).
30. *Id.* at 39–40. *See also In re* Boyer, 636 P.2d 1085 (Utah 1981).
31. FLA. STAT. ANN. §§744.102(5), 744.331(1) (West Supp. 1984).
32. "Gravely disabled" is recommended by the Suggested Statute on Guardianship. *See Legal Issues in State Mental Health Care: Proposals for Change— Guardianship,* MENTAL DISABILITY LAW REPORTER 2(4):444 (January/Febru-

ary 1978) [hereinafter cited as *Proposals for Change—Guardianship*].

33. For definition of "lack the capacity," *see id.* at 450, and SCHMIDT, *et al., supra* note 6, at 191. Arguably, this criterion is a "constitutional precondition" to intervention in an individual's life by court order. *See Legal Issues in State Mental Health Care: Proposals for Change—Civil Commitment,* MENTAL DISABILITY LAW REPORTER 1(1):89–93 (July/August 1977). *See also* Colyar v. Third Judicial District Court, 469 F. Supp. 424 (D. Utah 1979); Kinner v. State, 382 So.2d 756 (Fla.2d D.C.A. 1980).

34. CAL. WELF. & INST. CODE §§5008(h) 5350 (West 1972).

35. BROWN, *supra* note 16, at 287.

36. *See Proposals for Change—Guardianship, supra* note 32, at 450; SCHMIDT, *et al., supra* note 6, at 191.

37. *Proposals for Change—Guardianship, supra* note 32, at 133, 450; SCHMIDT, *et al., supra* note 6, at 192.

38. A Los Angeles study involving over 1,000 guardianship and conservatorship filings found that in 84 percent of the cases, the only persons present at the hearing were the judge, petitioner, and petitioner's attorney. National Senior Citizens Law Center, untitled, unpublished study, cited by Horstman, P.M., *Protective Services for the Elderly: The Limits of Parens Patriae,* MISSOURI LAW REVIEW 40(2):215, 235 (Spring 1975). Alexander and Lewin found that alleged incompetents are frequently not brought to court and if they were, only 16 percent had guardians ad litem appearing for them at the hearing. ALEXANDER, LEWIN, *supra* note 17, at 25.

39. FLA. STAT. §744.331(4) (1979) states: "The hearings shall be conducted in as informal a manner as may be consistent with orderly procedure and in a physical setting not likely to have a harmful effect on the mental health of the alleged incompetent."

40. Horstman, *supra* note 38, at 235.

41. *See* ALEXANDER, LEWIN, *supra* note 17, at 59; Horstman, *supra* note 38, at 236, 245; Solender, E.K., *The Guardian Ad Litem: A Valuable Representative or an Illusory Safeguard?,* TEXAS TECH LAW REVIEW 7(3):619 (Spring 1976).

42. *See* Alexander, G.J., *Foreward: Life, Liberty, and Property Rights for the Elderly,* ARIZONA LAW REVIEW 17(2):267 (1975).

43. *See* Horstman, *supra* note 38, at 260; Mitchell, *supra* note 10, at 459.

44. Mitchell, *supra* note 10, at 456–59.

45. *See, e.g.,* Levy, R.J., *Protecting the Mentally Retarded: An Empirical Survey and Evaluation of the Establishment of State Guardianship in Minnesota,* MINNESOTA LAW REVIEW 49:821 (1965).

46. *Id.* at 881; Mitchell, *supra* note 10, at 454.

47. Perlin, M., *Representing Individuals in the Commitment and Guardianship Process,* in K. FRIEDMAN, LEGAL RIGHTS OF MENTALLY DISABLED PERSONS (Practicing Law Institute, New York) (1979) at 501. Such practice in mental disability cases is not only unprofessional, but also probably unconstitutional. State *ex rel.* Memmel v. Munday, 249 N.W.2d 573 (Wis. 1977), *affirming,* No. 441-417 (Wis. Cir. Ct., Milwaukee Cty., August 18, 1976), *cited in* MENTAL DISABILITY LAW REPORTER 1(3):183 (1976). A vigorous and sophisticated public defender reduced the involuntary commitment rate to 2 percent following this

litigation. Zander, T., The Mental Commitment Law as Scapegoat (Milwaukee, Wis.) (August 1979). *See also In re* Paunack, 355 So.2d 1195 (Fla. 1978).

48. *See* SCHMIDT, *et al., supra* note 6, at 149–64; Final Report of the Grand Jury, Dade County, Fla. (Nov. 9, 1982) at 26–36. *See* Miami Herald, November 10, 1982, at D–1; Editorial, Miami Herald, November 11, 1982; *see generally* Sherman, R.B., *Guardianship: Time for Reassessment,* FORDHAM LAW REVIEW 49(3):350 (December 1980).

49. Eleven states have adopted the Code in significant part: Alaska, Arizona, Colorado, Idaho, Maine, Minnesota, Montana, Nebraska, New Mexico, North Dakota, and Utah.

50. *See* AMERICAN BAR ASSOCIATION COMMISSION ON THE MENTALLY DISABLED, DEVELOPMENTAL DISABILITIES STATE LEGISLATIVE PROJECT, GUARDIANSHIP AND CONSERVATORSHIP (ABA, Chicago) (1979) at 75–167 [hereinafter cited as DEVELOPMENTAL DISABILITIES STATE LEGISLATIVE PROJECT]; *Guardianship and Conservatorship Act: Introduction and Short Form Model Statute,* MENTAL DISABILITY LAW REPORTER 3(4):264 (July/August 1979); *Proposals for Change—Guardianship, supra* note 32, at 444–48; Legal Research and Services for the Elderly, National Council of Senior Citizens, Inc., *Guardianship and Conservatorship,* in LEGISLATIVE APPROACHES TO THE PROBLEMS OF THE ELDERLY: A HANDBOOK OF MODEL STATE STATUTES (1971) at 119; Regan, Springer, *supra* note 8, at 75.

51. *See* SCHMIDT, *et al., supra* note 6, at 179–203. This model was introduced by Representative Kirkwood during the 1980 Florida legislative session as House Bill 539. One review of the model statute, while complimenting the provision of due process protection, seems to suggest that it does not go far enough. National Senior Citizens Law Center Washington Weekly (April 18, 1980) at 4–5.

52. The American Bar Association in August 1980 adopted as policy a resolution (Report No. 111) urging states to enact laws calling for limited guardianship, where appropriate, to help persons with diminished capacity to live in the general community with maximum self-sufficiency. *See* FLA. STAT. ANN. §343.12(2) (West Supp. 1984). *But see* Axilbund, *supra* note 5 (indicating infrequent use of limited guardianship in the 12 to 16 limited guardian states). To the extent that all-or-nothing guardianship is a deterrent to adjudication of incompetency in cases of partial incapacity, limited guardianship increases the necessity for procedural protection because the risk of erroneous adjudications increases. Also, despite a presumption of competency, partial incompetency may taint, both legally and practically, those capacities that are not adjudicated. The Florida Bar's Committee on the Mentally Disabled has engaged in extensive preparation of a partial guardianship bill that enjoys widespread support, except, so far, from the Real Property, Probate, and Trust Law Section.

53. Twenty-two states offer the proposed ward the right to a jury of peers. DEVELOPMENTAL DISABILITIES STATE LEGISLATIVE PROJECT, *supra* note 50, at 5.

54. *See* Lessard v. Schmidt, 349 F. Supp. 1078, 1101 n.33, 1102 (E.D. Wis. 1972),

vacated, 414 U.S. 473 (1974), *remanded,* 379 F. Supp. 1376 (E.D. Wis. 1974), *vacated,* 421 U.S. 957 (1975), *remanded,* 413 F. Supp. 1318 (E.D. Wis. 1976). *See also* Note, *The Fifth Amendment and Compelled Psychiatric Examinations: Implications of Estelle v.* Smith, GEORGE WASHINGTON LAW REVIEW 50(2):275 (January 1982).

55. *See* Ennis, B., Litwack, T., *Psychiatry and the Presumption of Expertise: Flipping Coins in the Courtroom,* CALIFORNIA LAW REVIEW 62(3):693, 708–11 (May 1974).

56. *See generally* SCHMIDT, *et al., supra* note 6.

57. Florida contains a disproportionate number of older persons who are geographically separated from family and friends.

58. This group consists primarily of people who had been involuntarily committed, but released without the simple restoration of competency. FLA. STA. §744.464 (1979).

59. *See* Schmidt, Peters, *supra* note 12.

60. *See* FLA. STAT. §394.471 (1979) relating to the validity of prior involuntary placement orders. This section converts pre-1972 involuntary placement to voluntary placements but does not restore corresponding pre-1972 incompetencies. *See In re* Gamble, 394 A.2d 308 (N.H. 1978) (state's responsibility to provide guardians for indigent incompetent residents of state mental health hospitals). *See also* Vecchione v. Wohlgemuth, 377 F. Supp. 1361 (E.D. Pa. 1974), 426 F. Supp. 1297 (E.D. Pa. 1977), *aff'd,* 558 F.2d 150 (3rd Cir. 1977), *cert. denied sub nom.* Beal v. Vecchione, 434 U.S. 943 (1977) ($9.1 million in Social Security benefits ordered returned to incompetent mental patients through state compensated guardian officers where benefits were taken without a hearing).

61. The current statute requires a guardian advocate to be appointed upon any finding of incompetency to consent to treatment. *See* FLA. STAT. §§394.459(3)(a), 394.467(3)(a), 394.467(4)(h) (1982). There is difficulty finding willing and responsible persons to serve as guardian advocates where there are no family, friends, or compensation. FLA. STAT. §393.12(2) (1980), creates a demand for guardian advocates of the retarded.

62. *See* SCHMIDT, *et al., supra* note 6, at 86–87, 128.

63. *Id.* at 193.

64. An up-to-date model public guardianship statute is available for guidance. *See* discussion, *supra* note 51.

65. In other parts of the country, some banks will profitably service small estates that are grouped together. Another idea is such service as a required public contribution. For additional discussion about the alternatives to public service, *see* Schmidt, W., *et al., Alternatives to Public Guardianship,* STATE & LOCAL GOVERNMENT REVIEW 14:28 (1982).

66. *See* FLA. STAT. §744.305 (1982).

67. *See* SCHMIDT, *et al., supra* note 6, at 149–56.

68. *See* National Center for Law and the Handicapped, Guardianship of the Mentally Impaired: A Critical Analysis (1977); Alexander, G.J., *On Being Imposed Upon by Artful or Designing Persons—The California Experience with the*

Involuntary Placement of the Aged, SAN DIEGO LAW REVIEW 14(5):1083 (July 1977); Alexander, G.J., *Who Benefits from Conservatorship?,* TRIAL 13(5):30 (May 1977); Bell, W.G., Schmidt, W., Miller, K.S., *Public Guardianship and the Elderly: Findings from a National Study,* THE GERONTOLOGIST 21:194 (1981); Coleman, L., Solomon, T., *Parens Patriae "Treatment": Legal Punishment in Disguise,* HASTINGS LAW QUARTERLY 3(2):345 (Spring 1976); Effland, R.W., *Caring for the Elderly under the Uniform Probate Code,* ARIZONA LAW REVIEW 17(2):373 (1975); Frachter, W.F., *Toward Uniform Guardianship Legislation,* MICHIGAN LAW REVIEW 64(6):983 (April 1966); Hodgson, R.J., *Guardianship of Mentally Retarded Persons: Three Approaches to a Long Neglected Problem,* ALBANY LAW REVIEW 37(3):407 (1973); Kart, Backham, *Black-White Differentials in the Institutionalization of the Elderly,* SOCIAL FORCES 54:901 (1976); McDougal, M.S., Lasswell, H.D., Chen, L.C., *The Human Rights of the Aged: An Application of the Norm of Non-Discrimination,* UNIVERSITY OF FLORIDA LAW REVIEW 28(3):639 (Spring 1976); Morris, G.H., *Conservatorship for the Gravely Disabled: California's Nondeclaration of Nonindependence,* SAN DIEGO LAW REVIEW 15:201 (1977); Pickering, C.L., *Limitations on Individual Rights in California Incompetency Proceedings,* UNIVERSITY OF CALIFORNIA AT DAVIS LAW REVIEW 7:457 (1977); Report of the ABA Committee on Legal Incapacity, *Guardianship of Property of Incompetents,* REAL PROPERTY, PROBATE & TRUST JOURNAL 9:535 (Winter 1974); Report of Committee on Problems Relating to Persons under Disability, *Conservatorship: Present Practice and Uniform Probate Code Compared,* REAL PROPERTY, PROBATE & TRUST JOURNAL 5:507 (Spring 1970); Rohan, P.J., *Caring for Persons under a Disability: A Critique of the Role of the Conservator and the "Substitution of Judgment" Doctrine,* ST. JOHN'S LAW REVIEW 52(1) (Fall 1977); Regan, J.J., *Adult Protective Services: An Appraisal and a Prospectus,* in NATIONAL LAW AND SOCIAL WORK SEMINAR: PROCEEDINGS AND PROSPECTS (University of Southern Maine, Portland, Me.) (1982); Regan, J.J., *Protecting the Elderly: The New Paternalism,* HASTINGS LAW JOURNAL 32(5):1111 (May 1981); Comment, *An Assessment of the Pennsylvania Estate Guardianship Incompetency Standard,* UNIVERSITY OF PENNSYLVANIA LAW REVIEW 124(4):1048 (April 1976); Comment, *North Carolina Guardianship Laws—The Need for Change,* NORTH CAROLINA LAW REVIEW 54:389 (1976); Comment, *Probate Code Conservatorships: A Legislative Grant of New Procedural Protections,* PACIFIC LAW JOURNAL 8(1):73 (January 1977); Note, *The Disguised Oppression of Involuntary Guardianship: Have the Elderly Freedom to Spend?* YALE LAW JOURNAL 73(4):676 (March 1964).

19

Functional Evaluation of the Elderly in Guardianship Proceedings

Bobbe Shapiro Nolan, J.D.

Guardianship has traditionally been presented by courts and in the literature as a benevolent mechanism[1] through which those who cannot protect themselves will be assisted through surrogate management of their assets,[2] their persons,[3] or both.[4] While notice has been taken of the significant deprivation of property[5] and liberty[6] inherent in a total guardianship,[7] authorities recognize the sad necessity of imposing plenary external control[8] over some of us when sufficient need is shown. The power to do so is grounded in the state's police power and the traditional role of the state as *parens patriae.*[9]

THE GUARDIANSHIP DILEMMA

Although the tradition of guardianship is old and established, the institution has been criticized recently. Notwithstanding the benevolent intent of most guardianship statutes, of the parties who petition for guardianship,[10] and of the professionals who recommend that guardianship be imposed, guardianship can be a form of social control. People whose actions are approved or go unnoticed within their milieu do not become incompetent wards. People who do what professionals advise seldom find themselves the subject of guardianship proceedings.[11] The statutes themselves testify to the normative quality of their restrictiveness.[12] Only the individual whose behavior passes the limit of social tolerance experiences society's benevolent control through the probate court's intervention.

Reprinted with permission of the American Society of Law & Medicine from LAW, MEDICINE & HEALTH CARE, October 1984, pp. 210–18.

Courts tend to disclaim the social control function of guardianship; for example, one court noted that while poor business judgment would be an insufficient reason for appointing a guardian, the fact that the defendant's second, much younger husband was arguably misusing some of her wealth and that the defendant suffered from a tremor due to arteriosclerosis was sufficient.[13] Similarly, the giving of gifts by the elderly, which could be regarded as normal, can become dissipation of assets of vulnerability to designing persons in the eyes of the court when guardianship proceedings are brought.[14] Particularly in the case where guardianship is sought for the elderly, it seems that the prevention of socially disapproved role behaviors becomes an important court function.[15]

Some commentators have related this judicial function to a social devaluation of the elderly, who are viewed as useless and burdensome.[16] Other commentators postulate social oppression of all nonproductive classes of people, noting restrictions on the privacy and liberty of the mentally and physically handicapped; appropriation of the estates of the elderly, mentally retarded, and mentally ill; and limitations upon the civil rights of minors and other groups considered incompetent.[17]

Probate court judges who decide guardianship cases labor under a terrible load. Criticisms in the legal literature have been levelled against statutory wording and procedural weaknesses.[18] The devastating potential impact of an incompetency adjudication also cannot be ignored.[19] The judges encounter tremendous caseloads and can give only limited time to deliberations in each case.[20] They may decide guardianship cases with an almost complete lack of evidence, as was found by one state appellate court which reversed the probate court's determination.[21] Finally, the decision is essentially a prediction of future behavior,[22] a difficult task for anyone lacking prescience or even extensive training in the assessment of human behavior.[23]

In order to decide whether an alleged incompetent needs the protection of a guardianship so much that the concomitant sacrifice of his liberty, privacy, and property rights is justified, the judge must draw inferences from evidence that often is limited both in substance and in reliability. Guardianship petitions customarily recite only the barest facts supporting the alleged incompetence; in many states, they are couched in the words of the statute, circular and conclusory though this may be.[24] The evidence presented at the hearing is in many cases uncorroborated.[25] Frequently, the hearing is *ex parte;* neither the judge nor any other officer of the court has observed the defendant's behavior.[26] Even in the rare case where a guardian *ad litem* has been appointed, it appears that this officer tends to view himself as an objective or neutral party rather than as an advocate for the defendant's interests.[27] Sometimes the defendant's attorney (where there is one) sees as his duty the representation of the best interests rather than the expressed desires of the defendant.[28] Thus, the trial judge in a guardianship hearing suffers under any or all of the following handicaps:

1. the allegations of defendant's incompetence lack specificity
2. the evidence is hearsay
3. the petition is uncontested
4. even if contested, the defendant does not always appear
5. there is no disinterested evidence of defendant's behavior
6. the role of the guardian *ad litem* is incompletely fulfilled
7. the defendant's attorney fails to advocate effectively for the client's expressed interests

This article does not purport to offer a detailed analysis or critique of guardianship statutes, due process concerns that are important to the guardianship process, or the motivations of those who initiate, administer, and enforce the process. Rather, the foregoing summary provides a background for the discussion of a mechanism which could improve guardianship proceedings. This mechanism, the functional evaluation of the prospective ward, can provide the information needed by a fact finder to apply fairly the statutory standard for incompetence that is effective in a particular state. This article argues that a functional evaluation of the alleged incompetent provides an essential element in the process of deciding whether a guardian is needed. The article explores the way that a functional evaluation is affected by the various statutory definitions of incompetence, the components of a functional evaluation, and the uses of functional evaluation data in the hearing.

CONTENT OF THE FUNCTIONAL EVALUATION

The functional assessment concept, while arguably a new one for attorneys, is well known among human services advocates. Students of nursing, counseling, and social work have routinely been instructed regarding the importance of functional assessment and the techniques for carrying out the evaluation. Physical and occupational therapists concentrate heavily on specific components of functional ability. It is evident that there is no lack of expertise; thus, it is surprising that such expertise is so seldom sought in guardianship proceedings, with the result that nurses and social workers are apparently unaware of this potential use of their knowledge.

Information gathered in a functional assessment describes how the individual is managing his tasks of daily living and to what extent he is satisfied with his circumstances and abilities. There are many detailed assessment frameworks available, which have varied emphases and aims.[29] In general, however, information is sought regarding the defendant's basic needs: income adequacy and spending patterns (physical ability to manage currency and check writing, whether pension checks arrive consistently); adequacy of food, clothing, and shelter (ability to buy, transport, store, and prepare food; ability to eat; choice of diet; ability to dress and undress; adequacy of laundry facilities and their use; upkeep of shelter; warmth and ventilation; cleanliness of environment; safety of home). The evaluator also assesses physical functioning (ability to walk, climb stairs, reach, bend, get in and out of chair and tub); sensory functioning (ability to see, hear, feel, react in ways that do not endanger his health or safety). In addition, the defendant's access to helpful resources such as friends, relatives, physicians, emergency facilities, transportation, and the like is considered. The defendant is asked about his satisfaction with present circumstances, his desire for change, and what specific assistance he would like to have.

A very thorough evaluation would also explore such emotional factors as loneliness, anxiety, and life satisfaction. If a mental health assessment has not been made separately, the evaluator can explore orientation to reality, memory functioning, reasoning ability, abstract reasoning, and other components of mental status.[30] In many cases, however, it is advisable to leave detailed mental health assessment to experts in psychology and psychiatry.[31]

THE TECHNIQUE'S METHOD

These parameters are assessed through several complementary techniques. The evaluator observes the defendant throughout the evaluation. He or she invites self-report by the defendant, whose own view of circumstances should be given a presumption of validity unless clear evidence refutes it. The evaluator also observes the defendant's environment. He or she may gather data from others who know the defendant, such as friends, relatives, and care givers. He or she may use formal tests, such as the Short Portable Mental Status Questionnaire[32] or the Older Americans Resources and Services Multidimensional Functional Assessment Questionnaire,[33] which have been developed for such situations.

The functional assessment differs from other sorts of evaluations and diagnostic methods primarily in its focus on *resulting behavior*. The functional evaluator records the extent to which a subject carries out activities of daily living effectively. Thus, for example, when the defendant is disoriented as to date and time but uses newspapers and television announcements as cues to compensate for his deficit, functional evaluation would credit the adaptation as an effective use of resources. In contrast, a formal mental status evaluation would note the disorientation negatively. The functional evaluator is less interested, therefore, in the cause of disability, the prognosis, or the potential for treatment. These considerations may be relevant to the eventual determination of incompetency, but are not part of the behavioral evaluation.

Another example should clarify this point. An elderly person may fail to utilize his upstairs bathroom for any of a number of reasons: failing memory, physical weakness, amputation of a limb, arthritis, fear of falling, failure to recognize his need to use the toilet, or knowledge that the plumbing is clogged. Our evaluation of whether that decision is competently made will depend on the use of resources: has he or she found alternative ways of keeping him or herself and the environment clean? That is the *functional* determination.

If the evaluator has doubts about the validity of defendant's self-report, he or she can ask the person to demonstrate some of the activities involved. When dealing with elderly individuals, some clinical judgments may influence the evaluator's choice of method. Ordinarily, it is expedient to conduct the evaluation at the defendant's residence;[34] after all, it is the defendant's ability to maintain himself in this environment that is under scrutiny. If the subject's energy level is limited, it may be necessary to conduct the assessment in several stages. Indeed, the validity of the assessment may well be enhanced by seeing the defendant several times since a "one-shot" interview is susceptible to manipulation. There need be no secrecy about the purpose of the evaluation, for the defendant should have received notice of the pending proceedings and may be eager to prove his or her ability to manage independently.[35]

RESULTS OF THE EVALUATION

Whether the evaluator should draw a conclusion from this assessment is open to debate.[36] To some extent, the appropriateness of a recommendation or conclusion will depend on the role that the evaluator is assigned to play in the guardianship hearing process. If the evaluator is viewed as an expert witness, a conclusion would be admissible when properly framed. For example, such a conclusion would be admissible when it is within the evaluator's area of expertise, is based on the relevant facts, and is not a conclusion of law or an "ultimate fact." Where the evaluator is an agent of the court analogous, for example, to a presentence investigator, another set of expectations comes into play. A discussion of who should gather and present functional assessment data occurs later in this chapter.

Regardless of how the evaluator presents the findings, he or she should be measuring the defendant against the presumption of competency (whatever the standard for competency is in a particular state), not against any theoretical image of high-level wellness.[37] The evaluator must be aware that he or she is measuring not whether the defendant could function better, nor whether he or she needs the assistance of community agencies. Rather, the evaluator is measuring whether this person's functioning is on a level so minimal that he or she should no longer be allowed to bear responsibility for his or her own decisions.

STATUTORY STANDARDS

The usefulness of the functional evaluation in guardianship proceedings depends on the state statute governing the imposition of guardianship. Thus, this article now turns to a discussion of the various sorts of guardianship statutes and their effects on the availability of functional evaluations.

Statutes on guardianship attempt to define the point at which society ceases to regard an individual as competent to continue bearing responsibility for his or her own decisions.[38] The historical roots of these definitions evidence the colorful,[39] if stigmatizing,[40] language of our ancestors, as well as the law's struggle to encompass the specifics of human behavior in applicable generalizations. Modern efforts, while earnest, are only slightly more meaningful. Generally, statutory definitions seem to be ambling toward a combination of elements: the defendant's management of his activities of daily living seem inadequate or unsafe to interested, actively involved observers; the defendant's behavior may be due to factors beyond his control;[41] and it is more likely than not that the defendant's condition interferes with his ability to avoid becoming a public charge financially.[42]

Because guardianship statutes are based entirely on state law, there are 50 variations on the theme. In the main, however, the standards fall into three classifications: the traditional causal link statute, the Uniform Probate Code type (which also contains a causal link, but to different effect), and the functional disability or therapeutic type. Each is discussed below.

THE CAUSAL LINK STATUTE

The traditional standard, once used in almost all states, survives in the Ohio statute:

> "Incompetent" means any person who by reason of advanced age, improvidence, or mental or physical disability or infirmity, chronic alcoholism, mental retardation, or mental illness, is incapable of taking proper care of himself or his property or fails to provide for his family or other persons for whom he is charged by law to provide. . . .[43]

In this statute, the ward must have a diagnosis (all the specified conditions with the exception of "improvidence" and "advanced age"[44]), presumably obtained through a proper medical workup. Evidently, the legislature considered that a condition beyond the ward's control was a necessary element in the process. The diagnosis must be the *cause* of the socially disapproved behavior. Therefore, one who failed properly to care for himself or herself or his or her property, but who was able to do so (that is, he or she chose to be deviant), should not be declared incompetent. The definition thus excludes the sociopathic personality and should exclude the eccentric who knowingly chooses to care for himself or herself "improperly" or who disposes of his or her property in unusual ways.[45]

In states where such a causal link statute is in force, evidence from the functional evaluation can help to establish whether the defendant is taking "proper" care of him or herself and his or her property.[46] The evaluation is a description of behaviors, not a diagnostic procedure. When performed objectively and carefully, the evaluation supplies data to the judge who must decide whether the behaviors constitute improper care of self and property, whether the improper care is due to incapability, and whether the incapability is caused by the diagnosis/condition.[47] At least one commentator has noted that a detailed analysis of the facts in guardianship hearings seldom appears in reported opinions.[48] It seems likely that one reason for judges' analytical silence is a dearth of behavioral information at the hearing. Judges cannot base detailed analysis on a vacuum.[49]

THE UNIFORM PROBATE CODE

The Uniform Probate Code emphasizes lack of cognitive and communicative ability as a necessary criterion for incompetence. Many states have grafted local variations onto this standard, which was an attempt to require some objectively observable behavior as evidence of incapacity. The terminology has also been changed in the periodic attempt to escape the acquired stigma of older wordings.[50] The Utah statute is a typical example:

> "Incapacitated person" means any person who is impaired by reason of mental illness, mental deficiency, physical illness or disability, advanced age, chronic use of drugs, chronic intoxication, or other cause (except minority) to the extent that he lacks sufficient understanding or capacity to make or communicate responsible decisions regarding his person.[51]

It should be noted that these decisions concern only the person of the defendant; that is, his or her self-care, safety, and comfort. Financial management capability is not under scrutiny except insofar as it may affect personal care. An examination of the language of the Utah statute shows that the label has changed but the causative conditions are familiar. The causative condition, however, does not lead to inability to care for oneself or manage one's property; instead, it leads to a lack of understanding or an inability to make or communicate decisions considered by others to be responsible.[52]

Where the allegedly incapacitated individual is impaired by one of the listed diagnoses but can understand and communicate his or her decisions, the only question of law or fact is whether such decisions are responsible. In other circumstances, the judge must once again make the causal link between the diagnosis and the lack of understanding or decision-making ability, as well as the wisdom, responsibility, or social acceptability of the decisions made.

It is worth noting that interpretations of the Uniform Probate Code standard have varied widely among the states where it is in effect. The constructions of "sufficient understanding" and "responsible decisions" are highly subject to value judgments. One state has restricted application of the incapacity standard to those situations where the health or safety of the defendant was endangered. The Utah Supreme Court held that to avoid unconstitutional overbroadness, the determination of inability to make "responsible decisions" can be applied only if the defendant's "decision making process is so impaired that he is unable to care for his personal safety or unable to attend to and provide for such necessities as food, shelter, clothing and medical care, without which physical injury or illness may occur."[53]

Some states that use the Uniform Probate Code, while not limiting the application of the definition as carefully as the Utah court, have sought to limit the effect of the guardianship statute by requiring that a guardianship be selective,[54] in the nature of a protective order,[55] and that particular powers vested in the guardian be specified in the order. Other powers may be retained by the ward.[56]

Functional evaluation of the defendant is particularly useful in states with this sort of statutory definition for incompetence. With so many factual findings required, the presentation of unadorned medical diagnoses or conclusory anecdotal evidence is clearly insufficient to prove an even *prima facie* case. Information obtained from the functional evaluation would assist in determining the extent of the impairment, the level of defendant's understanding, his or her ability and willingness to communicate his or her decisions, and the quality of those decisions. The functional evaluator thus assesses the effectiveness of the defendant's decisions. Do they deprive the defendant of the necessities of life? Are they consistent? Does the defendant have reasons for his or her decisions? It should be left to the finder of fact whether such decisions are reasonable.

THE FUNCTIONAL OR THERAPEUTIC APPROACH

A current trend in gerontological and mental health circles favors a broader, nondiagnostic or therapeutic[57] approach, as adopted in New Hampshire:

> "Incapacity" means a legal, not a medical disability and shall be measured by functional limitations. It shall be construed to mean or refer to any person who has suffered, is suffering, or is likely to suffer substantial harm due to an inability to provide for his personal needs for food, clothing, shelter, health care, or safety or an inability to manage his or her property or financial affairs. . . ."

> "Functional limitations" means behavior or conditions in an individual which impair his or her ability to participate in and perform minimal activities of daily living that secure and maintain proper food, clothing, shelter, health care, or safety for himself or herself.[58]

These are the sorts of parameters evaluated in a functional assessment. The New Hampshire statute requires that specific acts or occurrences of incapacity or functional limitation be included in the complaint,[59] that such occurrences have taken place within six months of the filing date,[60] and that at least one act have occurred within 20 days of the filing.[61] Thus, some notice of recent behavior deemed harmful by the prospective guardian is afforded to the defendant.[62] While the medical diagnosis may be relevant to the prospective ward's ability to care for him or herself, it is in no way determinative. The defendant's ability to manage his or her life is what is under scrutiny;[63] the presumption of competency cannot be overcome without specific behavioral manifestations documented in a statement accompanying the complaint[64] and proven beyond a reasonable doubt at the hearing.[65]

This statute mandates that a functional evaluation be made and formally considered. The analysis shifts, then, to consideration of who will make the evaluation, under what circumstances it should be done, and the implications of relying on this evaluative process.

IMPLICATIONS OF USING FUNCTIONAL EVALUATIONS

There can be little doubt that there is considerable potential for violation of the defendant's constitutional rights in the guardianship process. Even without formal functional evaluation, the defendant's exercise of privacy rights, liberty, and property rights can become a part of the accusations against him. When a functional evaluation becomes a mandatory or recommended part of the proceedings, as under the Uniform Probate Code, the potential for violation of defendant's rights increases.[66] Before use of the functional evaluation becomes widespread, we should consider seriously this potentiality for violating the defendant's rights.

By its very nature, the functional evaluation could violate the defendant's privacy interest. The potential ward has a common law and statutory interest in being left alone,[67] as well as a fundamental constitutional right to privacy in his or her familial and procreative activities.[68] Both of these areas are scrutinized in a properly conducted functional evaluation.[69] The evaluator investigates whether the defendant has resources for filling his or her needs for love and belonging; although the defendant may refuse to answer, such a refusal is likely to be construed as a manifestation of paranoia. The interest in being left alone is violated by the very effort to make the functional evaluation, for the evaluator is required to be persistent and thorough.

Because it is the defendant's competency that is the matter in controversy, all of his or her behavior apparently falls within the discovery rules,[70] at least in states where the federal discovery model has been adopted. This implies that the plaintiff can be assisted by the court to conduct an inquiry into defendant's most intimate concerns, and that a proper defense might require even more intimate revelations of competent conduct.[71]

Although the determination of incompetency is in no way a criminal proceeding, the result in terms of the defendant's liberty interests may be very similar. He or she may be deprived of control over residence, associations, property, diet, and ability to go where he or she wishes. Functional evaluation of behavior, in these circumstances, could be seen as a sort of self-incrimination, performed under the compulsion of the discovery rules in violation of defendant's interests. In view of the potential deprivation of liberty, perhaps some due process protection should be given to the defendant's revelations during a functional evaluation,[72] even before a determination of incompetency is made.[73]

Nevertheless, the serious potential deprivations of liberty and privacy do not preclude a formal functional assessment if the defendant objects. Regardless of the defendant's objections, the court will make an evaluation of his or her ability to function when it determines whether the defendant is incompetent. The question is not whether an evaluation should be made but, rather, whether the evaluation that is made will occur with or without valid and reliable information. Because these hearings are so often conducted *ex parte*, with the complaint's unsupported allegations attested to only by conclusory written statements from physicians, any descriptive data can only improve the defendant's chances of a fair and informed verdict.

WHO SHOULD PERFORM THE EVALUATION?

If we grant that it is desirable to perform a functional evaluation, the question remains as to who should gather this information. The underlying question, which seems to cause some discomfort, is whether an evaluation of the defendant's functioning in a proceeding benevolent and protective in intent should be a tool of the adversarial process—and whether this process should be adversarial.

Clearly, the legal philosophy behind the organization of the guardianship hearing influences the way in which functional evaluation data are gathered and used. If the proceeding is strictly adversarial, the parties would be free to gather functional information, each with his or her own interest in mind, and to present such information in the light most favorable to his or her case. If, on the other hand, the information is to be considered neutral (as, for instance, when the court calls its own witness or demands its own investigation), the mode of presentation of the information must vary. The possibility that a fragile defendant could be adversely affected by being subjected to repeated functional evaluations by various experts should also be considered.

As a society, we need to come to terms with the purpose of procedural safeguards in these proceedings, and to use them properly or to change them. If we accept the desirability of the traditional adversarial process, evidence regarding the prospective ward's functional adequacy can be presented by either party or sought independently by the court. Nevertheless, the source of the evidence requires serious consideration, as there are disadvantages to each potential source. These disadvantages bring into question, again, the usefulness of the functional evaluation.

The person petitioning for guardianship must include in the complaint an allegation[74] of the defendant's inability to manage his affairs. The allegations tend to be anecdotal; the hearsay character of the evidence has been stressed earlier. If the plaintiff wishes to obtain a comprehensive functional evaluation of the potential ward, the previously discussed privacy and quasi-self-incrimination considerations come into play. In the event that the defendant resists the plaintiff's investigation, the court's enforcement may be sought—a situation distasteful to some courts and attorneys. When the plaintiff is a relative, usually with a future interest in the estate and certainly with a present interest in managing the person and/or the estate, an evident conflict of interest taints his or her role as objective assessor of defendant's competency. One may question whether the plaintiff should be required or permitted further to endanger these essential relationships by investigating the functional behavior of the potential ward. Of course, it may be that bad feelings are inevitable whenever persuasion fails and people must turn to the law; here, guardianship proceedings are no different from other legal encounters.

Similar problems may arise if the functional evaluation is performed by the guardian *ad litem*. This individual, usually an attorney, is supposed to represent what is in the defendant's interest, not necessarily what the defendant desires.[75] Guardians *ad litem* tend to take a neutral stance, regarding themselves as court representatives and investigators. In the end, their testimony is likely to support imposition of the guardianship.[76] It would be unusual for such an individual to have extensive expertise in the functional evaluation of competency, although if he or she did, the court could request that he or she perform such an assessment. Failing that expertise, however, it would seem inappropriate to rely on the guardian *ad litem* for functional evaluation data.

The defendant's counsel can gather information to counter the plaintiff's allegations of incompetency and indeed, in the classic adversary model, that is exactly what he or she should do. If the defendant does not desire a guardianship or wants only a limited guardianship, his or her counsel has a duty to present what evidence he or she can to support the presumption of competency. Here, expert testimony regarding defendant's functional performance may be the key to continued independence. There are community resources, such as senior citizens' centers, schools of nursing and social work, or public health departments, which can supply a person qualified to make such observations if the defendant will waive the professional duty of confidentiality.

THE ROLE OF THE COURT

The final evaluation of the defendant's abilities is, of course, for the court, but the court could also gather evidence. Guardianship decisions in some states require the judge to observe the defendant; in other states this is discretionary.[77] Where the defendant has not answered the complaint or has refused to appear at the hearing, presumably the court would have to visit the defendant—often a time-consuming and uncomfortable procedure for probate court judges, who are seldom trained in the multidimensional assessment of human functioning. The judge might be more willing to observe the defendant if he had already received a comprehensive evaluation from a trained assessor. In addition, not all judges consider observation of the defendant desirable; in one case, the judge refused to allow testimony or observation of the defendant, even when requested on the record.[78]

The court can obtain its own expert witnesses and can compel medical and psychiatric examinations.[79] Some judges have required that court-appointed physicians examine the defendant even when medical testimony was presented by the parties.[80] In cases where little credible evidence is provided by the parties, it would be more efficient for the court to require an objective evaluation than to award the guardianship as a precautionary measure or to dismiss the case to be brought again in the near future.

In states which have adopted the Uniform Probate Code, the court is either enabled or mandated to utilize the services of a court visitor.[81] This trained individual visits the defendant, his or her present residence, the proposed guardian, the proposed residence, and may interview the physician. The court visitor's findings are presented to the court.[82] The visitor can be a court employee or an employee of a designated public or charitable agency, but is regarded as a representative of the court itself, not of the parties. Cases involving the testimony of a court visitor have not yet been reported, so the likely conflicts and problems with this sort of evaluation can only be imagined. The main drawback at present is probably funding of the service, which can be expensive, and for which means of payment may not have been provided by statute.[83]

In the sense that court-obtained information is, theoretically, neutral, it appeals to many as a possible reform in guardianship hearings. Once the desirability of a comprehensive functional evaluation is established, it seems logical that it be done by the court's agent. This has the benefit of supplying the same information to all, untainted by conflict of interest. Social service and health care professionals are likely to agree, recognizing that they are the people most likely to be carrying out the evaluations.[84]

The assignment of such information gathering to the court's agent has the disadvantage of weakening the adversary system. The report of the court visitor or other agent is likely to be accorded greater deference than any evidence presented by the parties. Social service professionals, like many care givers, tend to attribute greater dependency to clients than do the clients themselves.[85] The professionals also demonstrate mainstream social values and a desire to see clients achieve better living standards.[86] Laudable though such attitudes may be, their influence on recommendations regarding potential wards must be recognized as a threat to the wards' personal liberty and autonomy.

Once the information from the functional evaluation has been presented in court, the judge's deliberations may be affected by it in various ways. Precisely what it is the judge must decide in a guardianship hearing will vary by state. Notwithstanding the difficulty of generalizing among diverse statutes, the lack of clarity in published opinions with regard to what is being determined, as discussed earlier, is truly regrettable. To facilitate analysis, judges might document whether each segment of the definition of incompetency or incapacity has been proven; in practice, one seldom sees such attention to detail. Other questions that seem to have been addressed by judges include: whether defendant would be better off with a guardian;[87] whether defendant could manage with the help of third parties without the imposition of guardianship, and whether this should be considered in the definition;[88] whether defendant might need a guardian in the future;[89] and whether defendant needs to be in a mental hospital.[90]

It is the judge's concept of what he or she is supposed to decide that will affect his or her use of whatever evidence he or she has heard, including the functional assessment data. The strength of a functional evaluation is that it can aid in answering these questions by providing detailed information about an elderly person's day-to-day functioning, which is the most basic concern of the competency evaluation. The probate judiciary, now so burdened by uncertainty in guardianship hearings, may be encouraged to use the information appropriately.

This chapter has explored the uses of a technique, the functional assessment, in the guardianship process. In view of the many criticisms expressed with regard to the conduct of a guardianship hearing in the United States, it would be presumptuous to present the functional evaluation as a cure-all. The technique does potentially threaten the individual rights and privacy of the person assessed. The technique has promise, however, as a way of providing real information to the court and the parties. Its wider use, while not a substitute for procedural reform, would facilitate just and informed decisions in incompetency hearings.

NOTES

1. The institution dates at least to Roman times, and apparently had as its root the protection of the ward's property. S.J. BRAKEL, R.S. ROCK, THE MENTALLY

DISABLED AND THE LAW (University of Chicago Press, Chicago, Ill.) (rev. ed. 1971) at 250.

2. Guardianship of the estate is authorized in all states. Where the Uniform Probate Code has been adopted, guardianship of the estate is termed conservatorship and the conservator takes on the duties of a trustee. UNIFORM PROBATE CODE §5-147. This distinction is immaterial to the thrust of this paper; thus, the terms "guardian" and "conservator" will be used interchangeably as will be the terms "ward," "incompetent," and "incapacitated person." On guardianship of the estate, *see* Effland, R.W., *Caring for the Elderly under the Uniform Probate Code*, ARIZONA LAW REVIEW 17(2):373–412 (1975); Note, *Legislation: The New York Conservator Law*, BUFFALO LAW REVIEW 22(1):487–98 (Fall 1972) [hereinafter referred to as *New York Conservator Law*]; Comment, *An Assessment of the Pennsylvania Estate Guardianship Incompetency Standard*, UNIVERSITY OF PENNSYLVANIA LAW REVIEW 124(4):1048–79 (April 1976) [hereinafter referred to as *Pennsylvania Estate Guardianship*].

3. Guardianship of the person involves such decisions as where the ward will live, who will care for him, and what activities he will be permitted. *See* Pickering, C.L., *Limitations on Individual Rights in California Incompetency Proceedings*, UNIVERSITY OF CALIFORNIA AT DAVIS LAW REVIEW 7:457–86 (1974) [hereinafter referred to as *California Incompetency Proceedings*].

4. In some states, if the court does not stipulate which type of guardianship is ordered, a statutory presumption favors "full" guardianship of both person and estate. *See, e.g.,* OHIO REV. CODE ANN. §2111.06 (Page Supp. 1983):

> If the powers of the person appointed as guardian of a minor or incompetent are not limited by the order of the appointment, such person shall be guardian both of the person and estate of the ward. In every instance the court shall appoint the same person as the guardian of the person and estate of any such ward, unless in the opinion of the court the interests of the ward will be promoted by the appointment of different persons as guardians of the person and of the estate. . . . A guardian of the person shall have the custody and provide for the maintenance of the ward. . . .

5. In states adopting the Uniform Probate Code, title to the ward's property is placed in the conservator. In more traditional states, disposition of the ward's property is subject to supervision of the court; any substantial alteration in the property requires specific permission. Effland, *supra* note 2, at 379.

6. An incompetent in most states is not free to determine his own place of residence, to vote, marry, drive, choose agents, or enter into contracts. Note, *The Disguised Oppression of Involuntary Guardianship: Have the Elderly Freedom to Spend*, YALE LAW JOURNAL 73(3):676–92 (March 1964) [hereinafter referred to as *Disguised Oppression*].

7. *See* Frolik, L.A., *Plenary Guardianship: An Analysis, A Critique, and a Proposal for Reform*, ARIZONA LAW REVIEW 23(2):599–660 (1981) (advocating a more limited model for guardianship designed to supplement the deficits exhibited by the ward). *See also* Comment, In re Boyer: *Guardianship of Incapacitated Adults in Utah*, UTAH LAW REVIEW 1982(2):427–43 (advocates the limiting of guardianship to deficits of the ward).

8. Even where only a conservatorship of the estate is imposed, control over the ward's activities can be extremely broad:

Seldom will there be a need to appoint a guardian for an elderly person, however, since appointment of a conservator will be adequate in most situations. The conservator's powers are ample to enable him to arrange whatever physical care is necessary, typically nursing home care. . . . The only real legal need for a guardian might arise when consent to medical treatment is required, but physicians and hospital administrators often are content with the signature of a spouse, or an adult child on behalf of the parent.

Effland, *supra* note 2, at 378–79 (citation deleted).

9. In contrast to civil commitment of the mentally ill, which relates more to police power and protection of the public, guardianship's purpose is protection of the helpless ward and his property. *See* Horstman, P.M., *Protective Services for the Elderly: The Limits of Parens Patriae,* MISSOURI LAW REVIEW 40(2):215, 217–25 (Spring 1975); Regan, J.J., *Protective Services for the Elderly: Commitment, Guardianship, and Alternatives,* WILLIAM AND MARY LAW REVIEW 13:569–622 (1972).

10. Occasional examples of plaintiffs motivated apparently by greed do appear. *See In re* Guardianship of Tyrrell, 190 N.E. 687 (Ohio 1963). Nonetheless, most petitioners for guardianship are acting out of concern for defendant's welfare. *See* BRAKEL & ROCK, *supra* note 1, at 260–61.

11. For an example of what can happen when medical treatment is refused, *see In re* Brooks' Estate, 205 N.E.2d 435 (Ill. 1965); Alexander, G.J., *Remaining Responsible: On Control of One's Health Needs in Aging,* SANTA CLARA LAW REVIEW 20:13, 44–45 (1980).

12. *E.g.,* OHIO REV. CODE ANN. §2111.01(D) (Page Supp. 1983) (requiring "proper" care of self or property); UTAH CODE ANN. §75-1-201(18) (Supp. 1983) ("responsible" decisions); N.H. REV. STAT. ANN. §464-A:2(VIII) (1983) ("proper" food, clothing, shelter, etc.).

13. Guardianship of Walters, 231 P.2d 473 (Cal. 1951).

14. *Disguised Oppression, supra* note 6, at 683; Annot., 9 A.L.R.3d 811–15.

15. Mitchell, A.M., *Involuntary Guardianship for Incompetents: A Strategy for Legal Services Advocates,* CLEARINGHOUSE REVIEW 12(8):451, 456–57 (December 1978).

16. *See generally* R. BUTLER, WHY SURVIVE? BEING OLD IN AMERICA (Harper & Row, New York) (1975).

17. *E.g.,* R.L. BURGDORF, JR., THE LEGAL RIGHTS OF HANDICAPPED PERSONS: CASES, MATERIALS AND TEXT (Paul H. Brookes, Publisher, Baltimore, Md.) (1980) at v, 1–52.

18. *See generally* Frolik, *supra* note 7; Dewey, F.A., *Civil Incompetency in Ohio: Determination and Effect,* UNIVERSITY OF CINCINNATI LAW REVIEW 34(4):419, 420 (Fall 1965); Zenoff, E.H., *Civil Incompetency in the District of Columbia,* GEORGE WASHINGTON LAW REVIEW 32:243, 244 (1963).

19. In the writer's personal experience, knowledge of such an adjudication can be lethal. The writer has known as least three wards whose physical conditions were not terminal but who refused to eat and died within two weeks of notice that guardianship had been imposed.

20. *See* Sherman, R.B., *Guardianship: Time for a Reassessment,* FORDHAM LAW RE-

VIEW 49(3):350, 351 (December 1980); Dewey, *supra* note 18, at 460, 461, n.51.

21. *In re* Conservatorship of Browne, 343 N.E.2d 61 (Ill. App. 1976). *See* Dewey, *supra* note 18, at 435 (in regard to judicial hospitalization).

22. *Pennsylvania Estate Guardianship, supra* note 2, at 1070–71 (discussion of difficulties in predicting behavior).

23. Prediction is problematic even for those with such training, however. *See, e.g.,* Leifer, R., *The Competency of the Psychiatrist to Assist in Determination of Incompetency: A Sceptical Inquiry into Courtroom Functions of Psychiatrists,* SYRACUSE LAW REVIEW 14(4):564, 574–75 (1963); Ennis, B., Litwack, T., *Psychiatry and the Presumption of Expertise: Flipping Coins in the Courtroom,* CALIFORNIA LAW REVIEW 62:693–752 (1974).

24. *See* Frolik, *supra* note 7, at 604; Zenoff, *supra* note 18, at 243–46; Dewey, *supra* note 18, at 434.

25. *See* Mitchell, *supra* note 15, at 451–55.

26. Dewey, *supra* note 18, at 434; Sherman, *supra* note 20, at 351.

27. Frolik, *supra* note 7, at 634–36; Zenoff, *supra* note 18, at 252.

28. Frolik, *supra* note 7, at 629–33. *See also Pennsylvania Estate Guardianship, supra* note 2, at 1049–50, n.14, *citing* UNIVERSITY OF MIAMI LAW CENTER, SIXTH ANNUAL INSTITUTE ON ESTATE PLANNING §72.1502 (1972); *Disguised Oppression, supra* note 6.

29. For a small sample, *see Older Americans Resources and Services (OARS) Multidimensional Functional Assessment Questionnaire,* in MULTIDIMENSIONAL FUNCTIONAL ASSESSMENT: THE OARS METHODOLOGY: A MANUAL (E. Pfeiffer, ed.) (Center for the Study of Aging & Human Development, Duke University, Durham, N.C.) (1975); Remnet, V.L., *The Home Assessment: A Therapeutic Tool to Assess the Needs of the Elderly,* in NURSING AND THE AGED (I.M. Burnside, ed.) (McGraw-Hill, New York) (1976) (assessment includes home safety and cleanliness, interpersonal relationships and pets, general health, personal care and safety, mobility, dietary needs, financial management, use of defense mechanisms); D.W. SMITH, C.P.H. GERMAIN, CARE OF THE ADULT PATIENT: MEDICAL SURGICAL NURSING (Lippincott, Inc., Philadelphia) (1975) at 61 (a partial list of items that are assessed includes physical agility, habits conducive to health maintenance, psychological orientation (sociability, memory, interest in the world, use of spare time), compensation for physical and psychological disability, access to and quality of relations with others, financial resources, and physical environment); M.O. WOLANIN, L.R.F. PHILLIPS, CONFUSION: PREVENTION AND CARE (Mosby, St. Louis, Mo.) (1981) at 58–78 (assessment of the elderly should include cognitive domain, reality domain, tests of perception, physical abilities to perform tasks of daily living, social interactions, structure and physiology, life history).

30. *See* Pfeiffer, E., *A Short Portable Mental Status Questionnaire for the Assessment of Organic Brain Deficit in Elderly Patients,* JOURNAL OF THE AMERICAN GERIATRIC SOCIETY 23(10):433–41 (October 1975) (ten-item test with demonstrated correlation to clinical diagnoses).

31. *But see* Leifer, *supra* note 23 (questioning scientific standards of psychiatry).

32. *See* Pfeiffer, *supra* note 30.

33. *See* MULTIDIMENSIONAL FUNCTIONAL ASSESSMENT, *supra* note 29.
34. Statutes that mandate court visitors require that the visitor visit the defendant's present place of residence, although the interview with defendant need not take place there. MONT. CODE ANN. §72-5-315(3) (1983); N.D. CENT. CODE §30.1-28-03(2) (Supp. 1983); UTAH CODE ANN. §75-5-303(2) (1978).
35. The writer's own bias in conducting such evaluations and the bias exhibited therein should be made clear. I routinely take care to inform a guardianship defendant that I will make every effort to see him as competent. This enhances trust and enables defendant to demonstrate his best. I have found that deficits severe enough to mandate a recommendation that defendant be found incompetent cannot be easily disguised. If a case falls on the borderline, the presumption of competency should prevail.
36. In some states, a court visitor or court-appointed evaluator is mandated to report his findings from a series of interviews to the court. *See* N.D. CENT. CODE §30.1-28-3(2 & 3) (Supp. 1983); COLO. REV. STAT. §15-14-303(2)(e) (Supp. 1983); MONT. CODE ANN. §72-5-315(3) (1983).
37. "High level wellness," a term of art in the health care field, refers to fulfillment of one's complete potential. H.L. DUNN, HIGH LEVEL WELLNESS (W. Beatty Co., Arlington, Va.) (1971). The level of wellness will vary with the individual, but competency evaluation measures the individual's distance from the *floor*, or minimally required level, not from the ceiling of high-level wellness.
38. *See* Comment, *Appointment of Guardians for the Mentally Incompetent*, DUKE LAW JOURNAL 1964:341, 343–44 [hereinafter referred to as *Appointment of Guardians*]. This article discusses where that point may be, and notes that "tests generally indicate no measuring standard to which his ability to manage ordinary affairs must conform." *Id.* at 343.
39. *E.g., In re* Emsweiler, 8 Ohio N.P. 132, 11 Ohio Op. 10 (1901) ("a gibbering slobbering lemon-headed wildman"). *See also Appointment of Guardians, supra* note 38, at 343 ("insanity, idiocy, lunacy, imbecility and unsoundness of mind").
40. *See* BURGDORF, *supra* note 17, at 3–14; Note, *Guardianship in the Planned Estate*, IOWA LAW REVIEW 45:360, 367 (1960).
41. Generally, consciously chosen aberrant behavior is excluded if not caused by an illness (e.g., alcoholism, mental illness) or a condition (e.g., mental retardation, old age) recognized in a statute. The right to be eccentric is intended to be protected. *See In re* Boyer, 636 P.2d 1085, 1089 (Utah 1981).
42. *See, e.g.,* OHIO REV. CODE ANN. §2111.01(D) (Page Supp. 1983). Many states have dropped this provision, concentrating only on the defendant's ability to care for himself.
43. *Id.* (Page Supp. 1983). For an excellent analysis of the application of this statute, *see* Dewey, *supra* note 18; *Disguised Oppression, supra* note 6, at 676.
44. For a suggestion that "advanced age" as the sole classification may be unconstitutional, *see Pennsylvania Estate Guardianship, supra* note 2; Dewey, *supra* note 18, at 423. *See also In re* Irvine's Guardianship, 52 N.E.2d 536 (Ohio App. 1943) (advanced age insufficient basis without allegation of mental

illness). *Accord In re* Guardianship of Gallagher, 441 N.E.2d 593 (Ohio App. 1981).

45. *See, e.g.,* A.M. ROUSSEAU, SHOPPING BAG LADIES (Pilgrim Press, New York) (1981).

46. *See* Frolik, *supra* note 7, at 604; "The decision whether to approve the guardianship should be based upon the quality of the individual's decisions and behavior rather than on identifying the cause of the erratic decisionmaking or behavior." Where this argument is accepted, clearly, functional evaluation data are needed.

47. Sometimes the causal linkage requirement is ignored or misplaced in reported opinions. *See Pennsylvania Estate Guardianship, supra* note 2, at 1060. *See also In re* Estate of Stevenson, 256 N.E.2d 766 (Ill.), *cert. denied,* 400 U.S. 850 (1970). "The justification for the appointment of a conservator is founded primarily on the incapability of managing one's person or estate and not on the cause of that incapability." 256 N.E.2d at 769. *See also* Oak Park Trust & Savings Bank v. Fisher, 225 N.E.2d 377, 384 (Ill. App. 1967) (medical testimony causally linked defendant's cerebral arteriosclerosis and her inability to manage her estate).

48. *Pennsylvania Estate Guardianship, supra* note 2, at 1060, *citing* Siegel's Estate, 82 A.2d 309 (Pa. Super. 1951).

49. *See In re* Conservatorship of Browne, 343 N.E.2d 61 (Ill. App. 1976). The only evidence submitted to the probate court was the petition and affidavits from two physicians alleging that appointment of the conservatorship would be in Browne's best interest, but giving no factual supporting data. The appeals court reversed the appointment, citing lack of evidence on which it could be based.

50. *See* BURGDORF, *supra* note 17, at 46–49.

51. UTAH CODE ANN. §75-1-201(18) (1978).

52. It is slightly more complicated in Montana: "Or which cause has so impaired the person's judgment that he is incapable of realizing and making a rational decision with respect to his need for treatment." MONT. CODE ANN. §72-5-101(1) (1983).

53. *In re* Boyer, *supra* note 41, at 1089. *See* Fazio v. Fazio, 378 N.E.2d 951 (Mass. 1978).

54. In favor of limited guardianship, see Frolik, *supra* note 7, at 652–59.

55. MONT. CODE ANN. §72-5-316(1) (1983).

56. *Id.* §§72-5-316 (2 & 3) (1983). *But cf.* COLO. REV. STAT. §15-14-304(4) (Supp. 1983) (if limits of guardianship are not specified, guardian shall have full powers and duties).

57. Frolik gives the label "therapeutic." Frolik, *supra* note 7.

58. N.H. REV. STAT. ANN. §§464-A:2(VII)(XI) (1983).

59. *Id.* §464-A:2(III).

60. *Id.* §464-A:2(XI).

61. *Id.*

62. *In re* DeLucca, 426 A.2d 32 (N.H. 1981).

63. *But see* Frolik, *supra* note 7, at 628. This author argues that this consideration can be repressive; "*any* behavior that is self-harmful gives reason for state

intervention. . . . In the therapeutic state, one is not 'free' to act in a manner harmful to oneself." (italics in the original).

64. N.H. REV. STAT. ANN. §464-A:4(III) (1983).

65. N.H. REV. STAT. ANN. §464-A:8(IV) (1983).

66. *But see In re* Joyce, 19 Ohio Op. 506 (Ohio 1970) (examination or observation of defendant not a violation of constitutional rights if by court order).

67. Warren, S.D., Brandeis, L.D., *The Right of Privacy,* HARVARD LAW REVIEW 4(5):193–220 (December 15, 1890); RESTATEMENT (SECOND) OF TORTS §652b (1976).

68. Eisenstadt v. Baird, 405 U.S. 438 (1972); Griswold v. Connecticut, 381 U.S. 479 (1965); Roe v. Ingraham, 480 F.2d 102 (2d Cir. 1973).

69. *See* explanations of functional assessments, *supra* note 29, and accompanying text.

70. FED. R. CIV. P. 26(b)(1): "Parties may obtain discovery regarding any matter, not privileged, which is relevant to the subject matter involved in the pending action. . . ."

71. Some guardianship statutes make provision for closure of the hearing on defendant's request or that of his attorney or guardian *ad litem. See* MONT. CODE ANN. §72-5-315(4) (1983); COLO. REV. STAT. §15-14-303(4) (1983); N.H. REV. STAT. ANN. §464-A:8(VI) (1983) (provisions for confidentiality of findings).

72. Murphy v. Waterfront Comm'n of New York Harbor, 378 U.S. 52 (1964); Counselman v. Hitchcock, 142 U.S. 547 (1892).

73. *See* Katz v. Superior Court of City and County of San Francisco, 141 Cal. Rptr. 234 (Cal. App. 1977). The appellate court stated that "liberty is no less precious when forfeited in a civil proceeding than when taken as a consequence of a criminal conviction. . ." and imposed "the test of certainty [that is] applied in the criminal law because fundamental rights are at stake." *Id.* at 234, 243.

74. The defendant may not be the only one needing protection. *See* Rau v. Tannenbaum, 444 N.Y.S.2d 635 (N.Y. App. Div. 1981) (plaintiff who was not judged incompetent because guardianship proceedings were dismissed by agreement was permitted to sue his physician for breach of the physican/patient privilege for testifying against him in the guardianship hearing).

75. Oak Park Trust & Savings Bank v. Fischer, 225 N.E.2d 377, 381 (1967). *See* Frolik, *supra* note 7, at 633–34, *quoting* AMERICAN BAR ASSOCIATION COMMISSION ON MENTALLY DISABLED, MODEL STATUTE §3(19) (1979): "The function of the guardian ad litem is to assist individuals to determine their interests and, if they are incapable of doing so, of acting in their stead."

76. Mazza v. Pechacek, 344 F.2d 666 (D.C. Cir. 1956).

77. *See In re* Guardianship of Corless, 440 N.E.2d 1203, 1207 (Ohio 1981) (requiring judicial observation). *Accord In re* Guardianship of Gallagher, *supra* note 44. *Cf.* Myers' Estate, 150 A.2d 525 (Pa. 1959) (trial court's observation was a significant but discretionary factor in the upholding of the incompetency determination).

78. *See Appointment of Guardians, supra* note 38, at 347 n.44, *citing Tyrrell, supra* note 10; *In re* Slamey, 146 N.E.2d 466 (Ohio App. 1957) (error to refuse to

allow defendant's attorney to examine, but decision reversed on other grounds).

79. *In re* Estate of Stevenson, *supra* note 47; *In re* Estate of Liebling, 254 N.E.2d 531 (Ill. App. 1970). *See, e.g.,* COLO. REV. STAT. §15-14-30 (1974); NEB. REV. STAT. §30-2619 (Supp. 1983); N.M. STAT. ANN. §45-5-303 (1978).

80. *In re* Guardianship of Corless, 440 N.E.2d 1203 (Ohio App. 1981).

81. *Compare* N.D. CENT. CODE §30-1-28-03 (Supp. 1983) (both court-appointed physician and court visitor mandatory) *with* IDAHO CODE ANN. §15-5303 (Supp. 1983) (court visitor mandatory, but social or charitable agency may perform function to avoid undue delay or expense) *and* HAWAII REV. STAT. §560:5-303(b9) (Supp. 1983) (visit by court officer if so ordered by the court).

82. *See* UTAH CODE ANN. §75-5-303(2) (1978); N.D. CENT. CODE §§30.1-28-03(2 & 3) (Supp. 1983).

83. *See* Comment, *House Bill 2002: The Protection of Persons under Disability and the Management of Their Property,* LAW AND SOCIAL ORDER 1973: 435–53. Some states have amended their court visitor provisions to encourage use of charitable organizations as functional evaluators. *See, e.g.,* IDAHO CODE ANN. §15-56-303(b) (Supp. 1984). North Dakota not only encourages use of charitable or public agencies, but also allocates costs of guardianship hearings, first to the incapacitated person if the court finds him able to pay, second to his spouse or parents, third to the state department of human services. N.D. CENT. CODE §§30.1-28-03(3 & 4) (Supp. 1983). *See also* Effland, *supra* note 2, at 385–86, n.92.

84. It is not irrelevant that court-ordered functions are usually paid by someone, public or private, and that payment will be enforced. Social agencies, hard-pressed by federal funding cutbacks, are unlikely to oppose such a contract.

85. M. BLENKNER, *et al.,* PROTECTIVE SERVICES FOR OLDER PEOPLE: FINAL REPORT: FINDINGS FROM THE BENJAMIN ROSE INSTITUTE (Benajamin Rose Inst., Cleveland, Oh.) (1974) at 183–85 (concluding that the result of social service assessment and intensive protective services was an increased rate of institutionalization and mortality for the experimental group in the Institute's study). *See also* Frolik, *supra* note 7, at 615–18.

86. *See* BLENKNER, *et al., supra* note 85.

87. *See In re* Wilson's Guardianship, 155 N.E. 654, 655 (Ohio App. 1926).

88. *See Pennsylvania Estate Guardianship, supra* note 2, at 1065–68; *In re* Schmidt's Guardianship, 352 P.2d 152, 154 (Or. 1960); Guardianship of Estate of Brown, 546 P.2d 298 (Cal. 1976).

89. *See Pennsylvania Estate Guardianship, supra* note 2, at 1070–72.

90. *See* United States v. Brawner, 471 F.2d 969 (D.C. Cir. 1972).

20

Adult Protective Services:
Convincing the Patient to Consent

Marshall B. Kapp, J.D., M.P.H.

Adult protective service systems in many of our states have been subjected to a good deal of public criticism. Much of this denunciation, particularly that emanating from civil libertarians who advocate on behalf of the legal and ethical rights of older citizens, centers on the legal aspects of protective services, and especially on the legal authority of the state to intervene unilaterally in the private life of an unwilling, protesting older individual.

Except in the most compelling of circumstances, society should avoid the coercive elements of protective services. Often overlooked, however, by commentators, policy makers, and care givers alike, is that protective services may be, and in the vast majority of instances are, accepted voluntarily (and gratefully) by the older recipient. A mentally competent individual may voluntarily give informed consent in the medical sphere, as well as in others, to the receipt of services that he or she currently needs. Additionally, legal mechanisms frequently enable a competent independent adult to foresee and prepare for the possibility that he or she might become incompetent and dependent, by providing for a substitute decision-making process of the individual's own choosing.

Health care professionals have an essential role to play, in appropriate circumstances, in encouraging their competent older patients (and almost all patients are competent for most of their lives) to accept, voluntarily, intelligently, and thoughtfully, necessary and available protective services, on either a present or a future basis. This function is generally ignored or consciously avoided by many health care professionals. The intent of this chapter is to emphasize the importance of this role and to encourage its fulfillment.

Reprinted with permission of the American Society of Law & Medicine from LAW, MEDICINE & HEALTH CARE, September 1983, pp. 163–67, 188.

WHAT ARE ADULT PROTECTIVE SERVICES?

Professor John J. Regan, who has written much on this topic, has defined adult protective services as "a system of preventive, supportive, and surrogate services for the elderly living in the community to enable them to maintain independent living and avoid abuse and exploitation."[1] Regan has characterized the system as containing two elements that can be combined in various ways: (1) the coordinated provision of services to adults at risk, and (2) the actual or potential transfer of authority for decision making for elderly individuals.[2]

The first element of protective services can involve a whole spectrum of social services, which are best provided in a coordinated fashion by a single caseworker or organizer. In fact, many state protective services statutes require that agencies both coordinate the casework and deliver the services.[3]

Several stimuli have inspired the creation of state programs for these social services. The recent trend, substantially slowed lately, towards deinstitutionalization of patients from large public mental health facilities into often unready communities, has provided an ample source of older candidates for these social programs. Another stimulus has been the general rise in the number of people who are very old and at high risk for health, social, economic, environmental, and legal problems.[4] Since the early 1970s, the federal government has made available funding for adult protective services through subchapters of the Social Security Act (Grants to States for Services)[5] and the Older Americans Act (Grants for State and Community Programs on Aging).[6] In the past decade, almost half of the states have responded by enacting a wide variety of programs under the rubric of adult protective services.[7]

LEGAL INTERVENTION

The second component of an adult protective services program, the authority given to an individual or state agency to intervene on behalf of the client, is the focus of this section. This transfer of authority typically occurs when a patient, while still competent, grants this power voluntarily and informally to a known and trusted individual, often a family member. As will be discussed later, where the patient desires a more formal arrangement, he or she may bestow power of attorney upon another individual. Occasionally, an agency providing adult protective services may identify an elderly person who requires public assistance, who has not given power of attorney to another individual, and who refuses to accept the proffered assistance. If regular intervention appears necessary, protective services statutes permit the social service agency to intervene and to seek appointment of a substitute decision maker.[8]

Laws regarding adult protective services exhibit a great deal of variety in dealing with recalcitrant elderly patients. Most use the traditional methods of legal intervention into the personal lives of individuals—involuntary commitment and guardianship/conservatorship. Other states, however, have specific, separate laws—either in addition to the traditional laws or as substitutes for them—for obtaining court orders in various situations, e.g., orders for institutionalization, for emergency services, where there is imminent danger to the patient's health or safety, or for entering the home of an uncooperative patient.[9]

Statutes with these special procedures have frequently bypassed many of the protections found in most guardianship laws.[10] For instance, rarely do these special statutes require notice of the filing of the petition to the patient/client, the presence of the patient at the hearing, the person's right to counsel, or a specific evidentiary standard of proof.[11] When some mention of these rights is made, it is generally done in a cursory and vague fashion.[12] Although a full hearing is contemplated and available, it frequently becomes the public agency's *ex parte* presentation of testimony to a sympathetic court which routinely issues the orders for protective services precisely as requested by the agency.[13]

After a court order is issued, few limits are imposed on the agencies that provide services. As Regan has noted, because adult protective services are so poorly defined in many statutes,[14] the term can refer to almost any kind of social service, including property management and medical care. Unless the court orders only specific services, the agency has enormous freedom. A protective services order may, therefore, be used as authority to transfer the person to a health care institution or boarding home.[15] In this regard, a health care professional should, as a matter of standard practice, ascertain the exact nature and scope of a protective services order before accepting as legally effective the authorization of a state social service agency offered as a substitute for the elderly patient's informed consent.

Another problem with these court orders stems from the discontinuous nature of the judicial role. Once a court issues an order for protective services, the court retains no further responsibility toward the patient, even though the order is generally of indefinite duration. For example, the agency need not file periodic reports about the patient's status or condition, nor is it required to seek regular renewal of the order.

Finally, the special protective services statutes under discussion here do not impose on the public agency an explicit fiduciary obligation similar to that ordinarily assumed by a guardian or conservator.[16] The agency is not mandated by statute to act in the best interests of the patient nor to use the substituted judgment test, i.e., to determine how the patient would choose to act if competent, in making decisions concerning his or her care. Rather, the agency's only explicit duty is to provide the services authorized in the court order.

Those states that have created new proceedings for court orders have attempted to create eligibility standards for identifying the candidates for protective services. These standards have generated substantial controversy. Most of these states follow the same statutory pattern which allows enormously broad discretion. First, standards are given for certain behavioral disabilities, such as an inability to provide for one's own care.[17] Statutes usually list the causes for this incapacity, which must be documented by the agency trying to obtain the court order. Most of these causes involve impairment of mental function, but are extremely general.[18] In a few instances, proof of physical impairment alone is sufficient for intervention when this condition leads to self-neglect or victimization by others.[19]

Some respected commentators have severely criticized protective service systems that coerce patients' participation through the special eligibility criteria and abbreviated procedural mechanisms just described.[20] The negative argument usually raised against involuntary guardianship, i.e., it imperils the individual's right to self-determination in major life decisions,[21] may also be applied with even greater logical force to protective service systems which involve even looser eligibility standards and less extensive procedural protections, especially in the area of emergency intervention.

VOLUNTARY TRANSFERS OF DECISION-MAKING AUTHORITY

Thus far, most of this discussion has focused on the variety of ways in which society is empowered to intervene in the life of an elderly individual without that individual's acquiescence. It is possible, however, and usually desirable from a philosophical and a clinical perspective, for many older, partially disabled individuals to voluntarily relinquish certain decision-making powers and to accept certain services willingly.[22] This, in fact, is what most elderly do when confronted by the problem.

All adult protective service statutes provide for the proposed patient's voluntary acceptance of offered services. Coercion through guardianship or specially devised procedures is mandated only where such acceptance is withheld.[23] Thus, it is a simple process for an older person to accede willingly to the overtures of the initiating public social service agency.

Whether or not adult protective services are needed, an older person may, for a variety of reasons, be willing to give up some or all decision-making authority, on either a temporary or a permanent basis. This transfer of power may be accomplished through the legal device of "power of attorney."

The ordinary power of attorney is, in essence, a written agreement, authorizing a close relative, an attorney, a business associate, or a financial advisor (or "attorney-in-fact") to sign documents and conduct transactions on the individual's (or the "principal's") behalf.[24] The individual can delegate as much or as little power as desired and revoke the arrangement at any time.

In its traditional form, the power of attorney has two major drawbacks that often render it an unsuitable method of providing necessary services for the elderly on a voluntary basis.[25] First, the person creating the power must, at the time of signing, have the legal capacity to make a contract. Should there be any doubt as to the individual's mental competence at that time, the validity of the power of attorney is open to challenge. If the challenge is successful, any transaction completed under the agreement might be cancelled.

Second, the power of attorney established under most state laws ends automatically upon the death or disability of the principal.[26] Thus, an elderly person who establishes a power of attorney to help in managing personal affairs is peremptorily cut off from such assistance at exactly the moment that assistance is most needed.

In an effort to overcome at least this latter deficiency, the National Conference of Commissioners on Uniform State Laws (a highly respected private body of legal scholars) has proposed, as part of the Uniform Probate Code, a Durable Power of Attorney Model Law.[27] This law also exists as a separate, free-standing proposed act, an alternative for the 35 states which have not adopted the Uniform Probate Code.[28] The act provides that a person may either (1) expressly confer authority on an attorney or agent to act for the principal, notwithstanding the later disability or incapacity of the delegating individual, or (2) state that the power of attorney shall become effective only in the event of disability. The durable power of attorney may be revoked at any point before incompetency begins.

This model law is the basis for the proposal that state legislatures employ the probate code to create a "living will"—a document that would allow individuals to direct, through the appointment of an agent who is given general instructions, the making of medical decisions and the management of their property for them in case of future incompetency.[29] This is related to, but distinct from, the "living will" concept popularly discussed in the context of terminating medical treatment.[30] Used in the probate sense, the living will would enable competent individuals to plan for the contingency of a future life in which incompetence may be a part, just as the living will in the "natural death" context enables competent individuals to plan for the contingency of a future terminal illness and simultaneous incompetency. The Model Health Care Consent Act, also drafted by the National Conference of Commissioners on Uniform State Laws, attempts to accomplish the same objective by providing for the appointment of a "health care representative."[31] Support for the enactment and use of legislation creating the durable power of attorney is building rapidly throughout the United States,[32] and this concept has been adopted by a majority of state legislatures,[33] several of which[34] are modeled on the Uniform Durable Power of Attorney Act.[35]

The power of attorney, in both its regular and durable forms, has traditionally been used for purposes of managing financial assets, but recently a movement to apply it to medical decision making has begun to develop. There would seem to be no reason in common law that the power cannot be granted for purposes of controlling medical treatment decisions following the onset of incompetence. Research reveals no statute expressly preventing such use, and it is likely that courts confronted by the issue will decide that difficult medical decisions are properly included within the general grant of a durable power of attorney.[36] The Model Health Care Consent Act notes, in commentary, that "the power to make such a designation [of a substitute medical decision maker] exists in jurisdictions that have statutes similar to the Uniform Durable Power of Attorney Act."[37] The document goes on to say:

> Section 6 [Health Care Representative] is consistent with the Uniform Durable Power of Attorney Act. The appointment made under this section would be given effect without this Act in a jurisdiction that has enacted the Durable Power of Attorney Act. By incorporating this section into the Act, the power of appointment will be brought to the attention of persons not aware of the Durable Power Act.[38]

If an individual can accept or reject medical care while competent, it follows that his or her chosen agent should have similar authority upon the individual's incapacity. Certainly, self-determination is better served when a competent individual dictates who will make treatment decisions for him or her after incompetence begins, rather than when that decision is left to a court. This was certainly the assumption of the President's Commission for the Study of Ethical Problems in Medicine and Biomedical and Behavioral Research in its recent examination of this subject.[39] However, until the issue is finally resolved in one's own jurisdiction, either by carefully worded statute[40] or by judicial pronouncement, specific enumeration of the agent's (or "attorney-in-fact's") medical treatment authority should be included in the power of attorney document.

Without question, the power of attorney mechanism entails a potential for serious abuse in some cases. This weakness is inherent in a voluntary procedure that was specifically designed to avoid the rigors and formality accompanying the creation of a guardianship. It is possible for a susceptible, suggestible older individual to be psychologically or physically pressured into signing over the power of attorney to an unscrupulous person whose chief concern is not the best interests of the older individual. Even where the original execution of the power of attorney is proper, the attorney-in-fact may nevertheless exercise that power in a manner that is deleterious to the principal's well-being. Because of this potential for abuse (or neglect) and the substantial societal values that it implicates, judicial scrutiny over, and possible intervention, into the execution or operation of a power of attorney must always be a possibility. Probate courts must remain available as legal forums where concerned relatives, friends, and service providers (including health care professionals) may petition for formal review of and, if necessary, reversal of a power of attorney arrangement that is deemed to disserve the older person. But such situations are likely to occur rarely. We must presume that many elderly individuals will be able to locate a trusted, competent, and honest relative or friend to whom power may be delegated safely, and that serious abuse of that fiduciary relationship necessitating judicial involvement will happen less rather than more frequently. This presumption is more preferable than a rejection of the power-of-attorney model on the grounds of potential abuse, since the latter position would more certainly consign older individuals to the considerable expense and tribulations of formal guardianship proceedings the first time that an important life decision needs to be made and the person's mental competency is questioned. A presumption of autonomy and good judgment, with occasional after-the-fact court intervention, better serves the elderly than a presumption of exploitation and bad judgment with a greater likelihood of before-the-fact judicial intrusion.

ROLE OF THE HEALTH CARE PROFESSIONAL

Physicians and other health care professionals who provide primary care to older people at risk of mental disability can and should recommend to these patients use of the durable power of attorney device. This advice goes directly to the heart of the health care professional's role toward an elderly patient. In all situations, but even more so when the patient is older, health care professionals must strive to avoid seeing themselves and acting as mere technologists remedying individual adverse patient episodes. Rather, the health care professional must become involved in the totality of the elderly patient's life, and must contribute as a supporter, counselor, advocate, and planner. Part of this planning obligation requires the health care professional to encourage and assist the elderly patient (and the patient's family) to prepare for the unhappy future contingency of a life in which decisions must be made but where the patient may be mentally unable to make them. The health care professional should discuss with the older patient and interested family members, compassionately and honestly, this possibility and potential ways to address it. In this way, agonizing crises, in a large number of situations, may be foreseen and averted before they happen.

The health care professional is particularly important in this planning process, both because of the high respect which he or she will ordinarily be accorded by the elderly patient and his or her family, and because the provider often has intimate contact with the older patient and the family at precisely the "teachable moment," such as admission to a nursing home, when a major life event compels the older patient and the family to plan and make serious arrangements for the future. Further, health care professionals are frequently in a unique, central position to identify those older individuals who, either today or likely in the near future, meet the eligibility criteria for, and could significantly benefit from, the intervention of an adult protective services program.

Finally, the potential contribution of the health care professional in service planning and placement activities for the current or future dependent elderly should not be neglected. The ultimate goal is not to obtain the protective services, whether on a voluntary or an involuntary basis; rather, the key is to ensure the quality and appropriateness of the services provided to the elderly individual. Social service agencies are not to be used as a convenient dumping ground for unwanted elders, and it is just as possible for an older person without personal resources to be harmfully "dumped" into the community as into a nursing home or public mental institution.[41] The older individual is entitled to reasonable continuity of care from his or her health care professionals, and these professionals are ethically and legally obligated, under the principle of "nonabandonment,"[42] to supply that continued care directly, or to facilitate its provision by other competent, willing health care professionals whose services are acceptable to the concerned older person.

Both legally and ethically, the health care professional owes the older patient a continuing involvement in that person's quality of life, and this obligation extends to the securing of appropriate protective services which the patient needs. Ethical principles of autonomy (respect for dignity and self-determination) and beneficence (helping those in need) support an active role for the health care professional. Arguably, this legal duty falls within the fiduciary obligation, which is part of the care giver/patient relationship, to provide services that meet acceptable professional standards and that affirmatively promote the patient's best interests.[43]

Why, then, do health care professionals so often fall short of fulfilling this obligation at a desirable level?[44] First, there may be ignorance of the legal and ethical issues involved and of the potential remedies available. Even where there is not ignorance, there is frequently apprehension among health care professionals, both toward the issues themselves and toward the patients and their families with whom these issues should be discussed. Issues raised by the present or future need for basic services by previously independent individuals, particularly when compounded by actual or anticipated serious mental dysfunction, are complex and rather unpleasant matters with which to grapple. The narrow role of objective scientists, adopted by many health care professionals, confines them to dealing strictly with the purely clinical aspects of the patient's medical ailments, and severely hinders adequate performance in the voluntary protective services area. Finally, many health care professionals may be unaccustomed to and uncomfortable with the sort of intricate interprofessional coordination that is required in a successful comprehensive plan of voluntarily accepted adult protective services.

Addressing these obstacles presents an interesting, and imperative, challenge for health care professionals. It is hoped that these care givers will permit and encourage advocates (both attorneys and others) for the elderly to work with them in arriving at practices that best serve both the human needs and the legitimate rights of older citizens.

CONCLUSION

Health care professionals who have practices involving elderly patients must become familiar with the various mechanisms for substitute decision making outlined, and with their legal, ethical, social, and clinical implications. These professionals can contribute greatly to the creation of substitute decision-making arrangements that ensure as much as possible continued respect for the individual autonomy and freedom of their older patients while caring for their basic human needs in a thorough and humane manner.

NOTES

1. Regan, J., *Intervention Through Adult Protective Services Programs,* THE GERON-
TOLOGIST 18(3):250, 251 (1978) [hereinafter referred to as *Intervention*], *citing*
G. MATHIASEN, GUIDE TO THE DEVELOPMENT OF PROTECTIVE SERVICES FOR
OLDER PEOPLE (National Council on Aging, Washington, D.C.) (1973); J.
REGAN, G. SPRINGER, PROTECTIVE SERVICES FOR THE ELDERLY (Special Senate Committee on Aging, 95th Cong., 1st Sess.) (Committee Print) (July
1977).
2. *Intervention, supra* note 1, at 251.
3. *Id. see, e.g.,* CONN. GEN. STAT. ANN. §46a-17 (West Supp. 1983); WIS. STAT.
ANN. §55.02 (West Supp. 1982). *See generally* Regan, J., *Protecting the Elderly:
The New Paternalism,* HASTINGS LAW JOURNAL 32(5):1111 (May 1981) [here-
inafter referred to as *Paternalism*].
4. *See Paternalism, supra* note 3.
5. 42 U.S.C.A. §§3021 *et. seq.* (Supp. 1983).
6. 42 U.S.C.A. §§1397 *et seq.* (Supp. 1983).
7. *See, e.g.,* N.Y. SOC. SERV. LAW §131 (McKinney 1982 & Supp. 1983). *See
generally* J. BURR, PROTECTIVE SERVICES FOR ADULTS: A GUIDE TO EXEM-
PLARY PRACTICE IN STATES PROVIDING PROTECTIVE SERVICES TO ADULTS IN
OHDS PROGRAMS (Administration on Aging, Washington, D.C.) (1982).
8. *Intervention, supra* note 1, at 251.
9. *See, e.g.,* ALA. CODE §38-9-1-11 (Supp. 1982); MD. ANN. CODE art. 88A
§§106–110 (1979 & Supp. 1982); N.H. REV. STAT. ANN. §§161-D:1:6, 465-
A:12 (Supp. 1981). *See also Paternalism, supra* note 3, at 1117–19.
10. *See, e.g.,* OHIO REV. CODE ANN. §2111.02 (Page 1982) (providing for assistance of legal counsel); OHIO REV. CODE ANN. §2111.04 (Page 1982) (requiring prior notice to the proposed ward). *See generally* Kapp, M., *Legal
Guardianship,* GERIATRIC NURSING 2(5):366 (October 1981). For arguments
that current guardianship laws provide inadequate protection, *see* Mitchell,
A., *The Objects of Our Wisdom and Our Coercion: Involuntary Guardianship for
Incompetents,* SOUTHERN CALIFORNIA LAW REVIEW 52(5):1405, 1432–33
(July 1979); Mitchell, A., *Involuntary Guardianship for Incompetents: A Strategy
for Legal Services Advocates,* CLEARINGHOUSE REVIEW 12(8):451, 459 (December 1978); Horstman, P., *Protective Services for the Elderly: The Limits of
Parens Patriae,* MISSOURI LAW REVIEW 40(2):215 (Spring 1975).
11. *See, e.g.,* FLA. STAT. ANN. §410.104 (West Supp. 1983) (no mention of any
procedural rights for the proposed ward).
12. *See, e.g.,* N.C. GEN. STAT. §108A-106 (Supp. 1982) (emergency intervention
may be ordered where "there is *likelihood* that the disabled adult *may* suffer
irreparable injury or death if such order is delayed") (emphasis added).
13. *Paternalism, supra* note 3, at 1117.
14. *See, e.g.,* TENN. CODE ANN. §14-25-102(9) (Supp. 1980) ("services aimed at
preventing and remedying abuse, neglect, and exploitation").
15. *Paternalism, supra* note 3, at 1118.
16. *See, e.g.,* OHIO REV. CODE §2111.13 (Page 1982) (duties of guardian of person); OHIO REV. CODE §2111.14 (Page 1982) (duties of guardian of estate).

17. *See, e.g.,* OKLA. STAT. ANN. tit. 43A §803(4) (West Supp. 1982–83).

18. *See, e.g.,* UTAH CODE ANN. §55-19-1(1) (Int. Supp. 1983) (impairment described as "infirmities of aging"); MD. EST. & TRUSTS CODE ANN. §13.705(b) (Supp. 1982) ("senility"); FLA. STAT. ANN. §410.102(1) (West Supp. 1983) ("advanced age").

19. *See, e.g.,* S.C. CODE ANN. §43-29-30(1) (Law Co-op Supp. 1982) ("individual is unable to provide for his own protection").

20. *See, e.g.,* Horstman, *supra* note 10; *Intervention, supra* note 1.

21. *See, e.g.,* Atkinson, G., *Towards a Due Process Perspective in Conservatorship for the Aged,* JOURNAL OF FAMILY LAW 18(4):819 (1979–80); Frolik, L., *Plenary Guardianship: An Analysis, A Critique, and a Proposal for Reform,* ARIZONA LAW REVIEW 23(2):599 (1981); Rohan, P., *Caring for Persons Under a Disability: A Critique of the Role of the Conservator and the "Substitution of Judgment Doctrine,"* ST. JOHN'S LAW REVIEW 52(1):1 (Fall 1977); Sherman, R., *Guardianship: Time for a Reasssessment,* FORDHAM LAW REVIEW 49(3):350 (December 1980).

22. *See* Alexander, G., *Premature Probate: A Different Perspective on Guardianship for the Elderly,* STANFORD LAW REVIEW 31:1003 (July 1979); *See* T. GUTHEIL, P. APPELBAUM, CLINICAL HANDBOOK OF PSYCHIATRY AND THE LAW (McGraw-Hill Co., New York) (1982) at 241 (the primary negative impact on the individual of involuntary guardianship is the experience of coercion).

23. *See, e.g.,* ALA. CODE §38-9-4(a) (Supp. 1982) ("All protective services shall be in conformity with the wishes of the person to be served unless the person is unable or unwilling to accept such services. . . .").

24. H. BLACK, BLACK'S LAW DICTIONARY (West Pub. Co., St. Paul, Minn.) (5th ed. 1979) at 1055.

25. J. REGAN, G. SPRINGER, *supra* note 1, at 45.

26. *See* RESTATEMENT (SECOND) OF AGENCY, §122 (American Law Inst. Publishers, St. Paul) (1958).

27. UNIFORM PROBATE CODE §§5-501-505, UNIFORM LAWS ANN. 8:28 (West Supp. 1983).

28. UNIFORM DURABLE POWER OF ATTORNEY ACT, UNIFORM LAWS ANN. 8:81 (West Supp. 1983).

29. *See* Alexander, *supra* note 22; Libow, L., Zicklin R., *The Penultimate Will: Its Potential as an Instrument to Protect the Mentally Deteriorated Elderly,* THE GERONTOLOGIST 13(4):440 (Winter 1973); Miller, B., *The Michigan Medical Decision Treatment Act,* in DILEMMAS OF DYING: PROCEDURES AND POLICIES FOR DECISIONS NOT TO TREAT (C. Wong, J. Swazey, eds.) (G.K. Hall & Co., Boston) (1981); Relman, A., *Michigan's Sensible "Living Will,"* NEW ENGLAND JOURNAL OF MEDICINE 300(22):1270 (May 31, 1979).

30. *See generally* Rosoff, S., *Living Wills and Natural Death Acts,* in LEGAL AND ETHICAL ASPECTS OF TREATING CRITICALLY AND TERMINALLY ILL PATIENTS (AUPHA Press, Ann Arbor, Mich.) (1982) at 186. *See also* Kapp, M., *Response to the Living Will Furor: Directives for Maximum Care,* AMERICAN JOURNAL OF MEDICINE 72:855 (1982).

31. National Conference of Commissioners on Uniform State Laws, Uniform Health Care Consent Act, approved and recommended for enactment in all the states at its annual conference, Monterey, California, July 30–August 6,

1982, *reprinted in* PRESIDENT'S COMMISSION FOR THE STUDY OF ETHICAL PROBLEMS IN MEDICINE AND BIOMEDICAL AND BEHAVIORAL RESEARCH, DECIDING TO FOREGO LIFE-SUSTAINING TREATMENT (U.S. Gov't Printing Office, Washington, D.C.) (1983) at 423–28 [hereinafter referred to as FOREGOING TREATMENT].

32. *Id.* at 145–48. "The Commission therefore encourages the use of existing durable power of attorney statutes to facilitate decisionmaking for incapacitated persons. . . ." *Id.* at 149. Lombard, J., *et al., Legal Problems of the Aged and Infirm—The Durable Power of Attorney—Planned Protective Services and the Living Will,* REAL PROPERTY, PROBATE AND TRUST JOURNAL 13(1):1 (Spring 1978).

33. *See, e.g.,* VA. CODE §§11-9.1, 11-9.2 (Supp. 1983).

34. CAL. CIV. CODE §§2400-2407 (West 1983); KAN. STAT. ANN. §§58-610-617 (Cum. Supp. 1982); MASS. GEN. LAWS ANN. ch. 201B, §§1-7 (West 1983–84); WIS. STAT. ANN. §243.07 (West 1982).

35. UNIFORM DURABLE POWER OF ATTORNEY ACT, *supra* note 28.

36. D. MEYERS, MEDICO-LEGAL IMPLICATIONS OF DEATH AND DYING (Lawyers Coop., Rochester, N.Y.) (Cum. Supp. 1982) at 50–51.

37. NATIONAL CONFERENCE OF COMMISSIONERS ON UNIFORM STATE LAWS, UNIFORM LAW COMMISSIONERS' MODEL HEALTH CARE CONSENT ACT (Chicago, Ill.) (1982) at 4.

38. *Id.* at 16.

39. FOREGOING TREATMENT, supra note 31, at 145–48. "[T]he Commission's conclusion that both instruction and proxy directives are important for medical decisionmaking that respects patients' wishes. . . ." *Id.* at 145.

40. Delaware's natural death act explicitly provides for the appointment of an agent for medical decisionmaking if the patient becomes incapacitated. DEL. CODE ANN. tit. 16 §2502(b) (1982).

41. RETURNING THE MENTALLY DISABLED TO THE COMMUNITY: GOVERNMENT NEEDS TO DO MORE (Comptroller General's Office, Washington, D.C.) (1976).

42. See generally on abandonment, G. ANNAS, L. GLANTZ, B. KATZ, THE RIGHTS OF DOCTORS, NURSES AND ALLIED HEALTH PROFESSIONALS (Avon Books, New York) (1981) at 249–51.

43. See generally on the care giver/patient relationship, S. FISCINA, MEDICAL LAW FOR THE ATTENDING PHYSICIAN (Southern Illinois University Press, Carbondale, Ill.) (1982) at 3–32.

44. *See* Kapp, M., *Promoting the Legal Rights of Older Adults: Role of the Primary Care Physician,* JOURNAL OF LEGAL MEDICINE 3(3):367 (September 1982).

Section V

Elderly Decision Making in Health Care

21

Some Legal and Moral Issues Surrounding Informed Consent for Treatment and Research Involving the Cognitively Impaired Elderly

Nancy Neveloff Dubler, LL.B.

The cognitively impaired elderly represent a class of persons for whom the law has yet to create proper supports and protections in regard to consent to or refusal of treatment, and participation in research protocols. State statutes have largely ignored or inadequately addressed the issue of elderly persons with declining or diminished cognition and intellectual capacity.[1] There is some case law offering guidance on decisions for patients clearly incapable of deciding, but it is scanty.[2] There is virtually no analysis of the legal powers of involved family or even of the range of acceptable choices available to a court-appointed guardian (that is, one legally empowered to make decisions about care and treatment).

Neither practitioners of law nor ethical analysts have adequately explored this issue or offered guidelines necessary both to permit the most individually appropriate and beneficial treatment for the individual and to support research which may be of little individual benefit but could be of great societal importance. Thus, problems surrounding the care of the impaired elderly arise both in the context of treatment and of research. This chapter will begin with a discussion of some issues affecting treatment and conclude with some thoughts on research.

The questions to be addressed are four. First, who can give consent for those persons, mainly elderly, who have impaired abilities, are demented, or have diminished, declining, or extinguished competence? Second, at present, who consents to or refuses suggested interventions? Third, who should provide the proper authority if we could refashion a balance between competing interests and create procedures to support those values inherent in the doctrine of informed consent? And finally, how can we proceed to fashion protocols, create legislation, or prepare litigation to move closer to an adequate set of guidelines for treatment and research? That is, how can we establish guidelines which protect patients from unnecessary interventions, facilitate needed care, and possibly permit some limited kinds of research?

TREATMENT

It is now firmly established in law that adult persons of sound mind who are neither incarcerated nor institutionally confined have a significant, but not absolute, legal and moral right to consent to diagnosis, care, and treatment and the concomitant right to refuse them.[3] The theory, however, is often undermined in practice by the inability of patients, in the face of catastrophic illness and personal weakness, to insist upon these rights. Physicians and care givers are also disinclined to provide adequate support for the *process* of informed consent.[4] There is little in the role modelling, socialization, scientific training, or paternalistic outlook of care givers—especially physicians—to encourage them to assist patients in exercising these rights. This does not imply that informed consent is an undesirable ideal. Rather, the formal right has not been provided with sufficient structural support in the initial and continuing education and training of those who must cooperate in its implementation.

Thus, even with competent adults, the exercise of informed consent requires skill, wisdom, personal force, and courage from the patient (and his or her family) and acceptance, support, and respect from the care givers. These reciprocally necessary resources and attitudes are often lacking in both patient and provider. As is patently obvious to those who work in health care institutions, the doctrine is honored more often in the breach than in the observance.

Informed consent encounters many obstacles because it embodies an attempted reordering of power relationships. It grants rights to patients, the rights to consent to or refuse treatment, and it imposes corresponding duties upon care givers, the duties to provide and explain the information that is material to the choices to be made by patients. Informed consent is thus a mediating principle. It empowers the patient at the same time that it limits the possible range of actions of care givers. It attempts to redress the imbalance of power created by medical training, medical institutions, social class, and the process of illness itself. It enforces and enhances the fiduciary nature of the physician/patient relationship.

Cases exploring the doctrines of informed consent and refusals rely heavily on concepts of autonomy, self-determination, and the constitutional right to privacy.[5] Those cases which attempt to extend the essence of these concepts to incompetent persons have relied mainly on the doctrine of substituted judgment.[6] Not surprisingly, the cases have focused not on patients of diminished or declining capacity but on those who are clearly unable to make decisions for themselves and are rendered incompetent by extreme congenital retardation,[7] by the end stages of dementia,[8] or by the existence of a comatose or permanently vegetative state.[9]

Since one of the possible treatment decisions, i.e., nontreatment, will often lead to the death of the patient, these cases arise in situations of extreme moral discomfort and grave anxiety about legal rights and liability. Various state courts which have considered these issues have arrived at markedly dissimilar conclusions about substantive legal principles and mandated procedures.[10] Some states rely heavily on their courts to make such decisions;[11] others require clear prior direction from the person when he or she was competent.[12] Still others invoke committees to confirm the prognosis of hopelessness and to permit a guardian to refuse care.[13]

The vast majority of intellectually compromised geriatric patients, however, are not totally incompetent. Rather, they are affected by confusion, fluctuating cognitive and reasoning abilities, diminished personal force, and declining individual advocacy skills. Yet, many of these patients do possess, at times, sufficient "competence" to make decisions for themselves.

In the way language is generally used, and as the term is employed by judges, mental competence assumes a set of skills and abilities. Indeed, our legal system presumes that all adults are competent, unless declared incompetent by a court. (The correct plane of language for all other persons is capable or incapable. The term competence is so widely used and abused, however, that its common rather than its more precise meaning is used here.) Physicians and judges call patients competent if they are oriented to time and place, if they are capable of understanding the diagnosis and prognosis of their illness and the risks and benefits of alternative treatments, and if they have reasonably intact judgment. Scholars in law, medicine, and psychiatry have described patients as functionally competent if they can "make a choice," arrive at a "reasonable outcome,"[14] or address "emotionally neutral" issues in a reasonable fashion.[15]

There are older patients, once successfully functioning adults, who may and should be treated as currently competent, even if they lack some of the skills referred to above. The reason for creating such a rule would be to amplify diminishing voices and support residual autonomy.

This argument assumes that competence is really an interaction of the abilities of the patient and the setting in which those skills are used.

Competence is, in a descriptive rather than a normative sense, a combination of a patient's linguistic and affective expression and the commitment of care givers. Competence is thus a societal artifact. It is both the expression of the patient and the decision of providers whether to accept or reject that expression. It is a function of patient ability and provider power. Thus, competence is a shorthand phrase for a set of values that are one ingredient in the decision whether to accept or contest a patient's expression of choice. Other factors may include provider judgments on health status, prognosis, and possible life span.

Competence is a relative matter, dependent upon the gravity and complexity of the decision to be made. A patient may be competent to choose whether to wear green or blue sneakers and incompetent to choose between possible medical interventions. A patient may, again descriptively, be competent to consent to a treatment and yet not competent to refuse.

Given the gray miasma surrounding the meaning of the term and the dynamic power relationships inherent in its use, certain geriatric patients of compromised skill and some disorientation should still be "deemed" competent, i.e., capable of making certain decisions. For, as competence is relative, elderly persons with clear personal value systems and a demonstrated or documented pattern of preference should be treated as competent, even if they have some diminished abilities and perhaps impaired judgment.

This suggestion is a somewhat radical departure from the usual argument. However, experience indicates that it is the best way of protecting patients' values in intimidating and alien surroundings. It may be argued that this insistence on the competence of those elderly persons of diminished ability unnecessarily confuses present competence with the separable issue of honoring the past wishes of presently incompetent patients. However, the theory seems worth advocating as a way of insuring that the statements of the elderly are given proper weight and value.

This analysis suggests that competence, or decision-making capacity, properly varies with the sort of decision required. Competence is not a fixed attribute but rather a flexible concept dependent upon both the patient's abilities and the sort of decision required. Risk is one factor requiring greater intellectual ability; complexity is another. Often a patient's decision-making ability will be questioned only if he or she rejects medical advice, especially if that rejection endangers life. However, such decisions, if not clearly based in stable and considered judgments, should be more troubling.

Thus, part of the answer to the question, "Who can make decisions?" is "the patient." Indeed, there are patients with diminished capacity and some dementia who are unable to articulate risks, consequences, and benefits but who, from the wellspring of their being, express clear and distinct choices. These expressions of authenticity, which I categorize as "sedimented life preferences," are related to long-held life values and should be honored.

For example, a patient may be demented but may know that he never wanted surgery. Consider the case of Mr. X, 82 years old, febrile, with blood in his stool, admitted to an acute care institution. He was charming, personable, adamant about refusing surgical interventions, and severely demented. He was disoriented to time and place. Yet he said, "I know I never wanted surgery;" his daughter supported this statement. His earlier pattern of actions—e.g., leaving other medical institutions against medical advice when surgery was urgent—was consistent with his present refusal. This continuity of lifestyle pattern was evidence of a definitive choice by Mr. X.

Such strong preferences often survive major cognitive deficits and should be given effect, especially if supported by statements of family and friends. Thus, who can make decisions? First, we must acknowledge the individual patient's right to decide, provided he or she is capable under some definition, including the ability to express a "sedimented life preference." Second, if that person is clearly and totally *incompetent,* many states, as previously noted, have provided for the appointment of a person or committee or combination who may, through the doctrine of substituted judgment, attempt to decide and seek judicial recognition of what the incompetent would have decided were he or she able. Finally, in some states a prior explicit directive, a living will, the appointment of an agent, a durable power of attorney, or the proper execution of a statutory statement of intent, may control. [16]

These last developments are increasingly important, for they permit and require a prospective approach to the determination of values. These resources need more attention, and are clearly the most reliable route for the protection of autonomy. For, despite the advocacy expressed in this chapter, reliance on "sedimented life preferences" is risky. It assumes the expression of consistent preferences, which is often not the case, and ignores problems of depression and the volatility of mental status. It probably also requires some third-party confirmation for the legal and moral comfort of care givers, especially in situations where a refusal is expressed and the outcome of respecting it is likely to be grave. Thus, increased focus on determining and recording the individual's expressed preference, either before dementia or during its milder and more benign phases, is critical.

Absent clear preference, and absent a legally appointed decider, who can provide consent for the elderly of diminished capacity or mild dementia? The answer in law is unclear. [17] Families often make such decisions. Under the broadest definition of the common law, we assume their ability to give, although not necessarily to withhold, consent for care.[18] This approach sees the common law not only as a specific case or statute but rather as the reflection of the norms of society. Participants in the health care system act as if families have the right to speak for their incapacitated elderly relatives. Perhaps the general acceptance of that rule has fashioned a new sort of common law. In most jurisdictions, however, this custom has neither legislative nor judicial support.[19] The only clear legal solution would be for a guardian or conservator to be appointed by a court of appropriate jurisdiction, but even that person may not possess unfettered decision-making authority.

Thus, who does make decisions for these patients? At the present moment, practically everyone is involved: close family, distant family, care givers, administrators, and whoever else may exist in the "partridged pear tree" of medical decision making.

Who should make decisions for these patients? First, who should *not* make the decisions? These sorts of health care decisions are peculiarly ill-suited to the judicial process—that is, for consideration by courts. In theory, judicial forums should provide very real benefits, since we assume the adversary system is the process best suited to expose the truth. Additionally, courts offer the possibility of a prescribed route for appeal and review of decisions.[20] On the other hand, it can be argued that courts are distant from the decisions, staffed by persons who lack medical knowledge and training, expensive, cumbersome and difficult to spur to immediate action, public and thereby invasive to privacy in the most exquisitely personal decisions, subject to political climates and thus to the abuse of special interests and lobbies, and staffed by individuals of varying judicial and moral temperament and widely ranging analytical ability. Despite these reservations, there is a class of patients, primarily the long-term institutionalized, retarded, and mentally ill, who are demonstrably so vulnerable to abuse that public judicial process is required.

For these reasons, and with some qualification, I advocate a marked preference for more private and flexible solutions which, by and large, are lodged within health care institutions. The doctrine of substituted judgment can be useful for this purpose—it is designed to discover and give effect to the silenced voice of the now-incompetent. It can and should be expanded to permit those of diminished capability to exercise, through the action and support of others, those preferences which would have been decisive for them. However, this expanded doctrine must be accompanied by specific procedures for application and review.[21] It will require the barriers of silence which surround terminal care to be dismantled. It will impose upon care givers, and most especially upon long-term care institutions, the added obligation to determine beforehand those facts and values of each patient that will be relevant to later decisions. It will require providers at long-term care institutions to discuss the processes of illness and dying with patients and their families.

Caring institutions must establish guidelines and procedures which indicate who must be involved in the decision making; what sort of process of consultation, review, and appeal should be provided; what standards exist for decision making; what is the role of independent advocates in complex cases; and what sort of issues finally must be referred to the courts. For many long-term care institutions, this will require new approaches to patients and new training for staff.

RESEARCH

Let us turn briefly to issues of including elderly patients of diminished or declining ability in research protocols. By and large, given the historic inability of the federal regulatory system to tailor consent regulations to certain problematic groups of patients, e.g., the mentally ill,[22] institutional review boards (IRBs) operate under certain highly questionable legal assumptions on the abilities of persons to provide consent. Federal regulations now provide that, absent a "legally authorized representative,"[23] only the contemporaneous legally effective informed consent of the individual will suffice to permit entrance into a research protocol. But since a legally authorized representative is defined by reference to state law, and since most states have not seen fit to address the problem, IRBs have been left to operate in a legal lacuna when the proposed research subject is an elderly individual with compromised mental competence.

The same definitions of competence proposed for diagnosis and treatment could be expanded to research. However, this informal conceptual expansion, which can be accomplished in the context of diagnosis and treatment, might well violate federal regulations.[24] Thus, I would argue that research generally should not proceed with patients of diminished capabilities who cannot balance for themselves individual risk and benefit against societal gain.

There is one category, however, in which research is critical, the condition of dementia is central, and in which the organ affected must be studied: namely, senile dementia of the Alzheimer's type (SDAT). Its inherent connections with human consciousness, memory, and affective ability preclude conclusive preliminary animal research. SDAT patients are, by current definition, launched on an inexorable path of declining competence. These are preeminently those persons who, in advanced stages of the disease, require institutionalization in chronic care facilities.

Federal regulations have not addressed the complexity of research with this category of patient. The horrible nature of this disease, its ability to destroy humanness, and its undermining of family and self, together compel the conclusion that research on this catastrophic illness should proceed. This, however, sets the stage for an explicit conflict between the requirement for informed consent and the possible benefits of research to the patient or to others. It would thus be a worthwhile task to create guidelines and offer regulations which could make a clear-cut distinction between, on one hand, invasive and risky research and procedures which could never be appropriate for the unconsenting and, on the other hand, other sorts of interventions posing minimal risk for which third-party consent might be appropriate.[25]

Guidelines and regulations concerning SDAT research should be created for the following purposes:

1. To express a preference for research with patients who are competent, or who are otherwise relatively less vulnerable to abuse— considering, again, that competence varies with the demands of the situation

2. To identify individuals who are favorably inclined to participate in research and to provide mechanisms, either through the appointment of agents or the execution of durable powers of attorney, to ensure contemporaneous consent for future participation

3. To assure that all research protocols involving patients with diminished capacity have adequate mechanisms to assess competence, assure the adequacy of the consent process, and ensure the continued ability of the subject to decline participation, or to withdraw from the protocol

4. To indicate special considerations, limitations, and permission for research involving patients who are not capable of granting consent, especially for invasive or intrusive research with substantial risk and great possible benefit to the patient[26]

Regulations could be drafted giving preference to the noninstitutionalized and requiring close inspection of institutional sites. Investigators could be encouraged to devise long-range, long-term protocols for which valid consent could be obtained from patient subjects with early diagnoses. This would permit potential subjects to consider the issues before the ability to do so is diminished or extinguished. In cases where research can only proceed with subjects of already diminished capacity, research protocols should specify the level of competence required. Note that with research, as with diagnosis and treatment, the requisite level of competence will be partly a function of the complexity and risk posed by a choice. The determination of a subject's capacity to consent need not be related to an assessment of an overall state of competence, but only to decision-specific abilities. In any event, however, refusal to participate at any point in the research should be controlling. Researchers and institutions must therefore provide for independent monitors or auditors who can ensure that diminished expressions of refusal, like diminished abilities to consent, are respected.

CONCLUSION

It is time for our legal system to deal with the needs and abilities of the cognitively impaired elderly. Certain impaired elderly have the capacity, and thus "competence," to make choices regarding their own health care, despite cognitive defects. Legal supports and protections must be enacted to give them the power to do so. In addition, specific criteria are needed to define the parameters of allowable human research, so that disease entities such as SDAT may be addressed by researchers. With developments such as these, we, as a society, will be able to care better for the ever-increasing number of elderly in our population.

NOTES

1. Case law and statutes have generally treated a patient's capacity to make health care decisions in a rather black and white manner; a patient is presumed "competent," and therefore capable of making a decision, unless declared "incompetent" by a court of appropriate jurisdiction. Unfortunately, scant legal analysis exists, either in case law, statutes, or legal treatises, regarding the appropriate legal weight for decision-making capacity of those individuals, particularly the elderly, who cannot properly be identified with either of these labels.
2. *See In re* Welfare of Colyer, 660 P.2d 738 (Wash. 1983); *In re* Storar, 420 N.E.2d 64 (N.Y. 1981); *In re* Spring, 405 N.E.2d 115 (Mass. 1980); *In re* Dinnerstein, 380 N.E.2d 134 (Mass. 1978); Superintendent of Belchertown State School v. Saikewicz, 370 N.E.2d 417 (Mass. 1977) [hereinafter referred to as Saikewicz]; *In re* Quinlan, 355 A.2d 647 (N.J. 1976) *cert. denied sub nom.* Garger v. New Jersey, 429 U.S. 922 (1976).
3. The foundation for these rights was set down in a classic statement by Judge Cardozo: "[E]very human being of adult years and sound mind has a right to determine what shall be done with his own body." Schloendorff v. Society of New York Hospital, 105 N.E. 92, 93 (N.Y. 1914). *See generally* Meisel, A., *The "Exceptions" to the Informed Consent Doctrine: Striking a Balance Between Competing Values in Medical Decisionmaking,* WISCONSIN LAW REVIEW 1979 (2):413–88; Canterbury v. Spence, 446 F.2d 772, 790 (D.C. Cir. 1972); Re-

garding the right to refuse treatment, *see generally* Saikewicz, *supra* note 2; Quinlan, *supra* note 2. *But see* State Department of Human Services v. Northern, 563 S.W.2d 197 (Tenn. Ct. App. 1978); Application of the President and Directors of Georgetown College Inc., 331 F.2d 1000 (D.C. Cir. 1964).

4. For an excellent new book on the disinclination of physicians to sustain a dialogue with their patients, *see* J. KATZ, THE SILENT WORLD OF DOCTOR AND PATIENT (Free Press, Riverside, N.J.) (1984); *see also* PRESIDENT'S COMMISSION FOR THE STUDY OF ETHICAL PROBLEMS IN MEDICINE AND BIOMEDICAL AND BEHAVIORAL RESEARCH, MAKING HEALTH CARE DECISIONS (U.S. Gov't Printing Office, Washington, D.C.) (1982) at 89–92.

5. The constitutional right to privacy, though not explicitly enumerated in the Constitution, has been recognized in several state and federal decisions. *See* Saikewicz, *supra* note 2, at 424–26; Quinlan, *supra* note 2, at 647; Roe v. Wade, 410 U.S. 113, 152–54 (1973); Eisenstadt v. Baird, 405 U.S. 438, 453 (1972); Griswold v. Connecticut, 381 U.S. 479 (1965).

6. *See In re* Spring, *supra* note 2, at 119–20; Saikewicz, *supra* note 2, at 431.

7. Saikewicz, *supra* note 2, at 420.

8. *In re* Spring, *supra* note 2; *In re* Dinnerstein, *supra* note 2.

9. *In re* Quinlan, *supra* note 2.

10. For example, the role of hospital ethics committees versus the role of courts is a hotly contested issue. *See* Saikewicz, *supra* note 2, at 434–35. More recently, the controversy over the removal of intravenous feeding tubes has led to conflicting results in New Jersey and California. *See,* Annas, G., *Nonfeeding: Lawful Killing in CA, Homicide in N.J.,* HASTINGS CENTER REPORT 13(6):19–20 (December 1983). However, the New Jersey Supreme Court in 1985 reached a conclusion consistent with the California court. *Compare* In the Matter of Conroy 486 A.2d 1209 (N.J. 1985) and Barber v. Superior Court, 147 Cal. App. 3d 1006, 195 Cal. Rptr. 484 (1983).

11. Saikewicz, *supra* note 2, at 433–35.

12. *In re* Storar, *supra* note 2, at 72.

13. *In re* Quinlan, *supra* note 2, at 668.

14. Roth, L.H., Meisel, A., and Lidz, C.W., *Tests of Competency to Consent to Treatment,* AMERICAN JOURNAL OF PSYCHIATRY 134(3):279–84 (March 1977).

15. Abernathy, V., *Compassion, Control and Decisions About Competency,* AMERICAN JOURNAL OF PSYCHIATRY 141(1):53, 57 (January 1984).

16. As of August, 1984, 22 states had enacted some type of "Living Will" legislation (also known as "Natural Death" or "Right-to-Die" acts). Conversation with Concern for Dying, 250 West 57th St., New York, N.Y. 10107. Several additional states have joined this list since then. In addition, California recently became the first state to enact comprehensive legislation establishing a specific durable power of attorney for health care. Chapter 1204 of the 1983 California Statutes. For a review of this statute, *see* Steinbrook, R., Lo, B., *Decision Making for Incompetent Patients by Designated Proxy: California's New Law,* NEW ENGLAND JOURNAL OF MEDICINE 310(24):1598–601 (June 14, 1984). Pennsylvania has a similar statute, as does Virginia.

17. *See* Meisel, A., Kabnick, L.D., *Informed Consent to Medical Treatment: An Analy-*

sis of Recent Legislation, UNIVERSITY OF PITTSBURGH LAW REVIEW 41(3): 407, 459 (Spring 1980).

18. *Id.* at 459–60.
19. *Id.*
20. *See* Baron, C.H. *Medical Paternalism and the Rule of Law: A Reply to Dr. Relman,* AMERICAN JOURNAL OF LAW & MEDICINE 4(4):337, 346–50 (Winter 1979).
21. PRESIDENT'S COMMISSION FOR THE STUDY OF ETHICAL PROBLEMS IN MEDICINE AND BIOMEDICAL AND BEHAVIORAL RESEARCH, DECIDING TO FOREGO LIFE-SUSTAINING TREATMENT: ETHICAL, MEDICAL AND LEGAL ISSUES IN TREATMENT DECISIONS (U.S. Gov't Printing Office, Washington, D.C.) (1983), at 132–34 [hereinafter cited as FOREGOING TREATMENT]
22. *Id.* at 23–28.
23. 45 C.F.R. §46.116, 1983.
24. Responding to inquiry from the President's Commission regarding the fate of regulations governing research with the mentally impaired, the Department of Health and Human Services stated that the basic regulations governing human subjects experimentation adequately address the issue of such research. The President's Commission, and other prominent authorities, strongly disagreed, and called for additional regulations. *See* FOREGOING TREATMENT, *supra* note 21, at 23–28.
25. For a suggested set of guidelines for research on SDAT patients, see Melnick, V.L., et al., *Clinical Research in Senile Dementia of the Alzheimer Type: Suggested Guidelines Addressing the Ethical and Legal Issues,* JOURNAL OF THE AMERICAN GERIATRICS SOCIETY 32(7):531–36 (July, 1984).
26. *Id.*

22

Ethical Aspects of Decision Making for and with the Elderly

Terrie Todd Wetle, Ph.D.

The first premise of this chapter is that, ideally, there should be no ethical issues unique to decision making and the elderly. Once one has left childhood, age, in and of itself, should have no influence on the ethics involved in decision making regarding treatment, nontreatment, and the distribution of health resources. When physical or mental impairment preclude an elder's ability to make decisions, the same ethical considerations applied to other adults should be applied to that elderly individual. Unfortunately, a variety of societal beliefs and circumstances may converge to create bias against the older person, thereby placing elders at special risk for harm in the decision-making process.

AUTONOMY AND THE ELDERLY

Geriatric care and treatment decisions are influenced by a number of factors, including an unprecedented number of individuals living into very old age, the growing and much publicized "scarcity" of health resources, an increased prevalence of chronic disease and disability in later years, and the ageism of health care providers and the elderly themselves who assume that to be old is to be sick, forgetful, and dependent. Because of the pervasive influence of these factors, health care for the elderly must be examined in light of relevant societal values and ethical considerations. Nowhere is this more important than in decisions regarding consent to and refusal of medical treatment. As John Stuart Mill said, "Neither one person, nor any number of persons, is warranted in saying to another human creature of ripe years, that he shall not do with his life for his own benefit what he chooses to do with it."[1]

The concept of personal autonomy is the most basic ethical foundation for requiring consent before medical treatment. In turn, the concepts of bodily integrity, religious freedom, and individual self-determination have each been used to support the concept of personal autonomy. Autonomy is the individual's right to self-determination, the right to make one's own choices.[2] This means that decisions are voluntary and intentional and are not the result of coercion, duress, or undue influence. In a technical sense, few, if any, decisions are truly autonomous. The individual is constrained by available choices and his or her own strengths and weaknesses and is additionally influenced by the wishes of others.

For the elderly, however, not only are the available choices fewer, but the wishes of others are quite likely to take precedence. Assaults on an individual's freedom may take rather subtle forms. For instance, an individual may receive less than complete information concerning the purpose or risks of a diagnostic procedure, or the physician may automatically include adult children in discussions on test outcomes and treatment options. Assaults on autonomy may also be more blatant. A physician may choose not to include the elderly person in treatment decisions and may ignore the expressed wishes of the individual about treatment, placement, involuntary hospitalization, or institutionalization.

PATERNALISM AND THE ELDERLY

The motivation behind the erosion of an elderly person's autonomy is often paternalistic. Paternalism is the interference with the "liberty of action of an individual and is justified by reasons referring exclusively to the welfare, good, happiness, needs, interests, or values of the person being coerced."[3] At times, however, a facade of paternalism may cover motivations which have less to do with the good of the individual than with some perception of the good of the institution, the care provider, the family, or society in general. Paternalism is most likely to occur in circumstances in which the individual is unable, because of cognitive impairment, lack of consciousness, or extreme physical disability, to make decisions for him- or herself. Unfortunately, a paternalistic approach is often taken with older persons even when there is no evidence to indicate that the individual's decision-making capability is compromised. It is likely that this practice is based on the ageist assumption that to be old is to be incompetent. Interestingly, with younger adults we assume competence to participate in the decision-making process unless there is considerable evidence to the contrary.

Paternalism toward the elderly is prevalent, in part, due to society's wish to protect its older citizens. Such protection, however, carries with it the potential to harm. First, by not including the older person in the decision-making process, decisions are made for that person without all of the relevant information. The missing information may include the individual's wishes, fears, expectations, financial situation, circumstances at home, and symptoms of disease. An elder who says, "I don't want an operation for this breast cancer," may actually be saying that she is fearful of the pain of surgery, that she could not tolerate the disfigurement of such surgery, or that she does not believe the operation would make any difference in comfort or survival. She may also be saying that she does not believe that she is worth the surgeon's or care provider's time and efforts. Each meaning requires a different response. The only way that we can determine each individual's meaning is by careful interaction with, and inclusion of, the elder in the decision-making process.

Second, if the elderly are not included in the decision-making process they may acquire a sense of dependency termed "learned helplessness."[4] Simply stated, if an individual is treated as helpless, his or her behavior is quite likely to change to meet that expectation.

THE COMMON GOOD

Trained professionals usually believe that their expert advice is valuable; therefore, they are disturbed when patients or their families make choices that go against the expert's judgment. It follows then that efforts to have an individual adjudicated incompetent are most often triggered when an individual chooses not to take an expert's advice. Justification is often based on the argument that the substitute decision maker knows what is best for the patient, an argument strengthened by claims that personal autonomy may be compromised in favor of the common good. Widely acknowledged circumstances in which the common good supersedes personal autonomy include the quarantine of patients with highly contagious diseases and the confinement of mentally ill individuals who are a physical threat to others. This common good argument is also used to justify placing some elders in nursing homes once it becomes more expensive to maintain them at home than in an institutional care facility.

The common good argument has also been raised in cases where patients refuse treatment by suggesting that health care professionals may use cost as a factor in making treatment decisions. For example, consider Mrs. G., a 76-year-old woman with diabetes, who has already had a below-the-knee amputation and who refuses to consent to similar surgery on her other leg. After a number of hospital stays for sepsis of this leg and other complications, Mrs. G. is brought to the hospital in a coma. Following discussions with a distant niece, the surgery is performed. Mrs. G. recovers and, with rehabilitation, adjusts well to a second prosthesis.

Medicare billings total more than $62,000. Some observers would argue that this amount represents an ethically avoidable expenditure of public funds.

In these times of budget austerity, it becomes difficult to unquestioningly uphold the patient's right to refuse treatment, particularly when such a refusal may result in large and avoidable expenditures of public monies. Given current efforts to limit Medicare and Medicaid spending, circumstances such as Mrs. G.'s are likely to receive close scrutiny.

DIFFERENT PROFESSIONAL PERSPECTIVES ON DECISION MAKING

In discussions of consent to and refusal of treatment, the focus has generally been on the patient/physician relationship and on such issues as truth-telling, the rights and responsibilities of the respective parties, and the role of expertise. The latter focus is certainly important because the physician's scientific role is so large; that is, he or she can make diagnoses and intervene in matters of health. Furthermore, the public and the courts generally respect the expertise of the physician.[5] I contend, however, that the sphere of discussion should encompass a much broader range of actors. Nurses, allied health professionals, social workers, clergy, and lawyers each have a part to play in the decision-making process. With special, although often conflicting, sets of professional philosophies, practices, and ethical codes, these individuals can bring important views and values to complex decisions. This becomes particularly obvious when we look at the refusal of treatment and care.

Take, for example, the case of Ms. B. She lived for many years with her brother who had a history of multiple hospitalizations for schizophrenia. Because of her own frail health and problems with mobility, Ms. B. had not been out of her apartment for more than five years, depending totally upon her brother for shopping and errands. When her brother was hospitalized once again because of his bizarre behavior, including an assault on a neighbor, the landlord began eviction proceedings and called a local agency to seek assistance with Ms. B. The landlord's concern for Ms. B.'s welfare was, in part, due to the stench of garbage coming from the apartment. In addition, he reported that no one had been in or out of her apartment in more than a week. A social worker was dispatched to evaluate the situation but was initially refused entry to Ms. B.'s apartment. Eventually, on the third try, Ms. B. agreed to talk with the social worker but refused to accept any needed services except for a legal aid attorney to fight the eviction. A week later, Ms. B.

fell and was hospitalized. The attending physician, alarmed at her physical condition, had Ms. B. sent to a nursing home to protect her from
further harm. The social worker was angry with the attorney for not
fighting institutionalization of Ms. B. and angry with the physician for
not considering community-based alternatives. The physician was angry
with the social worker for blatantly neglecting Ms. B.'s needs. The attorney was angry with the physician for not consulting her regarding the
placement.

Each of the professionals involved in the case had a different perspective and approach to Ms. B. The social worker, trained to act as an
advocate in seeking assistance for the client, even when the client refused
assistance, hoped that by early intervention a more serious and perhaps
irreversible crisis might be avoided. The attorney's role was to execute the
client's wishes as the client expressed them. The physician, believing that
the patient's competence was compromised, wanted to protect the patient
from further harm. Each was acting within the ethical code of his or her
own profession; each was trying to do what was "right" for the patient.

Ordinarily, decision making rarely involves explicit discussion and
consideration of the professional values involved. We often assume that
the various actors in the decision-making process hold common values,
with priorities similar to our own. Because these assumptions are rarely
verbalized, confusion and anger are likely to occur in situations where
our values are rejected and an undesired course is taken. Therefore, to
avoid such confusion, there should be a careful clarification of the assumptions, values, and ethics held by each of the participants in the
decision-making process. This need not be a time-consuming, heavily
philosophical discussion. It can consist of relatively simple statements on
feelings and motivations. Although discussions can be on a case by case
basis, they may be more productive when multidisciplinary teams of service providers discuss values and ethical considerations in a more general
structure, for example, at periodic rounds or case review sessions. This
clarification of values within and between professional disciplines, and
among providers, families, and clients would provide a framework and a
common language for discussion when conflicts in the decision-making
process do occur. The expressed wishes of the patient should be central
to such discussions.

WHEN CONSENT IS NOT CONSENT

Autonomy in decisions to accept or refuse treatment or care assumes
both that the individual has adequate information with which to make a
decision and that the decision-making process is free of undue influence
or coercion. However, the ageism of professionals, society, and elders

themselves can alter both the presentation and the interpretation of relevant information. First, there are well-documented gaps in the professional training of physicians, nurses, social workers, and others who provide care to elderly patients.[6] These include lack of information on atypical presentation of disease in the elderly, interaction of multiple pathologies, and the influence of age on response to pharmaceutical or surgical intervention. These gaps lead to mistaken beliefs, misunderstandings, and negative assumptions regarding the appropriateness and efficacy of treatment for the elderly. Further, negative clinical experiences of care providers in serving older clients/patients may reinforce pre-existing negative attitudes and practices, e.g., that elders are mostly sick or confused. Thus the information provided to the patient regarding diagnosis, treatment, and prognosis may be incomplete, biased, or wrong. Societal and individual beliefs about what constitutes a life worth living may also influence the options offered to elder persons. Statements such as "She's already lived a long and full life, why make her suffer through surgery" would never be made about a 20-year-old. This may indicate a devaluation of the later years of life, and it certainly indicates a bias against intervention.

Older adults are more likely than young adults to be financially or physically dependent on others.[7] An individual who is not self-sufficient will quite likely choose different treatment alternatives than one who is self-sufficient. Those individuals who are financially dependent on their children, for example, may feel constrained to choose treatment options which are less expensive but perhaps less desirable. In a similar manner, elderly persons who are dependent on their families for personal care may choose a care option such as institutionalization which reduces their dependency on family members, but leads to decreased quality of life. Independent elders fear becoming dependent on others for their care and reflect this fear in treatment decisions. They may, for example, refuse services in their homes or placement in nursing homes because of fear of losing their independence. Moreover, because a larger proportion of elders are likely to be dependent on their families than are younger adults, dependency is often assumed to be a natural and inevitable characteristic of old age. This assumption influences both individual treatment decisions and the distribution of resources among types of care providers. The institutional bias in public support of health care services compounds the problems resulting from these dependency assumptions.

ELDERLY IN INSTITUTIONS

The elderly in institutional settings are at a particularly high risk of compromising their autonomy when making decisions on consent to or

refusal of treatment. The very nature of the institutional setting rein-
forces negative feelings of dependence, encourages learned helplessness,
and takes away from the individual all but the most trivial decisions.[8]
Further, few nursing home residents actually choose the physician responsible for their care. The lack of regular interaction between physicians and nursing home residents makes it unlikely that a trusting
relationship will be developed. Compounding these barriers to autonomy, a large proportion of residents in institutions have some impairment of cognitive function. The presence of large numbers of cognitively
impaired persons in institutional settings has two major impacts on
clinical decision making. First, an individual patient's values and wishes
are difficult to ascertain. Second, given the fact that many nursing home
residents are impaired in cognitive function, all residents are thus assumed to be similarly impaired.

Nursing home resident/patient rights groups continue to fight an
uphill battle to educate the administrations and staffs of institutions.
They argue that many nursing home residents are able to pursue meaningful and active lives, maintain contact with the outside world, and make
decisions independently regarding treatment and care. We owe it to ourselves to provide the resources to effectuate this potential.

CONSENT FROM THE COMPROMISED INDIVIDUAL

The question of competence to participate in decision making is of central importance when addressing ethical considerations in health care
decisions. A patient's competence is variable and exists on a continuum;
as such, it may fluctuate from moment to moment and from day to day, or
may show a trend in one direction or another over time. For example, the
patient with Alzheimer's disease is likely to follow a somewhat predictable
downhill course. On the other hand, patients with confusion resulting
from an acute illness may be expected to improve in cognitive function as
the illness is resolved. In addition, an individual considered competent to
perform one type of task may not be competent to perform another. A
woman who is unable to manage her daily financial matters may be quite
able to discuss and refuse surgery.

There are several standards for determining competence. Some
standards emphasize a high degree of personal autonomy while others
are very paternalistic.[9] For the most part, the greater the risk related to
the decision, the more stringent is the standard of competence. Generally, every effort should be made to assist even the most minimally competent individual to understand the nature of his or her disease, the likely
risks of intervention, and the prognosis with and without interventions,
and to elicit a preference for action. The President's Commission for the

Study of Ethical Problems in Medicine and Biomedical and Behavioral Research has stated that "incapacity [should] be treated as a disqualifying factor in the small minority of cases," and that "[to] the extent feasible people with no decision-making capacity should still be consulted about their own preferences out of respect for them as individuals."[10]

There will be some persons who are unable to participate in the decision-making process because of physical illness, cognitive impairment, or loss of consciousness. For these individuals, surrogates may provide important information regarding previously stated preferences, previous behaviors, and lifestyle choices. In the absence of stated preferences, therapeutic activism is indicated—including thorough and appropriate assessment and treatment. However, there are circumstances in which forgoing treatment may be the most compassionate and appropriate intervention.

QUALITY OF LIFE

There are those who have argued that, in the absence of a stated preference, we must assume a desire to live.[11] The sanctity of life is a central value in the Judeo-Christian system. Yet adults of all ages, and particularly elders, express a fear of being maintained in a vegetative state. Advances in medicine and technology, for the first time, offer us the option of maintaining life well beyond loss of mobility or meaningful cognitive function. Patients in chronic comas and near coma states may be maintained for years in a half life/half death state. The time honored rule of medical ethics, to preserve life if at all possible, is now viewed in a new light, and many would argue that decisions to forgo treatment may indeed be based on the quality of life of the patient.

The concept of an acceptable or adequate quality of life is different for every individual. Determination of the quality of life is difficult, particularly when the nature of a patient's impairment compromises the patient's ability to describe the quality of life he or she experiences. Some severely impaired elders may appear to be quite comfortable, taking pleasure in simple things like meals, while others may appear to be suffering horribly, striking out at staff, crying and screaming, and bruising and tearing their own flesh. For some, these behaviors are alterable only with large doses of psychotropic medications that may have serious detrimental side effects.

CONCLUSION

In weighing the ethical aspects of medical decision making for the elderly, we must determine how aggressive we should be in providing treatments or interventions that would prolong a life of seeming agony. We must decide who we should involve in such care decisions. Finally, we must consider society's interests, as well as those of concerned individuals.

Once again, we must recognize that resources are scarce. Is it in the public interest to aggressively treat and prolong the lives of seriously impaired elders when such prolongation exacerbates the already spiraling costs of nursing home care? Decisions on such issues are made daily; better stated, nondecisions are made daily in nursing homes and hospitals across the country. These decisions frequently result in the nontreatment of elderly patients and residents. Some nontreatment decisions are based on compassion, caring, and full consideration of the ethical issues and value conflicts involved. Others are made as a matter of expedience, with little consideration and less discussion.

Compassionate caretaking requires that decisions be made with consideration of the many relevant points of view, involving in the process family members, care providers, clergy, and if possible, the elder himself or herself directly or by surrogate. Decisions should be made on a case-by-case basis with clearly stated policies concerning the decision-making process. Nonetheless, these difficult and sometimes tragic choices should remain, subject to social and legal review, the responsibility of primary care providers and family members.

NOTES

1. J. MILL, ON LIBERTY (John Parker and Son, London, Eng.) (2d ed. 1859).
2. Miller, B.L., *Autonomy and Refusal of Life Saving Treatment*, HASTINGS CENTER REPORT 13(4):22–28 (August 1983).
3. Dworkin, G., *Paternalism*, THE MONIST 56(1):64–84 (January 1972).
4. Thornton, J.W., Jacobs, P.D., *Learned Helplessness in Human Subjects*, JOURNAL OF EXPERIMENTAL PSYCHOLOGY 87:369(1971).
5. Dyke, A., *Ethics and Medicine*, LINACRE QUARTERLY (August 1973), *reprinted in* ETHICS IN MEDICINE: HISTORICAL PERSPECTIVES AND CONTEMPORARY CONCERNS (S.J. Reiser, A.J. Dyke, W.J. Curran, eds.) (MIT Press, Cambridge, Mass.) (1977).
6. Libow, L., *The Issues in Geriatric Medical Education*, GERIATRICS 32(2):99–102 (February 1977).
7. National Center for Health Statistics, 1977. National Health Survey, unpublished data as reported in P. FOX, LONG-TERM: BACKGROUND AND FUTURE DIRECTIONS (U.S. Department of Health and Human Services, Washington, D.C.) (1981).
8. *See* Besdine, R.W., ch. 23 of this text.
9. Stanley, B.H., Stanley, M., *Psychiatric Patients in Research: Protecting Their Autonomy*, COMPREHENSIVE PSYCHIATRY 22(4):420–27 (July/August 1981); Roth, L.H., Meisel, A., Lidz, C.W., *Tests of Competency to Consent to Treatment*, AMERICAN JOURNAL OF PSYCHIATRY 134(3):279–84 (March 1977).

10. PRESIDENT'S COMMISSION FOR THE STUDY OF ETHICAL PROBLEMS IN MEDI-
    CINE AND BIOMEDICAL AND BEHAVIORAL RESEARCH, MAKING HEALTH CARE
    DECISIONS, VOLUME I (U.S. Gov't Printing Office, Washington, D.C.) (1983)
    at 3.
11. For a discussion of this view *see* R.M. VEATCH, A THEORY OF MEDICAL ETHICS
    (Basic Books, New York) (1981) at 27–49.

23

Decisions to Withhold Treatment from Nursing Home Residents

Richard W. Besdine, M.D.

The identification of ethical issues or dilemmas inherent in clinical decisions about medical care of an old person is likely to improve that care. A substantial literature has arisen recently concerning ethical components in the process of decision making in clinical medicine for patients of all ages.[1-9] Issues of equal access to services, individual versus collective responsibility, individual autonomy, and the locus of decision making have been identified and discussed with a new vigor born of their previous neglect, especially in patients who are old.[10,11] Several clinical and academic centers have developed ethics projects exclusively concerned with care of the elderly. But the set of medical ethics problems faced in decisions to withhold diagnostic and therapeutic interventions in the long-term care institution has not been adequately addressed. That long-term care institutions, including nursing homes and chronic-care hospitals, serve one and one-quarter million older Americans at any one time, and that one in five individuals beyond age 60 will be admitted to a nursing home, demonstrate the need for this question to be raised.

Until now, the focus of ethical controversy has usually been concentrated on hospitalized, acutely ill, elderly individuals whose care has raised ethical concerns among care givers, families, or professionals who have identified themselves as ethically or philosophically interested. In the acute hospital the severity and rapidly evolving nature of disease dominates the situation. Ethical concerns often surface during hectic, active phases of illness and are addressed concurrently with the urgent care demanded by the patient's condition. Serious clinical decisions with

Reprinted with permission of the W.B. Saunders Co. from the JOURNAL OF THE AMERICAN GERIATRIC SOCIETY 31(10):602–6 (October 1983).

ethical implications must be made under severe pressures of time and psychologic stress arising from the institutional context. In long-term care institutions, care providers, unencumbered by the pressure of time restraints, face ethical dilemmas that usually arise in the context of deciding whether resuscitation, diagnosis, or medical treatment should be withheld from an individual on the basis of a moral judgment. Good medical care of nursing home residents requires physician advocacy for comprehensive diagnostic and therapeutic services aimed at improved enjoyment of life for the resident. In the most sensitive and sensible treatment settings, nursing home residents are encountered whose physical or psychologic suffering, debility, and poor prognosis raise questions about withholding treatment. The existence of these impaired individuals demands that we address their distress and generate guidelines for their moral and ethical medical management. When the individual, regardless of diagnosis, is able to understand the issues, he or she always decides; but when unable to participate in decision making, the individual must be spoken for by others.

In short, the moral and ethical questions that arise in providing medical care for impaired elderly nursing home residents must be identified and addressed. Failure to deal with ethical components of clinical decisions produces unreasoned care and intense frustration among caregivers.[12]

THE COMPLEXITY OF ETHICAL ISSUES
RAISED BY NURSING HOME CARE

Living in a nursing home introduces confounding issues to any discussion of the ethical components of the medical care of its residents. First, entering a nursing home intrinsically represents a substantial loss of personal autonomy, which influences all aspects of an individual's life. One especially relevant aspect of restricted autonomy is the likelihood that physicians caring for nursing home residents are not chosen by the residents and are not familiar with the residents' personalities and preferences. Second, by virtue of requiring care in a nursing home, its elderly residents have a generally acknowledged diminution of enjoyment of life. Most people would prefer to live elsewhere. The chronicity and permanence of the losses suffered by many nursing home dwellers is a discouraging prospect. Third, the high prevalence of dementing illness and of dependent behavior in the nursing home population means that many residents will be unable to participate in the decisions about their own care and will require substitute decision makers to be assembled. Fourth, many nursing home residents receive public funds to support their care, encouraging public concern about consumption of limited resources. Fifth, nursing home residents are extremely old, averaging 82 years of age nationwide. Advanced age alone may often provoke discussions of limitation of treatment should new illness develop or chronic illness worsen.

Thus we find in the nursing home large numbers of people whose continuing clinical care is likely to raise major and complex ethical concerns.[13] The concentration of ethical dilemmas among elderly nursing home residents requires attention on at least two levels. First, because these issues are complex and emotionally charged, health professionals need assistance in addressing them. Second, as places in which ethical dilemmas arise often, nursing homes provide a fruitful sociocultural "laboratory" in which problems in biomedical ethics can be identified and studied.

DECISIONS NOT TO RESUSCITATE, HOSPITALIZE, OR TREAT

THE NURSING HOME CONTEXT

Most decisions to withhold treatment in the nursing home emerge in the following three categories: do not resuscitate (DNR); do not hospitalize (DNH); and do not treat(DNT). Most limited and least relevant to the nursing home is the decision to withhold resuscitation; more relevant to nursing home residents and their physicians are the ethical components of decisions to hospitalize or not to hospitalize a resident and thus limit treatment to that available in the nursing home, and of decisions to initiate or withhold medical treatment.

Do-not-resuscitate decisions were first considered in acute hospitals, where they are a major ethical issue.[14] When a decision is made to write a DNR order, that order is usually of brief duration: either an arrest occurs, resuscitation is withheld, and the patient dies, or the crisis passes without cardiac or respiratory arrest and the patient improves. In the latter instance, the DNR order is no longer relevant and is rescinded. The ability immediately to detect cessation of respiration or heartbeat allows dramatic resuscitative interventions that employ an array of sophisticated equipment and personnel. After initial resuscitation, life-support machinery, drugs, and professionals continue to be available; this permits survival of resuscitated patients in spite of catastrophic damage to numerous vital functions. Although outcomes of resuscitation are discouraging, cardiopulmonary resuscitation (CPR) and other heroic interventions are correctly administered to the sickest acute hospital patients because those few who will survive with good quality of life are not prospectively identifiable.[15] In the acute hospital, DNR decisions are made after careful discussion by the patient and care givers, during which comprehensive information about the illness being treated and its prognosis and the mechanics of resuscitation are provided. When the patient is unable to decide because of unconsciousness or inability to understand, family members and other concerned individuals are asked to assist in the delicate and difficult process.[16] In either case, information is provided and decisions are made quickly.

In the nursing home, DNR orders are considered by physicians whose decision-making model is based on acute hospital experience. However, most features of the DNR decision are different in the nursing home. First, the capacity to detect, treat, and maintain nursing home residents who have cardiac or respiratory arrest is sharply limited. Long delays prior to initiation of CPR are likely to limit successful outcomes. The technology and personnel required for successful resuscitation are rarely available, so that resuscitated patients must be transferred to an acute hospital for continued maintenance and surveillance. Second, nursing home residents for whom DNR orders are considered usually manifest a different array of impairments than acute-care patients. Rarely are they in the midst of devastating and fluctuating acute illness. Instead, DNR discussions usually arise in the nursing home when the life of a slowly declining resident is sufficiently painful or tragic that death appears to offer awaited release from suffering.

IMPLEMENTING ETHICAL DECISIONS

The mechanism for implementing decisions to restrict treatment in the nursing home, whether DNR, DNH, or DNT, has features that differ from the hospital process. Care givers, overwhelmed by the perceived suffering or poor life quality of the resident, usually raise the issue of withholding resuscitation among themselves first. If the resident can comprehend the issues, he or she is given relevant information and asked to decide. If unable to participate, usually because of severe dementia, a substitute decision-making mechanism must be created. In either case, if ethical concerns are addressed methodically, ample time is usually available for all questions to be considered and implications to be pursued. When the individual cannot decide, factors that are considered include assessment of physical or emotional pain, prognosis, and the risks and distress produced by the intervention itself. In these cases, any evidence of the individual's own preference that can be documented by personal communication or a "living will" should be sought.

Because the pressure of an abrupt acute illness may deprive participants of adequate time for discussion of all aspects of the case, suffering individuals who may have limited ability to participate in decisions should be identified routinely in the process of assessment and care planning. Prospective identification of such residents allows time for all relevant individuals to gather for discussions in which the issues can be clarified without necessarily having to specify comprehensively what illnesses should or should not be treated. Adequate data can be collected free of the time pressure usually found in acute clinical settings. In addition, if the ethical components of a clinical decision are not identified before the decision has to be made, clinical situations can evolve with startling rapidity and produce frustrating and discouraging outcomes. For example, the recognition that an intubated patient on a respirator who has stroke disability and pneumonia and who requires intravenous or nasogastric nutrition should not have been treated at all is a destructive and unhappy event. All interested individuals among care givers, family, friends, clergy, and institutional administrators should participate, and unanimous decisions usually are required. In the few, unusual long-term care institutions capable of managing acute medical illness, DNR situations arise during urgent treatment in much the same way as in acute hospitals.

In nursing homes, DNR decisions, though of great moral weight, have little practical importance in the management of illness. Because resuscitation must be administered within moments of the crisis and because most situations require sophisticated equipment and personnel, prompt detection of arrest and successful resuscitation are rare events in nursing homes. The major impact of writing a DNR order for a nursing home resident is not to deprive that person of an important chance of surviving a cardiac or respiratory arrest, but rather it allays anxiety among staff concerning their responsibility should that individual die under observation or be found to have recently died. Honest acknowledgement of this reality helps nursing home staff deliver better care.

Ethical dilemmas that do commonly arise in the medical management of severely impaired nursing home residents concern whether the treament for a disease should be administered or be withheld to allow death to occur. The clinician at the bedside must be aware of the ethical impact of initiating treatment for an illness which, though medically treatable, is occurring in a setting of inexorable deterioration. Withholding therapeutic measures that are within the scope of usual medical care, e.g., intravenous fluids or antibiotics, may be considered when the individual is judged by reasonable measures to be suffering and beyond hope of recovery and to be living a life that he or she would not want to continue. If there is ethical uncertainty about the appropriateness of treatment, equal attention should be given to decisions to initiate diagnostic evaluation. Undertaking diagnostic tests in patients whose identified diseases will not be treated is irrational and without value, and is particularly senseless when the studies are unpleasant, dangerous, or expensive. For those residents who are unable to participate in decisions about treatment and whose lives appear to be very painful to them, discussion of whether to limit treatment should precede any clinical decisions.

THE DECISION TO HOSPITALIZE

Inextricably linked to discussions of whether to treat technologically treatable disease of a suffering nursing home resident is the question of whether to hospitalize that individual. Adequate treatment of many acute illnesses requires the resources of an acute hospital. Through prior discussion it may be possible to identify residents for whom the experience of hospitalization would be more confusing and painful than the therapeutic gain would warrant. For these individuals discussion and clarification of their status can simplify management decisions that may arise if acute illness occurs. Two other aspects of hospitalization of the nursing home patient must be factored into the ethical decision making. First, in addition to diagnostic and therapeutic benefits, hospitalization poses substantial risks. The occurrence of falls, nosocomial infections, and adverse drug reactions during hospitalization are more common and severe in frail elderly individuals.[17] Second, when the nursing home resident returns to the home after hospitalization, he or she is likely to be a nosocomial infection hazard to fellow residents because of resistant microbial flora acquired in the acute hospital.

THE ALLEVIATION OF SUFFERING IN LIMITED TREATMENT

Implicit in any discussion of limiting specific treatment is the expectation that suffering and distress will continue to be sensitively assessed and treated when detected. The limitation of certain kinds of medical treatment does not mean a patient should receive limited care or caring. The opposite should be true, especially in the nursing home. Proper use of morphine or psychoactive agents is essential in providing genuine rather than lip service comfort to the patient who is not receiving specific treatment. Family and patient require more, not less, access to professional staff for counseling and support once limitation of treatment decisions have been made. The needs of the staff for counseling and support must be considered.[18] Aggressive remediation of discomfort, through skin care, turning, bowel and bladder management, and mouth and eye hygiene are persuasive and comforting to a family anxious about the condition of their elder, and are necessary to ensure minimal distress for the resident.

In spite of sensible decisions to limit treatment, comfort of the patient may demand specific therapeutic interventions for an unexpected, intolerably painful illness. For example, an episode of pneumonia may cause chest pain or respiratory distress that care givers and family may decide should be treated with antibiotics, analgesics, and oxygen. A sudden mechanical intestinal obstruction may require an unplanned laparotomy for lysis of adhesions. Diabetic gangrene of a toe or foot may require amputation to relieve pain and malodorous drainage. Decisions to withhold treatment cannot be absolute. Unpredictable medical developments may well dissolve the most resolute unanimity of physician and family not to treat a hopelessly suffering old person. However, when it is appropriate that the decision to limit specific treatment remains firm in the nursing home, assiduous attention to comfort measures and relief of suffering may represent fulfillment of the institution's central mission of caring.

DEVELOPING AN INSTITUTIONAL FRAMEWORK FOR ETHICAL DECISION MAKING

Once they have identified the sorts of ethical issues that arise during clinical care of incapacitated elderly nursing home residents unable to make a decision about the limitation of treatment, it is easier for care givers in the nursing home to deal with this crucial aspect of good long-term care. Primary care professionals are usually the first to sense an ethical problem in an individual resident's care, although occasionally a family member will raise the issue. In either instance, meetings in the nursing home of involved care givers and concerned family to share information and establish trust are essential. Participation in discussions of life-and-death decisions is draining for everyone, and the identification of those individuals in the nursing home who have a special interest in and knowledge of these problems can be helpful to the principals involved. An ethical issues team, preferably including a physician, nurse, and social worker, eases both the process of determining whether a resident's case should be pursued and the deliberations following an affirmative decision. Although staff time is already heavily burdened in nursing homes, the importance of these ethical issues and the unhappy outcome of their neglect make the provision of an ethical issues team an essential concept for long-term care.

Activities in the nursing home concerning a decision to withhold treatment should involve the primary care personnel who know the resident best on a routine basis. Periodically, the nurse, social worker, and, if involved, the physician, should meet and review each resident in their care. As in DNR decisions, factors to be considered include current physical or emotional suffering, level of intellectual impairment, previously expressed wishes of the resident and family, prognosis for future decline, an overall assessment of quality of life, and any other relevant data about the resident. If the resident is able to state his or her wishes, that preference is dominant. If the primary care team expresses concern about application of resuscitation or less heroic therapeutic measures, a member of the ethical issues team should be involved. If preliminary agreement is reached that a decision not to resuscitate, not to transfer to an acute hospital, or not to initiate treatment in the nursing home is advisable, a meeting is arranged with family for the staff to discuss the resident's situation. At this meeting, efforts are made to understand the family's expectations, preferences, and perceptions and to reach agreement on an appropriate course of action. In such delicate and portentous discussions, care givers must avoid even the suggestion of coercion or deceptions and, if disagreements develop, the ethical issues team should be brought in. If agreement is achieved, three possible orders can be written in the chart of the resident. As was already discussed, DNR means that the resident's record clearly indicates to all personnel that cessation of life should not produce any therapeutic response. A DNH order means that the resident should not be transferred to the hospital. If acute events develop that make care givers question the continuing validity of a DNH order, as many of the participants in the original decision as possible should be reconsulted. When a decision has been made to withhold specific treatment for foreseeable illnesses in the nursing home, the DNT order is an indicator of the need to consider treatment of any new or flaring illness in light of the discussions that generated the DNT decision. The DNT order is less clear than either DNH or DNR, but still reflects a clear, ethically based decision about the resident's condition. All residents who have had a DNR, DNH, or DNT order written should be routinely and regularly reviewed for the continuing appropriateness of the order.

NOTES

1. T.L. BEAUCHAMP, J. CHILDRESS, PRINCIPLES OF BIOMEDICAL ETHICS (Oxford University Press, New York) (1979).
2. ENCYCLOPEDIA OF BIOMEDICAL ETHICS (W.T., Reich, ed.) (Oxford University Press, New York) (1979).
3. Callahan, D., *Contemporary Biomedical Ethics,* NEW ENGLAND JOURNAL OF MEDICINE 302(22):1228 (May 29, 1980).
4. R. VEATCH, DEATH, DYING AND THE BIOMEDICAL REVOLUTION: OUR LAST QUEST FOR RESPONSIBILITY (Yale University Press, New Haven, Conn.) (1976).
5. Siegler, M., *Decision-making Strategy for Clinical-Ethical Problems in Medicine,* ARCHIVES OF INTERNAL MEDICINE 142:2178 (1982).
6. Kass, L.R., *Ethical Dilemmas in the Care of the Ill: What is the Physician's Service?* JOURNAL OF THE AMERICAN MEDICAL ASSOCIATION 244:1811 (1980).

7. Jackson, D.L., Younger, S., *Patient Autonomy and "Death with Dignity": Some Clinical Caveats,* NEW ENGLAND JOURNAL OF MEDICINE 301(8):404 (August 23, 1979).
8. Bok, S., *Personal Directions for Care at the End of Life,* NEW ENGLAND JOURNAL OF MEDICINE 295(7):367 (August 12, 1976).
9. Pellegrino, E.D., *Medical Ethics, Education, and the Physician's Image,* JOURNAL OF THE AMERICAN MEDICAL ASSOCIATION 235:1043 (1976).
10. Wetle, T.T., Besdine, R.W., *Ethical Issues,* in HEALTH AND DISEASE IN OLD AGE (Rowe, J.W., Besdine, R.W., eds.) (Little, Brown & Co., Boston) (1982) at 425.
11. Daniels, N., *Am I My Parent's Keeper,* MIDWEST STUDIES IN PHILOSOPHY 7:517 (1982).
12. Lo, B., Johnson, A.R., *Clinical Decisions to Limit Treatment,* ANNALS OF INTERNAL MEDICINE 93:764 (1980).
13. Brown, N.K., Thompson, D.J., *Nontreatment of Fever in Extended-Care Facilities,* NEW ENGLAND JOURNAL OF MEDICINE 300(22):1246 (May 31, 1979).
14. Rabkin, M.T., Gillerman, G., Rice, N.R., *Orders Not to Resuscitate,* NEW ENGLAND JOURNAL OF MEDICINE 295(7):364 (August 12, 1976).
15. Thibault, G.E., *et al., Medical Intensive Care: Indications, Interventions, and Outcomes,* NEW ENGLAND JOURNAL OF MEDICINE 302(17):938 (April 24, 1980).
16. Suber, D.G., Tabor, W.J., *Withholding of Life-Sustaining Treatment From the Terminally Ill, Incompetent Patient: Who Decides?,* JOURNAL OF THE AMERICAN MEDICAL ASSOCIATION 248(19):2431 (1982).
17. Steel, K., *et al., Iatrogenic Illness on a General Medical Service at a University Hospital,* NEW ENGLAND JOURNAL OF MEDICINE 304(11):638 (March 12, 1981).
18. Hilfiker, D., *Allowing the Debilitated to Die: Facing Our Ethical Choices,* NEW ENGLAND JOURNAL OF MEDICINE OF MEDICINE 308(12):716 (March 24, 1983).

24

The Clinical Determination of Competence

Charles M. Culver, M.D., Ph.D.

This chapter will focus on the concept of competence and on its measurement in the clinical setting. Competence is an important concept because of the role it plays in determining whether a patient is able to give a legally and ethically valid consent or refusal to a proposed medical test or treatment. Being clear about these matters is particularly critical in caring for elderly patients, who are often treated as if they are less competent than younger people and less competent than they actually are. It will be useful for our later discussion to review briefly the components of valid consent.

VALID CONSENT OR REFUSAL

The term "valid consent" seems preferable to the more commonly used term "informed consent" for two reasons. First, the latter term implies, incorrectly, that giving patients adequate information is the principal or only criterion for whether the consent process has been carried out in a valid fashion. Second, the term "valid consent" suggests an accurate and useful similarity to terms as "valid contract" and "valid will". All of these terms refer to a process that, in order to be valid, must satisfy certain explicit criteria.

There are three explicit criteria which must be met before a patient's consent or refusal is valid:

1. The patient must receive *adequate information* about the proposed treatment. Adequate information includes, at a minimum, knowl-

*Preparation of this chapter was aided by a grant from The Ira W. DeCamp Foundation.

edge about the probable known risks and benefits associated with the proposed treatment, associated with any rational alternative treatment(s), and associated with no treatment at all. Patients should also be told whether there is a good reason to believe that the probable morbidity and mortality risk would be significantly less at some other medical center or in the hands of some other practitioner than those being suggested.[1]

2. *No coercion* should be used in obtaining consent, since to be valid a consent must be voluntary. "Coercion" is a term sometimes used broadly, but a narrow definition of it is intended here. Coercion refers to the use of such powerful negative incentives (for example, threats of physically hurting a patient, or of depriving a patient of his or her freedom) that it would be unreasonable to expect a patient to resist them. Coercion is sometimes morally justified (see below), but the "consent" that follows it is not valid.

   Coercion is not commonly used in obtaining consent. Psychiatrists occasionally coerce suicidal patients when they threaten such patients with commitment to a state hospital if they will not continue their "voluntary" treatment elsewhere. It would be coercive to threaten a nursing home resident with the loss of his or her single room if he or she did not cooperate in taking prescribed medications.

   It is not coercive for a health care provider to recommend a particular treatment, or even to argue for it strongly. Most patients want to know what treatment the health care team thinks is best. What is important is that the patient be clearly informed of all alternatives, not just the ones being recommended, and know quite clearly that the final decision is his or hers.

3. Finally, in order for a consent or refusal to be valid, a patient must be *competent to give a valid consent or refusal.*

If any of these three criteria is not satisfied, then the patient's consent or refusal is not valid. Under unusual circumstances, which will be mentioned later, it is morally justified to treat in the absence of a valid consent, but one should always be aware that one is doing so, and be able to defend that action according to certain explicit criteria. Whenever possible, a valid consent or refusal should be obtained.

COMPETENCE TO CONSENT OR REFUSE

What is meant by "competence"? First, competence is best regarded not as a global characteristic of patients. It is not the case that all patients can be divided into two groups, the competent and the incompetent, and that every patient in the former group is competent to do everything, and no patient in the latter group is competent to do anything. It is much more useful to ask about any particular patient whether he or she is or is not competent to perform some specific activity. A particular patient, for example, might be quite competent to feed him- or herself, but incompetent to perform some abstract intellectual task.

To decide whether a person is competent to perform some activity, one must first establish explicit criteria which, if satisfied, will document competence in that activity. For example, in most jurisdictions there are statutory criteria for being competent to make a valid will: one must know what one's assets are and who one's natural heirs are (i.e., who would inherit in the absence of a will), and one must know at the time of making a will that one is indeed making a will. If these criteria are satisfied, then a will has been made competently. The will may be challenged on other grounds, but not on the basis that one was incompetent to make it.

Competence to consent to or refuse treatment may most usefully be defined and measured in terms of how adequately a patient understands and appreciates the information that must be given to him or her during the consent process.[2] Patients who adequately understand the information about risks and benefits of the proposed treatment, of alternative treatments, and so forth, and who appreciate that this information applies to them at the current time, are fully competent. Patients who understand and appreciate significantly less of the information may be only partially competent, and some patients, of course, are not competent at all. Thus, patients may be divided into three groups with respect to their competence to consent or refuse.

1. Some patients are completely *incompetent* to consent or refuse. Either they may be comatose and completely unaware of their surroundings, or they may have limited cognitive abilities (for example, be able to recognize their spouse's face) but still be unable to consent or refuse. If one were to suggest a treatment to a patient in this category, the patient either could not answer or could answer only in some random fashion. There are many elderly patients in this category.

2. A second category of patients is partially competent; they are *competent to give a simple consent or a simple refusal,* but not a valid consent or a valid refusal. These patients understand that they are being asked to consent or refuse, and they superficially do consent or refuse; however, in fact they lack the capacity to understand and appreciate the information given them during the consent process.

There are very many elderly patients in this category. The dementias and deliria to which the aged are prone are apt to compromise competence for a long time before they eliminate it entirely. One example would be a man with multi-infarct dementia who agrees without hesitation to carotid arteriography but can repeat back little of the information about the risks of the procedure which have been explained to him. Ostensibly, he is consenting, but he has not adequate understanding of the relevant information. His is a simple, but not a valid, consent. It does not seem morally justified to treat patients just on the basis of a simple consent. These patients, by definition, do not adequately understand and appreciate the risks to which they will be exposed, and it does not seem justified to place them in jeopardy. In order to treat them, one must obtain a valid proxy consent from some third party, either a relative or a guardian.

Another example of a patient in this category would be a woman with a hypoxic delirium from cardiac failure, who summarily refuses all medications and has no understanding that she is ill and that people want to help her. Her refusals count as simple, but not as valid, refusals.

3. Finally, the majority of patients are *competent to give a valid consent or a valid refusal*. These patients are fully competent: they do understand the necessary information and appreciate its relevance to their current situation. The capacity both to understand and appreciate the relevant information is necessary to establish full competence to consent or refuse; understanding alone is not sufficient. For example, an elderly delusional man might be capable of thoroughly understanding and even repeating back the information he is given about a proposed treatment; however, he may believe that he is invincible and that none of the risks he has been told could ever happen to him. His consent to (or refusal of) the treatment should be classified as simple, and not valid.

It is necessary to have a threefold classification of competence in order to describe adequately the patients one encounters. This is nowhere more true than with elderly patients, so many of whom are partially but not fully competent.

An important point that sometimes arises in clinical practice concerns a patient who is agreed to be competent to give only a simple refusal but who gives a simple consent to treatment decisions. Suppose, for example, that a somewhat demented elderly man has only a limited understanding and appreciation of his circumstances. He refuses a suggested treatment, but rather obviously does not understand very much about the malady from which he suffers or the consequences of refusing treatment for it. It would be correct to say of him that his refusal was a simple but not a valid one. Now suppose that for some reason this same patient, without any alteration in his cognitive status, suddenly consents to the treatment which he has up until now been refusing. His consent, just like his prior refusal, would be only a simple and not a valid one. It would not be justified to proceed to treat him, since a simple consent does not by itself justify treatment. Yet there is a temptation, especially among care providers, to take any consent by a patient as being valid and justifying treatment, and to inquire into a patient's competence only in instances of treatment refusal.[3]

However, if a patient is competent to give a valid refusal and subsequently changes his or her mind, ensuing consent would almost always be valid as well. Suppose a depressed elderly woman will likely die without a particular treatment but likely will have a long life expectancy with it. She refuses the treatment because she does not want to live. Her refusal may be quite valid; she may understand and appreciate as much about the consequences of her decision as her physicians do, and thus be fully competent. If she subsequently changes her mind, because of the persuasive powers of her physicians or because her depression lessens, her consent would then be valid and treatment could proceed.

RATIONALITY AND IRRATIONALITY

In order to understand fully the concept of being competent to consent or refuse, it is useful to see how competence differs from rationality. These two terms are not synonyms, though they are sometimes loosely used as such. Competence refers to a patient's ability to make a treatment decision; rationality is a characteristic of that decision once it is made. Thus patients who are competent to give either a simple or valid consent or refusal may make treatment decisions which are either rational or irrational. The two concepts are independent. A patient may be fully competent to make a valid refusal that is seriously irrational. Another patient may be competent only to give a simple consent, but that simple consent may be quite rational.

What is an irrational decision or action? Only a brief account will be given here. A simple way of defining an irrational action is that it involves jeopardizing or hurting oneself pointlessly, as in "cutting off one's nose to spite one's face." An irrational decision (and some treatment refusals are irrational decisions) is one that likely will lead to one's suffering evils (harms) without any compensating benefit.

A more precise way of expressing this idea is to say that a decision or action is irrational if its foreseeable results are that the person will suffer evils without an adequate reason. The evils of most frequent concern in a medical setting are death, physical and mental pain, physical and mental disability, and deprivation of freedom or opportunity. It is irrational to act in a way, or to make a decision, that increases the likelihood that one will experience any of these evils, unless one has an adequate reason for doing so.

Adequate reasons are conscious beliefs about the compensating benefits probably to be obtained by acting in a way that admittedly will cause one to experience evils. Adequate reasons change what would otherwise be irrational actions into rational actions. For example, if I were to have my leg cut off for no reason at all, that would be a clear instance of irrational action. By contrast, if I suffer from an osteogenic sarcoma of a bone in my leg, and I agree to have my leg amputated to try to prevent the metastatic spread of the cancer, that would be a rational decision on my part. My belief that the loss of my leg may prevent my death is an adequate reason.[4]

It would rarely if ever be irrational for a patient to consent to a suggested treatment, because competent physicians rarely if ever suggest irrational treatments. An irrational treatment would be one that, on balance would be expected to cause much more harm than it could alleviate, and competent physicians rarely suggest treatments of that kind.

Refusing a treatment can be either an irrational or a rational act. Suppose an elderly man in generally good health and spirits contracts pneumococcal pneumonia. After the diagnosis is made, appropriate antibiotic therapy is recommended to him, but he inexplicably declines to be treated. He is warned that he may well die without treatment and is asked why he is refusing. He acknowledges he may die, but can give no reason for his treatment refusal. Since he is making a decision which will probably result in his death, and since he can give no reason for this decision which involves adequate compensating benefits to him, his refusal would be irrational. Suppose, by contrast, that this same man is terminally ill with a painful and debilitating neoplasm and contracts pneumococcal pneumonia. He refuses antibiotic therapy, preferring to die now rather than endure several more weeks or months of further pain followed by his certain death. He has an adequate reason for declining the antibiotics, and his refusal of treatment would be quite rational.

CASE EXAMPLES

The following cases, which were referred to the ethics advisory committee of our hospital for an ethics consultation, illustrate the application of many of the above concepts.[5]

Mr. Jones was a 67-year-old retired farmer who lived alone and had no close relatives. Two years previously he had had a skin lesion which proved to be a malignant melanoma. This was treated with surgery and chemotherapy. However, his cancer had recently recurred and was now more widespread than before. At the time of his current admission his cancer was judged to be incurable. His physicians recommended further excisional surgery and another course of chemotherapy, feeling these procedures would afford him considerable relief from his pain and might even extend his life by many months. Mr. Jones declined these treatments, however, and said he simply wanted to go home and await his death.

There is, except in very rare cases, no moral or legal justification for over-ruling the treatment refusal of a competent patient. But was Mr. Jones competent? His physicians were unsure. He had had two strokes during the past year, and these had left him with some mild but definite intellectual impairment; for example, he could not perform mental calculations nearly as well as he previously did, and his recent memory was somewhat impaired. However, he seemed to understand his medical situation adequately. The dilemma his physicians felt, and which they presented to the ethics consultant, was whether it was justified to regard Mr. Jones as competent to make a treatment refusal. Can an intellectually impaired man make a valid refusal? Were they morally justified in not treating?

The ethics consultant felt that Mr. Jones's treatment refusal was valid. Being competent to make a valid refusal depends on being able to understand and appreciate the information one has been given about the probable consequences attendant upon that refusal and upon alternate courses of action. Mr. Jones seemed entirely competent in that regard. The fact that his competence in some other areas was compromised had no direct bearing on his competence to make this treatment decision. The consultant also felt, as did Mr. Jones's physicians, that the patient's treatment refusal was rational and that no attempt should be made to overrule him, and that no very strong attempt be made to change his mind.

Mrs. Smithers was a 62-year-old widow who lived alone. Her only fairly close relative was an older brother who lived 200 miles away. Mrs. Smithers was admitted to the hospital by her internist. It was determined after a day of testing that she was suffering from a serious kidney infection. Appropriate antibiotic therapy was suggested to her. To her physician's surprise, she refused treatment. She claimed that she knew she could not be seriously ill, and she was especially sure that nothing could be wrong with her kidneys.

Over the next several days, the ward staff tried very hard to persuade her to accept treatment. It became apparent as they talked further with her that she had several other delusions about her life. Her physician also discovered that she had been treated years before at another hospital for a psychiatric illness in which she had also had delusional ideas. Her physician asked her if she would be willing to see a psychiatrist on this occasion. She firmly refused either to see a psychiatrist or to take any psychiatric medications.

The staff requested an ethics consultation. Mrs. Smither's condition was deteriorating rapidly and she could well go into renal failure and die within a few days or a week. The staff had called her brother to see if he would try to influence her, but he was unwilling to become involved, saying his sister had always been strong-willed and full of peculiar ideas, and he had never been successful in arguing with her. How should the staff proceed?

The ethics consultant felt, first of all, that Mrs. Smither's refusal of treatment was a simple, but not a valid, refusal. While she may have had some understanding of the information she had been given, she had no apparent appreciation that this information applied to her. Her simple refusal also appeared to be irrational. Not being treated would lead almost certainly to her death, and there was no adequate reason for dying that she gave or that the staff could imagine. In fact, in her conversation she never mentioned wanting to die at all.

The consultant felt that treating Mrs. Smithers against her wishes was morally justified. Not only was her refusal seriously irrational, but the evils involved in forcing treatment seemed much less severe than the evil (death) which treatment would probably prevent. It seemed morally justified to cause her to suffer mild to moderate amounts of evil in order to prevent her death in a setting where she had no rational desire to die.[6] The hospital counsel also felt that treating Mrs. Smithers against her wishes was appropriate, and steps were taken to have the court appoint a guardian who could give proxy consent for treatment.

CONCLUSION

The above guidelines should prove useful for almost all situations in which a patient's competence needs to be clinically assessed. The guidelines are based on a conceptual analysis of competence; no attempt has been made to summarize the plethora of legal definitions of the term. The law generally does not deal with the concept of partial competence, although clinicians in their day-to-day practice do treat partially competent and fully competent patients differently. Also, statutory law rarely, if ever, makes a distinction between competence and rationality, although judges in their written opinions often do.

When dealing with elderly patients, it is particularly important to use a clear and precise concept of competence. There is a danger of mistakenly classifying older persons as less competent than they actually are. This may be partly due to general stereotypes about the aged, but just as often it seems due to mistakenly believing that because an older person is not competent to do some things, he or she is also not fully competent to make medical decisions. Being clear about the criteria of competence to consent or to refuse, and realizing that partial competence is not equivalent to incompetence, are two important ways to guard against errors in classification and the unjustified paternalism that frequently flows from them.

NOTES

1. For a fuller discussion of the criterion of adequate information and the concept of valid consent, *see* C. CULVER, B. GERT, PHILOSOPHY IN MEDICINE (Oxford University Press, New York) (1982) at 42–63.
2. For a review of various definitions of competence to consent or refuse, *see* Roth, L.H., Meisel, A., Lidz, C.W., *Tests of Competency to Consent to Treatment,* AMERICAN JOURNAL OF PSYCHIATRY 134:279–84 (1977). For more recent reviews of several philosophical and legal definitions of competence, *see* T.G. GUTHEIL, P.S. APPELBAUM, CLINICAL HANDBOOK OF PSYCHIATRY AND THE LAW (McGraw-Hill, New York) (1982) at 215–21; PRESIDENT'S COMMISSION FOR THE STUDY OF ETHICAL PROBLEMS IN MEDICINE AND BIOMEDICAL AND BEHAVIORAL RESEARCH, MAKING HEALTH CARE DECISIONS, VOLUME I (U.S. Gov't Printing Office, Washington, D.C.) (1983) at 55–62 and 169–75.
3. *See* Lane v. Candura, 376 N.E.2d 1232 (Mass. App. 1978). A patient, Mrs. Candura, originally consented to an operation and then changed her mind. Her daughter filed a petition seeking appointment as the patient's temporary guardian with authority to consent to the operation on behalf of the patient. Until Mrs. Candura changed her original decision and withdrew her consent to the operation, her competence was not questioned. The Probate Court entered an order to appoint the daughter temporary guardian, but the decision was reversed on appeal.
4. For a fuller discussion of the definitions of rationality, irrationality, and adequate reasons, *see* CULVER, GERT, *supra* note 1, at 20–41.
5. For further examples of making treatment decisions based on a patient's level of competence and the rationality of his treatment decision, *see* Culver, C.M., Gert, B., *Basic Ethical Concepts in Neurological Practice,* SEMINARS IN NEUROLOGY, 4:1–8 (1984).
6. For a full discussion of when it is morally justified to treat patients against their will, *see* CULVER, GERT, *supra* note 1, at 143–63.

Appendix A

The Supportive Care Plan— Its Meaning and Application: Recommendations and Guidelines

The Task Force on Supportive Care*

Several incidents involving the withdrawal of treatment and/or the ordering of supportive care for nursing home residents came to public attention in the spring and summer of 1981, raising serious concerns among advocates, attorneys, and health care professionals about the use of supportive care orders. It appeared that there was little consistency or consensus with respect to the meaning or application of the supportive care concept.

In response to such concerns, a task force of interested individuals— long-term care staff and administrators, consumer advocates, medical, legal and social service professionals, and government agency officials— was convened to identify and discuss issues raised by the use of supportive care. The task set by the group was to make recommendations and propose a set of guidelines for the provision of supportive care in long-term care settings.

As used in this document, supportive care means the concept of providing care and medical treatment to preserve comfort, hygiene and dignity, but not to prolong life. The DNR (do not resuscitate) concept must be clearly distinguished from supportive care. While the phrase "supportive care" may have negative or misleading connotations, it was the consensus of the task force to use the term for want of any better one.

Reprinted with permission of the American Society of Law & Medicine from LAW, MEDICINE & HEALTH CARE, June 1984, pp. 97–105, 134.
*The Task Force on Supportive Care is an independent group formed in Minneapolis-St. Paul, Minnesota in 1982. Names and affiliations of group members may be found at the end of this appendix.

It is hoped that a common understanding will develop through continuing re-examination and refinement of the concept, and by consistent usage.

It is acknowledged that decisions regarding the continuance or discontinuance of treatment are commonly made in long-term care settings. The need to make such decisions results from advances in medical technology and treatments which have increased the ability to prolong life, even in situations where the prognosis is hopeless and further treatment offers no benefit to the resident.

Such advances have raised serious questions about, and conflicts among, fundamental principles and values including:

— the preservation and protection of life
— the promotion of individual and familial autonomy
— safeguarding the rights of all parties
— maintaining ethical integrity and the highest standards of practice of health care providers
— the affirmation of compassion and humane considerations
— the equitable allocation of resources

Particularly difficult ethical and legal questions are raised when incompetent or not fully competent residents are involved.

We have agreed that certain principles are fundamental in all supportive care situations:

1. Any decision regarding supportive care must be made on a case by case basis with full participation of all parties, and a thorough discussion of all concerns. All supportive care plans must be individualized.
2. The resident who is competent has the final decision as to the extent of care, or withdrawal, withholding, continuance or initiation of treatment. Regardless of the degree of competence, the resident should be involved in the decision-making process to the fullest extent possible.
3. The individual's values, religion and life philosophy must always be respected.
4. Wherever there are serious doubts or questions, the balance in the decision-making should be struck in favor of preserving life.
5. Finally, in all instances, the comfort, hygiene and dignity of a resident must never be compromised, and personal decision making and individual choice must be paramount.

The task force further agreed upon the following:

1. We recommend a principled approach to decision making in advance or by proxy, such as the use of living wills, advance directives, proxy decision making, or other means of conveying a person's wishes to his family and physician regarding the prolonging of life or the withholding of treatment.

2. We recommend the formulation and adoption of institutional policies and procedures to address the issues raised in the initiation and provision of supportive care.

3. We recommend that long-term care facilities establish interdisciplinary biomedical ethics committees to assist in developing and implementing supportive care policies.

This document is our first attempt to address some of the problems faced by those involved in a supportive care situation. It is directed to residents, their families and friends, health care providers and long-term care facilities to provide a basis for discussion, and assistance in making and carrying out supportive care decisions.

We have addressed only those circumstances involving competent or formerly competent adults in long-term care settings. We do not address situations involving individuals who were never competent (newborns, mentally retarded), nor do we address supportive care in acute care settings—although similar principles and procedures may apply.

This document makes recommendations and proposes guidelines for discussion and decision-making when a supportive care plan is considered. It first defines *what supportive care is*, by making a basic statement of philosophy and by outlining care and treatment which typically will be given or withheld under a supportive care plan. It then discusses *for whom supportive care might be considered* by outlining several major categories of medical conditions which may make consideration of a supportive care plan appropriate. Finally, the remainder of the document sets forth *procedures to be followed* whenever a supportive care plan is considered.

While this document does provide a guideline for decision making, it cannot eliminate the significant ethical, religious, medical and legal questions inherent in supportive care situations, nor will its use assure certainty in complex medical or legal cases.

I. WHAT IS SUPPORTIVE CARE?

A decision to provide supportive care to an individual means a decision to provide care and treatment to preserve comfort, hygiene and dignity, but not to prolong life. Supportive care is not considered to be part of the concept of euthanasia or causing death, but rather should be viewed as not extending life in hopeless situations. See Section II, For Whom Supportive Care Might Be Considered.

Once it has been determined that supportive care is appropriate, after utilizing the decision-making procedures outlined below, written orders for the individual plan of care must be established. The primary aims of a supportive care plan should be to promote the dignity of the individual and to minimize pain or discomfort. There should also be active support for the psychological, social, emotional and spiritual needs of the individual and family.

An individual supportive care plan for a resident in a long-term care facility should include consideration of the following guidelines:

A. A specific disease or life-threatening condition which could end life but which does not cause pain or discomfort normally would not be treated. For example, pneumonia not causing dyspnea or pleuritic pain would not be treated.
B. Specific medical conditions which compromise comfort, hygiene, and dignity would be treated. For example, oxygen would be provided to alleviate dyspnea; pneumonia causing pleuritic pain would be treated; a clear airway would be maintained as by suctioning; localized infections and fractures would be treated.
C. Specific nursing care for comfort, hygiene, bowel care, skin care, passive range of motion (PROM) and positioning, and catheter care would be given.
D. Hospitalization or more extensive medical intervention would not ordinarily be indicated. There may be exceptions to this (see above).
E. In most cases, a resident with a supportive care plan would have a do not resuscitate (DNR) order in the medical record.[1]
F. Life sustaining nutrition and hydration needs would ordinarily be met. There is no consensus within the task force on the controversial issue of when and under what circumstances food and fluids may be withheld. We do agree, however, that the existence of a supportive care plan does not in itself predetermine whether artificial means of providing fluids and nutrition will be continued or discontinued. Each individual case must be given careful and sensitive consideration.
G. The resident and family shall have as much control as possible over the care and activity level of the resident.

II. FOR WHOM SUPPORTIVE CARE MIGHT BE CONSIDERED

Residents in long-term care facilities who fall within the following major categories of medical conditions may be considered *potential* candidates for supportive care plans, when there exists clear documentation of the medical condition, and a high degree of certainty of the diagnosis and prognosis. Our intent in setting forth these categories is to limit rather than expand the numbers of long-term care residents who may be considered for supportive care plans.

A. *Terminally ill and imminently dying,* for example, from cancer or cardiac disease.
B. *Severe and irreversible mental disability,* where the resident demonstrates a significant inability to communicate, or to interact meaningfully with the environment, and an unawareness of self and/or the environment; for example, those with presenile and senile dementia (Alzheimer's disease) and cerebral vascular disease (strokes).[2]
C. *Severe and irreversible physical disability,* where there may exist normal mental functioning but, because of pain and suffering, or severe motor impairment, the resident demonstrates a significant inability to interact physically in a meaningful way with the environment; for example, spinal cord injury, head trauma, emphysema, and amyotrophic lateral sclerosis.[3]

III. Procedures for Initiation of a Supportive Care Plan

A. *When a supportive care plan should be considered.* There is no need for any haste in evaluating a resident for initiation of a supportive care plan. Time should be allowed to carefully and thoroughly consider all aspects of the resident's condition.
  1. A supportive care plan is generally inadvisable as part of the initial admission care plan. Before the appropriateness of supportive care can be fully determined, a complete medical record, including a full analysis of rehabilitative potential, should be created within the long-term care setting itself. However, in some cases a supportive care plan on admission may be appropriate depending on the resident's condition, previous course of care, completeness of previous record, and so forth. The physician and the facility should be open to full discussion of the issue if it is raised at admission.
  2. We recommend that the facility not affirmatively suggest the initiation of a supportive care plan. Such a plan is a very personal medical, religious and ethical matter for the resident, family and attending physician. However, we do recommend that the facility staff be open and receptive to discussions of death and the dying process. The facility staff may serve as a valuable resource to residents and families,

but should also act as a champion for any rehabilitative potential that may exist.

3. If a resident is admitted to a facility with physician orders for a supportive care plan, we recommend that the order not be followed without going through the decision-making process outlined below, or, at the very least, without thoroughly assuring, and carefully documenting, that a decision-making process raising all relevant issues had previously been undertaken. In all cases, the facility should clarify the orders received so that no ambiguity exists about the intentions of the physician and the resident.

B. *Participants in a supportive care decision.*

1. *Resident:* The resident must always be involved to the fullest extent possible, even if the resident is under guardianship. The procedures recommended here are intended to involve all interested persons to the fullest extent possible in the final decision so that all viewpoints are represented and thoroughly aired, and so that legal risks are minimized if the resident is unable to make the final decision.

Since supportive care may be viewed by some as placing a resident in a life-threatening situation, any such plan for an incompetent or questionably competent resident involves considerable exposure to serious legal risks. Such a plan may, however, be in the best interests of the resident if all viewpoints, including medical, religious, ethical and personal, as well as legal, are weighed against one another.

There is some question under guardianship law as to whether a guardian of a person has the legal authority to consent to a supportive care plan. Therefore, while these guidelines recommend having a guardian appointed if at all possible, a guardian's consent is not an absolute guarantee of proper authority to undertake a supportive care plan.

a. Competent resident: When the resident is clearly competent, the resident has the full authority to make the decision on a supportive care plan, one way or the other.

b. Questionably competent resident: When there are questions about the resident's competence, but the resident is not under guardianship and is still able to express his or her wishes, the following principles should govern:

   i. If the resident does not want a supportive care plan, no plan should be initiated.

   ii. If the resident seems to want a supportive care plan, the initiation of a guardianship for the resident should be encouraged so that someone is legally designated to speak for the resident.

      iii. If the resident seems to want a supportive care plan and if guardianship is not a viable alternative, a supportive care plan may properly be initiated after thorough family, physician, staff and Bio-medical Ethics Committee involvement, as outlined below.

  c. Incompetent resident not under guardianship: If the resident is clearly incompetent but not under guardianship, and the resident is unable to express himself or herself, the following principles should govern:

      i. Without a guardian, no one is legally authorized to speak for the resident. This situation involves serious risks for the physician, the facility and the family. However, we all agree that an incompetent resident should not be deprived of the right to a supportive care plan merely because of incompetence. Therefore, we recommend the initiation of a guardianship for the resident, so that someone is legally authorized to speak for the resident.

      ii. If guardianship is not a viable alternative, but a supportive care plan seems highly appropriate under all the circumstances, a supportive care plan can be initiated after the careful involvement of family, interested parties, staff, physician and biomedical ethics committee. Be aware, however, that such a situation does pose great risks to all involved.

      iii. If there is no guardian and no family to involve in the decision-making process, but a supportive care plan seems highly appropriate, a physician and a facility should carefully consider whether to initiate a supportive care plan without receiving court approval. In this case, the involvement of the biomedical ethics committee is particularly important and strongly recommended. Facilities and physicians are cautioned, however, that deciding against a supportive care plan in highly appropriate circumstances because of potential legal risks for themselves may in itself violate the rights of the resident, both legally and ethically.

  d. Incompetent resident under guardianship:

      i. The consent of both the guardian and the resident should be obtained, if the resident can in any way express his or her wishes. The family should be involved as outlined below.

      ii. A guardian may wish to seek probate court approval of a supportive care plan; however, at this point, it is not at all clear how the court would view such a request.

2. *Family and interested persons:*

  a. Whenever possible, unless the resident is clearly competent and forbids it, the family should be fully involved in the decision-making process. All family members who are involved with the resident's care and activities should be included, and all family members as close or closer in degree of relationship to the resident as the involved persons should be notified of the discussion. Any other family members who may reasonably wish to be included in the decision-making process should also be notified.

b. Other persons or groups involved in the resident's care and/or activities, or in support of the family should also be involved.

c. We recommend that the resident's attending physician take primary responsibility for the notification and involvement of family and others. Each physician and facility could, however, develop cooperative procedures in this respect.

3. *Resident's attending physician:*

a. A supportive care plan should be initiated by orders of the resident's attending physician only, never by the facility medical director unless the medical director is the attending physician.

b. If the resident and family are strongly in favor of supportive care and the physician is not, they have the right to consult another physician whose philosophy is more akin to their own. However, the resident and family should be strongly encouraged to consider why the physician is opposed and we encourage the involvement of the biomedical ethics committee.

c. If the physician questions a family's motivation for initiation of a supportive care plan, or if there is irresolvable conflict among family members, the matter should be referred to the facility biomedical ethics committee for additional guidance.

4. *Long-term care facility involvement:*

a. Administrative and professional staff:

i. The director of nursing services, the resident services director and the social services director, or their delegates, should be involved in the discussion. Minimally, the administrator should be informed of the existence of the discussion.

ii. General supportive care policies should be developed, along with a basic evaluation sheet, to ensure that all relevant information is gathered and assessed.

b. Direct care givers: Input should be solicited from those directly involved in care of the resident as they may notice small details or patterns of significance in the condition of the resident. Careful note should be given to the observations and opinions of the direct care givers, particularly when they conflict with the recommendation of the resident or the physician that a supportive care plan is appropriate.

c. Medical director: The medical director of a long-term care facility should not direct a supportive care plan unless he or she is
also the resident's attending physician.

We recommend involvement of the medical director in each
supportive care decision-making process, but do not see this as
an absolute requirement. He or she should at least be informed
of the existence and progress of the consideration, and should be
available for counsel or conflict resolution, if necessary.

The medical director should participate in the development
of, and ultimately approve, all general supportive care policies
developed by the facility.

d. Biomedical ethics committee: We encourage consideration of
each potential supportive care plan by an interdisciplinary biomedical ethics committee. In most facilities, the beginnings of
such a committee may already exist (e.g., utilization review).

Even when it is quite certain that a competent resident may
authorize a supportive care plan for himself or herself, we nevertheless would encourage committee review. In cases of questionably competent or incompetent residents, we feel it is very
important to have the committee's more objective involvement.

While the use of a facility's utilization review committee as a
biomedical ethics committee may be reasonable for the present,
we would recommend future development of an expanded committee to include lay, religious, medical, legal and other professional representation.

C. *Supportive care decision-making process*

1. The decision-making process should be designed to encourage full
discussion of all relevant facts and options so that the meaning and
significance of supportive care is fully understood by all participants, and to ensure that all views are expressed and weighed, and
so that full documentation of the plan will be possible. The following steps are recommended:

a. The issue is raised by the resident, family or physician.

b. The attending physician and facility should obtain complete medical and psycho-social information from the resident's records, at
both the hospital and the long-term care facility. Observations and
other comments which may not be completely reflected in the
medical records should be solicited from direct care givers.

c. The physician and/or facility staff should privately discuss the
potential supportive care plan and the significance with the resident, if at all possible, so that an assessment can be made in the
absence of any pressure by family members.

d. The physician should participate in a full discussion with family members and/or other interested and involved persons, with the consent of the resident if competent. Other family members should be notified of the discussions by the physician.

e. The resident's physician and facility staff should discuss the issue thoroughly among themselves. The facility should assure itself that full discussion between the physician and the resident and family has taken place.

f. All issues should be raised and discussed with facility staff in a care conference format.

g. The proposed plan should be considered by the biomedical ethics committee, particularly if the plan is for an incompetent or questionably competent resident.

2. General admonitions:

a. Document *all* conferences carefully and thoroughly.

b. Do not force a final decision too soon after all discussions have taken place. Let all involved have time to mull matters over.

3. Conflict resolution principles:

a. If the resident can express himself or herself and does not want a supportive care plan, it should not be initiated, or, if initiated by the physician, it should not be carried out by the facility.

b. If the resident and family want a supportive care plan and the resident's physician will not initiate one, the resident and family have the right to consult another physician. In such cases, however, the facility should ensure that the initial physician's concerns and viewpoints are fully considered.

c. If the resident is unable to express himself or herself and family seems to be pressing for a plan, the physician and facility should carefully weigh all factors before initiating and carrying out the plan to ensure its appropriateness. The physician and facility should carefully consider the family's intentions and motivations and should refer the case to the biomedical ethics committee before initiating the plan.

d. If there is an intra-family dispute over the appropriateness of a plan, we recommend careful consideration by the physician and facility as this poses a great risk of legal challenge. We also recommend utilization of the biomedical ethics committee or other facility or community resources to resolve the conflict prior to initiating the plan.

e. If the facility staff, medical director or biomedical ethics committee do not concur with the resident, family or physician on the appropriateness of a plan (for example, if the facility feels significant rehabilitation potential exists), the facility should forcefully express such opinion to the resident, family and physician to ensure that its objections are heard and understood. The facility may choose to refuse to implement the plan and recommend discharge, or may even consider resort to the courts.

D. *Documentation of a supportive care plan.*

1. Physician authorization for a supportive care plan should be a specific, *individualized* set of orders, stating explicitly what will and will not be done for the resident. It must be part of the medical record. An order saying just "Supportive Care" (unlike "DNR") is not sufficient.

2. Written authorization for the plan should be obtained from the resident whenever possible, even if under guardianship. The guardian should also authorize the plan.

3. Written acknowledgment of the plan should be obtained from those interested persons who have been involved in the decision-making process whenever possible.

4. The specific plan and the facility policies on supportive care should be given to the resident and family so that no ambiguity exists.

5. The decision, the nature of the plan, and other relevant matters should be thoroughly discussed with all staff involved with the resident.

E. *Re-evaluation of a supportive care plan.*

1. The plan must be re-evaluated whenever the facts or conditions which led to the initial plan change, or whenever the resident, family or other involved person requests it. The same persons should be involved in re-evaluation as were included in the initial decision.

2. The supportive care plan should be reviewed periodically, when the general plan of care is reviewed. We recommend review on a 30-day basis, in any event.

3. We recommend that criteria and an input sheet be developed for re-evaluation, to ensure that direct care givers are given guidance on what changes in conditions to look for.

IV. CONCLUSION

The task force does not view these recommendations and guidelines as the definitive resolution of the dilemmas raised by the supportive care concept, but rather as part of an ongoing dialogue on supportive care issues and practices. Comments are welcome and may be directed to individual members of the task force.

The recommendations and guidelines set forth in this report represent the views of the signatories as individuals. They do not necessarily reflect the policy of any institution, professional organization or governmental agency with which the signatory is affiliated.

NOTES

1. *See* Minnesota Medical Association, DNR Guidelines (adopted by the Board of Trustees of the Minesota Medical Association) (January 1981).
2. The life of a physically or mentally disabled person is just as valuable as that of a person described as normal or healthy. It is not appropriate to consider a supportive care plan on the basis of a physical or mental disability alone.
3. *Id.*

TASK FORCE ON SUPPORTIVE CARE

Barbara J. Blumer, J.D.
Broeker, Hartfeldt, Hedges & Grant
Bloomington, Minnesota

M. Chervenak, J.D.
Legal Aid Society of Minneapolis
Minneapolis, Minnesota

Ronald E. Cranford, M.D.
Associate Physician in Neurology
Hennepin County Medical Center
Minneapolis, Minnesota

Julie L. Ditzler, R.N., B.S.N.
Resident Services Director
Cedar Pines Health Care Facility
Minneapolis, Minnesota

Jenean Erickson, R.N., FACNHA
Administrator
Yorkshire Manor
Minneapolis, Minnesota

Iris C. Freeman
Director
Nursing Home Residents'
  Advocates
Minneapolis, Minnesota

Paul Goldstein
Assistant Director of Social
  Services
Hennepin County Medical Center
Minneapolis, Minnesota

F. Allen Hester, J.D.
Adjunct Professor of Law
William Mitchell College of Law
St. Paul, Minnesota

Grace Nelson
Long Term Care Committee
Minnesota Senior Federation
Minneapolis, Minnesota

Pamela J. Parker
Former Long Term Care
  Ombudsman
Minnesota Board on Aging
St. Paul, Minnesota

Arnold Rosenthal
Director, Office of Health Facility
  Complaints
Minnesota Department of Health
St. Paul, Minnesota

Lisa Laffoley Schmidt, J.D.   Jim Varpness
Minnesota Legal Services Coalition   Long Term Care Ombudsman
Minneapolis, Minnesota   Minnesota Board on Aging
                                              St. Paul, Minnesota

Affiliations are provided only to aid in the identification of the signatories. The views expressed are not necessarily those of the organizations.

A NOTE ABOUT THE TASK FORCE ON SUPPORTIVE CARE

To the best of our knowledge, this document is one of the first practical attempts to deal with the issue of appropriate care for the elderly in the long-term care setting. Widely distributed in Minnesota, the document has been the subject of intense discussion by professional organizations and consumer groups, in part because the Task Force took positions on several controversial issues. The group is collecting all responses and plans to consider them in some formal way later this year. The publication here of the *Supportive Care Plan* is part of this effort to solicit responses from as many groups and individuals as possible.

No issue so dramatically illustrates the dilemmas presented by the increasing numbers of the elderly than that of how aggressively an individual should be treated when there is little or no hope of rehabilitation or restoration of mental or physical functioning. In 1981, The Minnesota Long Term Care Ombudsman Program was made aware of a number of instances in which orders were inappropriately given for reduced medical treatment for nursing home residents. These incidents, and others, prompted the Program, funded through the Older Americans Act, to facilitate a series of discussions among a number of Minnesota citizens involved with the care of the elderly. The group included nursing home resident advocates and legal representatives, consumers, nursing home professionals and legal representatives, physicians, social workers, clergy, and governmental officials charged with overseeing nursing homes in the state. Participation was fluid, and input was received from many other individuals.

This loosely-formed group focussed its discussion on the way in which orders for supportive care (less than maximally aggressive medical treatment) for nursing home residents were being written by physicians, discussed with residents and families, and implemented in nursing homes. The group met over eighteen months to explore how to better define supportive care, how to determine for whom supportive care may be appropriate, and how to arrive at and document supportive care decisions. The group found itself moving toward a consensus on key issues, and the *Supportive Care Plan* reflects that growing agreement.

The group's efforts were not commissioned or assigned by any governmental agency or professional organization, nor has the group requested endorsements from any professional organizations. The group feels that its guidelines should be used as a basis for initiating discussions with many different concerned professional and consumer groups. The group feels strongly that the matters dealt with in its report should not be the subject of any legislation or regulation, but should serve instead to support and encourage independent choices by the elderly.

We welcome all comments and encourage similar efforts by other groups. Comments from readers may be addressed to any of the individuals listed below, in care of the Task Force on Supportive Care, 2850 Metro Drive #800, Minneapolis, MN 55420.

Barbara J. Blumer, J.D.   Paul A. Goldstein
Ronald E. Cranford, M.D.   Pamela J. Parker

Appendix B

A Response to the Task Force on Supportive Care

Jane D. Hoyt, Ed.M., and
James M. Davies, M.A., L.P.N., J.D.

It is generally acknowledged that there has been misunderstanding about "supportive care" plans, and that guidelines would help clarify and direct the decision making process. However, the guidelines and recommendations contained within the *Supportive Care Plan,* proposed by the Task Force on Supportive Care, are confusing and discriminate against persons with disabilities. Implementation of the recommendations could lead to inadequate care and neglect of a very vulnerable segment of our population, nursing home residents who are severely mentally or physically disabled. Because of concern about these possible outcomes, the Nursing Home Action Group of Minnesota has drafted alternative guidelines.[1]

There are five basic deficiencies in the *Supportive Care Plan:* (1) it would allow violations of the civil rights of persons with mental and physical disabilities; (2) it lacks definitions for some important terms; (3) it lacks sufficient protections for incompetent or questionably competent persons; (4) its tone and content encourage patients or their guardians to choose death-allowing care; and (5) it lacks adequate provisions for review of the decision-making process.

DISCRIMINATION AGAINST PEOPLE WITH DISABILITIES

The most disturbing aspect of the *Supportive Care Plan* is that Section II, entitled "For Whom Supportive Care Might Be Considered," wrongly

Reprinted with permission of The American Society of Law & Medicine from LAW, MEDICINE & HEALTH CARE 12(3): 103–5, 134 (June 1984).

includes patients with severe and irreversible mental disabilities and patients with severe and irreversible physical disabilities "where there may
exist normal mental functioning. . . ." By categorizing individuals with
severe disabilities as potential candidates for supportive care only, the
Supportive Care Plan becomes discriminatory against persons with disabilities. Aggressive research and rehabilitation efforts have improved the
functioning of persons with every disease and disability cited in the
Supportive Care Plan.[2] Listed as "potential candidates for supportive care
plans" are victims of spinal cord injury, stroke, amyotrophic lateral sclerosis, emphysema, head trauma, and presenile and senile dementia. To
label individuals with these infirmities as "potential candidates for sup-
portive-care plans" discourages both professionals and consumers from
hope and positive action.

Some patients who may seem beyond hope do have potential for
rehabilitation. A registered nurse who had experience with rehabilitation
testified in court to this effect:

> I saw a lot of nurses who had run into people maybe two to five years after
> they had had a stroke . . . or some other type of brain damage or dysfunc-
> tion, and either a nurse or an aide or somebody would start to reach them
> in some way . . . it seemed as if a lot of these people took two to five years to
> get over the emotional adjustment to the trauma they had endured.[3]

Under the *Supportive Care Plan,* some individuals might be prematurely
denied life-maintaining care and treatment before they have a chance to
come to terms with their disability.

It is possible to develop guidelines that address the issue of treatment for dying adults while avoiding such discrimination. The guidelines
drafted by the Nursing Home Action Group (NHAG) are based on the
premise that the primary goal of health care givers is to encourage and
promote the best physical, mental, emotional, social, and spiritual health
of which each person is capable. The NHAG maintains that the criteria
for making decisions about technology and ordinary and "extraordinary"
treatment should be the same for all persons, regardless of physical or
mental disability. A "death-allowing care goal"—care in which treatment
is offered for comfort only but not for the purpose of maintaining life—is
permissible only if the individual's bodily condition becomes, irreversibly
and irreparably, terminally ill, and if death is imminent.[4]

Another shortcoming in Section II of the *Supportive Care Plan*
concerns an inconsistency. The long Preamble states that these guidelines
"do not address situations involving individuals who were never competent (newborns, mentally retarded)." However, since some incompetent
newborns and many mentally retarded persons become nursing home
residents, these individuals would very probably fall into the second or
third category of patients for whom supportive care might be considered.

THE NEED TO DEFINE TERMS

The *Supportive Care Plan* uses misleading and ill-defined terms. The term "supportive care" is itself very confusing, especially when people are facing a crisis; the *Supportive Care Plan* lacks a clear statement that "supportive care" may hasten death. To a frail person, the words "supportive care" may seem to mean the opposite of what is intended. A term like "death-allowing care goal," used in the NHAG Guidelines, is offered as a more accurate, properly descriptive term since such a care plan would allow death without preventive treatment and could hasten death.

Another shortcoming in this document is the lack of a section devoted to defining language used throughout. Such terms as "hopeless," "principled approach," "meaningful interaction," and "high degree of certainty" leave the reader with little certainty of what is meant.

Consumers must have access to the information necessary to make thoughtful, protective decisions. The information must enable them to understand clearly their physicians' and facilities' values and policies.

PROTECTION OF THE QUESTIONABLY COMPETENT PERSON

The *Supportive Care Plan* lacks sufficient protections for nursing home residents, especially those who are incompetent or questionably competent. It is well known that care and treatment in nursing homes often fall short of even minimal standards.[5] A 1982 study commissioned by the Health Care Financing Administration revealed that about 60 percent of the nation's doctors—the professionals who would have the most authority under the *Supportive Care Plan* for imposing "supportive care" plans— avoid nursing home residents.[6] Despite the clear evidence of problems in the care provided by nursing homes, there has not been a substantial improvement in the standard of care achieved in nursing homes.[7] Partial deregulation of the nursing home industry in the past few years has further threatened the health and well-being of nursing home residents.[8] The inception of the DRG system (diagnosis related groups) has caused advocates to worry that nursing home residents might be returned prematurely from hospitals to long-term care facilites.[9] If the environment needlessly causes or facilitates the patient's decline, then it is unconscionable to harm the victim further by imposing a supportive care plan. Society must focus on improving standards of care and treatment rather than on writing decision-making procedures which discriminate against persons dependent on poor-quality nursing homes or uninterested professionals.

Many nursing homes have difficulty in properly following laws and regulations which are simpler than the guidelines found in the *Supportive Care Plan*. Evidence of this problem is nationwide and includes state health department reports showing that many nursing homes do not properly implement laws and regulations. [10]

The NHAG Guidelines provide that a fair evaluation of the health condition of any nursing home resident should include, but not be limited to, the following questions as they affect the individual resident:

1. Do the facility's nursing care, medical care, and social services meet state and federal standards?

2. Does the environment encourage meaningful, supportive interaction between residents and others?

3. Are meaningful, life-enriching activities available for all residents at the facility, and are residents encouraged to participate?

4. Are all residents' civil and human rights fully protected? Are residents encouraged to exercise these rights?

5. Is the resident free of medications which may cause: diminished activity and/or diminished motivation and/or other debilitating side effects (such as lack of communication)? [11]

Such extensive considerations are lacking in the *Supportive Care Plan*.

The *Supportive Care Plan* needs to provide greater protection for residents who refuse treatment; the recommendations ignore many considerations that may arise in such situations. For example, the NHAG Guidelines propose that there should be detailed documentation in the medical record:

1. that the resident is legally *and* clearly competent

2. that the resident made the decision freely and without duress

3. that the resident's intentions have been clearly interpreted

4. that as ascertained by clinical evaluation, the resident is not suffering from psychological depression or the effects of chemical use

5. that the resident was, before refusing a treatment, fully informed of the range of available treatments and their consequences, as well as the consequences of nontreatment

6. that the resident was encouraged to, and given agreed-upon time to, reconsider the decision

7. that possible extenuating environmental factors (such as those enumerated in the paragraphs above) have been considered as potentially influencing the resident's decision

8. that the resident was given the opportunity to summon relatives, friends, advocates, or professionals for alternative counseling in the matter[12]

The Task Force gives essentially no acknowledgement to the regrettable fact that the immediate family does not always strive for the best interests of its members. Family members do not necessarily share the same values with respect to life-and-death decisions. To rely on the family, with no cautions regarding potential conflicts of interest, is untenable. Testimony before the U.S. House Select Committee on Aging in April 1980 and in March 1981 produced evidence of extensive abuse against the elderly within families.[13] In numerous states, the emergence of statutes for the protection of vulnerable adults, often based on child protection laws, reflects general recognition of and concern about abuse and neglect of adults with mental and physical disabilities.[14]

In contrast, the NHAG Guidelines stress that the best interests of the nursing home resident are paramount. The wishes of family and friends should be considered, but only insofar as they cleary reflect a sincere commitment to and understanding of the best interests of the resident. The wishes of family and friends to preserve life should be respected unless there is no beneficial medical way to do this. Decisions about nursing home residents who are severely disabled, who are poor, who leave inheritances, or who lack close relatives or friends should be monitored with particular care.[15]

When a major medical or life-and-death decision involves an incompetent or questionably competent person, the NHAG Guidelines suggest either that a sincerely interested family member or friend assume the responsibility of guardianship, or that a guardian *ad litem* be appointed. The NHAG Guidelines create an exception to the requirement of guardianship when the nursing home resident is irreversibly, irreparably, and terminally ill, death is imminent, and a "death-allowing care goal" is being considered.[16]

The terminally ill resident should, like all other nursing home residents, receive emergency treatment for an acute, reversible emergency or injury (such as accidental choking or bleeding) not related to terminal illness. This issue is not adequately addressed in the *Supportive Care Plan*.

ENCOURAGING HOPE FOR PEOPLE WITH DISABILITIES

Another deficiency in the Task Force's document is that it makes no recommendation that health care providers promote the value of life to patients with disabilities. Health care givers must be cautioned against promoting false despair. While allowing for decision making before the onset of disability, guidelines should also provide for the possibility that people may change their minds once disabled. The individual's new, positive opinion of self-worth, and of the value of life after disability, should take precedence over any earlier decision to decline or discontinue treatment if disability occurs.

THE NEED FOR UNBIASED REVIEW

The *Supportive Care Plan* lacks adequate provisions for overseeing the decision-making process. While it does suggest that there be a bioethics committee in each nursing home, no provision is suggested for ascertaining whether the decision-making process is properly reviewed by a group outside the facility. Furthermore, no suggestion is made about the exact composition, authority, duties, or accountability of these bioethics committees.

The Task Force suggests that such a committee could be, at least initially, the facility's already established utilization review committee. Clearly, however, consideration of potential supportive care plans by the utilization review committee could conflict with other considerations, such as cost containment, which are already that committee's responsibility. In order to ensure the utmost protection of nursing home residents, bioethics committees would have to be independent of utilization review committees, and they would have to be supervised by some external agency.

Given the very different standards of care at different nursing homes, the criteria for regulating such decisions should be made outside the nursing home. This would lessen the possibility that a committee might be responsible for validating its own decisions to impose supportive care plans. Adequate review could be ensured through several ways. The NHAG Guidelines propose a nursing home human rights committee to advocate the civil rights and quality of services due all residents.[17] The human rights committee would function independently of the facility, and would be staffed by family and friends of residents, rehabilitation personnel from outside the facility, community members, and religious leaders.

Numerous groups advocating the rights of elderly and disabled persons oppose the type of discrimination found in Section II of the *Supportive Care Plan*. On April 12, 1984, at the request of the Nursing Home Action Group, the Board of the United Handicapped Federation, representing 25 organizations in the Minneapolis–St. Paul metropolitan area, adopted an affirmative resolution supporting the following principles:

1. The life of a person with mental or physical disabilities has the same intrinsic value as that of a person described as normal or healthy or ablebodied.

2. The primary goal of health care givers should be to encourage and promote the best physical, mental, emotional, social, and spiritual health of which each person is capable.

3. Orders for the withdrawal of treatment or noninitiation of treatment should never be given because of physical or mental disability

4. Denial of essential, life-maintaining care and life-enhancing care because of mental or physical disabilities is a violation of basic civil and human rights.[18]

Certainly, no set of guidelines can resolve all questions raised by rapidly changing medical technology and by conflicting ethical values and medical opinions. It is hoped, however, that the *Supportive Care Plan: Its Meaning and Application* will be thoroughly revised to become clearer and more protective so that it does not jeopardize the lives of nursing home residents who have severe mental or physical disabilities.

NOTES

1. Nursing Home Action Group, Guidelines for the Provision of Medical Treatment and Nursing Care in Nursing Homes, Draft II (April 1984) (available from the Nursing Home Action Group, P.O. Box 65363, St. Paul, Minn. 55165)[hereinafter referred to as NHAG Guidelines].

2. *See, e.g.*, Task Force of the National Institute on Aging, *Senility Reconsidered: Treatment Possibilities for Mental Impairments in the Elderly,* JOURNAL OF THE AMERICAN MEDICAL ASSOCIATION 244(3):259–63 (July 18, 1980).

3. Hoyt v. St. Mary's Rehabilitation Center, Transcript at 15–16, No. 773555 (District Ct. Hennepin County, Minn. February 13, 1981).

4. NHAG Guidelines, *supra* note 1, at 10–11. The definition of the individual's bodily condition as "irreversibly, irreparably, and terminally ill, and death is imminent" is taken from Rabkin, M. T., *et al., Orders Not to Resuscitate,* NEW ENGLAND JOURNAL OF MEDICINE 295:364–66 (August 12, 1976).

5. *The Need for Annual Surveys,* in NATIONAL CITIZENS' COALITION FOR NURSING HOME REFORM, CONSUMER STATEMENT OF PRINCIPLES FOR THE NURSING HOME REGULATORY SYSTEM—STATE LICENSURE AND FEDERAL CERTIFICATION PROGRAMS (September 1983) at 102–4.

6. *Doctors, Nursing Homes at Odds,* St. Paul Dispatch, January 31, 1983, at 3A.

7. *The Long-Standing Deplorable Conditions in Nursing Homes Persist, Report Says,* Peninsula Times Tribune, August 18, 1983, at 1.

8. CENTER FOR THE STUDY OF RESPONSIBLE LAW, LEAVING THEM DEFENSE-LESS—REAGAN'S DRIVE TO DESTROY NURSING HOME LAW AND ORDER (Center for Responsive Law, Washington, D.C.) (March 1983).

9. *Patients May Feel Pain in Hospitals' Concern for Costs,* Minneapolis Star/Tribune, March 22, 1984, at 1B.

10. Annual Report, 1983, of Minnesota Office of Health Facility Complaints, Minnesota Department of Health, Minneapolis, Minnesota (prepared and submitted to the Commissioner of Health and to the Legislature) (March 1984) at 25–26.

11. NHAG Guidelines, *supra* note 1, at 11.

12. *Id.* at 8.

13. *Domestic Abuse Against the Elderly, Hearing Before the Subcommittee on Human Services of the House Select Committee on Aging,* 96th Cong., 1st Sess. (April 28, 1980); *Abuse of Older Persons, Hearing Before the Subcommittee on Human Services of the House Select Committee on Aging,* 97th Cong., 1st Sess. (March 23, 1981).

14. *See, e.g.,* CONN. GEN. STAT. ANN.§§469-14 to 25 (West Supp. 1980); MD. ANN. CODE art. 88A §§106-110 (1979); MINN. STAT. §626.557 (1980).

15. NHAG Guidelines, *supra* note 1, at 9.

16. *Id.*

17. *Id.* at 14.

18. Resolution adopted by the Board of Directors of the United States Handicapped Federation, St. Paul, Minnesota (April 12, 1984).

Selected Bibliography

Books

ADVOCACY AND AGE (P.A. Kerschner, ed.) (The Ethel Percy Andrus Gerontology Center, University of Southern California, Los Angeles) (1976).

THE AGE OF AGING: A READER IN SOCIAL GERONTOLOGY (A. Monk, ed.) (Prometheus Books, Buffalo, N.Y.) (1979).

AGING: PROSPECTS AND ISSUES (R.H. Davis, ed.) (The Ethel Percy Andrus Gerontology Center, University of Southern California, Los Angeles) (rev. ed. 1976).

J.B. AKER, A.C. WALSH, J.R. BEAM, MENTAL CAPACITY: MEDICAL AND LEGAL ASPECTS OF THE AGING (Shepard's Inc., Colorado Springs, Colo.) (1977).

L.H. BOWKER, HUMANIZING INSTITUTIONS FOR THE AGED (Lexington Books, Lexington, Mass.) (1982).

R.N. BROWN, THE RIGHTS OF OLDER PERSONS (Avon Books– ACLU, New York) (1979).

M. BUCKLEY, THE AGED ARE PEOPLE TOO: ABOUT WILLIAM POSNER AND SOCIAL WORK WITH THE OLD (Kennikat Press Corp., Port Washington, N.Y.) (1972).

ELDERLY LAW MANUAL (Legal Counsel for the Elderly, ed.) (The Counsel, Washington, D.C.) (1982 and Supp. 1983).

EPIDEMIOLOGY OF AGING (A.M. Ostfield, D.C. Gibson, eds.) (National Institute on Aging, National Institutes of Health, Bethesda, Md.) (1972)

C.L. ESTES, THE AGING ENTERPRISE (Jossey-Bass Publishers, San Francisco) (1980).

D.L. FRANKFATHER, M.J. SMITH, F.G. CARO, FAMILY CARE OF THE ELDERLY (Lexington Books, Lexington, Mass.) (1981).

J.G. GILBERT, THE PARAPROFESSIONAL AND THE ELDERLY (Panel Publishers, Greenvale, N.Y.) (1977).

GROWING OLD IN AMERICA (M. Stegel, N. Siegel, eds.) (Instructional Aids, Plano, Tex.) (1980).

B.R. HERZOG, AGING AND INCOME: PROGRAMS AND PROSPECTS FOR THE ELDERLY (Human Sciences Press, New York) (1978).

R.L. KANE, J.G. OUSLANDER, I.B. ABRASS, ESSENTIALS OF CLINICAL GERIATRICS (McGraw-Hill, New York) (1984).

R.L. KANE, D.L. SOLOMON, J.C. BECK, E.B. KEELER, R.A. KANE, GERIATRICS IN THE UNITED STATES: MANPOWER PROJECTIONS AND TRAINING CONSIDERATIONS (Lexington Books, Lexington, Mass.) (1981).

M.B. KAPP, A. BIGOT, GERIATRICS AND THE LAW (Springer Publishing Company, New York) (1985).

LAW OF THE ELDERLY (J.A. Weiss, ed.) (Practising Law Institute, New York) (1977).

LEGAL PROBLEMS OF THE AGED (Institute of Continuing Legal Education, Ann Arbor, Mich.) (1976) (two volumes of course materials).

G. LESNOFF-CARVAGLIA, HEALTH CARE OF THE ELDERLY: STRATEGIES FOR PREVENTION AND INTERVENTION (Human Sciences Press, New York) (1980).

B.A. LOCKETT, AGING, POLITICS AND RESEARCH (Springer Publishing Co., New York) (1983).

B.B. MANNARD, C.S. KART, D.W.L. VAN GILS, OLD-AGE INSTITUTIONS (Lexington Books, Lexington, Mass.) (1975).

B.B. MANNARD, R.E. WOEHLE, J.M. HEILMAN, BETTER HOMES FOR THE OLD (Lexington Books, Lexington, Mass.) (1975).

E.W. MARKSON, G.R. BATRA, PUBLIC POLICIES FOR AN AGING POPULATION (Lexington Books, Lexington, Mass.) (1980).

MODEL RECOMMENDATIONS: INTERMEDIATE SANCTIONS FOR THE ENFORCEMENT OF QUALITY CARE IN NURSING HOMES (American Bar Association Commission on Legal Problems of the Elderly, Chicago, Ill.) (1981).

R. MORRIS, ALLOCATING HEALTH RESOURCES FOR THE AGED AND DISABLED (Lexington Books, Lexington, Mass.) (1981).

F.E. MOSS, V.J. HALAMANDARIS, TOO OLD, TOO SICK, TOO BAD: NURSING HOMES IN AMERICA (Aspen System Corp., Germantown, Md.) (1977).

A.L. SAHS, E.C. HARTMAN, S.M. ARONSON, GUIDELINES FOR STROKE CARE (U.S. Government Printing Office, Washington, D.C.) (1976).

W.C. SCHMIDT, *et al.*, PUBLIC GUARDIANSHIP AND THE ELDERLY (Ballinger Publishing Co., Cambridge, Mass.) (1981)

E. SEYMORE, PSYCHOLOGICAL NEEDS OF THE AGED: A HEALTH CARE PERSPECTIVE (The Ethel Percy Andrus Gerontology Center, University of Southern California, Los Angeles) (1976).

ARTICLES

Age Discrimination in Employment Act Amendments of 1978: Tension Between Congress and the Courts, BRIGHAM YOUNG UNIVERSITY LAW REVIEW 1980(3):569–97 (1980).

Alexander, G.J., *Premature Probate: A Different Perspective on Guardianship for the Elderly,* STANFORD LAW REVIEW 31(4):1003–35 (July 1979).

Alexander, G.J., *Remaining Responsible: On Control of One's Health Needs in Aging,* SANTA CLARA LAW REVIEW 20(1):13–48 (1980).

Anderson, G.F., Steinberg, E.P., *Hospital Readmissions in the Medicare Population,* NEW ENGLAND JOURNAL OF MEDICINE 311(21):1349–53 (November 22, 1984).

Anderson, H.W., *Relief under the Age Discrimination in Employment Act of 1967,* BAYLOR LAW REVIEW 31(2):217–26 (Spring 1979).

Avorn, J., *Benefit and Cost Analysis in Geriatric Care: Turning Age Discrimination into Health Policy*, NEW ENGLAND JOURNAL OF MEDICINE 310(20):1249–1301 (May 17, 1984).

Birnbaum, H., Burke, R., Pratter, F., *Managing Programs for the Elderly: A Design of A Social Information System*, HEALTH CARE FINANCING REVIEW 5(2):11–23 (Winter 1983).

Birnbaum, H.G., Kidder, D., *What Does Hospice Cost?* AMERICAN JOURNAL OF PUBLIC HEALTH 74(7):689–97 (July 1984).

Bloom, M., *High Costs Trigger Funding Options*, MODERN HEALTHCARE 14(3):76 (February 15, 1984).

Bonanno, J.B., Wetle, L., *HMO Enrollment of Medicine Recipients: An Analysis of Incentives and Barriers*, JOURNAL OF HEALTH POLITICS, POLICY AND LAW 9(1):41–62 (Spring 1984).

Bracing the System to Care for the Elderly, PATIENT CARE 15(1):212–16 (January 15, 1981).

Brody, H., Lynn, J., *The Physician's Responsibility Under the New Medicare Reimbursement for Hospice Care*, NEW ENGLAND JOURNAL OF MEDICINE 310(14):920–22 (April 5, 1984).

Brown, D.S., *Housing for the Elderly: Federal Subsidy Policy and Its Effect on Age-Group Isolation*, UNIVERSITY OF DETROIT JOURNAL OF URBAN LAW 57(2):257–94 (1980).

Brown, R.E., *Examining Hospice Benefits*, RX HOME CARE 6(1):18–23 (January 1984).

Brown, R.N., *A Bill of Rights for Nursing Home Patients*, TRIAL MAGAZINE 13(5):22–28 (May 1977).

Budnick, L.D., Sticof, R.L., Ellis, F., *An Outbreak of Influenza A in a Nursing Home, 1982*, NEW YORK STATE JOURNAL OF MEDICINE 84(5):253–38 (May 1984).

Busse, E.W., *Longevity, Disability, and Retirement*, NORTH CAROLINA MEDICAL JOURNAL 45(3):181–83 (March 1984).

Butler, N.G., *Optimal Long-Term Health Care for the Elderly: An Acute Care Hospital's Perspective*, TOPICS IN HEALTH CARE FINANCING 10(3):57–65 (Spring 1984).

Butler, P.A., *Assuring the Quality of Care and Life in Nursing Homes: The Dilemma of Enforcement*, NORTH CAROLINA LAW REVIEW 58(1):1317–82 (August 1979).

Butler, P.A., *Financing Noninstitutional Long-Term Care Services for the Elderly and Chronically Ill: Alternatives to Nursing Homes*, CLEARINGHOUSE REVIEW 13(5):335– 76 (September 1979).

Butler, R.N., *Gerontology: A Long Neglected Part of Medicine*, FORUM ON MEDICINE 3(3):139–40 (March 1980).

Caldwell, J.M., Kapp, M.B., *The Rights of Nursing Home Patients: Possibilities and Limitations of Federal Regulation*, JOURNAL OF HEALTH POLITICS, POLICY AND LAW 6(1):440–48 (Spring 1981).

Cattani, L.J., *Alzheimer's Disease and Social Security Disability Benefits: A Case Study in Vermont*, VERMONT BAR JOURNAL AND LAW DIGEST 10(4):11–13 (September 14, 1984).

Charatan, F.B., *Geriatric Psychiatry: Psychosomatic Considerations*, NEW YORK STATE JOURNAL OF MEDICINE 80(7):1085–86 (June 1980).

Chavkin, D.F., Cypen, M.K., *Cost-Sharing Under Medicaid: Lessening the Impact On Institutionalized Recipients*, CLEARINGHOUSE REVIEW 12(5):285–91 (September 1978).

Cohen, E.S., *Old Age and the Law*, GENERATIONS 8(3):5–6 (Spring 1984).

Cohen, K.S., *Section 4(f) (2) of the Age Discrimination in Employment Act: Age Discrimination in Employee Benefit Plans*, WESTERN NEW ENGLAND LAW REVIEW 2(3):379–452 (Winter 1980).

Compensatory and Punitive Damages for Age Discrimination in Employment, UNIVERSITY OF FLORIDA LAW REVIEW 32(4):701–30 (Summer 1980).

Continuing-Care Communities for the Elderly: Potential Pitfalls and Proposed Regulation, UNIVERSITY OF PENNSYLVANIA LAW REVIEW 128(4):883–936 (April 1980).

Continuing Legal Education Projects on Law and Aging (Commission on Legal Problems of the Elderly, American Bar Association, Washington, D.C.) (preliminary packet, March 1981).

Cunningham, R.M., *What Old People Want: More Work, Less Talk*, HOSPITAL 54(10):85–89 (May 16, 1980).

Cushing, M., *Wronged Rights in Nursing Homes*, AMERICAN JOURNAL OF NURSING 84(10):1213–18 (October 1984).

Daniels, N., *Is Rationing By Age Ever Morally Acceptable?* BUSINESS AND HEALTH 1(5):29–32 (April 1984).

Denham, J.W., *Evaluating the Elderly Patient*, NORTH CAROLINA MEDICAL JOURNAL 41(5):315–16 (May 1980).

Dervin, J., Dervin, P., Jonsen, A.R., *Ethical Considerations in Eldercare*, in ELDERCARE: A PRACTICAL GUIDE TO CLINICAL GERIATRICS (O'Hara-Devereaux, et al. eds.) (Grune & Stratton, New York) (1981).

Developing a Handbook on the Rights and Problems of the Aged (Commission on Legal Problems of the Elderly, American Bar Association, Washington, D.C.) (preliminary packet, March 1981).

Dobrof, R., *Long-term Care Challenge: Rationalizing a Continuum of Care for Chronically Impaired Elderly*, MOUNT SINAI JOURNAL OF MEDICINE 47(2):87–95 (March/April 1980).

"Dumping" of Elderly Patients Tied to DRG Systems, INTERNAL MEDICINE NEWS 17(6):3, 64 (March 15–31, 1984).

Dunlop, B.D., *Expanded Home-Based Care for the Impaired Elderly: Solution or Pipe Dream?* AMERICAN JOURNAL OF PUBLIC HEALTH 70(5):514–19 (May 1980).

Edelman, T., *Access to Nursing Home Care for Medicaid Recipients*, in LONG TERM CARE AND THE LAW (J.W. Skiba, ed.) (Panel Publishers, Greenvale, N.Y.) (1979) at 191–99.

The Effect of Asset Transfers on Medicaid Eligibility, UNIVERSITY OF PENNSYLVANIA LAW REVIEW 129(4):882–910 (April 1981).

Eggers, P.W., Connerton, R., McCullan, M., *The Medicare Experience with End-Stage Renal Diseases: Trends in Incidence, Prevalence, and Survival*, HEALTH CARE FINANCING REVIEW 5(3):60–88 (Spring 1984).

Eisele, F.R., Hoke, R.R. *Health Care Policy and the Elderly: Toward a System of Long-Term Care*, JOURNAL OF HEALTH POLITICS, POLICY AND LAW 3(4):452–55 (Winter 1979).

Elder Abuse (An Examination of a Hidden Problem), A Report by the House Select Committee on Aging, 97th Congress, 1st Session (April 3, 1981).

Evashwick, C.J., Read, W.A., *Hospitals and LTC: Options, Alternatives, Implications,* HEALTH CARE FINANCIAL MANAGEMENT 38(6):60–70 (June 1984).

Faulkner, L.R., *Mandating the Reporting of Suspected Cases of Elder Abuse: An Inappropriate, Ineffective and Ageist Response to the Abuse of Older Adults,* FAMILY LAW QUARTERLY 26(1):69–91 (Spring 1982).

Fletcher, D.J., *Promoting Health in Elderly Patients,* GERIATRIC CONSULTANT 2(4):26–29 (January/February 1984).

Foerster, J., *A Study of Falls: The Elderly Nursing Home Resident,* JOURNAL OF THE NEW YORK STATE NURSING ASSOCIATION 12(2):9–17 (June 1981).

Fritz, D., *The Advocacy Agency and Citizen Participation,* JOURNAL OF HEALTH AND HUMAN RESOURCES ADMINISTRATION 1(1):79–108 (August 1979).

Frobsky-Komlos, P., *Home- and Community-Based Long Term Care for the Elderly Poor,* CLEARINGHOUSE REVIEW 18(4):377–79 (August–September 1984).

Gillick, M.R., *Is the Care of the Chronically Ill a Medical Prerogative?* NEW ENGLAND JOURNAL OF MEDICINE 310(3):190–93 (January 19, 1984).

Gottlieb, T.W., *Quality Assurance in a Long Term Care Facility,* QUALITY REVIEW BULLETIN 10(2):51–54 (February 1984).

Greene, J., *Nutritional Care, Considerations of Older Americans,* JOURNAL OF THE NATIONAL MEDICAL ASSOCIATION 71(8):791–93 (August 1979).

Grimaldi, P.L., *How Major Regulations Strive to Ensure Quality Care in Nursing Homes,* HEALTHCARE FINANCIAL MANAGEMENT 38(9):50–66 (September 1984).

Guardianship: Removal of Life Support Systems, GONZAGA LAW REVIEW 19:417–35 (1984).

Hadden, B.F., Cohen, J., *A New Campaign of Caring for the Aged,* JOURNAL OF HEALTH AND HUMAN RESOURCES 3(2):148–68 (November 1980).

Hartzler, J.E., *Life Care: An Industry with Unique Financial Characteristics,* HEALTHCARE FINANCIAL MANAGEMENT 14(7):76–82 (July 1984).

Havener, W.H., *Physician Attitudes Toward Caring for Older Patients,* OHIO STATE MEDICAL JOURNAL 75(11):708–9 (November 1979).

Health Care for an Aged Population—Report of the American Medical Association Board of Trustees (adopted by the House of Delegates) (December 1983). JOURNAL OF THE TENNESSEE MEDICAL ASSOCIATION 77(8):456–61 (August 1984).

Hickey, T., Douglass, R.L., *Mistreatment of the Elderly in the Domestic Setting: An Exploratory Study,* AMERICAN JOURNAL OF PUBLIC HEALTH 71(5):500–507 (May 1981).

Hirsh, H.L., *Transfer Trauma: Medicolegal Issues,* MEDICINE AND LAW 3(3):217–33 (May 1984).

Hollis, C.D., *Towards Resolving Inequitable Medicare and Medicaid Reimbursements,* JOURNAL OF THE MEDICAL ASSOCIATION OF GEORGIA 68(10):893 (October 1979).

Holmes, D., Terese, J., Holmes, M., *Differences Among Black, Hispanic, and White People in Knowledge About Long-Term Care Services,* HEALTH CARE FINANCING REVIEW 5(2):51–67 (Winter 1983).

Horowitz, A., Shindelman, L.W., *Social and Economic Incentives For Family Caregivers*, HEALTH CARE FINANCING REVIEW 5(2):25–33 (Winter 1983).

Horowitz, A., Ryan, J.B., *Structuring the Life-Care Contract to Minimize Financial Risk*, TOPICS IN HEALTH CARE FINANCING 10(3):66–76 (Spring 1984).

How Should Medicare Pay for Capital Costs? WASHINGTON HEALTH COSTS LETTER (supplement) (March 16, 1984) (a review of various proposals by health care associations and key individuals in the health care field).

Howard, E., *Mandatory Retirement: Traumatic Evidence of Age Discrimination*, TRIAL 13(11):46–51 (November 1977).

Iglehart, J.K., *Medicare's Uncertain Future*, NEW ENGLAND JOURNAL OF MEDICINE 306(21):1308–12 (May 27, 1982).

Iglehart, J.K., *Prospective Payment Panel Faces Key Decisions as New DRG System Develops*, FEDERATION OF AMERICAN HOSPITALS REVIEW 17(2):52–57 (March/April 1984).

Interspousal Income Deeming to Determine Medicaid Eligibility and Governmental Assistance: The Statutory and Constitutional Infirmities, UNIVERSITY OF CINCINNATI LAW REVIEW 49(3):636–54 (1980).

Jennings, M.C., Krentz, S.E., *Private Payment for Long-Term Care: The Untapped Mechanism*, TOPICS IN HEALTH CARE FINANCING 10(3):1–21 (Spring 1984).

Johnson, E.A., *The Basis of the Coming Medicare Crisis*, HOSPITAL AND HEALTH SERVICES ADMINISTRATION 29(3):26–35 (May/June 1984).

Johnson, R.L., *A Second Opinion: The Prospects of Medicare's Hospital-Insurance Fund*, HOSPITAL AND HEALTH SERVICES ADMINISTRATION 29(3):7–25 (May/June 1984).

Kane, R., *Assuring Quality of Care and Quality of Life in Long Term Care*, QUALITY REVIEW BULLETIN 7(10):3–10 (October 1981).

Kane, R., *et al.*, *The Future Need for Geriatric Manpower in the United States*, NEW ENGLAND JOURNAL OF MEDICINE 302(24):1327–32 (June 12, 1980).

Kapp, M.B., *Promoting the Legal Rights of Older Adults: Role of the Primary Care Physician*, JOURNAL OF LEGAL MEDICINE 3(3):367 (September 1982).

Kapp, M.B., *Protecting the Rights of Nursing Home Patients: Using Federal Law*, FLORIDA BAR JOURNAL, pp. 212–15 (March 1981).

Kapp, M.B., *Legal and Ethical Implications of Health Care Reimbursement by Diagnosis Related Groups*, LAW, MEDICINE & HEALTH CARE 12(6):245–53 (December 1984).

Kapp, M.B., *Legal and Ethical Standards in Geriatric Medicine*, JOURNAL OF THE AMERICAN GERIATRIC SOCIETY 33(3):179–83 (March 1985).

Kapp, M.B., *Nursing Home Patients' Rights to Physician Care*, GENERATIONS 8(3):30–33 (Spring 1984).

Katz, K.D., *Elder Abuse*, JOURNAL OF FAMILY LAW 18(4):695–722 (1979–80).

Kemanis, V., *A Critical Evaluation of the Federal Role in Nursing Home Quality Enforcement*, UNIVERSITY OF COLORADO LAW REVIEW 51(4):607–40 (Summer 1980).

Klein, R.A., Hooper, P., *Medicare's Restrictive Attitude Endangers Future Development of Special Care Units*, FEDERATION OF AMERICAN HOSPITALS REVIEW 13(4):37–40 (August 1980).

Klonoff, R., *The Problems of Nursing Homes: Connecticut's Non-Response,* ADMINISTRATIVE LAW REVIEW 31(1):1–30 (Winter 1979).

Komlos-Hrobsky, P., *Damages of Wrongful Termination of Disability Benefits: Overview of the Law,* BIFOCAL 5(1):5–7 (Spring 1984).

Lang, R.H., *Implementation of Comprehensive Service Systems for the Elderly and Chronically Ill,* JOURNAL OF HEALTH AND HUMAN RESOURCES ADMINISTRATION 4(4):415–50 (Spring 1982).

Lange, D.J., *Geriatric, Psychiatric, and Legal Aspects of the Mental State of the Aged,* LEGAL MEDICAL QUARTERLY 4:161–64 (Fall 1980).

Lawton, A.H., *Some Considerations of Bioethics in Geriatrics,* JOURNAL OF THE FLORIDA MEDICAL ASSOCIATION 69(4):3100–13 (April 1982).

Leap, T., Kovarsky, I., *The Age Discrimination in Employment Act and the Vocational Rehabilitation Act: A Proposed Consolidation,* LABOR LAW JOURNAL 31(1):13–226 (January 1980).

Ledbetter, R., *The Medicare Evolution,* PRIVATE PRACTICE 16(1):40–41 (January 1984).

Legal Services for the Elderly: Where the Nation Stands (Commission on Legal Problems of the Elderly, American Bar Association, Washington, D.C.) (August 1981).

Levin, M., *Neighborhood Development and the Displacement of the Elderly,* URBAN LAW ANNUAL 18:223–64 (1980).

Lind, S.E., *Transferring the Terminally Ill,* NEW ENGLAND JOURNAL OF MEDICINE 311(18):1181–82 (NOVEMBER 1, 1984).

LINEBERGER, P., *Recent Developments in Age Discrimination,* AMERICAN BUSINESS LAW JOURNAL 17:363–75 (1979).

Lockett, B.A., *Setting the Federal Agenda for Health Research: The Case of the Institute on Aging,* JOURNAL OF HEALTH POLITICS, POLICY AND LAW 9(1):63–80 (Spring 1984).

Loeser, W.D., *et al., Federal Regulation of Medical Practice in Nursing Homes,* FORUM ON MEDICINE 3(8):512–14 (August 1980).

Loeser, W.D., Kickstein, E.S., Schiavone, L.D., *Medicare Coverage in Nursing Homes—A Broken Promise,* NEW ENGLAND JOURNAL OF MEDICINE 304(6):353–55 (February 5, 1981).

Lubitz, J., Prihoda, R., *The Use and Costs of Medicare Services in the Last 2 Years of Life,* HEALTH CARE FINANCING REVIEW 5(3):117–31 (Spring 1984).

Lynch, R., Phillips, H., *Creation of the Department of Aging: Improvement and Expansion of Services to the Aging in Pennsylvania,* TEMPLE LAW QUARTERLY 52(4):990–1039 (1979).

Lynn, J.H., *Ethical Dilemma: Should Independence Outweigh a Patient's Safety?* MEDICAL ECONOMICS 61(9):158–66 (April 30, 1984).

Mancini, M., *Medicare: Health Rights of the Elderly,* AMERICAN JOURNAL OF NURSING 79(10):1810, 1812 (October 1979).

McConnell, S.R., *Assessing the Health and Job Performance of Older Workers,* BUSINESS AND HEALTH 1(7):18–22 (June 1984).

Medicare Trust Fund: Rx for Survival? FEDERATION OF AMERICAN HOSPITALS REVIEW 17(2):22–25 (March/April 1984).

Medicare: Use of Home Health Services, 1978, HEALTH CARE FINANCING NOTES (June 1980).

Medicare: Use of Home Health Services, 1978, HEALTH CARE FINANCING PROGRAM STATISTICS, pp. 1–24 (1982).

Meiners, M.R., *The State of the Art in Long-Term Care Insurance* (National Center for Health Services Research, Rockville, Md.) (April 1984).

Melkonian, D., *Meeting the Special Care Needs of the Elderly,* TRUSTEE 34(3):32–36 (March 1981).

Michigan's Bill of Rights for Nursing Home Residents, WAYNE LAW REVIEW 27(3):1203–28 (Spring 1981).

Mitchell, S.A., *The Potential Inequities of Medicare Waivers in DRG System Explored,* FEDERATION OF AMERICAN HOSPITALS REVIEW 17:89–92 (January/February 1984).

Model Recommendations: Intermediate Sanctions for Enforcement of Quality of Care in Nursing Homes, (draft report) (Commission on Legal Problems of the Elderly, American Bar Association, Washington, D.C.) (July 1981).

Monk, A., Kaye, L.W., *Patient Advocacy Services in Long-Term-Care Facilities: Ethnic Perspectives,* JOURNAL OF LONG TERM CARE ADMINISTRATION, pp. 5–10 (Spring 1984).

Moon, M., Sneeding, T., *Medical Care Transfers, Poverty and the Aged,* JOURNAL OF HEALTH POLITICS, POLICY AND LAW 6(1):29–39 (Spring 1981).

Myers, J.M., Drayer, C.S., *Support System and Mental Illness in the Elderly,* COMMUNITY MENTAL HEALTH JOURNAL 15(4):277–86 (Winter 1979).

National Senior Citizens Law Center, Transfer of Assets: New Penalties in SSI and Medicaid, CLEARINGHOUSE REVIEW 15(3):259–61 (July 1981).

Newman-Hafner, M., O'Bannon v. Town Court Nursing Center, Inc.: *Limiting the Due Process Rights of Nursing Home Residents,* SAINT LOUIS UNIVERSITY LAW JOURNAL 24(4):828 (March 1981).

Nursing Home Quality of Care Enforcement: Litigation by Private Parties; State Agency Enforcement Remedies, CLEARINGHOUSE REVIEW 14(7):622–99 (October 1980).

Nursing Home Transfer Cases, NURSING HOME LAW LETTER, 31:3–8 (May 1979); 32:1–8 (June 1979).

Olson, J., *To Treat or to Allow to Die: An Ethical Dilemma in Gerontologic Nursing,* JOURNAL OF GERONTOLOGIC NURSING 7(3):141 (March 1981).

Our Last Quarter of a Century, Welfare of Elderly Has Improved at the Expense of Children's Welfare, FAMILY PLANNING PERSPECTIVES 16(4):186–87 (July/August 1984).

Pegels, C.C., *Institutional vs. Noninstitutional Care for the Elderly,* JOURNAL OF HEALTH POLITICS, POLICY AND LAW 5(2):205–12 (Summer 1980).

Physical and Financial Abuse of the Elderly, Hearing before the Subcommittee on Retirement Income and Employment of the House Select Committee on Aging, 97th Congress, 1st Session (April 3, 1981).

Pillemer, K., *How Do We Know How Much We Need? Problems in Determining Need for Long-Term Care,* JOURNAL OF HEALTH POLITICS, POLICY AND LAW 9(2):281–90 (Summer 1984).

Podell, L.B., *Medicare Coverage of Hospital Care,* AMERICAN JOURNAL OF HOSPITAL

PHARMACY 41(5):942–44 (May 1984).

Podolsky, R., Mason, J.H., *Geriatric Discharge Planning and Follow-Up*, ILLINOIS MEDICAL JOURNAL 157(5):291–92 (May 1980).

Quality Control in Private Bar Programs for the Elderly (Commission on Legal Problems of the Elderly, American Bar Association, Washington, D.C.) (undated).

Quaranto, L., *Protective Services for the Elderly: Legislative Reforms*, ADVOCATE 10(2):22–27 (Spring 1979).

Rappaport, A.M., *Post Retirement Health Benefits: A New Quagmire*, BUSINESS AND HEALTH 1(5):25 (April 1984).

Regan, J.J. *Protecting the Elderly: The New Paternalism*, HASTINGS LAW JOURNAL 32(5):1111–32 (May 1981).

Reitz, R.A., Reitz, J.A., *Collective Bargaining in the Health Care Industry: Implications for the Long-Term-Care Administrator*, JOURNAL OF LONG TERM CARE ADMINISTRATION 12(1):11–19 (Spring 1984).

Reschke, M.W., *The Age Discrimination in Employment Act: Procedural and Substantive Issues in the Aftermath of the 1978 Amendments*, UNIVERSITY OF ILLINOIS LAW FORUM 3:665–702 (1979).

Riklan, M., *Urban Hospital Reaches Out to its Area's Aged*, HOSPITALS 54 (10):110–12 (May 16, 1980).

Robinson, P.K., *Facing Up To Health Care Costs of Retirees*, BUSINESS AND HEALTH 1(7):23–26 (June 1984).

Rowse, G.T., *Legal Services for the Elderly Under Title III of the Older Americans Act: Utilization of a "Means" Test*, CLEARINGHOUSE REVIEW 12(4):225–30 (August 1978).

Rubin, R.J., Helms, R.B., *Medicare Payment of Hospital Capital-Related Costs*, HEALTHCARE FINANCIAL MANAGEMENT 38(4):20–38 (April 1984).

Scanlon, W.J., Feder, J., *The Long-Term Care Marketplace: An Overview*, HEALTHCARE FINANCIAL MANAGEMENT 38(1):18–36 (January 1984).

Schuck, P.H., *The Graying of the Civil Rights Law: The Age Discrimination Act of 1975*, YALE LAW JOURNAL 89(1):27–94 (November 1979).

Shapiro, E., Roos, N.P., *The Geriatric Long-Stay Hospital Patient: A Canadian Case Study*, JOURNAL OF HEALTH POLITICS, POLICY AND LAW 6(1):49–61 (Spring 1981).

Shapiro, K.P., *Age Discrimination—Final Regulations*, JOURNAL OF PENSION PLANNING AND COMPLIANCE 5(4):350–53 (July 1979).

Sheeder, R.E. *Procedural Complexity of the Age Discrimination in Employment Act: An Age-Old Problem*, DUQUESNE LAW REVIEW 18(2):241–70 (Winter 1980).

Simon, M.M., *Estate Planning and Resource Maximization for the Elderly: Medicaid Considerations*, NEW HAMPSHIRE BAR JOURNAL 25(2):101–8 (January 1984).

Smith, V.A., *New Approaches to Patient Care Inspection in Nursing Homes*, JOURNAL OF THE TENNESSEE MEDICAL ASSOCIATION 77(1):36 (January 1984).

SNF Decertification: The Medicare-Medicaid Beneficiary's Entitlement to a Prior Hearing, NORTHWESTERN UNIVERSITY LAW REVIEW 74(3):440–67 (October 1979).

Somers, A.R., *The High Cost of Health Care for the Elderly: Diagnosis, Prognosis, and Some Suggestions for Therapy*, JOURNAL OF HEALTH POLITICS, POLICY AND LAW 3(2):163–80 (Summer 1978).

Somers, A.R., *Long-Term Care for the Elderly and Disabled: A New Health Priority*, NEW ENGLAND JOURNAL OF MEDICINE 307(4):221–26 (July 22, 1982).

Somers, A.R., *Why Not Try Preventing Illness as a Way of Controlling Medicare Costs?* NEW ENGLAND JOURNAL OF MEDICINE 311(13):853–56 (September 27, 1984).

Soroka, M., Newcomb, R.D., *Vision Care for the Nation's Elderly: A Plea for Policy Direction*, JOURNAL OF HEALTH POLITICS, POLICY AND LAW 6(1):73–86 (Spring 1981).

Special Issue on Age Discrimination, JOURNAL OF COLLEGE AND UNIVERSITY LAW 5(3):161–216 (1978/1979).

Stanley, B., Guido, J., Stanley, M., *The Elderly Patient and Informed Consent*, JOURNAL OF THE AMERICAN MEDICAL ASSOCIATION 252(10):1302–6 (September 14, 1984).

Stark, A.J., et al., *Placement Change in Long-Term Care: Three Years' Experience*, AMERICAN JOURNAL OF PUBLIC HEALTH 74(5):459–63 (May 1984).

Swisher, C.M., *When Older Patients Don't Learn: Adopting Educational Efforts to Age*, RESPIRATORY THERAPY 14(1):73–79 (January/February 1984).

Thomas, J., Bobrow, M.L., *Targeting the Elderly in Facility Design and Case Studies*, HOSPITALS 58(4):83–123 (February 16, 1984).

Urban, A.J., *Nursing Home Patient Abuse Reporting: An Analysis of the Washington Statutory Response*, GONZAGA LAW REVIEW 16(3):609–36 (1981).

Wack, J., Rodin, J., *Nursing Homes for the Aged: The Human Consequences of Legislation-Shaped Environments*, JOURNAL OF SOCIAL ISSUES 34(4):6–21 (Fall 1978).

Wagner, A., *Cardiopulmonary Resuscitation in the Aged: A Prospective Survey*, NEW ENGLAND JOURNAL OF MEDICINE 310(17):1129–30 (April 26, 1984).

Ward, M.E., *Congregate Living Arrangements: The Financing Option*, TOPICS IN HEALTH CARE FINANCING 10(3):34–35 (Spring 1984).

Waters, G.E., Pursell, C.F., *Emotional Distress: The Battle over a New Tort Under Age Discrimination Continues*, LABOR LAW JOURNAL 30(11):666–79 (November 1979).

Weissert, W.G., *Rationales for Public Health Insurance Coverage of Geriatric Day Care: Issues, Options, and Impacts*, JOURNAL OF HEALTH POLITICS, POLICY AND LAW 3(4):555–67 (Winter 1979).

Weissert, W.G., et al., *Care For The Chronically Ill: Nursing Home Incentive Payment Experiment*, HEALTH CARE FINANCING REVIEW 5(2):41–49 (Winter 1983).

Williams, L.A., *Gerontology and the Law: A Selected Bibliography, 1982–1983 Update*, SOUTHERN CALIFORNIA LAW REVIEW 57:630–66 (1984).

Wilson, S.H., *Benefit Cutbacks in the Medicare Program Through Administrative Agency Fiat Without Procedural Litigation Approaches on Behalf of Beneficiaries*, GONZAGA LAW REVIEW 16(3):533–78 (1981).

Index

About the Editors

MARSHALL B. KAPP is Associate Professor of Legal Medicine at Wright State University in Ohio. He is the coauthor of *Geriatrics and the Law: Patient Rights and Professional Responsibilities* (Springer Publishing, 1985) and many articles. An active member of professional organizations, Professor Kapp was a participant at the 1981 White House Conference on Aging and was a Visiting Scholar at the Institute of Society, Ethics, and the Life Sciences of The Hastings Center in New York. He currently serves as cochairman of the American Society of Law & Medicine's Committee on the Legal and Ethical Aspects of Health Care of the Elderly in 1983. He received his B.A. from Johns Hopkins University, a J.D. from George Washington University and an M.P.H. from the Harvard University School of Public Health.

HARVEY E. PIES, Conference Co-Chair for the Conference on Legal and Ethical Aspects of Health Care for the Elderly, serves as Special Counsel, Health Industry Services, for the Blue Cross and Blue Shield of Florida. Prior to this, he was a Partner in the Washington Office of Gardner, Carton & Douglas and served as the Assistant Minority Counsel for Health to the United States Way & Means Committee. He is active on the Board of Directors of the National Health Lawyers Association and was on the Board of Directors of the American Society of Law & Medicine. He received his M.P.H. and J.D. from Harvard University.

A. EDWARD DOUDERA is former Executive Director of the American Society of Law & Medicine. He received a B.S. in business administration from Boston University in 1972 and a J.D. from Suffolk University School of Law. Mr. Doudera was Executive Editor of both the *American Journal of Law & Medicine* and *Law, Medicine & Health Care*. He has coedited several texts, including *Legal & Ethical Aspects of Treating Critically & Terminally Ill*

Patients, Defining Human Life: Medical, Legal, and Ethical Implications, and *Institutional Ethics Committees and Health Care Decision Making.* Before joining the American Society of Law & Medicine in 1977, Mr. Doudera was Associate Administrator for Research at Tufts-New England Medical Center.

DATE DUE

DEMCO, INC. 38-3012